MW01632881

EMMA
Hawai'i's Remarkable Queen

EMMA
Hawaiʻi's Remarkable Queen

a biography by
George S. Kanahele

THE QUEEN EMMA FOUNDATION

05 04 03 02 01 00 99 5 4 3 2 1

Library of Congress Cataloging-in-Publication Data
Kanahele, George S.
Emma : Hawai'i's remarkable queen / George S. Kanahele.
p. cm.
Includes bibliographical references and index.
ISBN 0–8248–2234–X (alk. paper)
1. Emma, Queen, consort of Kamehameha IV, King of the Hawaiian Islands, 1836–1885. 2. Queens—Hawaii Biography. 3. Hawaii—History—To 1893. I. Title.
DU627.17.E45K36 1999
996.9'027'092—dc21
[B] 99–13113
CIP

This book is printed on acid-free paper and meets the guidelines for permanence and durability of the Council on Library Resources.

Book design by Santos Barbasa and Brooks Bays
Cover design by Brooks Bays

Distributed by
University of Hawai'i Press
2840 Kolowalu Street
Honolulu, Hawai'i 96822

Contents

Foreword

Queen Emma was a remarkable woman. She was a true visionary and humanitarian, and her legacy has not only grown but prospered since her death in 1885. The queen loved Hawai'i and the Hawaiian people and devoted her life to good works and the purest of hopes for her Island home. Queen Emma Kaleleonālani was a daughter, wife, mother, statesperson, and role model who lived amongst her people with great humility and compassion. To tell of all the queen's charities would be impossible as they were unnumbered and many are now lost in time. Yet we can remember her loyalty to her people and to the church, her purity of life, and her kindly grace, as well as the many tragedies she endured in her short but eventful life.

On many occasions I have invoked the queen's spirit at Mauna'ala, the Royal Mausoleum, where Emma's body rests. In our dialogues she has guided me to remain true to her original vision of serving the Hawaiian people and ensuring their well-being in both spirit and health. She has reminded me that I have responsibilities as a Hawaiian and that her legacies—despite the complications of modern business—must preserve, protect, and perpetuate the health of all the people of Hawai'i, with special care for the needs of the native Hawaiians.

Sadly, a complete biography of Queen Emma's life and times had never before been written. To this end, I asked noted Hawaiian author and scholar George Kanahele if he would undertake the task to research and write Queen Emma's story from birth to death. George, a student of the queen's life, was excited with the project and the prospect of furthering the knowledge of one of Hawai'i's most loved and gifted queens. Over two years and thousands of hours of research are represented in this book, the most ambitious work ever written on the life of Queen Emma. The book gives great insights into how and why she developed into one of Hawai'i's greatest visionaries and leaders. It closely follows the triumphs and tragedies that shaped her life of charity and piety.

As stated in one of the queen's obituaries in 1885,

> The Queen is dead. We will not think of her as dead. Her good deeds will live after her, in them she will live, in that noble Hospital, in her Christian example she will live and those who knew her, loved her, cherished her can say with resignation;
>
> There is no death!
> What seems so is transition;
> This life is of mortal breath
> Is but a suburb of the life Elysian,
> Whose portal we call death.

The story of Emma is one to reflect upon and ponder. It gives inspiration and hope for all those who have endured hardships, and it exemplifies the power of the human spirit. Read and absorb the life of Queen Emma; it will bring historical and cultural perspective to one of Hawai'i's truly remarkable women.

Kenneth F. Brown

Preface

I became a serious student of Queen Emma in 1987 when I began consulting with The Queen's Medical Center on the uses of its fabulous heritage. Eager to learn as much as I could about the queen, I read every published source available. It did not take long because there was so little to read. With the exception of Alfons L. Korn's two books, *The Victorian Visitors* (1958) and *News from Molokai, Letters between Peter Kaeo & Queen Emma, 1873–1876* (1976), no one had ever attempted a definitive study of the life of Queen Emma.

When Kenneth Brown and I first discussed the project, this book was not supposed to be lengthy, not because of any arbitrary limits such as cost, but rather because, based on my familiarity with the sources, I assumed that not much information was available—a feeling that was shared even by my sponsors. In fact, I originally estimated a manuscript of not more than 400 double-spaced pages with fifteen chapters. So much for estimates based on faulty assumptions. As I and my team of researchers, including several Hawaiian language specialists, conducted our research, we found a significant amount of new information, especially for the period after the queen's marriage in 1856. While the newspapers, both English and Hawaiian, were extremely helpful, I found the mother lode of information in Queen Emma's intermittent diaries and extensive correspondence as well as in the private letters and journals of contemporaries who had some contact, directly or indirectly, with the queen and her husband, King Alexander Liholiho Kamehameha IV. In fact, I do not believe that we have exhausted the reservoir of information on Queen Emma. So, even though this book may be twice as long as initially projected, it may not be the last word on the subject—there are still gaps to fill, more stories to tell, and conclusions to challenge.

I started out writing with a specific audience in mind, namely, the employees and stakeholders of The Queen's Health Systems. After all, not only did they have a vested interest in the queen but also they had shown the greatest amount of due diligence. For example, The Queen's

Medical Center had just concluded nearly ten years of heritage-building —a process designed to raise the awareness and appreciation among its employees of the vision, mission, and values of the founders of the hospital. I had helped in writing brief biographies of the king and queen, in developing award-winning videos about the hospital's founding, and in creating the *wahi pana* (storied place) tour program for hospital employees. And even before I became involved, Margery Hastert, the volunteer historian in charge of The Queen's Historical Room, had devoted years to nurturing and preserving the corporate memory. Everyone in-volved with the hospital realized that its heritage had become a powerful force for instilling a greater sense of purpose and for unifying the various components of a system undergoing rapid growth and change in the turbulent healthcare industry.

But I quickly realized that the telling of Queen Emma's story is for a much wider audience. It is for all Hawaiians and Hawaiians-at-heart whose ancestral and cultural roots tap into the values and traditions she so nobly represented; it is for the students and teachers at St. Andrew's Priory that she helped to establish in 1867; it is for the adherents of what is now the Episcopal church in Hawai‘i that she co-founded with her husband, King Kamehameha IV; it is for the parishioners of St. Andrew's Cathedral that she inspired and helped to fund; it is for the Daughters of Hawai‘i who lovingly take care of her Summer Palace in Nu‘uanu and for the dedicated members of the Queen Emma Hawaiian Civic Club; it is for the gardeners and the botanists of the Islands who have honored her "green thumb" by naming plants after her; it is for the collectors and conservators of the Hawaiian artifacts that she treasured and sought to preserve; it is for the environmentalists whose cause she ennobled by her love for nature; it is for the adventurers who will find a kindred soul in her daring hikes and other explorations; and, last but not least, it is for the sick and the poor and all those devoted to their care.

Perhaps, it is for everyone.

Acknowledgments

Where does one start? Scores of people contributed to the writing, researching, editing, and production of this book. Because writers are only as good as their sources, I should start with Hawai'i's archivists and librarians, especially Jolyn Tamura and her staff at the Hawai'i State Archives, which holds most of the material on Queen Emma. I am sure they would join me in thanking The Queen's Health Systems for donating the funds necessary both to microfilm the vast collection of royal correspondence and to preserve the fragile original letters in protective coverings. Margery Hastert, the perennial and faithful volunteer historian at The Queen's Medical Center, was most helpful; as were John Breinich and Helen Wong Smith at the Hawai'i Medical Library.

I am also indebted to the librarians at the Hawai'i State Library and its branch in Kaimukī, Hawaiian Mission Children's Society Library, Bishop Museum Library, Hawaiian Historical Society, Hamilton Library at the University of Hawai'i, Daughters of Hawai'i library, St. Andrew's Priory library, and the Woodson Research Center of Rice University, Houston, Texas; University of Geneva Library; and Central Library, Zurich. I am also grateful for the help of Kalani Flores of the Kaua'i Historical Society, Jean Greenwell of the Kona Historical Society, and the staffs at the National Tropical Botanical Garden in Lāwa'i, Kaua'i, the Koke'e Museum in Koke'e State Park, and the National Park Service, John Young Homestead site, in Kawaihae.

I owe an enormous *mahalo* to the knowledgeable and insightful historians, writers, artists, legal scholars, psychologists, teachers, and students, whose minds and hearts I exploited shamelessly: chanter Ka'upena Wong, University of Hawai'i professors Lilikalā Kame'eleihiwa, Niklaus R. Schweizer, and Puakea Nogelmeier, historian Dr. Rhoda Hackler, psychologist Dr. Frances White, state archivist emeritus Agnes Conrad, historian-writer Bob Dye, scholar Linda Menton, attorney Robert Bruce Graham, Jr., architect Hideo Murakami, Episcopal historiographer Father Norio Sasaki, cultural consultant Kepa Maly, curator

Leiana Woodside, and Hilo Community College instructors Edward and Pua Kanahele.

I could not have written this book without the research assistance of Joanna Leiko Kanahele who devoted nearly two years to helping her father. She scanned or read nearly every microfilmed page of Honolulu's two main nineteenth century newspapers covering nearly fifty years, plus countless pages of archival material, documents, monographs, reports, ad infinitum. She is owed more thanks than I can possibly give her.

I am also indebted to Keali‘i Tongg, Kalama Cabigon, Kamaui Aiona, and Tracy N. Ku‘ulei Higashi who read and translated articles from the Hawaiian language newspapers. *Mahalo nui loa* to Pua Kanahele, president of the Edith K. Kanaka‘ole Foundation, who came to my rescue at crucial moments of my research. And to Renate Schuh of Geneva, Switzerland, I extend my thanks for her archival work.

The list of people who read all or parts of the manuscript is long: Richard Griffith, Kenneth Brown, Mike Walsh, Danielle Izat, Connie Black, Roy Cameron, Diana Davids, Dan X. Hall, David Kennedy, Rianna Williams, Ka‘upena Wong, Agnes Conrad, Rhoda E. A. Hackler, Niklaus Schweizer, Nona Irvine, Joel Kennedy, Sabra Kauka, Kalani Flores, Jean Greenwell, Mary Yamashiro, Rita Hew Len Sweeney, Ivan Lui-Kwan, and Helen Wong Smith. I thank them all for their time and friendly, though at times trenchant, criticism. To those whom I've forgotten to mention, *e kala mai ia‘u* (forgive me).

The book's cover—itself a glorious tribute to Emma—was created by Brooks Bays, designer and illustrator, School of Ocean and Earth Science and Technology (SOEST) of the University of Hawai‘i. His unique contribution gives a visual grace to the printed word. I also wish to give special mention to certain other individuals who provided their specialized skills so integral to this book. Naomi C. Losch painstakingly verified the Hawaiian words and phrases in the text and served as the Hawaiian language resource person throughout the production stages. The final manuscript copy was meticulously typed and formatted by Lois M. Bender. In his role as trouble-shooter and computer specialist, Chris Klutz-Simanu was responsible for a myriad of technical details and ultimately for the book's smooth transition from manuscript to electronic typesetting.

I little imagined how much work a good editor could put a writer through until I met Barbara Naudain. She has been absolutely meticulous in every detail and endlessly helpful with her incisive comments on successive drafts of the manuscript. What's right in this book is due in no small part to her. What's wrong, of course, is my responsibility.

Finally, I express my personal thanks—and the thanks of all who have inherited the benefits of Queen Emma's remarkable legacy—to The Queen Emma Foundation, under the able leadership of Chairman and Chief Executive Officer Robert Oshiro and Vice-Chairman Kenneth F. Brown, for the foundation's generous and unfailing support. Appreciation and recognition are also extended to Arthur Ushijima, president of The Queen's Medical Center, for inspiring the center's caregivers in honoring their founder's mission and vision.

My wife Jeanne and family patiently endured my long preoccupation with this book. Even though they know how much I love them, I hope that this recounting of the remarkable life of Queen Emma will be some compensation.

Note to Reader

Except for some personal names, the spelling of Hawaiian words in this book includes the *'okina* (glottal stop) and the *kahakō* (macron). However, all quotations—in both Hawaiian and English—appear intact to reflect their original text.

Chronology of the Important Events of Queen Emma's Life

January 2, 1836	Birth and adoption.
January 3, 1842–August 7, 1849	Attendance at Chiefs' Children's School.
Fall of 1849–1854	Home tutoring by Sarah Von Pfister and Dr. Rooke.
February 1854	Engagement to Alexander Liholiho.
June 19, 1856	Marriage and wedding at Kawaiahaʻo Church.
July 18, 1857	Death of uncle Keoni Ana and subsequent inheritance of Hānaiakamalama in Nuʻuanu Valley.
May 20, 1858	Birth of Prince Albert.
November 28, 1858	Death of Dr. Rooke.
August 1, 1859	Opening of Queen's Hospital's temporary facility on King Street.
September 11, 1859	Shooting of Henry Neilson
July 17, 1860	Laying of cornerstone of Queen's Hospital at Punchbowl site.
August 23, 1862	Death of Prince Albert.
October 11, 1862	Arrival of Bishop Staley and start of Anglican mission.
November 30, 1863	Death of King Kamehameha IV.
November 30, 1863	Accession of King Kamehameha V.
May 6, 1865	Queen Emma's departure for England.
September 9, 1865	Audience with Queen Victoria.
December 5, 1865	Arrival in Paris.
June 9, 1866	Audience with the Emperor and Empress of France.
August 8, 1866	Arrival in New York.
August 13, 1866	Reception at the White House with President Andrew Johnson.
September 22, 1866	Return to Honolulu.

March 5, 1867	Laying of cornerstone of St. Andrew's Cathedral.
May 30, 1867	Dedication of St. Andrew's Priory.
December 22, 1870–April 25, 1871	Adventures in Lāwaʻi, Kauaʻi.
December 11, 1872	Death of King Kamehameha V.
January 8, 1873	Election of Lunalilo as king.
February 3, 1874	Death of Lunalilo.
February 12, 1874	Loss of election to Kalākaua and the Riot.
April 1874	Trial of the rioters (so-called Emmaites).
November 5,–November 20, 1874	Grand tour of Oʻahu.
February 1876	Election of Queen Emma Party candidates.
February 1880	Election of Albert Kūnuiākea on Queen Emma Party Ticket.
September 4, 1880	Death of Fanny Kekelaokalani.
January–May 1881	Smallpox quarantine at Rooke House.
May 24, 1883	Death of Princess Ruth Keʻelikōlani.
February 1884	Disappearance of Queen Emma Party.
October 16, 1884	Death of Princess Bernice Pauahi Bishop.
April 25, 1885	Death of Queen Emma.

The Institutions Established *by* Queen Emma

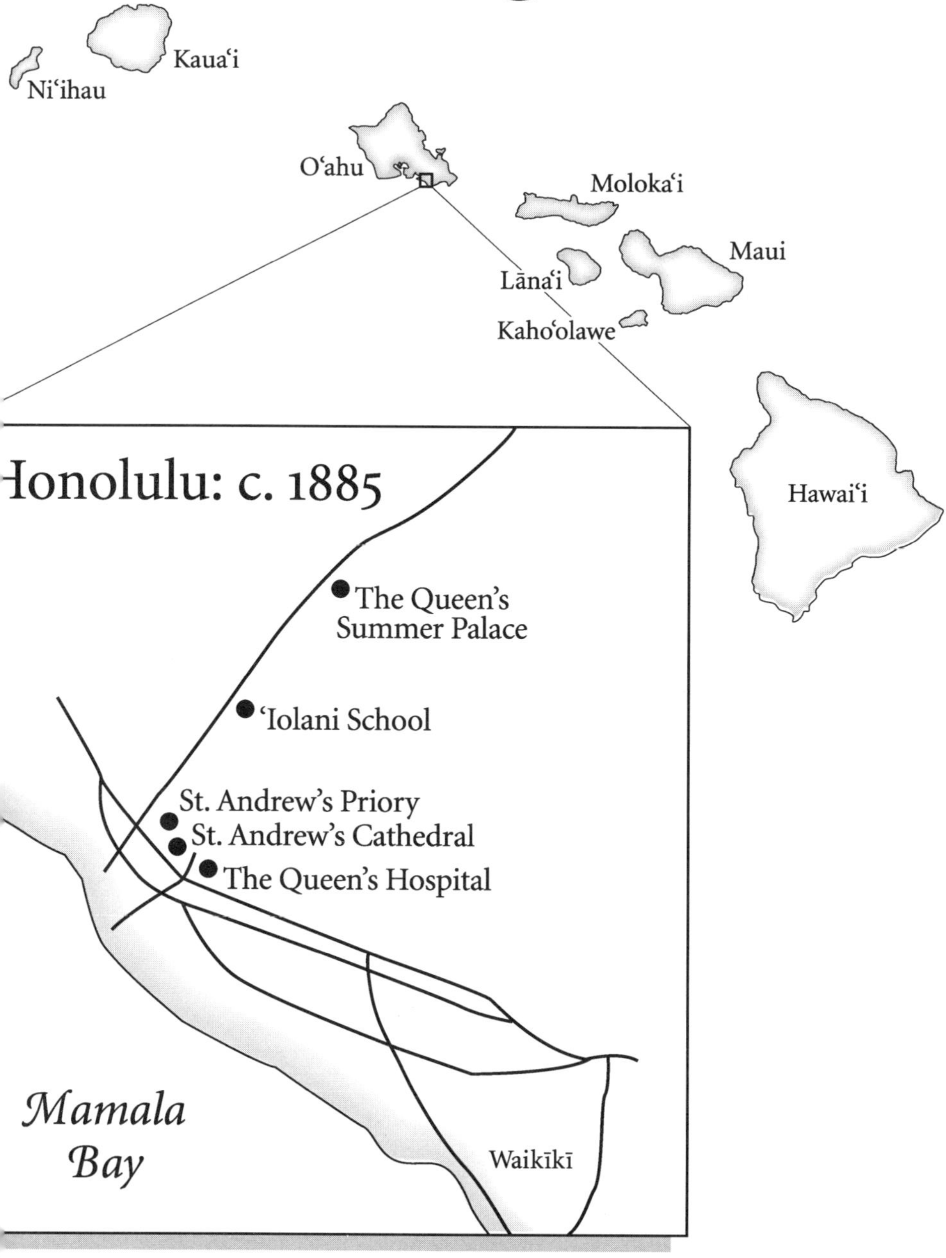

Kaua'i

Ni'ihau

O'ahu

Moloka'i

Maui

Lāna'i

Kaho'olawe

Hawai'i

Honolulu: c. 1885

The Queen's Summer Palace

'Iolani School

St. Andrew's Priory

St. Andrew's Cathedral

The Queen's Hospital

Mamala Bay

Waikīkī

1

The Beginnings

No auspicious events occurred on January 2, 1836, when Emma was born: no crackling lightning, no angry winds, no raucous thunder, no prophecy fulfilled—none of the portents *(hō ʻailona)* of a royal birth. It was unlike the night the Great Kamehameha was born when "a fiery star, trailing a flaming tail, was seen moving across the sky."[1] Even the birth of David Kalākaua—whom one day Emma would challenge for the throne—had been foretold.[2] Perhaps the signs were present, but no one recognized them or thought to record them—or maybe, even if she was destined to be queen, the gods chose to be silent. In any event, Emma Kalanikaumakaamano Naeʻa arrived unheralded but not unanticipated.

The Four Parents

Among the circle of people attending her birth were her intended adoptive parents, Dr. Thomas Charles Byde Rooke and Grace Kamaʻikuʻi Young, and her natural father, George Naeʻa. Her natural mother, Grace's sister Pane (or Fanny) Kekelaokalani Young, was, of course, in delivery.

Seven years before, Dr. Rooke was on a whaling ship serving as its youthful twenty-three-year-old surgeon when he arrived in the sailors' port of Lahaina, Maui, in 1829. Born in Hertford, England, to a physician father, he was educated at the Hertford branch of Christ's College Hospital, trained at St. Bartholomew's Hospital, and attended lectures on midwifery and surgery at the Royal College of Surgeons in London.

After receiving his degree at an early age, he decided to seek both adventure and his "internship" on board the whaling ship that brought him to Lahaina.[3]

After some new-found friends persuaded him to remain in the Islands, he settled in Honolulu, which at the time was a sprawling village with a few thousand inhabitants, including a couple of hundred foreigners—merchants, artisans, sailors, government emissaries, and missionaries. Somehow he caught the attention of the then sixteen-year-old King Kamehameha III and his advisers and was appointed as the court physician. The court considered his services so important that as an added inducement it arranged for Rooke to marry Grace. Rooke thus became one of only a handful of white men who were allowed to marry women of *ali'i* (chiefly) status and one of the few foreigners to swear allegiance to the king. (A law was later enacted that made this a requirement of anyone who wished to marry a Hawaiian woman or to accept a governmental position.)

Grace was the *hapa haole* (part-white) daughter of John Young and the High Chiefess Ka'ōana'eha, who was the niece of Kamehameha the Great. Fair-complexioned and blessed with fine features, she was born in 1808 in Kawaihae in Kohala, Island of Hawai'i. There on her father's homestead situated on a barren hillside overlooking the sea she was raised. At a tender age she was married to High Chief Kahekili Ke'eaumoku, the brother of the Queen Ka'ahumanu, but she was left a young widow when he died in 1823. Thus when Grace and Rooke were married in 1830, she was the only royal part-Hawaiian woman married to a white man.

Although intermarriage was uncommon at this time, the young couple seemed well suited to one another. Grace had a fair command of English, was acquainted with British ways, and probably felt socially equal (if not superior) to her husband (Rooke came from a family of commoners). For his part, Rooke was "a man of rare cultivation and refinement," with an outgoing and cheery disposition that complemented Grace's natural bashfulness.[4] His *'ehu* (ruddy) complexion may have endeared him to Hawaiians as much as his generosity.

At the time of their marriage in 1830 he operated a dispensary in a one-story, part-adobe structure on Union Street.[5] As only one of three Western physicians in all of Hawai'i, Dr. Rooke had more business than he could handle. And as a friend of the court, he was secure and comfortable. In fact, he had adapted so well to his new homeland that he wrote to his mother that he "shall never return to England."[6] The skies appeared bright for the Rookes except for one dark cloud: they could not have children.

The Adoption

Desperately wanting a child, the Rookes arranged to *hānai* or adopt one. Adopting each other's children was still common, although the missionaries were sternly opposed to its Hawaiian practice. All classes, especially the *ali'i,* indulged in *hānai.* For example, King Kamehameha III adopted Alexander Liholiho who became Kamehameha IV; the Queen Regent Kīna'u adopted Bernice Pauahi who became Mrs. Charles Bishop; High Chief Pākī and Chiefess Konia adopted Lydia who became Queen Lili'uokalani; Governor Hoapili adopted Lot who became King Kamehameha V; and the High Chiefess Ha'aheo adopted David who became King Kalākaua.

More often than not, adoptions occurred in the same *'ohana* or extended family. Therefore, it is not surprising that the Rookes chose to adopt one of their own. The natural choice of mothers was between Grace's two sisters: Pane (Fanny), the older (born in 1804), or Gini (Jane) Lahilahi, the younger (born in 1813). Exactly why they chose Fanny is unknown. It may have been because Fanny was a more serious, stable person and a Christian, while Jane tended to be "clever as well as a little frivolous."[7] As it turned out, Jane later became a mistress to Kamehameha III, though she was already married to Joshua Ka'eo, a lesser chief from the Island of Hawai'i. She bore the king a son, Albert Kūnuiākea (who would become Queen Emma's "prodigal cousin"). Another possible reason why the Rookes chose Fanny is that Jane might have promised her firstborn to their brother Keoni Ana, or John Kalaipaihala Young II, who did in fact adopt her first child, Peter Ka'eo .

Under Hawaiian custom, a child could not be adopted without the full consent of both true parents, lest some misfortune befall the child.[8] Fanny and Nae'a must have fully consented because they had promised the child before its birth to the Rookes. It would have been unthinkable to break that promise, but in parting with the child Fanny and Nae'a may have consoled themselves with the facts that they still had Polly, their firstborn, and that their adoptive child would probably have a better station in life with the Rookes, as well as be nearer the court in Honolulu.

In any case, it is said that as soon as the baby was delivered, the Rookes "immediately" wrapped her in "soft tapa" (bark cloth from the mulberry) and took her to their home nearby, a two-story frame building on Union facing Fort Street.[9] One should not take the term "immediately" too literally because it was customary to preserve the *piko* (umbilical cord), to bathe the infant and perhaps lightly oil it, to wrap it snugly in its tapa receiving blanket, to allow the mother to nurse it, and then to carry out the adoption ceremony.

When a child was handed to the adoptive parents, the natural parents would seal the act with the words "*Nāu ke keiki kūkae a naʻau.* I give you this child intestines and all."[10] (In Hawaiian symbology the intestines were believed to be the seat of emotions, intelligence, and character.) It was a solemn promise, a spoken contract, that was as binding as any modern legal instrument. This arrangement no doubt explains why the Rookes did not bother to sign a "legal" deed of adoption until December 30, 1851, fifteen years after the fact.

Royal Pedigree

Through the veins of Emma's mothers Fanny and Grace and her natural father Naeʻa flowed the blood of Hawaiian royalty. Naeʻa was the son of Kamaunu and Kukaeleiki, the daughter of Kalauawa, from the royal line of Kauaʻi chiefs.[11] Kukaeleiki was also the cousin of the High Chiefess Keōpūolani, the most *kapu* or sacred wife of Kamehameha I.[12] He was also descended from Kalanawaʻa, an Oʻahu high chief, and Kuaenaokalani, a Maui high chiefess who held the sacred rank of Kekapupoʻohoʻolewaikalā (a head so sacred that it could not be exposed to the sun except at dawn).[13]

Even more important than her father's lineage was her mother's because she had the blood of the Kamehamehas, the ruling dynasty founded by Kamehameha the Great when he unified the islands by defeating all dynastic rivals. Fanny's mother or Emma's grandmother was Mele or Mary Kuamoʻo Kaʻōanaʻeha, the daughter of High Chief Keliʻimaikaʻi ("the Good Chief")—Kamehameha's younger brother—and the High Chiefess Kalikookalani.

Kaʻōanaʻeha's royal status is attested to by the fact that when she was born, *pūloʻuloʻu* or *kapu* sticks with tapa-covered balls on the ends signifying a taboo were set up before the house and *pahu heiau* or *kapu* drums were beaten heralding her birth. As further confirmation of her high status, when her father died in 1810, she was reportedly the only person allowed to enter his premises, which had been declared *kapu.*[14] And when she died, she was honored by being buried in the Royal Mausoleum (then at the ʻIolani Palace site) with other royalty. (She is now entombed with her husband John Young at Maunaʻala.) These facts of

QUEEN EMMA

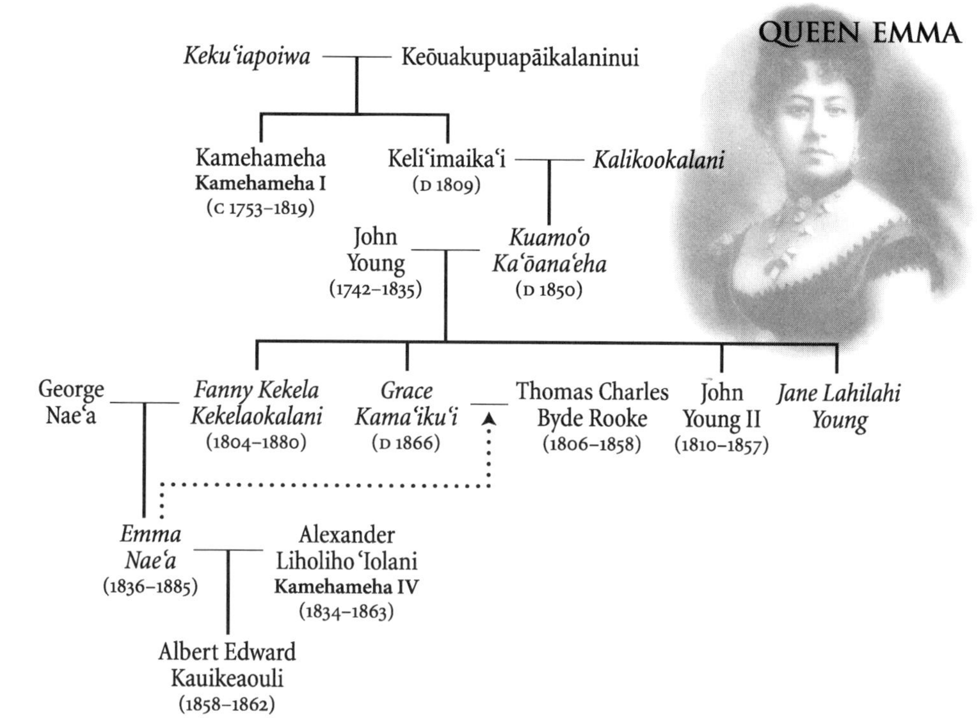

Keku'iapoiwa — Keōuakupuapāikalaninui

- Kamehameha, **Kamehameha I** (c 1753–1819)
- Keli'imaika'i (d 1809) — *Kalikookalani*
  - *Kuamo'o Ka'ōana'eha* (d 1850) — John Young (1742–1835)
    - *Fanny Kekela Kekelaokalani* (1804–1880) — George Nae'a
      - *Emma Nae'a* (1836–1885) — Alexander Liholiho 'Iolani, **Kamehameha IV** (1834–1863)
        - Albert Edward Kauikeaouli (1858–1862)
    - *Grace Kama'iku'i* (d 1866) — Thomas Charles Byde Rooke (1806–1858) [hānai: *Emma Nae'a*]
    - John Young II (1810–1857)
    - *Jane Lahilahi Young*

KING ALEXANDER LIHOLIHO KAMEHAMEHA IV

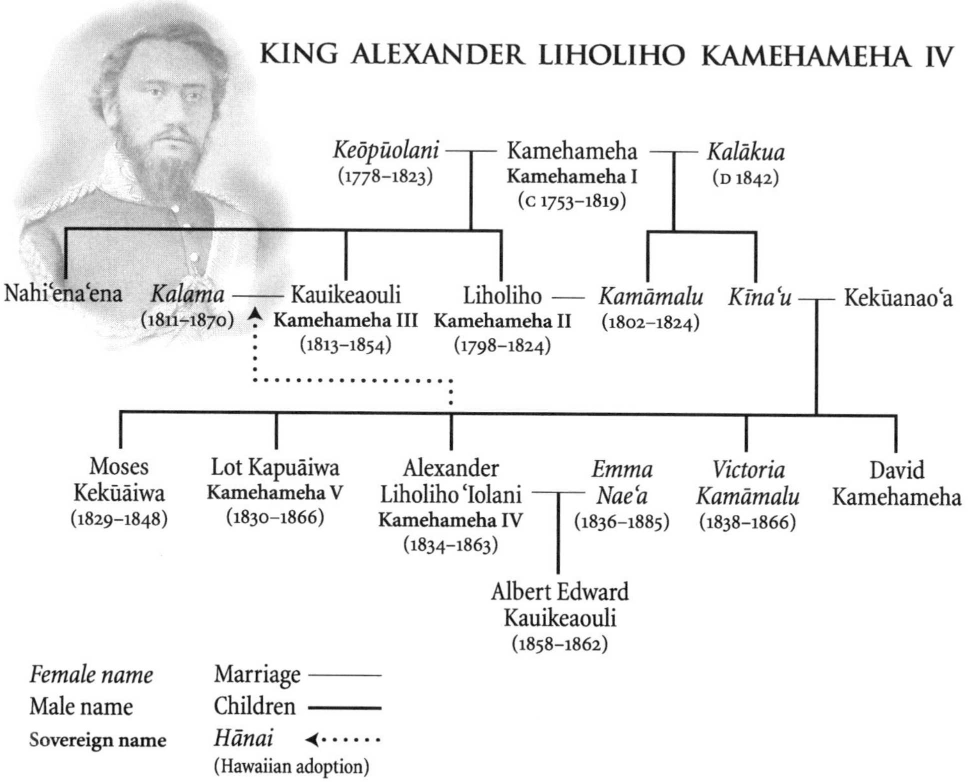

Keōpūolani (1778–1823) — Kamehameha, **Kamehameha I** (c 1753–1819) — *Kalākua* (d 1842)

Children of *Keōpūolani* and Kamehameha:

- Nahi'ena'ena
- Kauikeaouli, **Kamehameha III** (1813–1854) — *Kalama* (1811–1870) [hānai: Alexander Liholiho 'Iolani]
- Liholiho, **Kamehameha II** (1798–1824) — *Kamāmalu* (1802–1824)

Children of Kamehameha and *Kalākua*:

- *Kamāmalu* (1802–1824)
- *Kīna'u* — Kekūanao'a
  - Moses Kekūāiwa (1829–1848)
  - Lot Kapuāiwa, **Kamehameha V** (1830–1866)
  - Alexander Liholiho 'Iolani, **Kamehameha IV** (1834–1863) — *Emma Nae'a* (1836–1885)
    - Albert Edward Kauikeaouli (1858–1862)
  - *Victoria Kamāmalu* (1838–1866)
  - David Kamehameha

Female name	Marriage ———
Male name	Children ━━━
Sovereign name	*Hānai* ◄······ (Hawaiian adoption)

her royalty would be used later to defend Emma's genealogy against attacks by the Kalākauas and others.

Ka'ōana'eha may have also inherited from her father his compassion and goodness as illustrated in the story of how he got his name, "the Good Chief." High Chief Keli'imaika'i was the victorious commander of an expedition that conquered the lands of Kīpahulu and Hāna on Maui. Contrary to all previous practice, instead of punishing the people, he scrupulously respected their rights and property. As Samuel M. Kamakau, the historian, writes, "There was no sugar cane broken off, no potatoes dug up, no pigs roasted." The *maka'āinana* (common people) loved him and called him "the Good Chief" by which he was ever after known.[15] No wonder Kamehameha I considered him his favorite brother; indeed, he thought so highly of him that he was the one chief that he would not allow to work on the construction of the Pu'ukoholā *heiau* lest the work defile his *kapu* status.[16] According to the historian John Papa 'Ī'ī, Keli'imaika'i's *mana* (universal energy) was so powerful that "whatever he dedicated became very kapu." (He dedicated two bathing pools in Kawaihae, called Keli'ialalaho'ola'awai and Alawai, which were thereafter declared *kapu*.)[17]

Kamehameha I arranged, presumably in agreement with Keli'imaika'i, for the marriage of his niece Ka'ōana'eha to his trusted counselor John Young. She was only thirteen, but Hawaiians considered a girl to be grown up at that age. Kamehameha I considered his niece a "fine choice" for his white *ali'i*.[18]

John Young was a lowly seaman when he arrived in Hawai'i in 1790, only to be kidnapped by Kamehameha I's men and then impressed into the king's service. With his knowledge of cannons, rifles, fortifications, and military strategy, Young became indispensable to Kamehameha I's conquest of the Islands. No other man contributed more to Kamehameha I's military successes than John Young, although Isaac Davis, his fellow seaman who was also impressed into the king's service, played an important role.[19] The grateful king repaid his loyalty with lands, including the *ahupua'a* (a land division) of Kawaihae on the Island of Hawai'i and Hālawa on O'ahu, plus parcels on Maui and Lāna'i. The king also gave him important positions of authority and responsibility. For example, Young served as governor of the Island of Hawai'i from 1802 to 1812 and supervised the building of the fort in Honolulu in 1816.[20] When he died at the age of ninety-three, after forty-seven years of continuous service to the Kamehamehas, he had earned the right to be buried among Hawai'i's kings and queens in the palace grounds (from whence they were eventually moved to Mauna'ala, the Royal Mausoleum in Nu'uanu).[21] Except for his *haole* lineage, Emma's grandfather was a chief in every other respect.

To summarize Emma's royal pedigree, her two mothers, Fanny and Grace, were the granddaughters of Keli'imaika'i and the grandnieces of Kamehameha I. This lineage made Emma the great-granddaughter of Keli'imaika'i and the great-grandniece of King Kamehameha I. Were she not born to the high lineage of the Kamehamehas, there would be no great story to tell.

I Ke One O Kakuhihewa, On the Sands of O'ahu

Where was Emma born? Some people continue to question the place of her birth. Was it Kawaihae on the Island of Hawai'i? Or was it Kona? Lahaina on Maui? Or Honolulu—"*i ke one o Kakuhihewa,* on the sands of O'ahu"?

Marion Kelly, a well-known archaeologist formerly with the Bishop Museum, surveyed John Young's residence at Kawaihae in 1974 and speculated the following: "A grass-thatched house photographed at Kawaihae about 1889 has been identified as the house in which Queen Emma was born. Not everyone agrees today that Emma was born at Kawaihae, but if her mother lived there . . . it is possible that Emma was born there."[22]

Russell A. Apple, former historian for the National Park Service, stated in his 1978 study titled *Pahukanilua: Homestead of John Young,* "Tradition indicates that Emma was born at Kawaihae."[23] His cited source is Marion Kelly.

Much of the confusion about Kawaihae has been caused by two photographs, both taken by William Brigham, the Bishop Museum's first director, of the same grass hut mentioned by Kelly. (One of the photographs may be found on page 288 in Joseph Feher's book *Hawaii: A Pictorial History.*) Apparently, someone—whether it was Brigham is not known—added to the photograph the caption "Queen Emma's birthplace at Kawaihae, Hawai'i."

Another source claims she was born at Wai'aha in Kailua, Kona. "When we arrive at the pretty cove and white sand beach at Wai-'aha let us reverently pause, for we are at the almost unknown birthplace of the noble Queen Emma. . . .

"The whole area fronting the cove at Wai-'aha, between the point of Ka-lae-loa on the north and that of Kā'ili-punahele on the south, belonged to Queen Emma's ancestors up to her own time. Descendants of date-palms planted by Dr. Rooke still grow on the sand just back of Ka-lae-loa Point. . . ."[24]

Lahaina, on the surface, would appear to be a logical choice because it is where her natural parents resided. But only one person, the Reverend John Paul Engelcke, supposedly an "authority" on the life of the queen, thought she was born at Chief Pākī's house in Lahaina.[25] It should be noted, however, that by 1835 Pākī and Konia (the parents of Princess Bernice Pauahi Bishop, founder of the Bishop Estate/Kamehameha Schools) had settled in Honolulu. Their home *'Aikupika* was located only a short distance from the house of the Catholic sisters.[26]

The preponderance of evidence clearly favors Honolulu as the site of Emma's birth. The two Honolulu newspapers, the *Hawaiian Gazette* and the *Daily Bulletin*, reported, when they published the queen's obituary on April 29 and May 18, 1885, that the house in which Emma was born was located in Honolulu "makai of the premises now occupied by the Catholic sisters" (which was adjacent to today's Catholic Cathedral on the *ma uka* end of Fort Street Mall). Then there is the inscription on the silver plate of the queen's coffin that reads: "Emma Kaleleonalani Queen Dowager Relict of Alexander Liholiho, Kamehameha IV—Born, *Honolulu* January 2, 1836—Died Honolulu April 25, 1885" (italics added). Finally, Emma's adoption papers state that her birthplace was Honolulu.

There is a telling, albeit circumstantial, piece of evidence. It is this: John Young had died at the Rooke home on December 16, only three weeks before Emma's birth. He had been living there for some time under Dr. Rooke's care, and it appears that his family, including Fanny and Nae'a, had gathered in Honolulu, perhaps in anticipation of his death. In any case, they were present to attend his funeral. It is foolish to think that the Rookes would have allowed Fanny in her last stages of pregnancy to risk the health of *their* baby by sailing back in the rough channels to either Kawaihae or Lahaina. Obviously, the only sensible alternative for Fanny was to remain in Honolulu and have her baby there.

One of the strongest arguments for Honolulu as Emma's birthplace is her birth chant, *He Hānau no Kaleleonālani* (A Birth Chant for Kaleleonālani). Composed sometime after her death, it declares that she was born *"i ke one o Kakuhihewa"* or "on the sands of Kakuhihewa." Kakuhihewa was a famous chief of the ancient kingdom of O'ahu, which was a poetic metaphor referring to the Island of O'ahu—not Maui or

Hawai'i. No worthy composer of a sacred chant would have mistaken Kawaihae or Lahaina for Honolulu.

Finally, a puzzling set of questions remains about the house in which Emma was born. Exactly whose house was it? It wasn't the Rookes' house because after Emma's birth she was taken to their home nearby. Why didn't Fanny have her baby there in the first place? After all, it would have been much more convenient for Fanny to be there where one of the best physicians in Honolulu could look after her. The answer may simply be that there was no more room in the house. In addition to the Rookes, John Young was there seriously ill. Ka'ōana'eha was also there at his side. Under these circumstances, the house may not have been appropriate for an expectant mother. As it turned out, Young died in the home, and his funeral services were held there after his corpse had lain in state for nearly three days.[27] Because Hawaiians considered a corpse defiling, this may have dissuaded Fanny from staying there, even if the premises could have been purified by *pīkai* or sprinkling with seawater.

Rooke House

Shortly after Emma's birth, the Rookes moved into their new and spacious wood-frame mansion, one that Isabella Bird, who visited Queen Emma in 1873, described as "the most English-looking house I have seen since I left home, except Bishopscourt at Melbourne."[28] With its wide verandas facing Nu'uanu Valley, the two-story square-shaped structure, with each of its two floors measuring approximately fifty by fifty feet for a total of 5,000 square feet, was one of the largest private homes in Honolulu at the time. Its size was most likely dictated by Rooke's need for additional space for his medical practice and his extensive library, as well as for entertaining. Also on the property were a stable and coach house and the living quarters for a bevy of *kahu* or servants who typically served the royal or the affluent—categories that the Rookes by now fulfilled.

"Rooke House," as it came to be popularly called, was located on the *ma kai*-Waikīkī corner of Beretania and Nu'uanu and was bordered by Fort Street and Chaplain Lane. It occupied a one-and-one-half-acre parcel called Kaopuana ("Raincloud"), which was probably gifted to Rooke by his patron, the king. Later, he would lease or be given other royal lands in Nu'uanu Valley, partly as token payment for his services as court physician.

Rooke House, where Emma spent her childhood as well as her later years. Her father, Dr. Rooke, used the first floor as his clinic.

The nearest neighbors included fellow Englishman Henry Skinner, a businessman, whose house on the corner of Nuʻuanu and Chaplain Lane, was "one of the most pretentious mansions in the town" (it was built out of coral stone, the material of choice among foreign merchants).[29] The Reverend Samuel Damon, chaplain of the Seamen's Bethel, after whom Chaplain Lane was named, and the Reverend Lowell Smith, who presided at the original Kaumakapili Church located on Beretania Street, were also close neighbors.[30] On Fort Street were the previously mentioned Catholic Cathedral and the residences of American businessmen such as Charles Brewer, after whom C. Brewer & Co. was named, and Captain John O. Dominis, among others. Their closest *ali'i* neighbors included the High Chief Pākī and Chiefess Konia, Chief Levi Ha'alelea (he was the *konohiki* or land agent for High Chief Leleiōhoku, one of Kamehameha's grandsons, and the second husband to Kekau'ōnohi, one of Kamehameha's granddaughters), as well as Grace's sister and husband, Jane Lahilahi and Chief Ka'eo. Last but not least were the many commoners or *maka'āinana* who lived in their grass or adobe houses surrounding the white mansions.

Here then is the house and its immediate environs in which Emma would spend the first twenty years of her life. It was a world of contrasts and contradictions between the traditional and modern, the native and foreign, the *ali'i* and *maka'āinana,* the rich and poor, and the sick and the healthy. Here in Rooke House Emma's formative years would be shaped by the cosmopolitan forces represented by her mother and family, her learned physician-father, and the many guests, both local and foreign, who came to enjoy the Rookes' *ho'okipa* or hospitality.

2

Ulu Ke Keiki, The Child Grows

After Emma's birth, Grace, like most new mothers, would have reflected on the features of her child. She may have seen hints of herself, Fanny, or other members of her family reflected in Emma's fair skin and delicate features. Like all new mothers, Grace would have been thrilled to hear Emma's first coos and to see her first smiles. Unlike most new mothers, however, Grace would have been saddened by the fact she would never experience the intimate maternal feelings that come from breast-feeding.

Nuʻakea, the Goddess of Lactation

Wet nurses were common in old Hawaiʻi, which had many *hānai* infants. Those chosen few who breast-fed the infants of high-ranking *aliʻi* were called *nuʻakea* after the Goddess of Lactation who was called on both to help nursing mothers and to wean infants. (In Hawaiian mythology, she was the wife of Keoloewa, a ruling chief of Molokaʻi.) Being a *nuʻakea* was a high calling. In fact, because of the life-giving importance of their *waiū* (literally breast liquid), the breasts of the *nuʻakea* were considered sacred and *kapu* to others.[1]

Because Grace had no *waiū* to give Emma, the infant must have been nourished by these royal wet nurses. The alternative would have been to feed the child milk from a spoon or bottle. Although milk was available in Honolulu, obtaining a steady supply and keeping it fresh were difficult. Goat's milk was also available, but it tasted sour after a few hours and often caused *hī* (diarrhea) or *ʻea* (thrush). Even missionary mothers, who heartily disliked the practice of using native wet nurses, resorted to using their milk rather than goat's milk.[2]

Hawaiians believed that relatives of the infant's mother, even distantly related, would ensure that the *mana* (spiritual power) of the family line would remain pure. Although Grace's family was based on Hawaiʻi, relatives were available in Honolulu for this purpose. So from the time Emma was born and until she was weaned, Grace probably gave her over to *nuʻakea,* not without perhaps a bit of envy and anxiety. Unsettling questions must have worried her. Would she have to somehow compete for the child's affection? Wouldn't these women develop an emotional and sensory bonding that she as a barren, adoptive mother would never have? Grace knew that wet nurses commonly had a close symbiotic relationship with a child—one that would continue long after the infant had grown up. Hence the saying that wet nurses were *hoa ʻai wai,* "companions at the breast."[3]

When an infant was ready to be weaned, custom prescribed an *ukuhi* (or weaning) ritual in which prayers were offered to take away the child's desire for milk. Mary Kawena Pukuʻi, the revered modern Hawaiian scholar who was weaned in the same ritualized way in 1895, described the process as follows:

"Always, *ukuhi* began with *pule,* with prayer. *Kū* and *Hina* were invoked and asked to take away the child's desire for milk. A family senior or a *kahuna* sat facing the mother and the baby. Stones—two to represent the mother's breasts—were placed within the baby's reach. If the child grasped the stones and threw them away, the ritual was successful and the baby was ready for weaning. After another prayer, the *kahuna* or senior asked, 'Do you (naming the child) wish the desire for milk to go away from you?'

"The mother, speaking for the child answered, 'Yes.'

"And never more will you desire milk?

" 'Never,' answered the mother."

According to Pukuʻi, "The decision always was the baby's." (There were variations in the ritual using feathers, bananas, or flowers instead of stones.)[4]

Was Emma weaned with this customary ritual? Because the ritual involved prayers to the traditional gods, Dr. Rooke may have frowned on such a ceremony in respect of his Anglican beliefs. On the other hand, Grace, who remained close to her traditions, may have insisted on following the old ways. Dr. Rooke may have also resisted other practices for medical reasons. For example, he would have surely challenged and put a stop to *ho'opū'ā,* the practice of feeding babies, whereby a mother would chew a bit of solid food and then place it in the mouth of the infant being fed. It was believed that by absorbing this food the infant would also absorb the mother's character and personality. This practice might have been tolerable in non-pathogenic Hawai'i, but the epidemic spread of contagious bacteria in the 1800s made it dangerous and unhealthy.[5]

Nā Kahu, the Attendants

No ranking *ali'i* ever went without *kapu* (sacred prohibition) or *kahu* (attendant), especially the latter. From birth to death attendants always surrounded their chiefly masters, caring for their every need, desire, or whim. The higher the ranking, the more numerous the attendants and the more diverse their positions and duties. For example, when Queen Keōpūolani and her young son and daughter, Kauikeaouli and Nāhi'ena-'ena, once gave an audience to the missionaries, each had at least three attendants by their sides: one to fan, one to hold a spittoon in readiness, and one to flick flies away with a small feather *kahili.*[6] Not all *kahu,* however, performed such menial tasks. The great warrior Kekūhaupi'o was a *kahu* who trained the young Kamehameha,[7] and John Papa 'Ī'ī was already a teacher and judge when he was the *kahu* for the royal students attending the Chiefs' Children's School.[8] Royal students such as Alexander Liholiho, for example, had as many as thirty attendants in tow. Lesser ranked members of the chiefly class may have had only one attendant, but all ranking chiefs and chiefesses always had their *kahu.*

So it was for Emma, beginning with her royal wet nurse. Even after she had been weaned, at least one royal wet nurse would have probably stayed on as the principal *kahu.* She would have been responsible for Emma's feeding, bathing, dressing, disciplining, and other childcare functions; as such, she became, in effect, Emma's surrogate mother. Additional *kahu* would have done the household laundry, cleaning, cooking, and other domestic chores. Unfortunately, the identity of these early *kahu* is unknown, although the names of servants and retainers are frequently mentioned in Queen Emma's lifelong correspondence and in her will.

Massaging and Molding

Two things a mother or *kahu* would typically do to the body of a favorite *(punahele)* infant would be to massage it *(lomi)* and mold it *(kino pākō-*

lea). (*Kino pākōlea* also referred to correcting deformities and other rehabilitative practices.) Hawaiians practiced *lomi* for its physical as well as emotional benefits. In Emma's case her entire body would have been massaged daily to strengthen her limbs and to improve her circulation. Hawaiians also knew that *lomi* stimulated the infant's understanding of being loved and cared for. This daily deep and slow rhythmic touching conveyed a mother's aloha just like western-style hugging and kissing (neither of which Hawaiian women traditionally did).[9]

Puku'i relates how the bodies of favorite children were molded to approximate certain standards of physical beauty: "My people rolled the ends of fingers gently to make them taper . . . if the nose was *'ūpepe* (flat), they pressed it gently to make a sharper ridge. . . . Ears that stuck out were pressed back against the head, and when the baby was laid down, care was taken that the ears did not fold forward. . . ."[10] Puku'i recalls: "I never saw a Hawaiian in my childhood with ears that stuck out."[11]

Puku'i was talking about the 1890s and early 1900s, some sixty years after Emma's birth. So, while no direct information exists, it can be assumed that Emma was massaged or body-molded.

First Birthday Party

At the end of the child's first year—after the nursing, weaning, massaging, and molding—the family *'ohana* gathered to celebrate *Ka 'Aha'aina Piha Makahiki,* the Feast of the Fullness of the Year. It was a time for thanksgiving and for gift giving. Interestingly, the gifts were presented not to the child but rather to the family's poets, chanters, and dancers who attended on this special occasion to relate events of the child's *'ohana* and to honor the child's name in *mele inoa* (name chant).

Doubtless, the Rookes held such a feast at the beginning of 1837. After all, they had much to be thankful for: Emma was alive! As the missionary Artemas Bishop reported in 1838, "the great majority of children born in the islands die before they are two years old."[12] Indeed, the infant mortality rate was so high that microbiologist O. A. Bushnell uses the term "genocidal decline" in discussing Hawaiian infants in this period.[13]

The Rookes would have been happy to host the *'aha'aina,* especially Dr. Rooke who was always eager to play the role of the genial host, unlike Grace who was exceedingly shy and nervous.[14] Abraham Fornander, the foremost collector of Hawaiian lore, as well as both an employee and a friend of Dr. Rooke, described him as "affable and hospitable" and beloved by both natives and *haole.*[15] He entertained frequently and sometimes on a grand scale. The *'aha'aina* would have tested his hospitableness because the feasting and the fun might have lasted for an entire week![16]

In the midst of all the celebration, what did the family poets and chanters have to say about Emma? Did they recite her royal pedigree and speak of her birth in their chants? Did they also talk about her character? Was she quick and alert? Was she amiable and happy? Or was she stubborn and fussy? Did she take after a particular ancestor? Would she bring honor to the family and the Kamehamehas? Would her *haole* blood be in any way limiting? Who and what was she destined to be?

Unfortunately, nothing specific is known about what was said on the occasion of Emma's first birthday. Given their family bias, however, none of the poets and chanters would have denied that something special surrounded the child and her circumstances.

Bilingual Child

Emma grew up in a bilingual home. Her mother, Grace, spoke Hawaiian and some English; her father, Dr. Rooke, spoke English and some Hawaiian, and her attendants spoke Hawaiian. Because she heard these two languages every day, she naturally spoke and understood both languages as a child.

She learned to speak British English from her father who had been educated in London and Hertfordshire. She could not have had a better teacher than her doting father who, even if not always accessible, was always patient and interested. He spent many hours reading her stories from books in his large library including those that his mother in England had sent him for just that purpose. He may have also started teaching Emma how to read. If he did, no other royal child would have had that solid a start in English at such an early age. (Coincidentally, it is said that Alexander Liholiho was taught the language at the age of three.)[17] Emma would grow up to speak perfect English with a pronounced British accent.

While Rooke House may have been a bilingual home, Hawai'i was not a bilingual country. Although many Hawaiians, the *ali'i* in particular, had some knowledge of English, Hawaiian was the language spoken and written. Most foreign residents, including the missionaries, spoke and read Hawaiian. In fact, it was the missionaries who insisted on speaking and preserving the language as a matter of mission policy.[18] (By the 1840s the mission had translated, published, printed, and distributed more than half a million pages in Hawaiian, including the Bible and four popular newspapers.)[19]

Parental Activities

If Emma's physician-father was not always accessible, it was because he was busy with the king and members of the court, his private patients, shipping clients, business partners, and weather information users, among other responsibilities. His first priority was, of course, tending to his royal patients.

One of his most important but saddest consultations was attending to the birth in 1836 of the infant son of Princess Nāhiʻenaʻena, the king's sister. The king had announced that the child would be the heir to the throne—because he believed the child to be his—but the infant died after only a few hours. To make matters worse, Nāhiʻenaʻena fell seriously ill immediately after the birth. Dr. Rooke was unable to determine the cause of the illness and called in Dr. Ruschenberger, a visiting surgeon, to assist him. But her condition did not improve, and she died a few months later on December 30, 1836, causing a "great stillness" to fill Honolulu.[20]

Dr. T. C. B. Rooke, an Englishman, arrived in Honolulu on a whaling ship in 1830. When Emma was born in 1836, Dr. Rooke was the court physician.

Dr. Rooke's private practice continued to prosper among resident foreigners as well as natives. Regarding the doctor's Hawaiian patients, Fornander's biographer wrote, "Every day the grounds and verandas of his handsome residence, which was also his dispensary, were crowded with natives waiting to consult him" and "He gave freely of his services and his medicines to all who needed them, whether or not they were able to pay."[21] As for his foreign patients, Dr. Rooke treated many of the men and officers on the whaling and merchant ships, which led him to advocate the establishment of a hospital for British seamen in Honolulu. In 1838 he proposed to the British Consul in Honolulu that he would be willing to pay half the cost if he were allowed to treat "other than British subjects."[22]

In addition, Dr. Rooke supplied crews and shipping companies with drugs, medical equipment, and other provisions and also operated an export-import business trading in hides, butter, and "bear's fat," among other items. As a physician-entrepreneur, he was involved in several business partnerships and dealt with some of the biggest names in business: Henry Peirce, Henry Skinner, and Stephen McKintosh. He also formed a short-lived partnership with Dr. Parker Peabody, an American physician, whose part-Hawaiian daughter, Lucy Kaopauli Kalaniki'eki'e, would later serve as one of Queen Emma's maids-of-honor and as a *kahu.*[23]

Rooke's mother in England was so certain of her son's ultimate financial success that she wrote to her niece saying "His practice has increased so greatly that three out of the five medical men had been induced to leave the [Hawaiian] Islands to seek their fortunes elsewhere. . . . I think he cannot fail making a fortune."[24]

By 1844 Rooke already owned several properties and continued to acquire more in Nu'uanu Valley where he grew several crops including coffee and sugar. Viewed as a local expert on coffee, he once reported to the Royal Hawaiian Agricultural Society on the growing and marketing of coffee.[25] He was one of the first on the island to set up a mill.[26] He also managed Grace's lands in the *ahupua'a* of Hālawa, which she had inherited from her father John Young who in turn had been given the lands by Kamehameha I after conquering O'ahu in 1795. In 1847 Rooke was able to lay claim to Hālawa for Grace before the Board of Commissioners to Quiet Land Titles as part of the Mahele of 1848.[27]

For a while Rooke was also a part-time meteorologist for the *Hawaiian Spectator,* which regularly published his "General Table of Meteorological Observations at Honolulu."[28]

In the meantime, what were Grace's duties? In addition to caring for Emma and her husband, she had to manage the household, which included the servants and their respective families. If the Rookes were typical, the regular household staff comprised at least one or two nurses for Emma, a cook, a gardener, a stable or carriage attendant, and a cleaning woman. If each servant's family averaged four persons, the staff would total twenty-four persons. With Dr. Rooke and Emma, Grace was responsible for the caring and feeding of a twenty-four-member *'ohana.*

Grace also hosted, with her husband, the social events, dinners, parties, teas, and receptions for which they were well known. Steeped in the *ali'i* tradition of *ho'okipa* or hospitality, Grace was a gracious hostess. No less a host was Rooke, always elegantly dressed, who complemented his naturally shy wife with his open, gregarious, and forthright manner. Fornander states, "The doctor was also popular among the more worldly and sophisticated members of the foreign community, for he was affable and hospitable."[29] And Gorham Gilman, a business agent who lived in Honolulu in the 1840s, describes Rooke House as "one of the most hospitable in town" and adds that "the doctor's genial disposition made him many friends."[30]

Although the Rookes were noted for their hospitality, so were other members of Honolulu's affluent society such as the Pākīs, Dominises, Patys, and Skinners, not to mention the king. In the absence of theaters, restaurants, clubs, and other public or private social institutions, entertaining guests at home with plentiful food and stimulating conversation was the prevailing style. A hospitality circuit existed in Honolulu's high society in which each member had his or her turn to play the host. Their status games—like those of traditional chiefs—revolved around whose parties were the most entertaining and lavish. For the Rookes, however, being hospitable was perhaps not so much a matter of showcasing their status as simply affirming it.

Few Children, Many Adults

Emma's world was populated with many adults but few children. Royal children were handicapped by their *kapu* status when it came to playmates. Emma's were chosen from among a select few. One playmate was her cousin Peter Ka'eo, who lived a short distance away on Richards Street. The other royal children who resided in the neighborhood, such as Bernice Pauahi and Alexander Liholiho, were all several years older. She might have played with *haole* children, missionary or non-missionary, just as Alexander Liholiho or Lot did with James Dowsett.[31] But there were very few *haole* children at that time. And the nearby Damons and Smiths did not as yet have any children.

Had she been born a commoner, Emma would have been as free as other children. Because everybody was related to everybody else, children could roam where they willed. If a wandering child ended up at a neighbor's house a mile away, everyone knew the child would be safe and cared for. In this way children were exposed to many other children in many different situations.[32]

As an *ali'i* child, however, Emma was bound by jealously guarded bloodlines and royal protocols that limited her contact with other children. The world she experienced as a child was, for all intents and purposes, exclusively shaped by adults. She was thus a mature child of six when she entered the Chiefs' Children's School.

3

Ka ʻIke O Ke Keiki, The Child Learns

When Emma entered the Chiefs' Children's School in January 1842, she joined an elite group of sixteen royal children destined to lead the kingdom through perilous times. This unprecedented and short-lived experiment in education produced four kings, Alexander Liholiho (Kamehameha IV), Lot (Kamehameha V), William Lunalilo, and David Kalākaua; one queen, Liliʻuokalani; and a queen by marriage, Emma Rooke. In addition, there was a princess who might have been queen had she not refused the offer, Bernice Pauahi Bishop, the founder of the Kamehameha Schools. No school in Hawaiʻi, before or since, has ever produced the number or quality of royal leaders as did this special school.

The Tutorial Tradition

The Chiefs' Children's School was unprecedented because for the first time *aliʻi* children from different contending families were gathered together in one classroom. Traditionally, each autonomous chiefly family had educated and trained its own children. School was held at home or at the royal court or in other appropriate places. The approach was basically tutorial, using mainly the royal *kahu* as tutors. The *kahu* were experts in fishing, craftsmanship, oratory, medicine, warfare, and other subjects. For example, Kamehameha I was trained at the court of King Alapaʻinui for the first seven years of his life, and one of his principal tutors was his *kahu,* the famed warrior-chief Kekūhaupiʻo.

Apart from the personal attention a student received, one distinctive advantage of this "home schooling" approach was the infinite variety of real-life experiences that it offered. Any activity or situation—whether throwing a spear, making a surfboard, or planting taro—presented an opportunity for teaching and learning. While royal children were often difficult to discipline because of their sacred status, they too, like all Hawaiian children, learned by listening and observing in constant repetitious patterns. In an oral, non-literate culture, repetition was the most effective way to commit learning to memory. (Because Hawaiians did not have a written language until 1823, all knowledge had to be memorized.)

Despite all its advantages, the tutorial approach to chiefly education had one drawback: it did not further the cause of peace. In fact, it prevented chiefly families from coming together to discover and strengthen their common interests in the spirit of communal learning. The separateness exacerbated their distrust of one another, which contributed to frequent intertribal conflicts.

John Papa ʻĪʻī, who was one of the architects of the school, confirms this divisiveness when he tells us that the chiefs decided on establishing a school because "it was desirable that they [the chiefs' children] remain together, thereby retaining the harmony among them and discouraging rebellion of one against another. Rebellion and constant wars were common in olden times because, as the missionary William Richards[1] taught, the children of the chiefs were reared apart."[2]

A collegial approach was chosen after nearly thirty years of exposure to western-style classroom education. The start of schools in the Islands officially began in May 1820, when the missionaries established the first Protestant mission school in Honolulu, which had about thirty pupils. Over the next decade the missionaries, with the help of the chiefs, set up hundreds of schools, mostly one-classroom affairs, held indoors or outdoors, for teaching adults reading and spelling. By 1830 the schools had rendered virtually the entire adult population of 37,000 literate in Hawaiian.

During the next decade the emphasis shifted to educating children almost exclusively. Various schools were established: so-called "common" schools taught by Hawaiian teachers, and "select" schools, usually for boarders, taught and controlled by missionaries. By 1840 as many as 12,000 to 15,000 native children were being schooled.[3] This accomplishment can be credited to the support of the chiefs and to the single-minded determination and dogged faith of the missionaries.

The Cookes

The Chiefs' Children's School was officially established in 1839, when King Kamehameha III and the high chiefs secured the teaching services of two missionaries: Amos Starr Cooke and Juliette Montague Cooke. Some of their fellow missionaries protested the creation of a separate school for royal children because it promoted elitism, but an agreement was finally reached on the conditions that the chiefs (1) build a schoolhouse, (2) support the Cookes financially, and (3) sustain the Cookes' authority over the students.

The Cookes were somewhat ill-prepared for the task. For one thing, they had very little teaching experience. Before arriving in Hawai'i in 1837, Mr. Cooke had worked as a bookkeeper and clerk in a general store, while Mrs. Cooke had taught in a school for nine months. They had neither special teacher training nor the command of specialized knowledge in any secular subject. Moreover, they had little understanding of the chiefly system and even less sympathy for it.

The Cookes, however, were quite qualified to teach the Gospel of Christ, to convert the heathen "until Christ be formed in them." This was, after all, their missionary calling, and the school was a special means to fulfill that calling. In short, the Cookes were interested in saving heathen souls; the chiefs were interested in saving their own kingdom on earth.[4]

Why then did the chiefs entrust their children to this missionary pair? In the final analysis, it may have come down to character. The chiefs saw in the Cookes those qualities they deemed necessary to endure and persevere. Whatever their professional or cultural limitations, the Cookes' dedication was destined to exert enormous influence over the lives of the chiefs' children, some more than others.

The Schoolhouse

The new school was located at about the site of the present State Capitol of Hawai'i. Completed in early 1840, at a cost of $1,500, the building was square-shaped, with a courtyard and a well in the center. Its seventeen rooms included a large classroom, kitchen, dining room, sitting room and parlor, and living quarters for the students and the Cookes. The girls shared two rooms, each ten by sixteen feet. There was one playground for the students and another for the exclusive use of the Cookes' five children. The school's adobe walls were two feet thick (the partitions were one foot thick), and the pitched roof was thatched with *pili* grass. The entire complex was surrounded by a high wall, intended as much to keep people out as to keep them in. Amos Cooke, who also supervised the construction of the building, noted in his journal, "It is all cheap, yet nothing mean, all who call upon us are pleased with its style and simplicity."[5] Mrs. Cooke described it as "very comfortable."[6]

Most Royal Students

When Emma entered the school in January 1842, she was one of the last to do so, as most of the students had been there from its beginning in 1839. Those that preceded her included the three brothers, Moses Kekūāiwa, Lot, and Alexander Liholiho, their sister, Victoria Kamāmalu, Bernice Pauahi, William Charles Lunalilo, sisters Jane Loeau and Abigail Maheha, the brothers James Kaliokalani and David Kalākaua and sister Lydia Kamaka'eha (Lili'uokalani), Elizabeth Keka'anī'au, and Emma's cousin Peter Ka'eo. The last two to enter the school were Polly Pa'a'āina and John William Pitt Kīna'u.

Although no record exists of the selection process, there can be little doubt that the king and his high chiefs made the final decisions. Elizabeth Keka'anī'au Pratt, a former student, stated that "seven boys and seven girls were selected by [the king] personally. Every student was of *ali'i* status. Alexander was the crown prince, adopted by the childless King Kamehameha III and hence heir to the throne. Moses, who was adopted by the governor of Kaua'i, Kaikio'ewa, was the presumptive governor of the Island. Lot was the adopted son of Harriet Nāhi'ena'ena, but was raised by the governor of Maui, Hoapili, and was thus the presumptive governor of Maui. Victoria was eventually to succeed her mother, Kīna'u, as *kuhina nui* or co-ruler.

Bernice Pauahi was the biological daughter of the High Chief Abner Pākī and High Chiefess Konia, and the adopted daughter of Kīna'u. Lunalilo was the son of Chief Charles Kana'ina and Miriam Kekauluohi, the successor as *kuhina nui* to the Queen Regent Kīna'u. He was also the grand nephew of Kamehameha I. Jane Loeau and her half-sister Abigail Maheha were daughters of the Chiefess Liliha. Abigail was also the *hānai* daughter of the Chiefess Kekau'ōnohi, the youngest wife of the deceased Kamehameha II, who also was the governor of Kaua'i in 1842.

James Kaliokalani, David Kalākaua, and Lydia Kamaka'eha were the biological children of the High Chief Caesar Kapa'akea and his wife the Chiefess Keohokālole, a descendant of Keaweaheulu, a first cousin of Kamehameha I.

Elizabeth Keka'anī'au was the daughter of the High Chief La'anui and the High Chiefess Owana. Polly Pa'a'āina was the *hānai* daughter of

Bishop Museum

Emma was the hānai child of the Rookes. Emma's natural mother was Fanny Kekelaokalani Young, the daughter of John Young, counselor for Kamehameha I. Emma's natural father was High Chief George Naeʻa. At birth she was adopted by her mother's sister, Grace Kamaʻikuʻi Rooke and her husband Dr. T. C. B. Rooke. Dr. Rooke raised Emma to be very British; her adoptive mother Grace raised her to be Hawaiian.

the High Chief John Papa ʻĪʻī. John William Pitt Kīnaʻu was the son of William Pitt Leleiōhoku, who was a governor of Hawaiʻi Island, and Princess Ruth Keʻelikōlani, a descendant of Kamehameha I. And finally, there was Peter Kaʻeo, Emma's cousin.

To summarize, every student, including Emma, was of chiefly rank either by blood or adoption, with thirteen of the sixteen descended from the Kamehameha line. While they did not represent all of the chiefly children in the kingdom, they were, as Mrs. Cooke characterized them, "the hope of the nation."[7]

First Day at School

On January 3, 1842, Emma arrived for her first day of school in the midst of morning prayers. She was accompanied by her father, unlike every other child who had been accompanied by his or her *kahu,* in some cases dozens of them. In the early days of the school, the *kahu* were a major distraction for the Cookes. "From the commencement we have been watched as with 'eagle eyes' by the numerous *kahu,* who have been extremely jealous of us and our influence over the children."[8] The Cookes accused them of pampering the children, contaminating their innocent minds with superstitions, and trying to find as much fault as they could. On the other hand, the *kahu* had reason to resent the Cookes whom they accused of threatening their jobs, privileges, and status and even of abusing the children. The upshot of this struggle was that by the time Emma arrived, the *kahu's* presence had been greatly reduced.

At first glance, the fact that Emma's mother did not accompany her raises the question as to whether she had misgivings about Emma's matriculation. One can only speculate, but Grace must have been happy to have her daughter be admitted to the school and thereby to have her royal genealogy affirmed. Apparently, Emma started as a day student, but within a week after her matriculation she became a boarder, a decision that the government may have made because it paid the bill.

Her roommate was Elizabeth Keka'anī'au who was a year and a half older and who helped her to adjust. They became lifelong friends and in later years she said of Emma the student, "She was a great sympathizer and a sweet tempered girl. All those who knew her learned to love her."[9]

"She Has Not Yet Learned to Obey"

The first day at school can be painful for some children. Lili'uokalani, for example, states in her autobiography that she was traumatized. "I can recall that I was carried there on the shoulders of a tall, stout, very large woman. . . . As she put me down at the entrance to the schoolhouse, I shrank from the doors. . . . Crying bitterly, I turned to my faithful attendant, clasping her with my arms and clinging closely to her neck."[10]

Unfortunately, there are no recorded recollections about how Emma felt on her first day. It was probably not easy because she was closely attached to both her parents. This may explain the intriguing reference by Mr. Cooke sharply disapproving of her behavior. He recorded in his journal, just five days after Emma arrived, the following: "She has not yet learned to obey."[11]

How disobedient was she and why? The Cookes' journal is silent, but the fact that they chose to mention Emma at all suggests that she must have been more than a little disobedient, at least by their standards.

For the next year the Cookes make no mention of any misbehavior by Emma, but on January 30, 1843, the Cookes wrote, "Our souls have been much tried this evening by the going out of some of our number from our yard into our neighbor's. I put Moses in the carpenter's room, Jane in the carpenter's shop, Abigail in her room, Polly in the bathing house, & Emma in the grass house & punished her for several disobediences this day."[12] Again, except for being disobedient, the Cookes give no reason as to why she was punished. They provide a clue in June 1844, when Emma, Polly, and Elizabeth are punished because "they have had too much their own way for some months past."[13]

Thus, while the references are scant, Emma seems to have been a relatively mild thorn in the Cookes' side, sufficient to warrant a heart-to-heart talk with her father. "Last evening had some talk with Dr. Rooke about Emma. He had noticed the same that we had about her. It seems that Mrs. Rooke takes Emma's part. A sure way to spoil her."[14]

If the Cookes thought Emma was spoiled, that is what they thought of most, if not all, the *aliʻi* children. Mrs. Cooke wrote, "They [the chiefs] appear to love their children very much, but they have very imprudent ways of showing their love. They do very much as a child does when he wishes exceedingly to please a playmate—overdo—give them *everything* in their power without considering the circumstances or the possibility that they may regret this haste."[15]

The Cookes, along with their fellow missionaries, considered that Hawaiian children in general were wild and undisciplined and that royal children were even worse. Linda K. Menton, in her study of the Chiefs' Children's School, writes, "Obedience to adults, such as the Cookes envisioned it, was obviously not a quality inculcated in *aliʻi* children."[16] Exactly, because, unlike American children, *aliʻi* children were regarded as *kapu* or sacred subjects and therefore could not be disciplined as ordinary children. It would have been unthinkable, for example, for a *kahu* to strike a royal charge or even speak harshly to him or her, no matter how unruly the child.

The Cookes, however, did not hesitate to enforce the rules with punishments ranging from beatings with a ruler to depriving the children of meals or to confining them to their rooms or a grass house in the school yard for periods ranging from several hours to several days. On one occasion Mr. Cooke, while attending a church service with the children, "struck him [David Kalākaua] upon the face" for making noise.[17] On another occasion, Cooke wrote: "I became a little more stern with my scholars, & had to strike Moses to make him mind. To day I struck Alexander on the head & Moses replied, 'he keiki a ke aliʻi oia nei.' [He is a child of the chief.] I replied I was king of the school."[18] At one point Alexander and Lot tried to put a stop to the hitting by hiding

Mr. Cooke's ruler. Cooke wrote, "Found out that Alex & Lot had concealed my ruler & that Moses wished to return it to me, but was afraid to do so, lest the children should be displeased. A & L. said they were sorry."[19]

The brothers Moses, Lot, and Alexander were by far the most flagrant violators of the rules and hence received the most serious disciplinary action. Generally, the older students were more disobedient than the younger students, but among the latter, "Little Emma," as she was called at the school, seemed to be the most "wilful."

The Scholars' Routine

The daily (except Sunday) routine at school for Emma—and for every other student—was, of course, far different from that at home. She now had to awake at 5 a.m., followed usually by a walk or horseback ride. At 6:30 was morning devotion, which included prayers, readings from the Old Testament in Hawaiian, and memorizing a biblical verse in Hawaiian. Breakfast began at 7:00 and classes were from 9:00 to 12:00 noon. Another three hours of classwork filled the afternoon. Supper was at 5:30 p.m. followed by evening prayers and memorizing of scripture. (The same biblical verse learned in Hawaiian in the morning was memorized in English in the evening.)[20] The younger children went to bed at 7:00, and everyone else was in bed no later than 8:45 p.m.[21]

Occasionally, this timetable was suspended for special events such as the opening of parliament, the arrival or departure of a ship, the visit of the king, a funeral, or an occasional break to spend time with parents. Otherwise, the Cookes did not deviate from the schedule.

The intent of this untraditional routine was to instill in the young chiefs a new sense of time: clock time. Rather than live in traditional Hawaiian time, i.e., the natural cycles of sunrise and sunset, of lunar tides, of growing and spawning seasons, students now had to perform in mechanical time via seconds, minutes, and hours. If they were going to function in the western world, they needed to understand and adopt new habits of scheduling, meeting deadlines, being punctual, managing, and saving, not wasting, time.

This new order came with new rules—the new *kapu*—and one of the most important was punctuality. Status was no longer the determinant of when an event started, but rather it was a little brass school bell. As Mr. Cooke stated, students had to listen to "the bell in season & come quick."[22] Those who did not come quickly were punished. Anyone late to dinner, for example, simply went without. Queen Liliʻuokalani recalled in her autobiography "the instances in which we were sent hungry to bed" and blamed the Cookes for failing "to remember that we were growing children."[23] Because they were not allowed to eat between meals—which was contrary to the Hawaiians' custom of eating when they chose—the punishment must have been especially hard on all the children.

Punctuality required planning and managing their activities in which the beginning and ending as well as the duration of the activity were as important as its content. Students had an object lesson in "time management" in the minute-by-minute "Order of Exercises" that the Cookes prepared:

1	Singing & prayer	10	minutes
2	Reading Theology, dialog & questions	2	"
3	Reading Cain & Abel	8	"
4	Spelling	5	"
5	Spelling Kali ma	5	"
6	Show the writing B[ernice]	5	"
7	Sing "Twinkle Little Star"	5	"
8	Show the drawing books	5	"
9	Respite	5	"
	One school hour	50	"

Emma's formal education began in 1842 when she entered the Chiefs' Children's School. She was one of sixteen royal students including Alexander Liholiho, Lot, Bernice Pauahi, David Kalākaua, and Liliʻuokalani.

The Curriculum

The curriculum was divided between the secular, i.e., academic and political subjects, and the non-secular, i.e., religious and moral training. The former included reading, spelling, penmanship, arithmetic, geometry, algebra, physics, geography, history, bookkeeping, singing, and English composition. From time to time other subjects such as French and Spanish were taught by visiting foreigners. Special lectures were also given on various topics and events.

English was the most important subject not only because it was the medium of instruction but also because as future rulers who had to deal with foreigners they needed to be able to speak it. This was the major reason why the Cookes forbid the use of Hawaiian in the classroom although both the Cookes spoke fluent Hawaiian and used it with the children on many occasions.

Incongruously, although the students were being trained to rule, the curriculum did not include law, government, political philosophy, economics, business, or other subjects related to governing a nation, especially one that was experiencing rapid change.

In the classroom students were divided by their age and length of time at the school. The older group consisted of Moses, Lot, Alexander, William, Jane, Bernice, Abigail, and Elizabeth, all of whom were older than Emma by a few years. Emma was in the next class together with James, Peter, and David, while Victoria, Lydia, and Polly and John Pitt were in a still younger group (except for Polly who was born in 1832, four years earlier than Peter, Emma, or David).

By the time Emma entered the school, the older students were studying history, intermediate arithmetic, geography, grammar, and composition, among other subjects. Emma and her class started with basic reading, spelling, and beginning arithmetic. During her first year, for example, the class had read "Worcester's Second Reading Book," "Gallaudet's Book on the Home," and "Emerson's Arithmetic Part I."[24] These and almost all the textbooks at the school were American and used in the United States in the 1830s and 1840s; hence the students received a totally American education.

Because Emma had learned to speak perfect English at home, she was ahead of her "classmates," Peter, David, and James, in reading and spelling. This advantage was only temporary, however, because all the students learned to speak English quite well. In fact, by the end of her first year in 1842, the students spoke mainly English both in and out of class. Mr. Cooke reported to his superiors: "Most of their conversation among themselves is now in English. Indeed they are very fond of getting together in the school room soon after dark and the boys haranguing their little assembly in our language. We allow this for the sake of strengthening their lungs and facilitating their fluency in our mother tongue."[25]

Religious and Moral Training

Religious and moral training took precedence over secular education because the purpose of the school was "to teach them correct morals, and the religion of the Bible," as the newspaper *Polynesian* put it.[26] "The children of the chiefs," it continued, should "seek first the kingdom of God and his righteousness, imbibe the spirit of the gospel and avoid sin in all its forms, that they may eventually be qualified to take the lead of a civilized and Christian nation." While all the chiefs may not have agreed with this view, as far as the Cookes were concerned, the children served only "our Master in Heaven."[27]

God may have rested on the Sabbath, but not the Cookes and not the children. Even Mrs. Cooke admitted, "There is no day in which I am so much fatigued as the Sabbath."[28] The children attended the early morning Sabbath School taught by the Cookes and learned the scriptures and other religious (presumably Congregational) tenets. Then they attended Hawaiian church services, one in the morning and the other in the afternoon, and sometimes English-language services as well. Attendance at these services was not an idle manner of passing time. The Cookes regarded these services as additional scriptural lessons and as an important faith-building experience.

Emma was diligent in attending these services, though neither she nor any of the students had a voice in the matter. Mr. Cooke wrote, "The habit of always attending church has become so fixed that they do not imagine that they can stay at home."[29] For Emma, attending church was a habit she maintained throughout her life.

The biblical injunction "We will give ourselves continually to prayer" was one the Cookes shared with the children. They prayed often: in their morning and evening devotionals, at each meal, at bedtime, and on many special occasions that required divine guidance and protection. Like attendance at church, attendance at prayer services was not voluntary. Missing or being late to a prayer service was a punishable offense.[30] Nevertheless, the Cookes, obviously knowing that prayer could not be forced on the children, hoped that in time prayer would become a habit. Indeed, prayer did become an integral part of Emma's spiritual development.

Another important part of the children's religious and moral training was their involvement in the temperance movement. Shortly after Emma entered the school, the older children—Moses, Lot, Alexander, William, Jane, Bernice, and Abigail—joined the Children's Temperance Society, which prohibited both alcohol and tobacco. They also signed the temperance pledge.[31] The king and several chiefs also pledged abstinence. A "cold water army" was formed, and the children made a flag on which was inscribed the motto, "We will no more participate of that which can Intoxicate."[32]

A year later, the students were still keeping their pledge of "Teetotalism" but needed to be "lectured every day" on "Moral Purity." Mr. Cooke complained about the "improper conduct" of the students and had them sign a Purity pledge that read: "That we will not indulge in licentious conduct or conversation, and as far as in us lies, we will abstain from all impure thoughts, and we will also do all in our power to promote moral Purity among ourselves & others."[33] Mr. Cooke was hopeful but realistic when he wrote: "May they have grace to keep it. None of them have, as yet, obtained a new heart. This is the only secure remedy for the waywardness of youths and adults. Their knowledge of Scripture and consequently of the principles of our Holy Religion is daily increasing. But *knowledge,* alone, never yet saved a single soul, either civilized or heathen."[34]

The Cookes talked to the girls about "the subject of virtue" and especially "of their intercourse with the boys."[35] They tried to put a stop to boys visiting the girls in their rooms, one of which was Emma's. Mr. Cooke wrote, "This morning arose earlier than usual & called the children to go for a walk. Could not find Kali. He was afterwards found in Emma *ma* [and her group's] room, & I punished him very severely."[36] (Her roommate, Elizabeth Keka'anī'au, may have been with Emma and others at the time, which may be why she was not punished. Emma was only nine at the time.)[37]

The Cookes' sexual code was quite rigid, and despite their exhortations and punishments, several violations occurred. Jane and Polly had left the school at night to dally with someone's uncle.[38] Moses slipped away "to sleep with the Queen."[39] And Abigail Maheha had to leave "in prospect of becoming a mother."[40] In August 1844 Juliette Cooke wrote, "The most discouraging feature of our labor is that not one of our scholars is seeking the right way. I am afraid that their high stations will cheat them yet of heaven. We have daily evidences that they are depraved —totally depraved."[41]

A year later Mrs. Cooke wrote, "Our scholars are improving, they greatly need the Spirit's influence. Oh if they were only Christians how it would cheer us on in our labors! . . . They seem more like New England hardened hearers of the word. They pant for the pleasures of earth such as the civilized world chose as delightful. They would gladly if permitted attend the dancing school and join the balls which are more numerous here than anywhere in New England."[42] Mr. Cooke contributed to this assessment of the students when he remarked, "I am quite low-spirited this evening, in consequence of some mischief among our scholars. They are like a wild ass colt . . . deceitful above all things and desperately wicked."[43] Mrs. Cooke added her verdict: "Our interesting scholars . . . can converse intelligebly in English—read—write —cypher—parse—spell—study geography—sing—drawing (linear)—2 boys play flute & two girls play on a pianoforte—& nearly all ride horseback, etc., etc., but all this avails us nothing, comparatively, while we see them exposed to the damnation of hell. O Christians! pray for them."[44]

While the Cookes gave themselves a failing grade for religious and moral training, the chiefs must have approved their methods because no indication exists that they ever objected to the Cookes in any significant way.

Extracurricular Activities

Life in the Chiefs' Children's School was not entirely spent in a classroom or in a church. The days were filled with an eclectic range of recreational, social, vocational, artistic, and civic activities aimed at producing well-rounded future leaders. The Cookes were involved in many, if not most, of these activities, and surprisingly, so were the children's parents.

The number one extracurricular activity was keeping physically fit, which, in the words of the Cookes, consisted of "riding in the wagon, on horse back, walking early in the morning and just at evening, playing ball, rolling hoops, bathing and swimming weekly and innocent plays to keep them from sleeping during the day."[45] Mr. Cooke boasted that until the students came to the school they had never exercised so much.[46]

What they did most was horseback riding. Bernice Pauahi wrote in her diary that rising early and riding was the "usual" thing they did.[47] And "everyone" rode, including Emma. They went on rides of several miles. On May 28, 1842, for example, the Cookes wrote, "This morning we rode before breakfast . . . went as far as Dr. Rooke's."[48] Occasionally

Emma rode accompanied by her father.[49] Sometimes they even went to Kaniakapupu, the summer residence of Kamehameha III in upper Nuʻuanu Valley, approximately four miles away, where Alexander Liholiho was brought up and trained in the ways of a Hawaiian chief.[50]

The boys went often to Waikīkī to surf. The Reverend David B. Lyman, who accompanied them on one of their visits, described their "dressing apartment" (a thatched house located where the Royal Hawaiian Hotel is located today) among the "fine groves of Cocoanut trees & Kou trees" and their surfboards "12 to 20 feet long, more than 2 ft. wide & in the middle 5 or 6 inches thick," some of them "handed down to the royal family for years."[51]

Emma must have developed her love for music at the school because, as Mrs. Cooke wrote, "We encourage their finding amusement in music as it prevents idleness and gives a taste for rational pleasures."[52] Emma, like all her fellow students, had "a decided taste for music." She took piano lessons, learned to play well, and continued the piano into adulthood. She also played her accordion, which her father had "brought" to the school.[53] Emma particularly enjoyed singing. She had a fine voice, as did all the students.[54] Together they sang "excellently" and often entertained themselves as well as visitors to the school. In addition, Emma and the other students attended the popular "singing school" at the nearby chapel, which was but one of many singing schools established by the missionaries to teach their Hawaiian converts how to sing the *hīmeni* or hymns. Because the participants in the singing schools sang in Hawaiian, singing presented an unusual opportunity for the students to use their mother tongue.

Emma's musical education did not include learning any of the classical Hawaiian *oli* or *mele* (chant), the *pahu* (drum), *ʻohe hano ihu* (nose flute), *ipu* (gourd), or any other instruments. It was not because neither of the Cookes could teach the subject. They could have invited native performers to the school, just as they did foreign pianists and singers to entertain the students and their parents. The Cookes, however, did not do so because they regarded Hawaiian music and the hula in particular, like the rest of their missionary cohorts, as the "work of the devil."

Instead, the students' musical education was entirely western: from the hymns they sang in the singing schools, whether sung in Hawaiian or English, to the piano, accordion, flute, melodeon, and other instruments they learned to play, to the vocal and instrumental performances of visiting artists. Little wonder that Emma and most of the students grew up to be devotees of western music.

The girls also learned to sew, cook, clean, and do other housekeeping chores. Of course, under ordinary circumstances, no chiefly child would do any such work; that, after all, was the function of their servants. But with their *kahu* all but banished from the school premises, the young boarders had no choice. The Cookes were convinced that it was good for them to learn a new work ethic and that there is dignity in all work, no matter how menial. How willingly did Emma and the other girls perform their chores? If the uncomplaining Pauahi was any indication, they were all willing participants.[55]

Perhaps the most exciting and interesting times for the students were their trips to places on Oʻahu and the neighboring islands of Hawaiʻi, Maui, and Kauaʻi. One Oʻahu trip was made to Waikīkī where Emma and the children "bathed" and visited the *heiau* (Papaenaena) "where human victims were once offered."[56] A more extensive, nearly two-week Oʻahu trip took the students from Honolulu to ʻEwa, then Waialua, around to Hauʻula, Kāneʻohe, and Waimānalo, all by horseback.[57] Still another Oʻahu trip took them to Nuʻuanu for nearly ten days. As the school's physician, Dr. Rooke accompanied the students on most, if not all, such excursions.

Shortly after Emma matriculated, she and her fellow students journeyed to Lahaina to be with parents attending the regular parliamentary session. (The Cookes do not mention whether Emma had met her natural parents, Fanny and George Naeʻa, in Lahaina where they were domiciled.) Although the students enjoyed the sail over, the Cookes were miserable, suffering from seasickness and cockroaches that "made a road" of them. The children were happy to spend time not only with their parents but also with their *kahu,* as each child was allowed to bring along one servant. While in Wailuku, the children and the Cookes visited the girls' school run by the missionaries. The Cookes were struck by the orderliness of the girls and wished the chiefs "could do more for our school." A measure of the success of the twelve-day trip is revealed in Mr. Cooke's journal entry: "The children exhausted all their English over and over again in trying to tell me of the things that they had seen and heard. . . ."[58] The Cookes were so impressed with the royal treatment they received on Maui that on their return to Honolulu they reciprocated with an "excellent supper" for the king and the chiefs. Mrs. Cooke wrote: "The Chiefs always expect cake, and nice cake too. I had bread and butter, cup cake, cookies, fried cakes, sponge cake, crackers, cheese, tea and coffee. I used 40 eggs in my cookery, and the board was swept clean."[59]

In June of 1846 the students sailed to Hilo on the king's best schooner for a month-long trip to Hawai'i, Maui, and Moloka'i, accompanied by Dr. and Mrs. Rooke. Their first adventure was a trek from Hilo to the crater of Kilauea, a distance of eleven miles, which took a day and a half. The slow pace was due to the fact that, in Cooke's words, "Servants attended us almost beyond number."[60] Because not every one had a horse, some rode and some walked, including Mr. Cooke. As the group wended their way up the slope, "all" the villagers along the trail came to see "the people of high character." As soon as they approached the crater, according to Mr. Cooke, the larger boys immediately went to the edge of the crater where Alexander Liholiho lost his wide brimmed hat, which Cooke called "a sacrifice to Pele."[61] Alexander, as he later wrote to Mrs. Cooke, was very disappointed. He expected to see "fire & smoke issuing out of the volcano," but all he saw was "some little smoke issuing out here & there like so many chimmneys." It took them nearly a day to go around the crater.[62] That evening a weary Emma slept with her parents who were assigned to chaperon the girls, while the boys and *kahu* occupied a nearby grass house with John 'Ī'ī and Mr. Cooke. They returned to Hilo the next day and from there traveled on to Kealakekua to visit Captain Cooke's death site, then to Kailua, Kona, and finally to Kawaihae.

For the Rookes, Kawaihae was a homecoming, for among the welcoming party was Ka'ōana'eha, Emma's grandmother, whom she had not seen for some time. For Grace and Emma especially, the reunion with Ka'ōana'eha was a special pleasure during an otherwise arduous trip. Ka'ōana'eha happily entertained the entire group at her home one evening. Mr. Cooke's terse journal entry read, "We found old Mrs. Young here ready to receive us."[63] She was only fifty-five years of age at the time, but in the 1840s when Hawaiian mortality rates hovered around age forty, Cooke was correct in his use of the term "old." Since John Young's passing in 1835, she had continued to live in Kawaihae in her large airy grass house (rather than in her husband's stone house) situated on the rise overlooking Kawaihae Bay and seldom ventured far away to places like Honolulu.

As future leaders of the nation, the students were made acquainted with important civic or political events. One such event occurred on July 31, 1843, when Admiral Richard Thomas ended the five-month rule of the Islands by Lord George Paulet, a commander of a British vessel, and returned independence to a grateful Hawaiian people. The students observed the entire day and Emma had reason to be especially proud that day because Dr. Rooke was one of the two government witnesses (the other was Dr. Gerrit P. Judd) to the signing of the documents of restoration by Kamehameha III and Admiral Thomas.[64]

Epidemics of 1848

A series of epidemics broke out in Honolulu in 1848: first, a serious epidemic of diarrhea, then measles and whooping cough, and finally influenza. Nearly every child born in 1848 died from these diseases.

On October 19, Mr. Cooke wrote in his journal: "The streets of Honolulu indicate that many are confined to their houses from sickness of the measles called by the Hawaiians *Ma'i puu puu ula.*"[65] Students at the school did not escape: everyone, including Emma, caught the disease. All survived, except for Alexander's brother, Moses Kekūāiwa. This may have been the first time that Emma came close to understanding the plight of the Hawaiians. She heard her father report that 200 were dying in Hilo every week. She saw Amos Cooke going out to the sick to administer medicine he had made, including pills for diarrhea consisting of one part calomel, three parts opium, and four parts ipecac. Some students accompanied Mr. Cooke on these visits. He recorded in his journal: "One house on being entered was found to contain four dead bodies! They had perhaps starved to death! All sick at once; no one able to go for medicine or assistance." He described another case of a couple who were found in their home "locked in each other's arms dead."[66]

As far as the Cookes were concerned, caring for the sick was "an important part of a girl's education." But this lesson was one Emma had already learned at home from her physician father.

The Last Days of School

In the fall of 1848 the Cookes indicated that they would leave the school in a year. "As our scholars grow up, we find it more difficult to restrain them. Our two eldest boys are grown men as to size. Alexander is not yet 15, but he is almost 6 feet high and weighs 160 pounds. L. Kamehameha is 17, and is about the same size. I tremble to see them enter on the stage of action with uncircumcised hearts. . . ."[67]

A year later Mr. Cooke revealed the real reason for their departure: they were plain tired. In a letter to his mother-in-law, he wrote that they were ready "to give up our charge of the school & take some other labor that would not tax the entire and constant energies of both soul & body, day & night, month after month & year after year."[68] The government tried to persuade the Cookes to stay, even offering a salary increase, but they had made up their minds.

On August 7, 1849, Emma left the school for the last time (along with William, James, Peter, and David) and returned to her parents. There she would continue her schooling in the traditional tutorial method with a governess.

What impact did the school have on its students? The Cookes, of course, had but one objective: to produce "civilized and Christianized" young people. But, as author Linda Menton writes, "this achievement had cost more than a trifle. For in order to reach these goals the royal children had been almost completely cut off from their indigenous culture."[69] However, the students did acquire several skills: "They learned to read, write and speak English, while maintaining their first language. They learned how to behave according to Western standards. At ease with foreigners and high ranking dignitaries, they learned the skills of 'high culture.' They became accomplished musicians, and several later became composers and poets. Genteel and polite ladies and gentlemen, they were 'civilized' by Western standards. Whether such skills, however, were adequate for the very difficult task of ruling Hawaii for the next half century is less certain."[70]

Although much is known about the formal schooling of the *ali'i* children, it would be wrong to assume that their education was limited to that described in the journals and letters of the Cookes. For example, Alexander Liholiho, the future Kamehameha IV, was said to have been educated in two ways: "First he was trained to be a king in the western style. And then he was brought up here to the valley to his father's palace [in Upper Nu'uanu at Kaniakapupu] and trained as a Hawaiian chief."[71]

4

Growing Up

When Emma left the Chiefs' Children's School in the summer of 1849, she was already a teenager, thirteen years and eight months, to be exact. It was a marriageable age for Hawaiian girls of the time; consequently, Dr. Rooke saw to it that she would receive an "English lady's education" so as to become a "fit bride."[1] Instead of sending her to another day school, as the Pākīs had done for Liliʻuokalani by sending her to the Beckwith School, he engaged private tutors to educate Emma at home. History records the name of only one of these tutors: a genteel English woman, Mrs. Sarah Rhodes Von Pfister. During the critical years of Emma's adolescence, Sarah would become not only a tutor but also a trusted mentor and confidante.

An English Lady's Education

The fortuitous appearance of Sarah may have proved to Dr. Rooke that timing is everything. Sarah had moved to Oʻahu from Kauaʻi sometime in 1849, shortly after her American husband had been killed—stabbed to death by a drunken miner near Sutter's Fort, where he had gone to strike it rich in the California Gold Rush.[2] Widowed with two children, she had turned to teaching to support herself. When she arrived in Honolulu, she set up a "select" school for the children of Honolulu's elite, which was located on Smith and Beretania Streets near the Rooke House. It was an ideal happenstance for the Rookes and for Sarah.

Sarah was well suited for her special role on two counts. The first reason was that she was English, having been born, raised, and educated in England. She had a respectable background: her father was a high official of the Bank of England. Her brother-in-law, John Brown, was a well-known landscaper in charge of all the gardens and hothouses of Queen Victoria at Windsor Castle. Through his royal connections, Sarah became acquainted with the refinements of British etiquette and high society.

The second reason for Sarah's suitability was her knowledge and understanding of the "natives" and their ways. She had come to Hawai'i in the early 1840s with her sister and husband, John Brown, who had left England seeking, on his doctor's advice, a warmer climate. She accompanied the Browns to Kaua'i where they first settled in Hanalei. There Brown teamed up with Sarah's brother, Godfrey Rhodes, who had arrived in Hawai'i much earlier, to raise coffee. When the effort failed, he moved his family, along with Sarah, to the district of Wailua where he acquired some land and went into ranching.[3] He built a large frame house in Wailua, designed by an English architect, whose plans included a secret chamber where the family could hide in case they were "attacked by savages."[4] It was there that Sarah had met John R. Von Pfister who was in both the coffee and the sugar business. They married and had two daughters before he, like many other men in Hawai'i, caught gold fever and went to California where he met his untimely end.

Unlike Amos Cooke, Sarah did not keep a journal (or at least none is extant), so little is known of what she taught her most famous pupil, although some reasonably sound guesses can be made. Sarah and Emma must have spent considerable time reading, probably some of the English classics in Dr. Rooke's extensive library (as an adult, Emma continued to read the English classics). Reading aloud, particularly from the Scriptures, was a common practice, and the Anglican Book of Common Prayer was particularly popular in the Rooke household. Not surprisingly, Sarah was an Anglican herself.

English composition, grammar, and spelling along with geography and history, especially of Great Britain, would have been a natural part of the curriculum. Sarah may have also taught some beginning French not only because it was a language that English ladies learned but particularly because the French government insisted on conducting its affairs in Hawai'i in French. The rules of proper dress, make-up, posture, dining, and other social graces were an essential part of Emma's education. The use of proper manners was important not only to Sarah but also to Emma herself in becoming a defining part of Honolulu society—a society that she was to live in and to shape.

Sewing, which Emma enjoyed, was certainly one of the domestic skills in the curriculum. Earlier it had been taught and encouraged by Mrs. Cooke to all the girls who mended or made their own dresses. For Emma, who had a keen eye for fashion, sewing had both a practical and artistic utility. The combination of being fashion conscious and fastidious in her dress occasionally caused Dr. Rooke to complain about the bills for her finery.[5]

At that time sewing also had a social meaning in Honolulu. Almost every woman of any importance was a member of the Sewing Society. It was supposed to do sewing for the poor, but it was mostly a pretext for socializing. Its lady members met fortnightly at one of their homes, starting at 2:00 p.m. and ending at 5:00 p.m. with a substantial tea consisting of sandwiches and cold salads—and lots of chatter. Often they resumed at seven o'clock when their husbands and many young people arrived for games, musical numbers, and more chatter.[6] Emma regularly attended these meetings such as the one in February of 1854 held at the Pākīs where Mrs. Bernice Pauahi Bishop emceed.[7]

Because Emma was fond of music, it was natural for her to affiliate with the Amateur Musical Society. When it was established in 1853, Emma was one of its founding members, along with Bernice Pauahi Bishop and Sarah Von Pfister, and at seventeen years of age, she was probably its youngest member. The main purposes of the organization were improving the musical abilities of its members, holding public concerts and rehearsals, purchasing musical instruments, books, etc., and raising funds "to give permanency to the existence of a musical society in Honolulu." Emma also participated in several of its musical and theatrical performances.[8]

The society's thirty members met once a month, in private homes, including Rooke House. One of the rules was that "no dancing shall be allowed at the house where the Society assembles." But this was later changed when "the puritan element became less dominant" among its members.[9] Given her love of dancing, Emma no doubt welcomed the change.

It is not known exactly how long Emma's private education lasted, but it continued for at least four or five years or until her marriage. Nor is it known how much or how well Emma learned her lessons. It is certain though that Emma was constantly pushed by Sarah, who was a dedicated and demanding teacher. The story is told of how Sarah, while sailing from Kaua'i to O'ahu on a little schooner, kept the man at the wheel awake by prodding him with her umbrella because she had heard that the helmsmen on these schooners, when well offshore, invariably lashed the wheel and took a snooze. (Despite her prodding, the schooner went aground on Barber's Point, but they finally reached Honolulu by horseback.)[10]

Emma must have responded well to Sarah's tutoring because, based on the things she stood for in her adult years—Anglicanism, Victorian morality, the superiority of British parliamentary government to American republicanism, the English tradition of tea, and so on—she had indeed acquired an "English lady's education."

The fact that Sarah and Emma enjoyed a friendship that lasted for forty years suggests that Sarah was more than a tutor. She entered Emma's life when she needed a sympathetic and understanding ear. As an adolescent, set apart from everyone by her mixed ancestry, her *haole* father, and her upbringing, she must have often felt at sea, trying to measure her self-worth on the ebb and flow of her relationships with the people and the world around her, seeking reassurances about who she was, how she looked, or what others thought of her. In between the many hours of tutorials, Emma would have naturally turned to Sarah,

Emma as a Young Woman

many years older and wiser, to talk about the bewildering experiences of growing up. Sarah provided not only the intellectual nurturing but also the emotional sustenance that only a non-parental mentor could impart.

Medical Education

Another important part of Emma's home schooling came from an altogether different tutor, her father Dr. Rooke. Rooke House was an ideal setting for both teaching and learning: she was a curious, awe-struck student with a compassionate streak, and he was a doting and eager teacher dedicated to medicine. Their informal classroom was the clinic on the first floor. Nearly every morning he opened his doors to the lame, injured, or sick, and the wide veranda and grounds were crowded with patients and others who sought his help. Because almost all his native patients were too poor to pay, his clinic was free.[11] Dr. Rooke operated his clinic with perhaps one assistant and a willing and able teenage daughter at his side.

Under these circumstances Emma learned about the healing arts: how to recognize certain kinds of injuries or diseases and their cures, how to bring down the fever of a patient by applying a cooling cloth, how to bandage a cut or wound, how to mix medications and to apply the appropriate ones, and perhaps even how to apply a tourniquet or a splint to immobilize an arm or leg. She could have assisted her father in simple surgical procedures such as handing him instruments and gauzes, dabbing blood, or lancing wounds. And she also could have assisted during those most tragic and traumatic times of Hawaiian suffering—the epidemics. Inevitably, treating the sick must have been an integral part of her upbringing.

Deaths of Ka'ōana'eha and Kanehoa

A special patient who convalesced at Rooke House was Emma's grandmother, Ka'ōana'eha. She had been reluctant to leave Kawaihae and probably knew that she would not return—just as fifteen years before, her husband John Young did not return. At sixty-two and too ill to be cured, she died in Rooke House on January 22, 1850.

Ka'ōana'eha was buried the next day on the palace grounds by the Royal Tomb, without the high ceremony to which she was entitled by her high chiefly rank. Some wondered why a chiefess of her status would be buried so quietly. The official *Polynesian* did not make much of her death either, devoting just a few lines to her obituary.[12] It is said that this lack of respect indicated that she "was out of favor in Honolulu chiefly circles" partly because she preferred the traditional Hawaiian values, including the ancient religion, and had resisted Christianity and westernization.[13] For example, she defied convention when she took as her new name Mele Kuamoʻo, after the name of the battlefield where her brother Kekuaokalani, defender of the ancient *kapu* or sacred prohibitions, was killed leading the rebel forces against those of Kamehameha II in 1819. The extent of Emma's affinity for her grandmother is not known, but it would have been uncharacteristic of Emma to allow the conflict between her grandmother's traditionalism and her own Christian fervor to affect her love for her grandmother. She, after all, was quite close to the traditionalist cum iconoclast, Princess Ruth Keʻelikōlani, the king's half sister, who refused to speak English or to step inside a Christian church.[14]

One year later Emma experienced the death of a close family member: her half-uncle, James Young Kanehoa (the son of John Young by Namokuʻelua, his first wife). He was as colorful as Emma's other uncle, Keoni Ana, but she had little contact with him until the last six or seven years of his life. When he died on October 1, 1851, he too had been a patient at Rooke House.

Although born in Kawaihae, Kanehoa left the Islands at the age of nine and lived in the United States where he became a merchant mariner; for many years he sailed between Philadelphia, his home port, and England. Eventually, his experiences abroad and his fluency in English led to his becoming the interpreter for King Kamehameha II. After what proved to be an ill-fated journey to London in 1823, Kanehoa accompanied the body of his deceased king back to Honolulu. He then assumed a court position under the Regent Kaʻahumanu until her death in 1832. In the meantime, Kanehoa had married Sara or Kale Davis, the daughter of Isaac Davis, John Young's comrade in arms. For about the next ten years he lived in Lāwaʻi—a large *ahupuaʻa* that he owned—in the district of Kōloa, Kauaʻi, where he served as a judge for a time.

From 1845 on Kanehoa distinguished himself as he was appointed a member of the House of Nobles, then a member of the privy council, and finally a member of the original Land Commission. Concurrently with the last position, he served as governor of Maui from 1845 to the time of his death. The fact that his brother Keoni Ana was serving as prime minister during these years probably had some bearing in these appointments.

What is worth noting is that when Kanehoa was able to spend time in Honolulu, he got to know his niece well. Apparently, he was pleased with Emma because he made his wishes clear to his second wife the Chiefess Hikoni that his lands in Lāwaʻi should one day be given to Emma.[15]

A Father's Letter

Shortly after Kanehoa's passing, Dr. Rooke wrote to his "child" Emma in one of the few such letters extant.

> Lahaina Dec 22nd 1851
>
> My dear Emma
>
> I received your letter yesterday and am very sorry to hear of poor old Joe's accident. Take care of him. It makes me more anxious than ever to get back. It is my intention if I am not ordered to remain to return in the Kaluna. I may hopefully, come in the Harriette on Wednesday but I cannot place in dependence on the King's resolve. He is well now and might keep so if he likes. Fanny is quite well and desires her love to you and Mother.
>
> What a Lalau [blundering] Goose you are. I sent for a piece of narrow common bordering & you send me a piece of broad satin paper bordering & a fragment with the border cut off, but I suppose it is with you as others out of sight, out of mind. I will not trouble you again. Give my love to Mother and tell her that I hope to be with her soon for it is very dull here with nobody to speak to. William___________ was married on Thursday night by Mr. Baldwin after that they had quadrilles too and a great feast. I do not know how it went off, as I went to bed before supper. Was Mary Ii married yesterday to Mr. Griswold?
>
> The report here is that Hikoni [Kanehoa's widow] is going to marry Haalilea.
>
> God help you my dear child
> Your affectionate father
> T. Cha. Byde Rooke

Smallpox

In May 1850 King Kamehameha III established the Board of Health (the first in the United States) and appointed three commissioners: Dr. Gerrit P. Judd, William C. Parke (the kingdom's marshal), and Dr. Rooke who was selected its chairman. The board had just been established when it faced its first public crisis: the smallpox epidemic of 1853.

It was May when the brig *Zoe* landed a chest of clothes and other merchandise at the port of Honolulu. Shortly afterward the wearing apparel was auctioned, and within days the first cases of *maʻi puʻupuʻu liʻiliʻi* or smallpox were reported. Although the commissioners immediately initiated a strict quarantine of the infected areas and began general vaccinations, it was too late. The disease spread like wildfire and people "died like sheep." Within a month more than 400 had succumbed in Honolulu alone. The "whole medical staff of Honolulu" worked night and day without pay to battle the disease. Many ordinary citizens volunteered to nurse the sick. Forty houses in Waikīkī were converted to hospitals and another thirty on the ʻEwa side of Honolulu. Marshal William Parke described heartrending scenes: husbands and parents deserting their families and children; entire families falling sick at the same time; entering a house only to find dead bodies. Nearly 6,500 cases were reported of which 2,500 died, a death rate of almost 39 percent.[16]

Ironically, the most difficult part was not treating the sick but rather burying the dead. No one—not even those who had recovered from the disease—would help in this work. The commissioners were obliged to draft able-bodied men who had recovered to help, and if they refused they were fined or imprisoned. Parke himself went to his jail where he recruited six of his prisoners. Kamakau, the Hawaiian historian, who witnessed the epidemic firsthand, described the deathly scene: "The dead fell like dried *kukui* twigs tossed down by the wind. Day by day from morning till night horse-drawn carts went about from street to street of the town, and the dead were stacked up like a load of wood, some in coffins, but most of them just piled in, wrapped in cloth with heads and legs sticking out."[17] Parke's men buried forty to fifty corpses daily, and sometimes more, working often until midnight.[18]

Parke mentioned that many ordinary citizens volunteered to nurse the sick. Was Emma among them? It is understandable if Dr. Rooke, as a father, would have preferred to shield his daughter from the disease. But as a physician and as a commissioner, he was totally involved in everything related to the epidemic at some personal risk. It can be easily imagined that an empathetic Emma and other family members would have wanted to be at his side. This was not the first nor the last time that Emma would see the ravages of disease: the pitiful sight of deeply pitted faces of so many who had suffered and their homes shuttered or burned to the ground.

The extent of Emma's involvement notwithstanding, one fact is certain: by the end of her adolescent years, she had gained an appreciation of the plight of her people and the need for their care.

Death of Nae'a

Emma's natural father, George Nae'a, died on October 2, 1854, from leprosy, which he had contracted in 1838, two years after Emma's birth. Emma never knew her natural father because, so far as is known, he was not allowed to come in contact with Emma, which explains why his name has not been mentioned in any of the events related so far.[19] In fact, he may have continued to share a home with Fanny on Maui because it was not uncommon for spouses to *kōkua* or care for their afflicted mates. He does not appear to have been cut off from leading a productive life because Minister of Foreign Relations Robert C. Wyllie describes him as a "highly respectable Hawaiian."[20] Curiously, his apparent anonymity from Emma may have sparked the rumor that not he but Dr. Rooke had actually fathered Emma.[21]

Contrary to modern day claims, Emma's natural father was not the first Hawaiian to be diagnosed with the disease. Clarice Taylor, formerly a popular columnist on "Hawaiiana" for the *Honolulu Star-Bulletin,* once wrote that "He is famous in history as having been the first diagnosed case of leprosy in the islands. And it was he who gave the disease the name "*ali'i ma'i*" or "sickness of the chief."[22] According to Dr. Arthur A. St. Mouritz, a physician at Kalaupapa in the 1880s, several well-authenticated cases of leprosy appeared among Hawaiians as early as the 1820s.[23]

For Emma, the sequential deaths of her grandmother, uncle, and natural father ushered in the specter of mourning that would haunt the rest of her life.

5

Courtship and Marriage

Every popular modern story about Emma and Alexander Liholiho tells of their falling in love while they were students at the Chiefs' Children's School.[1] Because everyone loves romance, the story is easy to believe. The live-in school with close quarters would have been the ideal situation to get to know a person. As boarders the students lived, dined, studied, prayed, and played together almost daily. Consequently, all the students would have had ample opportunity to take the measure of one another. If Alexander had been attracted to Emma, he would have been captivated by her youthful beauty, talent, intelligence, and modesty. And, conversely, if Emma had been attracted to Alexander, she would have had every reason: he was already tall and handsome, brilliant, charming, and—the future heir to the throne.

Sweethearts at School?

Surprisingly little evidence exists to support the romantic notion of Alexander's and Emma's falling in love at school. For example, the Cookes, who had much to say about the encounters of their female and male students, never once hinted that Emma and Alexander had eyes for each other. There were many occasions, social and otherwise, when they were together, such as the regular Sunday processions to church when girls and boys marched side by side, but Alexander always walked with Abigail, followed by Lunalilo and Emma immediately behind.[2] There were the dinners with parents and the parties with the king that both

Emma and Alexander attended but always in the company of others.[3] In fact, the only mention of Emma ever being involved with a boy is when James (Kaliokalani or Kali), who was a year older than Emma, was caught in her room (apparently several of Emma's schoolmates were present) and punished "severely." Because no mention is made of Emma being even reprimanded, presumably she had done nothing wrong.[4]

As for Alexander Liholiho, apparently he did not take much notice of Emma. He was an upper classman, two years older and a grade or two above Emma, and was more often interested in the distractions outside the school's premises. Like many younger siblings, he tried to emulate his mischievous older brothers, Moses and Lot, carousing and drinking about town. Their frequent "night walks" reached the point where the Cookes demanded that the king intervene and stop the activity.[5] (Moses was eventually expelled for his misdeeds.)

Perhaps the most that could be said about Emma's and Alexander's relationship by the time they left the Chiefs' Children's School in 1849 was that they were just two friends who were attracted but not attached to each other.

Flirtations Abroad

When Alexander Liholiho and his brother Lot accompanied Dr. Gerrit P. Judd (Minister of Finance at the time) on a diplomatic mission to Europe and the United States from 1849 to 1850, he certainly was not thinking of Emma or any other female in particular. His personal journal reveals his thoughts. For example, in early June 1850, while visiting New York, he wrote how he danced with every young lady: "I considered myself quite enchanting, and thought that I had played my part of the Evening very well—but I soon found that I was to be conquered in the same manner, but the ransom was no trifling boquet [sic], nor some glowing promises ne'er intended to be kept, but it was to be my sword tassel around a fair lady's hand. It must be worn as a bracelet. She raise[d] it to her lips, and her thanks are overwhelming. But circumstances, of when, how, or where, are not to be related; neither are names allowed to be repeated. For it was a CONQUEST, a perfect one."[6]

Alexander wrote of another evening when he danced with a number of ladies: "I flirted with Miss Whistler, of which I hear she has boasted of having made a conquest of me. I say no such thing, it was her that was Captivated."[7]

On yet another occasion, while visiting Sacketts Harbor, New York, Alexander encountered "a very singular adventure" involving a married woman at a hotel. "Passing by the hotel, I was riding a little behind Lot, and had my pantaloons inside my boots. The lady we had seen earlier came out and greeted me saying, How do you do, Sir Knight? I carried the joke out by saying, Well, fair one, a thousand thanks for the kindness Your Ladyship has shown to a wandering knight.

"She said nothing, took off one of her gloves, threw it at me. I caught it, kissed it and then rode on. Looked in the inside, there were the initials of Mrs. C. G. Wordsworth. Hang my stars, and her too, to think of a married woman playing such a prank."[8]

At a reception in his honor in Brooklyn, his host toasted the "King of Hawai'i" and expressed the hope that Alexander in choosing his queen would remember the "democratic girls of the United States." Alexander rose and said: "Of all the ladies I have seen in my travels, none have struck me as beautiful and attractive as the ladies of the United States. They are gentle and good and lovely. They please me. They are queens and I hope American gentlemen honor them as such."[9]

This bit of flattery was the only reference in his entire journal to his "future queen." Had he thought of Emma, he probably would have mentioned her name at least once. Had he written a letter to her, he probably would have mentioned that; after all, he had written letters to the king, queen, John Young (or Keoni Ana, Emma's uncle), William Lunalilo, Victoria (his sister), and others.[10] And had he bought a gift for Emma, he probably would have mentioned it, just as he mentioned the gift his brother Lot had bought for Bernice Pauahi.

Courtship

Thus Alexander's courting of Emma must have started after his return to Hawai'i in September 1850. But between then and the time of their marriage an interval of six years occurred. When did Alexander Liholiho become serious about Emma? According to Charles de Varigny, the Frenchman who served in Alexander's cabinet as foreign minister and thus knew him well, Alexander did not take Emma seriously until 1855. As de Varigny stated in his book, *Fourteen Years in the Sandwich Islands, 1855–1868,* Alexander Liholiho became "tired of the easy pleasures to which he had devoted his youth" only after he assumed the kingship in January 1855. He "sincerely wished to reform his conduct and take care of his already threatened and uncertain health. . . . He was even more concerned with passing on his throne to an heir, and so was thinking of marrying and settling down. After some months of hesitation he found his choice for a wife in Miss Emma Rooke."[11] Needless to say, the young bachelor had a keen eye for beauty, and Emma at this time was described as being "beautiful," possessing a "sylph-like" figure, with fair "luminous" skin and "extraordinarily large" eyes and as being "graceful, intelligent and lively."[12] A slightly less flattering view was held by Henry Neilson, Alexander's private secretary, who described Emma as "not remarkably beautiful, but still good looking" and "rather short" for the king who was nearly a foot taller.[13]

Although de Varigny's account is logical, David L. Gregg, the American commissioner in Hawai'i, may have established the truth. A close friend of Alexander's, he wrote in his diary on February 2, 1854, the following: "Miss Rooke is said to be engaged to Prince Alexander, the heir to the throne."[14] More stock should be placed in Gregg because he was already posted in Honolulu at the time whereas de Varigny did not arrive in Hawai'i until 1855.

Indeed, if there is a correlation, as de Varigny implies, between Alexander's becoming serious about Emma and his assuming increasing official responsibilities, then his courting may have begun as early as April 1852 when he was appointed to the House of Nobles and to the privy council as honorary member.[15] Certainly the date was no later than April 1853 when the king named him to be his successor. From that date on, Alexander Liholiho was involved in every important governmental decision. This fact is supported by Gregg's observation that the king was "unwilling to have any final step taken when he [Alexander] is not present."[16]

Such were Alexander Liholiho's responsibilities as he pressed his courtship of Emma.

The Weight of the Kingdom

Even though he was only nineteen, Prince Alexander Liholiho faced some decisions that affected the very survival of the kingdom. The most important of these was the threat of annexation to the United States, which grew out of the political turmoil caused by the competing interests of the Americans, British, and French. The controversy with France over its demands for trading and diplomatic privileges, which Alexander knew all too well from his earlier mission to Paris, continued to plague the kingdom. No less serious was the threat to the kingdom's peace and security caused by the filibustering of California. By 1853 this problem had become so serious that Gregg's predecessor, Commissioner Luther Severance, tried to persuade the State Department to stop the filibusters. He feared that the menace from California was forcing Hawai'i into dependence upon the British and French for protection. At the same time American residents, who opposed Kamehameha III's tax and land policies, threatened to appeal to California for aid. By February of 1854, or about the same time Alexander became engaged, Honolulu was rife with rumors of possible revolution against the monarchy.[17]

In the midst of such threats, Kamehameha III and his ministers coolly calculated that the only way for the kingdom to survive was to draw up a treaty of annexation with the United States. Wyllie wrote that "colonial subjection to any European power would not be so favorable to the interests of the islands as their admission as a sovereign State of the United States. . . . There are no markets in Europe likely to afford such consumption of island produce at high prices as those of California and Oregon." Wyllie was even willing to advise the king to annex himself to Japan "if I thought that it would be best for him, the prince, the chiefs, the Hawaiians generally, and the future interests of the islands as an agricultural and mercantile state."[18] Thus, on February 6, 1854, the king, fearing a rebellion leading to anarchy, ordered Wyllie to open negotiations for annexation by the United States. To complicate matters, the British, and especially the French, consuls strongly opposed American control. Gregg charged that they had gone so far as to work hand in hand with the revolutionary leaders in stimulating unrest.[19]

Even with the positive support of Kamehameha III, Gregg's and Wyllie's efforts for annexation were frustrated by none other than Alexander Liholiho. The British Consul William Miller repeatedly raised the twin specter of American racial prejudice and slavery to frighten the Hawaiians, including Alexander. Hawaiians opposed American annexation on the same grounds, charging that American attitudes toward the blacks reflected American contempt for the colored races and that annexation would mean virtual enslavement, as well as the loss of their lands and their social and political liberties. Alexander Liholiho, who keenly remembered his experiences while traveling in the United States, did not need to be persuaded that the threat was real.

Lest Alexander's attitude toward foreigners be misunderstood, it is important to digress and consider his remarks on the subject. In his January 1855 inauguration speech as the new king, he stated:

> To be kind and generous to the foreigner, to trust and confide in him, is no new thing in the history of our race. It is an inheritance transmitted to us from our forefathers. The founder of our dynasty was ever glad to receive assistance and advice from foreigners. . . . I cannot

> fail to heed the example of my ancestors. I therefore say to the foreigner that he is welcome. He is welcome to our shores—welcome so long as he comes with laudable motive of promoting his own interests and at the same time respecting those of his neighbors. But if he comes here with no more exalted motive than that of building up his own interests, at the expense of the native—to seek our confidence only to betray it—with no higher ambition than that of overthrowing our government, and introducing anarchy, confusion and bloodshed —then is he most unwelcome.[20]

In his later analysis, Gregg maintained that the key reason for the failure of the treaty was the delaying tactic of Prince Alexander Liholiho, who, "so long as the circumstances held out the hope of a perpetuity of his dynasty," refused to complete the negotiations.[21]

"Stay the Wasting Hand"

The new king's maiden speech before parliament was also notable because it contained his first request for funding the establishment of public hospitals, although it was not the first time he had mentioned the need for hospitals. A year before his enthronement, he had addressed the annual meeting of the Royal Hawaiian Agricultural Society, stating that public hospitals should have been "called into existence even ten years ago or five" and that "unlike the good Samaritan, [we] have neglected our duty towards our neighbor."[22] But now as king, referring to the ravages of disease among native Hawaiians, babies dying of malnutrition and intestinal disorders, men and women dying or rendered sterile by venereal diseases, he declared: "A subject of deeper importance, in my opinion, than any I have hitherto mentioned, is that of the decrease of our population. It is a subject, comparison with which all others sink into insignificance; for, our first and great duty is that of self-preservation. Our acts are in vain unless we can stay the wasting hand that is destroying our people. I feel a heavy and special responsibility resting on me in this matter; but it is one in which you all must share; nor shall we be acquitted by man, or our Maker, of a neglect of duty, if we fail to act speedily and effectually in the cause of those who are every day dying before our eyes. . . . I would commend to your special consideration the subject of establishing public hospitals."[23] But the weak financial position of the government made it impossible to spare the money for building hospitals at the time. Four years would pass before the first hospital would be built but not without the help of his future wife.

"Dearest Emma"

If letters that begin with "Dearest" are evidence of a suitor's seriousness, then Alexander Liholiho was that by the fall of 1855. In September, while on a visit to Kona, Hawai'i, he wrote to Emma addressing her as "Dearest" and signing it with "Ever yours, Liholiho." A month later, while on another trip, he wrote again, this time addressing her as "My Dear Emma."[24] Although no sweet words of love or romance are mentioned, clearly he is writing to someone who is more than a friend.

While it is not known when or where Alexander Liholiho asked Emma to marry him, he may have proposed in a place not too far from the palace. The story goes that he and Emma were riding in Honolulu and stopped at the spring in Kamō'ili'ili (or Mō'ili'ili) to water and rest their horses. It was there, "where the coconut trees stood for so many years on the *ma kai* side of the old road," that he asked for her hand.[25]

In July 1855 the king informed the privy council of his intention to be married in the following January.[26] In a letter to Admiral Richard Thomas dated July 27, 1855, Foreign Affairs Minister Wyllie wrote that the king had just announced his intention to marry Emma Rooke whose "many naturally good qualities fit her for the high station of Queen."[27] Gregg confirmed the action but told his diary that the marriage "may chance to happen sooner."[28]

About the same time, Amos Cooke, writing to his sister, reported that he had heard about Alexander's intention to marry Emma, "one of our old scholars," and that he felt she would make "a suitable wife for a king" but wished that "they might both become Christians!"[29]

Although Gregg was uncertain about the wedding date, Cooke seemed certain that the couple would wed on January 2, 1856, which would have been Emma's twentieth birthday.[30] The Cookes may have obtained their information directly from Emma. She often visited their home; as Amos wrote, "[Emma] frequently calls upon us, tho [Alexander] never does."[31] Because the actual wedding took place in June, either the Cookes were mistaken or Emma herself may have been uncertain about the date.

Competing Suitors

Emma did not lack for admirers of either native or foreign origins. As one account stated: "Very naturally she had many admirers and the cultured home of Dr. Rooke was a much sought after privilege to visit."[32] After all, she was by all contemporary accounts "talented," "intelligent," "modest," and possessed of "a rare and delicate beauty."[33]

Emma mentions one of her possible admirers in her diary as she wrote: "Duddley took Mill & I out to ride on the plains and we were singing and making a noise the whole time."[34] A few days later she rode with Duddley again, this time on a "moon light carriage ride."[35]

One of her suitors was an English naval officer of the H.M.S *Amphitrite* who fell madly in love with her. Said he in one of his letters: "I have visited you very often of late, perhaps too often for the rigid etiquette of Honolulu, but if I have done so, Emma, you know the reason, your heart must have told you long ago, even if I had not, how much I loved you. . . .

"Just tell me that you love me, Emma, and you will make me so happy that I believe I could be almost brought to embrace that hirsute old monster of a skipper of ours and forgive him all his misdeeds. . . ."[36]

This was the incident Lady Franklin wrote about in 1861 while visiting Hanalei: "The King was a long time courting Emma. He had shewn great signs of admiring her but had not made any proposals, when one of the officers of a British man-of-war paid attentions to her which she willingly received. It is said she was ready to accept him when the King, stimulated by his perception of what was going on, offered his hand and carried her off."[37]

Were They Ever Betrothed?

Did Emma always believe that Alexander was the man she would marry? This possibility arises from the speculation that Emma and Alexander Liholiho had been betrothed to each other as infants.[38]

It was not uncommon for distinguished families to betroth their children, as in the case of Lot and Bernice Pauahi who had been betrothed at birth. A betrothal *(hoʻopalau)* ensured that the royal offspring would be marrying others of equal rank to maintain genealogical purity, to effect a political alliance, or to strengthen inter-family ties.[39]

The only known claim of Emma's and Alexander's betrothal was made in the Hawaiian newspaper *Ko Hawaiʻi Paeʻāina* in 1883 by the defenders of Emma's royal genealogy. It stated that Emma "while she was still in the womb . . . was betrothed by her parents" and that the betrothal "was set until they were married."[40] That is why, it alleged, King Kamehameha III, Alexander Liholiho's adopted father, had told Emma, "Don't give up on marrying Liholiho. Don't focus too much on his sexual affairs. Liholiho is such a young chief and wanders here and there. That is what young men do."[41]

No other evidence, however, exists to support the claim that they were betrothed. None of the contemporary writers or historians,

The Kamehamehas, who ruled the Islands for four generations, are renowned for their social and political advancements in the lives of their people. Of all the *aliʻi,* Queen Emma and King Kamehameha IV probably inspired the greatest personal admiration within their kingdom and beyond.

Hawaiian or European, such as Manley Hopkins, Charles de Varigny, and Samuel Kamakau, or diarists such as Amos Cooke and the American diplomat David Gregg, ever mentioned a betrothal. Furthermore, none of the correspondence, which consists of hundreds of letters written by Emma, Alexander Liholiho, and other members of the family, contains any hint of a betrothal. Moreover, had they been betrothed, this kind of information would have been disseminated widely, as in the case of Bernice's and Lot's betrothal a few years earlier. Yet no one seemed to have known about it. Finally, if Alexander Liholiho and Emma had known of their childhood engagement, they might have married earlier, being assured that their union was foreordained.

Opposition

In the High Chiefess Emma Rooke, according to de Varigny, "The king could not have made a better choice."[42] Robert Wyllie confirmed the Frenchman's verdict when he wrote to Admiral Thomas, "I have not heard anyone express any other opinion than that of approval of the young King's Choice."[43]

In fact, however, not everyone agreed. According to Lili'uokalani in her autobiography, "Some of those interested in the genealogies of the historic families of the Hawaiian chiefs, on hearing of his intended marriage, went to the king, and begged him to change his mind." When the king asked why he should, he was told, "Because, Your Majesty, there is no other chief equal to you in birth and rank but the adopted daughter of Paki," namely, Lili'uokalani herself. Despite this rather self-serving statement, she did say that the king "took offence at this counsel, and dismissed the objectors from his presence."[44]

One of the chiefs who condemned the marriage was none other than Lili'uokalani's natural father, the High Chief Kapa'akea. He had said that if neither the king nor any high chief wanted to marry his daughter, he would have her marry "some good white man" (as she eventually did).[45] Surprisingly, the other chief who opposed the match was the High Chief Joshua Ka'eo, the husband of Emma's aunt and the father of her childhood playmate Peter. The American Commissioner David Gregg recorded in his diary that although Ka'eo was glad that Emma was going to marry the king, he thought "her rank was not high as it ought to be for a Queen."[46]

It was probably some of these same detractors who ruined Emma's engagement party. Emma had overheard them whispering that the impending marriage would be improper because her lineage was not high enough and that she was unfit to be queen because she was *hapa haole* (part white). It is said she burst into tears and left the party with her embarrassed family. Although hurt, she would have to become accustomed to the situation because the whisperings would never quite go away.

Whatever her detractors may have said, the *Pacific Commercial Advertiser* spoke for the vast majority when it declared: "It is not saying too much that she is probably better fitted and more suitable for the station to which she has been elevated than any young lady in the Kingdom."[47]

The Wedding

On May 18, 1856, Prince Lot announced to the legislature what everyone already knew: the marriage of Alexander and Emma. Upon hearing the welcome news, the legislators called on King Alexander Liholiho, now King Kamehameha IV. They wished him great happiness and voiced the hope that the union would be fruitful for the perpetuation of the kingdom.

The wedding took place on the morning of June 19, 1856. The government declared the day a public holiday and appropriated $2,500 for the event. With all shops and stores closed, the government was assured of a large turnout. Indeed, the event drew huge and happy crowds who lined the processional route along King Street, which was covered with a carpet of rushes and grass to keep down the dust and smooth out the potholes.

The procession consisted of several carriages, one carrying Emma and her attendants and another the king with his brother Lot and his father Kekūanaoʻa seated beside him, followed by uniformed aides-de-camp on horseback, with a cavalry escort preceding and closing the procession. With the king wearing his Windsor uniform—a blue coat richly embroidered with gold lace running down to the feet, the large Hawaiian Star on his left breast, a plumed hat, and a small sword—the event could have almost been mistaken for a royal procession in London were it not for the colorful *kahili* bearers who marched along both sides of the carriages.

As the king passed in his carriage, the soldiers aligning the street and many spectators prostrated themselves "until their foreheads touched the ground." The *Polynesian* observed that while this ceremony was common in olden times, it was rare in the 1850s.[48]

The procession ended at Kawaiahaʻo Church where the ceremony was to be held. The church was packed with 500 people inside and 3,000 outside. Some guests refused to go inside for fear the building would collapse, although the king had previously had the structure checked to ensure that the galleries could bear the weight of such a crowd.[49]

The ceremony was an Anglican service, encouraged by Dr. Rooke who was a devout Anglican, and readily endorsed by both the bride and groom, even though they were not Anglicans at the time. Some members of Kawaiahaʻo, which was a Congregational bastion, wondered out loud as to why an Anglican ritual would be allowed in their church, but no one had the temerity to question the king. The service was performed by a non-Anglican, the Reverend Richard Armstrong, in both Hawaiian and English. The ceremony went well until Alexander Liholiho discovered that he had forgotten the wedding ring. The situation was saved when the Chief Justice Elisha Allen quickly and quietly slipped his own gold ring to the king as the ceremony proceeded.

Emma "presented a vision of unparalleled beauty" in her wedding gown. The *Polynesian* said, "The bride's dress offered unmistakable evidence of its Parisian origin. Nothing could have been more elegant, or have better suited her fairy-like proportions. The robe was of white silk, heavy and lustrous, trimmed with three flounces richly embroidered. The veil was of Brussel's point lace, confined to the hair by a wreath of roses and orange blossoms beautifully blended. Her jewelry consisted of a superb set of diamonds, elegantly designed. The *tout ensemble* [whole effect] was happy in the extreme."[50] The wedding, including the dress, cost the government $2,500.

Emma's three bridesmaids were Victoria Kamāmalu, sister of the king, Lydia Kamakaʻeha or Liliʻuokalani, and Mary Pitman, a close friend of royal blood. The inclusion of Liliʻuokalani is interesting because Emma must have considered her a close friend at this time.

After the ceremony, the newlyweds returned to the palace where they were toasted by the Diplomatic and Consular Corps. The French Commissioner, Mons. Emile Perrin, speaking in his halting English, congratulated the king on his choice of Emma in the mellifluous language of the diplomat: "In the numerous characteristics destined to charm, and the eminent goodness of heart which distinguish the partner this day chosen by your Majesty, we see with pleasure new guarantees of happiness and prosperity to the Hawaiian nation. For this we offer to Providence our sincere thanks."[51]

That evening a royal ball and supper was held at the palace for the 500 invited guests. The palace and grounds were illuminated and "presented a beautiful sight." So did the queen, dressed in her evening dress made of "an exquisitely airy fabric of lace embroidered in white silk and silver, interspersed with marabou feathers." The king and queen led the first quadrille, and everyone "kept dancing with great spirit to a late hour."[52]

A curious and awkward incident at the ball revealed the new queen's deferential but independent character. The French Commissioner, Mons. Perrin, asked the queen for a dance, but she demurred on account of fatigue. He insisted, but the queen refused again and again. David Gregg, who witnessed and recorded the incident in his diary, wrote that the queen asked him whether he considered her behavior to be proper. "Certainly," he replied, "he ought to have been content with a simple refusal." The queen then said, "I think so too. My excuse was sufficient, besides I do not care to dance with him at all, for I do not like him."[53]

The evening was capped with a blaze of brilliant fireworks from atop Punchbowl. The only event that marred the affair was that a few people complained the next morning about stomachaches caused by either the chicken or lobster salad.

The celebrations continued. The Americans gave a ball in honor of the marriage, which was followed by another ball given by the Germans. Not to be outdone, the Chinese put on a ball in grand style with "truly magnificent" decorations and sumptuous food.[54] Finally, the king decided to reciprocate with his own ball "regardless of expense," which turned out to be "a grand success" and which culminated the public celebrations.

Amidst the national festivities, Dr. Rooke[55] and Grace hosted a large *lūʻau* for their tenants, retainers, and household servants, all of whom had touched Emma's life in some large or small measure. It was typical of her parents to acknowledge those who often seemed to matter the least.[56]

6

The New Life at Court

Life at court would be drastically different from life at Rooke House. The context of Emma's young life would now be defined by the needs and expectations of an old monarchical order over which she had little control except the will power she could impose on it. In time she would muster that power, but in 1856 during the first months of her queenship she was content to learn what adjustments she would have to make. And the adjustments, big and small, were many: from how she dressed to how she was addressed, to what she could or could not do in public, and to which friendships she could cultivate, ad infinitum.

Incremental Adjustments

Up until June 19, 1856, people called her "Miss Emma Rooke," but now Emma had to become accustomed to people addressing her as "Queen." Newspapers and other public media addressed her as "Her Majesty the Queen," or when the king was included, "Their Majesties the King and Queen." Her native people now endearingly called her "Emalani" (heavenly Emma), a name that would be celebrated in *mele* (chant) honoring her henceforth.[1] Even the missionary Cookes recognized her new status and addressed her respectfully in their private journals and correspondence as "Her Majesty Emma" or "Queen Emma."

In addition to the verbal protocol, Emma also had to adjust to the spatial protocol. She was already accustomed to a certain amount of bowing and kneeling and having people keep their distance from her because of several *kapu* she had inherited from her own royal lineage. But the protocol of the court was far more exacting. For instance, commoners and even *ali'i* of lower ranks prostrated themselves before the king and kept a prescribed distance from his royal presence. The Hawaiian belief was that space around him was sacred and *kapu,* and to intrude on it would diminish his *mana* and defile his status. As queen, Emma enjoyed a similar protocol. Those who traveled with her had to walk in single file separated from her at the distance of her shadow. Her ladies-in-waiting would advance to within about four feet from where she was seated, sink to their knees, crawl the remainder of the distance, and then kiss her hand.

Needless to say, no one was put to death for violating *ali'i* protocol, as had been done in olden times. By the 1850s Hawai'i had all the trappings of a constitutional monarchy that limited the king's powers and recognized the equality of all persons. Many Hawaiians were more relaxed about how they complied with the royal protocols. In fact, the king was often content with extending a western handshake.

As for the foreigners, the British, who were accustomed to royalty, were respectful but not the egalitarian Americans who had no compunctions about ignoring royal etiquette. Sophia Cracroft, visiting from England, once remarked, "We are never so inclined to shew the usual marks of outward respect to the King and Queen as when in the presence of the badly behaved Americans." She longed to teach them proper manners. She was particularly incensed because she felt that "The Queen has such simple sweet manners that they are never reminded of the want of it by her."[2]

Emma also had to get used to her new residence, the first royal palace called 'Iolani (the royal hawk). Built in 1844 by Governor Kekūanao'a as a residence for his daughter Victoria Kamāmalu, it was selected to be the palace for Kamehameha III when the capital was moved from Lahaina to Honolulu in 1844.

The palace was a large stone structure with a basement and a first floor raised six feet above the ground, spacious royal apartments, and accommodations for the guards and household servants. Wide verandahs circled the entire house, and massive walls supported a upper story consisting of two rooms that were used for smoking and lounging in the heat of the day.[3]

The new occupants proceeded to redecorate the palace by filling it with handsome teakwood furnishings, satin draperies, and Persian carpets from Europe and China. The palace took on a "rich and gorgeous air" that it did not have before. To quench their thirst for reading, they also filled it with books, especially those by their favorite English authors ranging from William Shakespeare to Alfred Lord Tennyson. The other reading materials, which the king read religiously, included the London *Times,* the *Illustrated News,* the *Quarterly Review,* the *Edinburgh Review, Blackwood's Magazine,* the *Westminster Review,* and *Punch,* none of which were American.[4]

Rooke House was a home filled with memories of doting parents and solicitous servants, of aloha and compassion, of security and reassurance. Hence, for Emma, the transition was not easy: to leave twenty years of intimacy and familiarity for the publicness and showiness of a royal fishbowl, however palatial. The palace was not so much a home but an open arena where cabinet ministers, legislators, judges, diplomats, merchants, military officers, missionaries, and even commoners came to deal with the affairs of state. Its thick walls and lofty ceilings resonated with the stresses and strains of diplomatic intrigue, business deals, religious conflicts, court rivalries, and both national and personal tragedies. Though the palace was only a few blocks away from Rooke House, the distance might as well have been in miles.

How could Emma make a home for herself and husband and children here? The king must have shared this concern because he built Emma a separate and smaller royal residence next to the palace (near the site of the present Archives of Hawai'i). Interestingly, the house had two names: the *ma kai* side was named Kauluhinano (the growth of the male pandanus blossom) and the *ma uka* side, Ihikapukalani (heavenly splendor and sacred to the chief) where the queen had her private apartments. Here the king and queen would spend most of their time during his reign.[5]

Friends

Amidst the stream of people who called on Emma during the days immediately following the wedding was a group of Emma's "female friends," a cosmopolitan group that included *haole, hapa-haole,* and full-blooded Hawaiians.[6] Among her closest female friends—women who were near her age, were close to the court, and shared her Christian faith—were Victoria Kamāmalu, Elizabeth Keka'anī'au Pratt, Lucy Kaopauli Kalaniki'eki'e Peabody, Mary Pitman, Rebecca Gregg, Cornelia Hamlin, Annie Parke, and Alice Brown. Their opinions and manners may well have shaped those of the queen.

Emma's friendship with Victoria, who was two years younger, began when they were students at the Chiefs' Children's School and grew during Emma's courtship. Like Emma, Victoria was a Christian, a talented singer, and pianist. Though only sixteen when Alexander Liholiho became king, she had already been designated as his heir and now served in her brother's cabinet as *kuhina nui*. Emma probably spent more time with Victoria than any of her other lady friends because they attended many of the same family and official functions.

The High Chiefess Elizabeth Keka'anī'au Pratt, who was born in the same year as Emma but outlived her by forty-three years, was one of the Cookes' "old scholars." A bridesmaid at Emma's wedding, she frequently attended the queen as lady-in-waiting. She was the daughter of High Chief La'anui and High Chiefess Owana, one of the twin daughters of Jean Rives, a French adventurer and court favorite of Kamehameha II. Elizabeth's husband, Franklyn Seaver Pratt who was from Boston, was also a close friend of the queen.[7]

Lucy Kaopauli Kalaniki'eki'e Peabody, four years Emma's junior, was a high chiefess who served as one of Emma's maids-of-honor. Her mother was Elizabeth K. Davis, a granddaughter of Isaac Davis who, along with John Young, was an adviser and companion-in-arms to Kamehameha I. Her father, American physician Dr. Parker Peabody, was once involved in a business partnership with Emma's father, Dr. Rooke.

Mary Pitman, one of the queen's bridesmaids, was her first cousin. Mary's mother was the Chiefess Kino'oleoliliha from the Ola'a region of Hawai'i and the daughter of High Chief Ho'olulu whose lot was to conceal the bones of Kamehameha I in a secret hiding place. Kino'ole was the first wife of Benjamin Pitman, an American who owned a store in Hilo where he prospered until he left the Islands in 1861.[8]

Rebecca Gregg's friendship with Emma developed partly out of the excellent relationship that her husband had as an adviser and later minister to the king in spite of the king's unequivocal opposition to annexation by the United States. The Greggs were often houseguests of Their Majesties at their home in Kailua-Kona on Hawai'i and at their Nu'uanu summer home. Rebecca was frequently present at court functions and a chosen companion for rides with the ladies of the court. She even named one of their daughters Emma.

Cornelia Hamlin, Gregg's niece from California, accompanied them to Hawai'i in 1853. She also accompanied the Greggs on their first audience with King Kamehameha III when they met Prince Alexander for the first time. Commissioner Gregg thought Alexander would "compare favorably in intelligence and address with young men of any country."[9] It must have been shortly thereafter that Cornelia met Emma and became a close friend. When Cornelia married Captain William Babcock (a whaler) in January 1857, both the king and queen attended the wedding. The king even gave away the bride.[10] Gregg described Cornelia as being the "Queen's most intimate friend."[11] She fell in love with Hawai'i and remained until her death in 1915.

Annie S. Parke, five years older than Emma, had easy access to the court and hence the queen because of her husband's position. William Parke served both Kamehameha III and Alexander Liholiho as the kingdom's trusted marshal (a position he would hold until 1884). It was Annie who was commissioned to purchase the wedding trousseau for Emma and a wardrobe for Victoria on her trip to the U.S. mainland a few months before the wedding.

Alice Brown was the niece of Sarah Von Pfister, Emma's former governess. Her father was Thomas Brown, the royal gardener at Windsor Castle before he moved to Hawaii for his health in 1844. Alice was an Anglican, devoted to her faith and to helping the poor and the sick. These qualities must have attracted Emma to Alice.

Emma had other female friends, perhaps not as intimate, such as Bernice Pauahi Bishop and Princess Ruth Ke'elikōlani, and a few older friends who had little contact with the court such as Mrs. Juliette Cooke and Sarah Von Pfister.

She also had close male friends beginning with her cousin Peter, who was an aide-de-camp at the palace and one of several young men, including David Kalākaua, who surrounded the king and his personal staff. Others were Prince Lot, the king's older brother, American Commissioner David Gregg, Robert C. Wyllie, one of the king's most trusted and capable ministers, and her favorite uncle, Keoni Ana, whom a visiting English woman once described as "the handsomest man you could see anywhere."[12]

Social Life at *Aloali'i* (Court)

Many of Emma's friends naturally called on her at the palace, but, interestingly, it was the queen and king who often called on them, attending their parties, teas, and other events at their homes. For example, they went to parties at Prince Lot's, Victoria's, and Dr. Guillou's residences, attended meetings of the Amateur Musical Society at Mrs. Bishop's, visited the Greggs and Hamlins for tea, and stayed with the Pitmans, Titcombs, Woods, or Maninis on trips outside of Honolulu. Clearly, the exchange was not one-sided in favor of the royal palace. It was in keeping with the social conduct of the time; in fact, calling on friends and relatives was the predominant social activity. Thus, as Emma quickly learned, even though palace life was insulating, it was not isolating.

Western-style dancing was probably the most popular amusement of Honolulu's elite (except the missionaries, of course). There were the grand balls, smaller dancing parties, dancing lessons, and dancing practices. On June 26, 1856, for example, the queen and king attended a small dancing party at the residence of Dr. and Mrs. Charles F. Guillou, an American physician who tended to the dying Kamehameha III with Dr. Rooke. Among the party-goers were Prince Lot, Victoria, and Cornelia Hamlin. Most of the evening was devoted to practicing quadrilles. The quadrille's intricate steps[13]—performed by four couples—required more than average skill to perform; hence, many such gatherings were hosted by different favorites of the court for the "purpose of learning," as David Gregg put it.[14] Because the quadrille was designed for high society to dance in ballrooms, these dance practices were in effect preparations for the grand balls. Interestingly, public dancing was relatively new to the queen because the first time she danced in public was in June, a few days before her marriage.[15]

At least a half dozen of these grand balls were held between July and December 1856, all of which the king and queen attended. The American community held its Fourth of July Ball; five days later Victoria sponsored a special ball for Their Majesties' "dancing friends"; two weeks later the Germans held another ball honoring the king and queen; Mrs. Gregg's ball took place in September; the Chinese held their outstanding ball in November; and the king and queen followed with their own ball on November 28, "Hawai'i Day."

The Chinese business community (mostly three dozen Cantonese led by Chun Afong), eager to demonstrate their loyalty to the government and win its protection at the same time, put on a grand ball in honor of the king and queen. They invited everyone who wanted to attend or nearly a thousand people, far more than any other ball. To feed the throng, cooks prepared an array of "substantial dishes" that included six sheep and 150 chickens. These were placed on wonderfully decorated tables (which included three-foot-high pagodas constructed out of pastry and carved watermelons ornamented with dragons and all sorts of reptiles) that "groaned" under their combined weight.

Apart from dining, the main program consisted of dancing. Prior to the ball none of its Cantonese sponsors knew how to dance because it was socially unacceptable for a Chinese gentleman to dance with a member of the opposite sex. So for weeks, Afong and his cohorts dutifully learned how to waltz, polka, and schottische and perform a quadrille. Asing, a grocer, was selected to dance with the queen in the first set, but when time came to open the ball, a handsomer and younger businessman, who was more agile on his feet than Asing, escorted the queen to the floor.[16]

The *Pacific Commercial Advertiser* said, "Our Chinese friends may rest assured that if their efforts are any indication of their hearts, they as yet stand far above us outside barbarians in our efforts to 'honor the King.' "[17] The Hawaiian-language newspaper *Ka Hae Hawaiʻi* reported that the king and queen were pleased with the Chinese not only because of the great ball but "because of their great assistance to the government and their trading skills. Thus, the government takes great care of them."[18] Their efforts cost nearly $4,000, probably the costliest party in the history of the kingdom up until then, but they had achieved what they wanted—the king's respect and the government's support.

The king's and queen's ball was "a very fine affair," which opened with an immense quadrille, the queen leading off with General William Miller, the British Consul General, and the king with Mrs. Gregg. Seated at the royal dinner table were the queen's closest friends, Victoria, Cornelia, Rebecca Gregg, and Annie Parke, along with their partners. Also seated at the table was Dr. Rooke, but not Grace.[19]

The ball was the setting for another faux pas by the French diplomat Perrin, who, while dancing with a lady, asked, "Have you not observed the Queen's appearance?" The lady replied, "Certainly she looks remarkably well." "O," said he, "you do not understand. I mean, have you not remarked the prominence of her abdomen? She is going to have a keiki. The King will be quite a happy man."[20] Perrin was off the mark by more than a year.

Horseback riding was another popular royal pastime, though for Emma it had always been a regular activity. She loved to ride, sometimes alone, but now more often in the company of Alexander or friends such as Cornelia Hamlin.[21] An accomplished equestrian, she enjoyed the rhythm of a leisurely gait as well as the thrill of a galloping thoroughbred. However, Honolulu's streets were not always safe. The *Pacific Commercial Advertiser* warned its readers, for example, that it was dangerous to life and limb to cross Nuʻuanu or Beretania at dusk "as the natives seem to understand that that is the only hour when they can race with impunity."[22] One wag predicted a dire future for Hawaiians because of their love affair with horses when he said: "Nothing renders the Hawaiians' future prospects as dark as their rage for Horses."[23]

By the mid-1800s the horse meant far more than a recreational vehicle to Hawaiians: it was Honolulu's main mode of transportation. Although Emma had use of the royal carriages, she often rode horseback to her destination whether it was Waikīkī, upper Nuʻuanu, or Waiʻanae, twenty-five miles away. She did in fact go to Waiʻanae in July with the king for his health and rode horseback part of the way.[24] Because riding long distances, especially side saddle, can be strenuous, the queen must have been in fairly sound physical condition.

Official Duties

One of the first of many official duties that Queen Emma performed was the christening in late July of the steam-and-propeller-driven tugboat *Pele.* The boat, seventy-five feet in length and costing $16,000, was the "most substantial piece of ship-carpentry" ever executed in the kingdom. The *Pacific Commercial Advertiser* described the queen cracking a bottle of champagne over its bow "with a grace that drew forth applause from every side." ("Grace" or "graceful" was often used to describe the queen's actions.) While the paper praised the boat's construction, it noted that the name *Pele* (the fire goddess) did not meet with "a favorable reception."[25] Neither the queen nor king, nor Prince Lot nor Victoria, who were all in attendance, objected, and thus the name remained.

Two days after the christening, the king and queen received visits from the British, American, and other foreign representatives and consuls.[26] These receptions were usually held in the elegantly appointed throne room, which took up the entire left wing of the palace. On top of a dais at the far end of the room were two satin-covered chairs, which formed the throne, flanked with gold feathered *kāhili.* With its lush carpeting and the delicate Brattenburg lace curtains veiling the French windows, a visitor described it as resembling a drawing room in London or Paris, with added Hawaiian touches.[27]

The most exhausting official undertaking for the queen, if not for the king, during these first months was a grand tour of the kingdom to visit every Island, including the uninhabited islets of Lehua and Kaʻula, and nearly every village. In addition to the king and queen, the party consisted of Victoria, Keoni Ana, the queen's uncle, Governor Kekūanaoʻa, Caesar Kapaʻakea, the father of Liliʻuokalani, David Kalākaua, and Henry Neilson, the king's secretary, as well as nearly 200 servants, including their families. They all left Honolulu on August 7, 1856, packed

Bishop Museum

Emma as Queen

to the gills on the schooner *Maria,* which was refitted expressly for their convenience, and headed for Waimea, Kaua'i, where Captain Cook made his first landfall in 1778.[28]

All the past monarchs had conducted such tours to confer with their appointees, to see firsthand what was happening, and to meet and talk with their subjects, but between the many meetings and site visits, they also found time to sightsee and to play. On this tour, the royal party took a ten-mile detour from Waimea to visit Keonekani of Nohili or "the sounding sand of Nohili," now called Barking Sands. The name comes from an interesting phenomenon: when the sand dunes (which rise 100 feet or more) have the right humidity and salt content, you can shuffle your feet or clap your hands and the sound is that of a barking dog. After scampering up to the top of one of the dunes, the queen demonstrated that the sound could also be made in other ways. Henry Neilson wrote how amused he was at seeing Victoria, the queen, and her uncle Keoni Ana all lying on their stomachs on the sand; the queen was holding Victoria's feet and Keoni Ana was holding the queen's feet. Together they all slid down the dune making a "great noise."[29]

From Waimea the king and queen sailed to Ni'ihau, which at the time (1856) had a population of nearly 800 souls. The king took a special interest in Ni'ihau because, except for a fifty-acre *kuleana,* he owned the entire island; it was crown land, and those occupying the land were required to pay an annual lease. But from the outset, problems arose because Ni'ihauans refused to pay their rent. The previous year they did not pay one penny of lease rental but managed to donate several hundred dollars to their church.[30] The king may have been more frustrated than annoyed by the situation, but after a stay of two days the royal party departed with little rent money, a few of Ni'ihau's famous mats, and other *ho'okupu* or gifts. For the queen, who became an avid collector of Hawaiian craftworks, this first and only trip to Ni'ihau may have sparked her interest in its shell leis, design gourds, and mats.

The party proceeded to Ka'ula, twenty-two miles southwest from Ni'ihau. One mile long and half a mile wide, this bleak and barren rock was uninhabited except by tens of thousands of sea birds that the king had never before seen. The whole party was intent on setting foot on the rock, though there was no beach or inlet to anchor in. Only one point was accessible, and that only for a strong swimmer. Undeterred, the adventuresome king and many others in the party were able to fight the wild surf and climb onto the precipitous rocks. Both Emma and Victoria were eager to follow until they witnessed one of the girls being repeatedly dashed against the rocks. While the queen and the princess waited, the king and his companions went exploring while shooting rats.

Unlike Ka'ula, the landing at Lehua, an even smaller rock, located less than a mile offshore from the northern tip of Ni'ihau, was made easy by its open, crescent-shaped bay. Lehua was populated by large quantities of birds and rabbits, which were the offspring of stock left there some years ago. Everyone went onshore. While the king, having a gun and a good dog, went hunting for rabbits, the queen and the others amused themselves by running down the young rabbits.[31]

They returned to Waimea and then proceeded on horseback to the seaside village of Hanapēpē, about five miles south. The royal entourage was now swelled by Kaua'i's Governor Paulo Kānoa, his aides, and other local dignitaries. The procession must have been quite grand with the king and queen on their mounts leading scores of riders, including women dressed in their colorful and long flowing *pā'ū* (skirt) and horses bedecked with leis and other ornaments. The villagers feasted and entertained the group with, according to Neilson, "a good exhibition of native dancing, and music, in the ancient style."[32] This is one of the earliest references to the queen actually witnessing a performance of a traditional hula. Although Neilson fails to mention it, she must have enjoyed the entertainment as much as the king, notwithstanding the fact that it was against the law to dance the hula in public.

The royal party continued on to Kōloa to visit the plantation of Dr. Robert Wood, a friend of Dr. Rooke and the queen. Dr. Wood helped to host the entourage for the two days they spent there. The physician-turned-entrepreneur had previously headed the American Seamen's Hospital and opened the first public pharmacy in Honolulu in 1848 before moving to thriving Kōloa. While there Emma wrote to her father saying she had met Hikoni, the widow of her uncle James Young Kanehoa of Lāwa'i, and also that when they left Kōloa, 400 to 500 natives were present to bid them farewell. She added that she felt homesick from the moment her father had said good-bye to her in Honolulu and that, although the king was "pleasant" enough and she was "contented," being away from her parents and friends was something "new." Emma also remarked that "as girls always have more to fix, fuss and busy over than boys, you may easily know why Alex and the rest of them boys have had abundance of time to write or do anything they please." In concluding her letter to her father, she asked him to correct the mistakes and to let no one see her "shameful dirty letter."[33] Emma always felt self-conscious about what she perceived as her lack of proficiency in writing English. She once admitted: "I have thoughts as they formed themselves, not stopping to adjust them properly or see if the spelling is correct. As you know, I am not very good at it."[34]

From Kōloa Their Majesties and party proceeded to Nāwiliwili where Governor Kānoa was domiciled. While their party stayed at the governor's home on the beach, the king and queen stayed with their loyal supporter Judge Hermann A. Widemann and his Hawaiian wife, Mary Kaumana, in Līhuʻe. Remaining there for a week, the king toured the area and was impressed by the success of the sugar industry, which in no small measure was due to the efforts of Governor Kānoa, who had been appointed to his position by the king's father only ten years earlier.[35]

They next went to Wailua, Anahola, and Hanalei. Without railroads or stage coaches, the royal party traveled the entire thirty-mile route by horseback. (It was common then to ride thirty to forty miles on a good day.) To the king and queen who loved the astounding beauty of the area, Hanalei was worth all the effort. While there they stayed with the Charles Titcombs on their coffee plantation, which was adjacent to Robert Wyllie's vast estate. On one evening they went to nearby Makana (which was also named "Mount Rooke") to see the *ʻōahi* or fireworks display of lighted spears of wood being hurled from the peak and carried off by currents of air, sometimes far to sea, showering sparks all along the way.[36]

The party left Kauaʻi and arrived on September 15 in Honolulu where they stopped for a day to load on brandy and other provisions and then departed for the Island of Hawaiʻi. After a rough five-day passage, they arrived in Hilo where they were welcomed by the king's half-sister, Princess Ruth Keʻelikōlani, whom the king had appointed governess of Hawaiʻi the year before. They were hosted by the prosperous Benjamin Pitman and his Chiefess-wife Kinoʻole, who were the parents of Mary Pitman, the queen's bridesmaid. Neilson reported that they passed a week in Hilo without much activity, except for a visit to Mauna Loa, which had erupted the previous year. It produced a stream of lava that had cut a path nearly sixty miles long and five miles wide and had stopped perilously near Hilo. "We went quite close to the flow," he wrote, "and obtained specimens of the lava, and made impressions in it, whilst hot and soft, with coins, buttons, etc."[37] In Hilo the king made a speech in which he told his *haole* audience that "he embraced their knowledge, farming skills, and worship of *Akua*," but he warned them not to do "any kind of evil deeds."[38]

In 1856 Emma married Alexander Liholiho, King Kamehameha IV.

From Hilo they sailed to Kawaihae, where the queen's family homestead was located. For Queen Emma, little had changed since her visit as a Chiefs' Children's School student except for the passing of her grandmother. After tarrying a few days, the party traveled over the forbidding road, constantly uphill and across an ocean of stones and boulders, to Waimea where both the landscape and temperature dramatically change. (A person smothers in Kawaihae and chills in Waimea.) They stayed but a few days and returned to Kawaihae.

Neilson seemed to dismiss rather cavalierly the importance of Kawaihae and Waimea when he wrote that they "hurried" their visit because "Hawai'i is not so pleasant to visit as Kaua'i."[39] Neilson also said that Kaua'i was the most beautiful of the Islands, with better roads and finer scenery. It is not known whether both the king and queen shared in this assessment, although the queen would spend more time on Kaua'i than any other of the neighbor Islands.[40]

After leaving Kawaihae, they sailed to Lahaina, then to Lāna'i, back to Maui, over to Moloka'i, and finally to Honolulu, all in less than a month. The royal party arrived home on October 30, 1856, and were greeted by two royal salutes fired from the top of Punchbowl, one for the king and the other for the queen. Despite the weeks of living out of suitcases, the many miles of riding over rough roads and trails, and the countless conversations, meetings, receptions, ceremonies, and meals, the king described the trip as "highly agreeable"—and more than likely the queen agreed.[41]

Emma Street

Shortly after they returned, the young queen received a new mark of respect: something was named after her for the first time. On November 10 the privy council at the request of Prince Lot passed a resolution that named the street "leading up from Beretania by the King's gardens towards the western side of Punch Bowl Hill" as Emma Street.[42] It was but the first of many tributes, ranging from baby girls to ships, plants, associations, costumes, jewelry, horses, a park, and a hospital that would bear her name.

Thanksgiving on Christmas

The king and queen should have enjoyed this Christmas day of 1856 as their first Christmas together since their days at the Chiefs' Children's School. They did not, at least not officially, because King Alexander Liholiho decreed that December 25 would be celebrated as the kingdom's national day of Thanksgiving. Apparently, he accepted the persuasions of the missionaries who objected to Christmas on the grounds that it was a pagan celebration, but six years later he would rescind his decree and formally proclaim Christmas as a national holiday.

Victoria's Scandal

Rooke House had never been tainted with scandal, so Emma may not have been prepared for her first scandal at court. Prince Lot had invited to dinner Marcus Monsarrat, the English businessman who lived close to the palace and who just two weeks before had led a group of merchants in presenting a new carriage to Queen Emma on her twenty-first birthday. When dinner was finished, his guest said good night and took leave. But soon after, one of Lot's servants told Lot that the tall and handsome Monsarrat was in Victoria's room. He immediately went to her room and caught Monsarrat in the act of arranging his pantaloons. Enraged, Lot ordered him to leave and, if he did not, threatened to kill him. When the king later heard about the incident, he "blamed Lot for not shooting Monsarrat down like a dog."[43] The king then banished Monsarrat from the kingdom; when he later returned, the king had him arrested and banished again.

The incident was particularly embarrassing to the court because efforts were under way to arrange a match between Victoria and David Kalākaua; these plans were quickly aborted. As for Emma, she felt sorry for her friend but was sorely disappointed by her behavior and her culpability. For a while this incident, plus Victoria's intemperance, strained their friendship.[44]

The King's Birthday

The queen's first six months at court ended on a note of celebration when she and the entire nation celebrated the king's twenty-third birthday on February 9, 1857. It began with the customary gun salute from on top Punchbowl and with the birthday homages paid by his subjects. The formal well-wishing from his cabinet and foreign officials in the morning was followed by a noon reception. The king and queen then slipped away to Waikīkī to attend a *lūʻau* spread under an "immense *hau* tree" at the residence of Jonah Piʻikoi, a major Waikīkī landowner.[45] It was not the only *lūʻau* celebrating the royal birthday; Gregg reported that there were *lūʻau* all over Honolulu in every direction.[46] That evening another ball took place at the palace where Queen Emma danced the opening quadrille with the American Commissioner who confessed that

"Under her guidance, I managed to get along passably well."[47] The king and queen continued partying until the wee hours of the morning.

An Uncle's Legacy

While their subjects were celebrating their birthdays, the king and queen were agonizing over the deteriorating health of her uncle and his trusted adviser and minister, Keoni Ana. A sudden paralytic attack in January forced him to resign all his duties. It was a blow to the king who relied heavily on him, just as his adopted father (King Kamehameha III) had done. Despite the ministrations of Dr. Rooke and the caring of the queen, he never recovered. He passed away on July 18, 1857, his death, hastened by influenza, at the age of forty-seven.

Absolutely honest and loyal, Keoni Ana was one of the few men in the kingdom who had virtually no enemies. He was praised for his skills in reconciling conflicts, especially between foreign and native interests. The *Polynesian* declared that not only the king but also the people, both foreign and native, had lost an extraordinary servant.[48] The queen had also lost a beloved uncle.

Having no children (his wife, the High Chiefess Juliana K. K. Alapai was already dead), Keoni Ana bequeathed his estate to his two nephews, Albert Kūnuiākea and Peter Ka'eo, and to his niece. The queen received several *ahupua'a,* including Kawaihae totaling 10,615 acres and his mansion in Nu'uanu. With these bequests, Queen Emma had suddenly become a large landowner with the responsibilities of managing the land, its tenants, and its resources. As long as her father was alive, he would oversee the management of her properties. She had other important concerns, not the least of which was the gestation of her first child.

7

The Birth of an Heir

In over thirty years no reigning monarch had produced a legitimate heir. Many worried that the barrenness of the Kamehamehas would bring an end to their line. Some wondered whether it was due to a genetic flaw attributable to generations of royal inbreeding. Such worries were put to rest in August 1857 when Queen Emma learned that she was pregnant. The next nine months would be one of the most important periods in the life of the queen and in the rule of the Kamehamehas.

The Most Important Nine Months

The queen's official routine at first did not seem to change. In her first trimester she continued to attend many official and social functions. In early October, for example, she and her attendants accompanied the king and other high officials on board the visiting U.S. sloop-of-war *St. Mary's.* Despite the whisperings of annexationists and the ship's contingent of marines, the ship's captain had assured the king that he was there "to preserve and strengthen the friendly relations" between the two countries.[1] The royal party enjoyed the captain's "hospitalities" and remained on board for three hours of dining and talking. A few evenings later, Their Majesties attended a dinner and ball on board the *St. Mary's,* "the first gala night" for Honolulu in many months.[2] Dancing well past midnight, they did not leave until the party broke up at about 2:00 a.m.[3]

Throughout October the queen continued to receive official visitations by diplomats, ministers, admirals, captains, and other dignitaries.

Because scores of ships stopped in Honolulu for provisions, repairs, recreation, or on official visits, the most frequent callers at the palace were ship captains, such as Captains Davis of the *St. Mary's* and Mecham of the *Vixen.* Of the diplomats the American Commissioner, David L Gregg, frequently called on the king or queen for both official and social reasons.[4]

One party Queen Emma did not attend was a *lū'au* hosted by Prince Lot at his residence in Moanalua in late October. Apparently, only men, including the king, Commissioner Gregg, and several officers from visiting warships, were present at this overnight gathering. Gregg reports that the evening's entertainment included "a hulahula" with a large number and a variety of dances, which he described as "the finest" he had seen.[5] One of the foods commonly served at *lū'au* was roasted dog. Gregg's comment on this "prime favorite" was, "I assure you from experience that it's not to be despised."[6]

The queen's appointment calendar for November was equally busy. Interested in antiques and other valuables, she attended a crowded party that featured an auction of Japanese curiosities at the residence of the Consul for Chile, Mr. A. P. Everett, an American married to a Spanish lady.[7] She attended another auction at which her late uncle Keoni Ana's belongings were sold.[8] Accompanied by Lydia Pākī and Mrs. Bernice Pauahi Bishop, she also visited the British steamer *Vixen.*[9] It is not known whether she shared the sentiments of Commissioner Gregg who described this and similar occasions as being "invariably tiresome."[10]

On November 28 the king and queen held a royal dinner to celebrate the joint declaration of Great Britain and France to ensure the sovereignty of the Hawaiian Islands. Some of the queen's closest friends, Miss Miller, Mrs. Elizabeth Pratt, Mrs. Rebecca Gregg, and Lydia Pākī, were in attendance. Also present were Mess. Perrin and Gregg, who did not miss the opportunity to record in his diary that Mons. Perrin criticized the king's wine, made many offensive and impertinent remarks, and fell asleep in the drawing room in the presence of the ladies, including the queen.[11]

Pregnancy

Surprisingly, even after the fourth month of the queen's pregnancy, the fact that she was with child was not widely known. In a town where news and rumors traveled at dazzling speeds, such a singular development could have been expected to be public knowledge by this time.

None of the newspapers, the English or Hawaiian language, had published the news yet. Commissioner Gregg found out only at the end of November when he recorded in his diary on the 26th that he had just learned about the queen being in a "family way."[12] A few days later he wrote that Minister of Foreign Relations Wyllie had just been informed by the king that the queen was "*enceinte*" and in her fourth month of pregnancy.[13] The queen's family and close female friends, however, must have known earlier because Gregg reported that his wife had known about the queen's pregnancy "some time" before he did.[14]

Strenuous Trips

Despite her condition, the queen took two strenuous trips in December and January: the first to ʻEwa and the second to Hilo and Maui. The thirteen-day trip to ʻEwa with the king and entourage began with a steamer ride to Pearl Harbor and then a journey of about eight miles to the ranch managed by Captain John Meek. While the men rode horseback, the queen and ladies went by carriage.[15] The next morning they traveled by horse and carriage to the home of Paul Manini, about twenty-five miles away. While there the queen and ladies occupied a grass house, the king and Commissioner Gregg slept in the courthouse, and the rest of the party found quarters as best as they could. Gregg reported that the king, who seldom complained, was a bit unhappy with the reception they received.[16] On their return, they rode to the beach to board the boat that was supposed to be waiting for them. Instead, the boat was aground some miles away, which forced them to remain there overnight. They finally arrived in Honolulu the next evening.[17] Travel, in those days, even for the royals, was frequently unpredictable and frustrating.

Before the queen embarked on her second trip, she and the king hosted another major social event at the palace: a *lūʻau* to celebrate the national day of "fasting humiliation and thanksgiving" (December 31). About 700 people attended what Gregg described as "the most remarkable gathering" he had seen in the Islands. "A tent was erected 220 feet by 40, and along the centre was a platform about 6 inches high for the reception of dishes. At 3 a cannon gave the signal of readiness and soon after the retainers or people of different chiefs connected with the royal family in separate bands, made their appearance, each person bearing some fish for the table."[18]

The next day the queen joined the king in receiving New Year's wishes, and that evening they attended a party in Waikīkī that featured a midnight supper and "hulahula" for entertainment.[19] The following day was the queen's birthday celebration.

Their Majesties embarked for Hilo on January 21, 1858, on the *Vixen* as guests of its British captain. The royal party included Governor Kekūanaoʻa, the king's natural father, and Dr. and Mrs. Rooke.[20] The presence of Emma's father, who doubled as her obstetrician/pediatrician, and her mother, who rarely made such appearances, was a welcome bonus. The trip to Hilo included stops at Lahaina, Kealakekua, and Kailua, Kona, and took twenty-two days. In thriving Hilo the king and queen resided with Governess Keʻelikōlani, as they had done on their previous visit. Typically, such a trip would include meeting with district leaders, civil servants, and other officials, attending receptions and parties, and listening to petitions from the people. One of the petitions was a plea to the king and queen for help in building a bridge over the Wailuku river in Hilo to prevent any more needless drownings by people trying to ford the stream. The king promised to pay for part of its construction.[21]

A sad encounter involved Dr. Rooke and a girl suffering from syphilis. Upon seeing the patient, he said that she would die if not attended to but that with proper care, she would recover in a short time. He recommended the appropriate medicine, and the girl said she would take it if her mother approved. Her mother did not approve and was given till the next morning to reconsider her decision. She remained firm, however, apparently fearing that the foreign medicine would be worse than the disease.[22] It is not known what happened to the girl, but the king and queen were by now extremely aware that distrust of western physicians and drugs was pervasive throughout the native population.

The royal party left Hilo for Lahaina where they stayed for a few days, while celebrating the king's twenty-fourth birthday. The queen returned to Honolulu in "high health and spirits" and quite pregnant. After welcoming the queen home, Commissioner Gregg reported that she was "much larger, in that goodly way which promises increase to the world's population, than when I last saw her."[23]

For the next three months there would be no more strenuous trips, no late-night dancing, no grand royal dinners.

Rooke's Appointment to Privy Council

On March 31, 1858, the king appointed Dr. Rooke to the privy council, the highest body of royal advisers. He joined an illustrious group that included Prince Lot, Robert C. Wyllie, David Kalākaua, Mataio Kekūanaō'a, Jonah Pi'ikoi, John 'Ī'ī, Paul Nahaolelua (governor of Maui), Elisha H. Allen (chief justice), Richard Armstrong (minister of public instruction), and Charles G. Hopkins (editor of the *Polynesian*). While Emma may have influenced the appointment of her father, he qualified on his own merits. The *Polynesian* editorialized that Dr. Rooke was "so intimately connected with, and through his inclinations and family ties is so thoroughly involved in, the fate of these Islands," that no one could doubt his ability to advance the interests of the community.[24]

Preparations

Although the palace had not made any official announcement about the queen's condition, by March 1858 everybody knew from the "prominence of her abdomen." Charles de Varigny described the reaction of the people to the anticipated birth: "The joy of the royal household was shared by the entire country. It was evident that the birth of an heir to the throne would serve to preserve and consolidate the Kamehameha dynasty, already recognized and accepted by foreign powers, and very precious to the natives."[25]

Preparations for the expected event ran the gamut from creating new chants, special hulas, and ceremonies to making ready the royal nursery. *Haku mele* (composers) composed new *mele inoa* (name chant) to blazon the ancestry of the new chief-to-be in order to add *mana* and distinction to the baby. Hula masters and their dancers committed the chants to memory and performed dances celebrating the new birth.[26]

Ladies-in-waiting and other friends of Queen Emma busied themselves sewing clothes, booties, blankets, and other items. An Englishman commissioned the same Irish seamstress who had made Queen Victoria's coronation robe to make a christening robe out of Ireland's finest laces for the child.[27] Craftsmen made furniture for the nursery. Wilhelm Fischer, a German cabinetmaker residing in Honolulu, made a beautiful cradle of koa, inlaid with rosewood, that was shaped like an eggshell cut in two, lengthwise. It was a work of art that cost $600.[28]

Others in the meantime watched for omens, scanned the clouds and the sea, noted the winds and the rains, and listened for the other celestial nudgings. Some looked for the most auspicious signs indicating an extraordinary infant or *keiki.* Some hoped that the pregnant queen would avoid the portents of danger such as wearing a lei (this might make the umbilical cord wrap itself around the baby's neck), working with cord (if the actual cord kinked, the umbilical cord might also kink, killing the baby), and eating the *'ōhi'a 'ai,* the mountain apple, or the *humuhumu,* the trigger fish (the child might have a birthmark).[29] It is uncertain whether Queen Emma subscribed to these traditional beliefs in *hōʻailona,* or signs, but even if she had, the omens and the associated interpretations were so numerous that often no one could agree on their meaning.[30]

It was also customary for chiefs to ask for the privilege of bringing up a child while still in its mother's womb. It is not known whether anyone did, but even if they had, both the queen and the king would have certainly refused.

The Joyful Event

On May 20, 1858, the queen went into labor. Attending her in the royal chamber were her father and Dr. William Hillebrand. Waiting in the adjoining rooms of the palace were her mothers Grace and Fanny, aunt Jane Lahilahi, cousin Peter Kaʻeo, Prince Lot, Princess Victoria, Governor Kekūanaoʻa, and Queen Dowager Kalama, among others. About 6:10 p.m. Emma gave birth to a baby boy.

One of the first sounds the infant prince heard was the booming guns on Punchbowl that immediately announced his birth.[31] The royal salute signaled the start of several weeks of national thanksgiving and jubilation. Happily, the celebratory shots did not cause any needless deaths or injuries. People had complained of the danger because several innocent bystanders had been wounded or killed in the past.

The cheering crowd that had gathered at the gates of the palace spilled out into the streets to continue the celebration through the night. Early the next morning flags and colorful streamers fluttered from every staff. Foreign consuls and government officials proceeded to the palace to pay their respects. And shop owners unanimously agreed to declare their own holiday and closed their doors for the festivities.

In the afternoon a large number of foreign residents marched in procession to the palace, escorted by the uniformed Honolulu Rifles. Upon arriving at the palace, the volunteers lined up on both sides of the entrance while people entered the spacious reception hall, filling it to overflowing. Abner Pratt, the American Consul, was the first to speak on behalf of the group congratulating the king on the birth of a "Royal Son" and on "the comfortable condition of the fortunate and happy Mother." At the same time, somewhat inappropriately, he urged the king to "support those principles of morality and religion . . . in building up and permanently establishing primary schools, and other educational institutions and . . . in fostering industry, agriculture and commerce . . . until your national domain, shall export and import millions annually, and until your national government shall stand firmly upon a footing with the most-favored and enlightened nations of the world."[32]

The second spokesperson for the group was the Reverend Samuel C. Damon, a friend of both the king and the queen. He presented the king with a Bible and stated "should God permit the infant prince to live and become your successor," that he be imbued with the principles of the Gospel. The king expressed his gratitude and assured him that both he and the queen would teach their first-born Bible principles. Deeply moved, the new father stated: "The birth of the young Prince has placed me in a relationship to which I have hitherto been a stranger, and it has imposed upon me new responsibilities. . . . Gentlemen, you see me a proud father, and by these manifestations of your love for me and mine, you make me a proud King."[33]

At birth the Prince Royal was given the name Albert Edward Kauikeaouli (place in the blue sky) Leiopapa a Kamehameha (the beloved child of Kamehameha). Four days later, on the recommendation of the privy council, the title *"Ka Haku O Hawai'i"* or Prince of Hawai'i was bestowed on the infant. The privy council took delight (as well as a little license) in describing the happy mood of the nation in its congratulatory message to the king: "No event which has ever occurred in the history of these Islands, has been cause of a more general feeling of interest, or been hailed with more universal joy, among all classes of Your Majesty's subjects and the foreigners residing within Your dominions, than the birth of the young Prince."[34]

The celebration continued for several weeks as the welcome news spread by sea mail beyond Honolulu. Throughout the Islands feasts were held, toasts given, and prayers offered, including a Catholic mass held by Bishop Louis Maigret in honor of the Prince Royal. All the while representatives from the different Islands journeyed to the palace bearing gifts and conveying congratulations.

One extraordinary event was a public showing of the prince in mid-June, 1858, when he was less than four weeks old, to a delegation of foreign children. Accompanied by their parents and led by a boy bearing a silk flag, they marched to the palace along King Street. It may have been a "forced march" because the *Polynesian* stated that *"all children* of foreign parentage were expected to join in the procession." The little girls, all dressed in white, pushed their royal gift, a baby carriage, bedecked with flowers and ribbons. They were ushered into the reception hall, and there in the center of the room was the cradle crafted by

Fischer. A nurse then brought in the infant, accompanied by his *kāhili* bearers, and placed him in the cradle. A few minutes later, His Majesty entered, without the queen, followed by Prince Lot and several chiefs. Four-year old Henrique Everett addressed the king: "Sire: You would scarce expect one of my age to speak to a King, but I have come with the foreign children to see your little boy the Prince of Hawaii." The children then thronged around the cradle to see "a fat, healthy and exceedingly beautiful boy."[35]

At the beginning of the legislature in June, the king spoke movingly about his newborn: "Since the Legislature was last in session, it has pleased almighty God to bless me with a son. The birth of an Heir to the Throne is an event . . . inseparable from the future of our country's history. . . . Gentlemen, the child is yours as well as mine; the circumstances that attend his birth deprive me of an undivided interest in him, for if such be the will of Divine Providence, he will one day be to your Sons what I am to their Fathers. Destined as he is to exercise a paramount influence in years to come, I consecrate him to my people, and with God's help, I will leave unused no faculty with which I am imbued to make him worthy of your love and loyalty."[36]

The Queen Mother

The record is silent about how the new queen mother might have nurtured the child, whether she breast-fed him or whether she resorted to *nuʻakea* (wet nurse), whether she personally fed and bathed him, whether she tucked him into his cradle and sang lullabies to him, whether she massaged and molded his soft body—all tasks that would have taken considerable time but presumably given her considerable joy. Had Emma decided to limit the amount of her time and personal attention, she would have had two sound reasons: the pressure of her royal responsibilities and the availability of plentiful help. It appears she decided, with the concurrence of the king, to spend more time as a mother. This decision meant not only less involvement in official activities but also less reliance on overindulgent servants—a departure from ancient custom. This would not be the first such departure for this modern queen.

By late summer Queen Emma had regained much of her strength. She started horseback riding again with the king or lady friends on jaunts that took her as far as the royal residence in Waikīkī and her new home in Nuʻuanu. Horseback riding was her favorite sport; in fact, anything to do with horses appealed to her. So she was particularly pleased to learn that one of the most popular attractions at a recent art exhibition in San Francisco was a large painting of the royal family—the king and queen, Prince Lot, Princess Victoria, and Queen Dowager Kalama—all on horseback. The queen and her *ali'i* companions were complimented on their "style of dress and the ease and grace with which they sat their horses."[37]

Queen Emma also resumed some of her official duties, particularly the social functions. One of the first was hosting a dinner-dance for the departing British Consul-General William Miller and his niece, her close friend. The success of the affair did nothing to detract from the queen's reputation as a gracious hostess. The *Polynesian* wrote: "All the arrangements were excellent, and gave fresh evidence of that *savoir faire* which always makes the entertainments at the Palace so agreeable."[38] It paid another tribute to the queen by describing her as "a lady whose gentle disposition and unaffected kindness of heart have made her a favorite in the community."[39]

The forthcoming social season was predicted to be "one of the liveliest, as well as the busiest on record" for Honolulu.[40] Preoccupied with caring for her young prince, Emma may have felt a bit overwhelmed as she glanced at the crowded calendar of dinners, musicales, sewing circles, balls, and other activities.

What few plans she may have made were suddenly cancelled by the king's violent asthma attack in early September. His physician (Dr. Rooke) recommended several months of rest in the dry climate of Kailua, Kona. The king, queen, and the infant Prince Albert left almost immediately for Hawai'i. Accompanying them were Prince Lot, Governor Kekūanao'a, Princess Victoria, Dr. Rooke, Charles Hopkins, Mr. and Mrs. Gregg, several chiefs, and other members of the court, all together numbering about 200 people. While the queen may have preferred to remain in the palace and not expose the less-than-four-month-old prince to the rigors of ocean travel, the king's health was uppermost.

If King Alexander Liholiho wanted rest, according to his secretary Henry Neilson, Kona was the place: it was void of any distractions. He wrote, Kona was "so desolate that ennui was the order of the day. Nothing is to be seen but black masses of lava, heaved into all sorts of shapes . . . and scarcely a tree within miles." He complained that there was little to do and that "all grumbled at the want of amusement." Presumably "all" included the queen because, Neilson added, only the king "alone" appeared to be "contented" and "glad enough." The queen could not indulge in her favorite pastime because there was "not grass enough to feed a horse." But there were books to read, people to converse with, and the little prince to take care of—and to show off to all who came to see him.[41]

As for the king, he was "a great fisherman" and spent much of his time fishing with nets or rod and line. According to Neilson, His Majesty "stayed out for hours in the hot sun and often got nothing." The king also had fun because he enjoyed "upsetting the canoe" and seeing people tumble into the water.[42] Without the need to make speeches, conduct audiences, resolve conflicts, and so on, the king's "rest and recuperation" progressed well. His nervous tension subsided, and his asthma retreated for the time being.

On November 28, 1858, tragedy struck, ironically, not the patient but rather the physician. Dr. Rooke, who had been in failing health for a while, suffered a heart attack that morning and died a few hours later. He was fifty-two.

Although the king's original plan was to stay in Kona till January, he immediately ordered two ships to convey the royal party and his father-in-law's remains to Honolulu. Flags in the harbor area had been hoisted to welcome back the royal family, but when the schooner holding Dr. Rooke's remains came into view, the flags were lowered to half-mast.

Except for the death, the nearly three months of rest had been a happy sojourn. As the *Polynesian* put it on their return, "Their Majesties and the infant Prince appeared to be in the enjoyment of perfect health."[43]

In Memoriam

Fellow physician, Dr. Robert W. Wood, president of the Hawaiian Medical Society, wrote in his memoriam to Dr. Rooke:

> For several years [he] had ceased to use any efforts to secure his proportional share of the general practice of the town. But he retained to the day of his death the office of Physician to the Court and deeply impressed with the want of hospitals for sick natives, every morning threw open the doors of his dispensary to many who could not otherwise have procured advice or medicines. Besides the amount of physical relief which he thus achieved it must have been a balm to the minds of many suffering wretches to know that what they claimed as members of a community was accorded to them upon the broader though simpler basis of a common humanity. . . .
>
> We have lost not only the Senior member of our Profession here, whose labors among these people and community during his long

residence on these islands have secured for him an enduring place in the memory of the Hawaiian nation; but, also, a brother whose strict sense of professional propriety in his relations to us, as well as to those entrusted to his care, have won for him our lasting esteem and respect."[44]

Dr. Rooke was buried among the chiefs in the Royal Cemetery on the palace grounds. (His body was later removed to the Royal Mausoleum in Nuʻuanu where he lies beside his wife in the Wyllie Tomb, one of only four non-Hawaiians so honored.)

Had Dr. Rooke lived a few months longer, he would have witnessed the fulfillment of a life-long dream: the kingdom's first public hospital. It was established through the efforts of the king and queen but it was he who had planted the seeds of the idea in her heart.[45]

8

The Queen's Hospital

Four years had passed since King Alexander Liholiho had first asked the legislature to build and fund hospitals to "stay the wasting hand." Many supportive speeches were made and bills passed, but not one had been funded. Amid the wail of innumerable victims, not a single concrete step had been taken. At the end of December 1858, a month after Dr. Rooke's death, the *Pacific Commercial Advertiser* expressed the frustration and anger of many when it lambasted the government: "This talk about hospitals . . . is all bosh. Neither the ministry nor their organ care any more for a hospital for the suffering Hawaiians than they do for the Sepoys of India—at least so their acts indicate. The last Legislature voted the liberal sum of $5,000 for a Hospital for Sick Natives, on this Island and the first dollar has not yet been expended for that object though hundreds of natives had died purely from want of attention and medicine."[1]

No responsible person or party openly opposed the establishment of a public hospital, but *The Friend*'s soon-to-be hospital trustee the Reverend Samuel Damon urged that everything should be done to "prevent the need of a hospital." Most people seeking hospital care, he argued, "have no business there." They were sick because of poor eating habits, drunkenness, and licentiousness. He wanted preventive health measures such as good nutrition, exercise, sanitation, and clean air.[2] He made excellent sense of wellness, but that was the long view; now the cries of the sick and the dying were far too urgent to be ignored.

In January 1859 the hospital issue was referred to a joint committee consisting of Acting Minister of Interior David L. Gregg and Foreign Minister Robert C. Wyllie. Eight months before, Dr. Charles Guillou had recommended that a public fund-raising drive for the hospital be started and had urged the government to "Go to the ladies, go with the ladies" because these "good Genii of every community" would loosen every "gentleman's" heart and purse.[3] The committee took his advice and determined that if Queen Emma and other interested ladies would take charge, the hospital could be carried through. This was the first of many fund-raising campaigns for worthy purposes that she would be involved in during her lifetime.

Gregg and Wyllie then outlined a plan of operation, similar to the one that Dr. Guillou had outlined the previous year.[4] A dispensary would be set up at once, and the general groundwork would be laid for a hospital project. The ladies would be active in this latter phase. Then the legislature would appropriate government lands for support and levy a tax on each seaman sailing under the Hawaiian flag for a marine hospital fund. Patients requiring home treatment would be provided for according to circumstances until a suitable hospital could be built. But the plan still rested on legislative action.

The Legislation

It took the legislature 141 days in its "longest and most tedious session" to pass still another hospital bill, but this one was different: it allowed for the organization and incorporation of an association for the establishment of a hospital for sick and needy Hawaiians and granted it all necessary powers. If and when the corporation raised at least $5,000, the minister of interior could, with the king's consent, convey to it government lands (or their proceeds) of equal value. In case the lands should be granted, the Board of Health would have a proportionate voice in the management of the corporation. The law also permitted one hospital to be set up on each of the Islands of Maui, Kaua'i, and Hawai'i under similar conditions.

On April 20, 1859, King Kamehameha IV signed what he considered to be the most important act of the 1859 legislative session and immediately began work to force the legislature to provide the needed funds. According to the historian Ralph S. Kuykendall, the king "did this not alone in response to his own feeling of humanity but at the particular request of Queen Emma."[5] Beginning about April 28, he began soliciting subscriptions for the hospital. Accompanied by his secretary, who

So strong was the desire of the royal couple for Queen's Hospital that they personally canvassed the community for the original funds. Their quest—"to stay the wasting hand that is destroying our people"—is depicted in this painting by Peter Hurd.

carried a memorandum book in which to record pledges, the king visited business houses, professional offices, diplomatic representatives, and private citizens. The *Polynesian* described the scene as follows: "His Majesty, notebook in hand, has been seen in the most frequented parts of town, soliciting subscriptions to the hospital for his poor subjects. He accosted people, slipped into their homes and offices as he happened to pass. Upon foot and in the rain, he has worked many hours a day to accomplish his self-imposed mission."[6]

The *Pacific Commercial Advertiser* wrote: "During the past week the honored Chief Magistrate of the country appeared before the public of Honolulu in a new character, that of a solicitor of the charities of the residents on behalf of Hospital Institutions for the benefit of indigent sick."[7] And *Ka Hae Hawai'i* reported that "Our King . . . has gone among the foreigners and chiefs of this town, and because of their great aloha for him and the importance of this grand project, they have helped him considerably. . . ."[8]

One contemporary observer said of the king's success as a fundraiser: "He was a most pleasing conversationalist, and his power of persuasion was seldom exerted in vain. Generally dressed in white linen and a fine panama hat, and as little of the mark of his position as possible, he early won the confidence of those to whom he appealed."[9] However well disguised the king may have been, his Hawaiian subjects were probably shocked to see their king soliciting money on the streets of Honolulu.

To the astonishment of some of his sluggish legislators, within a week the king had collected more than $13,000 in amounts ranging from $5 to $500. He and the queen headed the list with pledges of $500 each. *Ka Hae Hawai'i,* impressed with the royal success, attributed it to the people's "great aloha" for the king.[10] The *Pacific Commercial Advertiser* attributed it to the "proverbial generosity" of the people and then posed the question: "when the Chief Magistrate, the King himself, takes upon himself the task of going about town, day after day, to collect subscriptions for so praiseworthy an object as the establishment of a hospital fund for Hawaiians, who can have the face to refuse, or rather who would refuse to give something or begrudge the sum he has submitted?"[11]

> Enthralled with the public response, the king, addressing the nobles and representatives, stated: I confess that the Act of your two Houses, which I regard with most complacency is that in which you commit the public treasury to the aid of hospitals. You Representatives, amongst whose constituents are those very persons for whom these places of refuge are principally designed, have expressed a kind and grateful feeling for the personal share which I and the Queen have taken in the labor of securing the necessary means for the establishment of a hospital in Honolulu. Whilst acknowledging your courtesy I wish to take this first public occasion to express the almost unspeakable satisfaction with which I have found my efforts successful beyond my hopes. It is due to the subscribers as a body, that I shall bear witness to the readiness, not less than the liberality with which you have met my advances. When you return to your several places let the fact be known, that in Honolulu the sick man has a friend in everybody—nor do I believe that He who made us all and to whose keeping I commend in now dismissing you, have seen with indifference how the claims of a common humanity have drawn together, in the subscription list, names representative of almost every race of men under the sun.[12]

The subscription list numbered 250 private individuals, government representatives and a few businesses.[13] The exact sum collected added up to $13,530, which exceeded the king's goal by $8,000.

Fund and Tax Raising

Although Queen Emma was not directly involved in the largely political decisions of the hospital's founding, she was extremely active in raising funds through benefit performances and fairs. A week after the birthday celebrations, the queen helped to organize a benefit concert for the "Hawaiian Hospital Fund" by the Amateur Musical Society, of which she was an active member. Two leading members of the concert were friends of Their Majesties: Eugene Hasslocher, the German maestro, and Madame Louise de Varigny, a talented pianist, who boasted that she played a piece by Goria on themes from Bellini seventeen pages long, alone and by heart, without a pause from beginning to end.[14] The well-attended affair cost a dollar.[15]

Their Majesties enjoyed the works of Weber, Beriot, Rossini, and other composers performed by local artists "whom the proudest court in Europe would have been proud to possess." As they left the hall, the band played "God Save the King" with lyrics written especially for the occasion.[16]

In conjunction with the hospital bill, the legislature sought to take care of the medical needs of a special group of natives, Hawaiian seamen. Their English and American counterparts had long been cared for in their own hospitals and by their own physicians. But the legislature rectified this imbalance with an Act "to Aid in the Establishment of Hospitals for the Benefit of Sick & Disabled Hawaiian Seamen." Approved by King Alexander Liholiho on May 13, it provided that each passenger arriving from a foreign port should pay a tax of $2.00 to the Collector of Customs for the support of such hospitals. (Was this Hawai'i's first tourist tax?) Additional revenue was expected from a tax on seamen sailing under the Hawaiian flag. The Civil Code of 1859 provided that (1) ship owners or masters arriving from foreign ports should pay twenty-five cents a month for each seaman employed on board since the last entry at any Hawaiian port and (2) masters of coasting vessels should pay, quarterly, twenty-five cents a month for each seaman employed. The tax was withheld from wages, and the funds realized were retained as a "Marine Hospital Fund" for the relief of sick and disabled seamen.

Organizing the Hospital

On May 24, 1859, the king and his cabinet met and decided without debate to name the hospital "The Queen's Hospital" or "*Hale Ma'i O Ka Wahine Ali'i*" (literally the Sick House of the Lady Chief).[17] It is noteworthy that in a town of gossipers and royal critics, no one ever questioned naming the hospital after the queen. The *Pacific Commercial Advertiser* confirmed what everyone seemed to know: "that the plan of erecting a general hospital originated in the heart of our noble queen."[18] The Hawaiian language newspaper *Ka Nūpepa Kū'oko'a* also credited the queen with the original idea. Using almost the same words, it said, "This fine deed originated within the heart of our Queen."[19]

For Hawaiians who were deeply aware of the mystical power in the names given to things—that words or names have their own *mana*—the name had more meaning than being a simple name. It meant investing the hospital and its people with the mantle of the queen's *mana*. The belief was that you could invoke that power if and when needed, provided you were worthy.

On May 25, the hospital subscribers met in the courthouse and passed several resolutions. They elected the king as president by acclamation and, thanking both the king and queen, named them Royal Patrons; organized themselves as a "body politic and corporate" to establish a hospital and to take "The Queen's Hospital" as its corporate name; and agreed to select the first trustees—ten chosen by the subscribers and ten by the minister of interior, for a total of twenty-one persons including the king.[20] The trustee selection process did not go smoothly; in fact, "hot words" were exchanged concerning various government appointees. Even the king lost his temper and administered sharp rebukes.[21]

The resolutions also outlined the duties and functions of the Board of Trustees, provided the means to secure a permanent site for a hospital, detailed the membership and voting rights of subscribers, as well as instructed the trustees to collect unpaid subscriptions. (Up to that time, only $695 of the $13,530 had been collected.)[22]

As to the composition of the 250 subscribers, about forty-six or less than 20 percent of the total were native Hawaiians. At least sixteen of them were of chiefly rank including the king and queen, Lot Kamehameha, Albert (the Prince of Hawai'i), Victoria Kamāmalu, the Queen Dowager Kalama, Grace Rooke, David Kalākaua and Lydia Pākī, and their father Kapa'akea, William Lunalilo and his father Charles Kana'ina, Governor Paulo Kānoa of Kaua'i, Governor Paul Nahaolelua of Maui, John William Pitt Kīna'u, and John Papa 'Ī'ī.[23] (Some notable *ali'i*—and family-connected—names, such as Ruth Ke'elikōlani, Jane Lahilahi, and Peter Ka'eo, among others, were absent.) Except for a few Chinese, the remaining 80 percent of the subscribers were Caucasians, the vast majority of whom were American. Of the $13,530 raised, at least $2,840 or 20 percent of the total came from native Hawaiians. The king's satisfaction with the fund-raising notwithstanding, one wonders how satisfied he was with the native Hawaiian participation, which, in proportion to its total numbers, was clearly limited.

The new trustees comprised the king, Prince Lot, William A. Aldrich, James W. Austin, Asher B. Bates, Charles R. Bishop, James Bissett, Samuel N. Castle, Rev. Samuel C. Damon, William L. Green, David L. Gregg, Heinrich Hackfeld, Edwin O. Hall, Theodore C. Heuck, H J. Holdsworth, John Ladd, John Montgomery, George M. Robertson, B. F. Snow, John T. Waterhouse, and William Webster. Apart from the king and Lot, there were no other Hawaiians.[24]

Thus trustees were scarcely representative of the general populace. They represented the rich, the famous, and the influential—the kingdom's "power elite." Eight were businessmen, namely, Charles Bishop, the founder of today's First Hawaiian Bank, Samuel Castle of Castle & Cooke, and Heinrich Hackfeld of today's AMFAC, Edwin O. Hall and John T. Waterhouse, merchants whose companies were later absorbed by Theo. H. Davies, William L. Green and James W. Austin, who were in the shipping business, and John Ladd of Ladd & Co. Heuck was an architect, Webster an engineer, and Damon a minister. The rest held government positions; for example, Gregg was the minister of finance, Robertson the chief justice, and Bates the attorney general. No women or physicians were on the board.

The work of organizing proceeded rapidly and successfully. On May 28, 1859, King Kamehameha IV instructed Gregg to prepare a memorandum for a hospital charter, which Gregg promised to deliver the next day. A week later in an evening meeting the trustees organized themselves, read, considered, and amended the draft of the charter, which the king then referred to a committee of five for study and report. When the committee met on June 6, a great deal of bickering took place. At one point the king "snubbed" a "very factious" Trustee Bates who "quarreled with everything."[25] By the next evening they were able to iron out their differences and agree on a charter. The subscribers met again on June 9 at the courthouse to approve the charter. With the king presiding, they approved the charter with only one minor amendment that allowed absent subscribers to vote by proxy.[26] On June 16 the privy council granted the charter that the trustees formally accepted thirteen days later.[27]

A little more than two months had passed from the day the king signed the hospital legislation to the privy council's authorization and the trustees' approval of the charter.

The Charter

The new charter spelled out the hospital's purpose as "the reception, accommodation and treatment of indigent sick and disabled Hawaiians, as well as such foreigners and others who may choose to avail themselves of the same. . . ." Although the hospital was intended to treat mainly Hawaiians, it was to be open to non-natives as well. This was reiterated by the trustees of the hospital four years later when the board "Resolved that all indigent sick and disabled Hawaiian subjects, native and naturalized, are entitled to receive accommodation and treatment at the Queen's Hospital. . . ."[28] Oddly enough, even with the queen's patronage, "the indigent sick and disabled Hawaiians" did not automatically include female Hawaiians. Not until the Board of Trustees' meeting on June 30, 1859, when it had to decide on whether to allow prostitutes to be treated, was the matter clarified about whether to admit "females as well as males."[29]

Contrary to a popular belief today, the charter makes no mention of "free treatment" for Hawaiians. However, as subsequent events would indicate, because it was a government-supported institution, the hospital would be required to provide "gratuitous" treatment to those unable to pay as long as the patient was properly admitted and the funds were available.

Apart from the usual legal powers accorded to trustees to set the bylaws and to appoint and terminate employees, and so on, the charter empowered the board to set up a temporary dispensary in Honolulu until a permanent facility could be built, to purchase a site and build and equip a permanent hospital, and to appoint a "medical attendant or attendants." In addition, the board was required to report semi-annually to the minister of the interior and to appoint a presiding officer in the absence of the king.

On June 29, the trustees formally approved the charter and then passed a set of bylaws the next day. The bylaws provided for a board secretary, treasurer, auditor, and an executive committee of five, all to be chosen annually by ballot by a majority; each member was to have one vote; the board would appoint a physician or physicians and determine their salaries; all contracts, excepting real estate, were to be limited to four years; and board meetings would be held monthly.[30]

On June 30 the trustees selected their first officers. The king was named president and subsequently was made "perpetual president."[31] (Thus Queen's is the only hospital in America that can claim to have had a king as its president.) The other officers were James Austin secretary, Charles Bishop treasurer, and William Green auditor.[32] Over the next two days the trustees also considered a petition presented by the subscribers supporting Dr. William Hillebrand as hospital physician; appointed a committee to draft a code to govern the internal direction and control of the hospital; directed the treasurer to deposit subscriptions in Mr. Bishop's bank; selected its executive committee consisting of Judge Robertson, Webster, Castle, Ladd, and Austin; and decided to rent from Mr. Thomas Thrum a temporary hospital building for $60 a month for at least six months. The trustees also temporarily adopted as the hospital seal a plain wafer but conferred with the queen regarding a permanent seal.[33] It was not until June 21, 1860, a year later, that the board adopted a seal bearing a profile of Queen Emma.[34]

Appointment of Dr. William Hillebrand

One of the trustees' first priorities was to appoint a physician to run the hospital. From the start there was considerable interest in the appointment among Honolulu's dozen or so doctors. The leading aspirants were Dr. Robert McKibbin, Sr. and Dr. Robert McKibbin, Jr., Dr. Charles Guillou, and Dr. Hillebrand, all of whom were professional colleagues and founding members of the Hawaiian Medical Society. At first Dr. McKibbin, Jr., who was the king's choice, seemed to have the best chance of appointment, but the board favored the "quiet, sober and practical" Hillebrand. The king was advised by Gregg to save face by either carrying McKibbin's election or by obtaining an agreement that the latter would not be a candidate. He refused to withdraw, and the contest went on. On July 20 the trustees set the physician's salary at $1,500 per annum, which the *Pacific Commercial Advertiser* criticized as too much money. But the trustees stuck to their offer in order to obtain the best medical attention for hospital patients.

By the 23rd of July McKibbin's case was beginning to look "desperate." Three days later the trustees chose Hillebrand. He received ten votes and McKibbin received nine. The king suggested the vote should be unanimous, and a formal ballot followed. This time Hillebrand won sixteen of the eighteen votes cast.[35]

The duties of the hospital physician, as set forth by the trustees in "Rules and Regulations for a Temporary Hospital and Dispensary," included the following: (1) fit up one room as a surgery and dispensary;

(2) select and arrange a proper supply of medicines; (3) attend the dispensary every day for not less than one and a half hours and not more than three hours at a time fixed and published by the executive committee (though shortly thereafter three hours' attendance was required); (4) prescribe appropriate medicines; (5) examine all patients asking for admission to the hospital, and in non-emergency cases the doctor should report to the next meeting of the executive committee; (6) admit patients without certificate of admission in cases of emergency, but in such cases the doctor should report to the next meeting of the executive committee, which would decide whether hospital care would be continued; (7) admit patients given admission certificates by the chairman of the executive committee and treat or attend them by day or night as necessary; (8) supervise the hospital and see that subordinates did their duty; (9) keep records of all cases cared for; (10) make weekly reports to the executive committee on business done and any other matters requiring action; (11) render accounts to the executive committee at the first meeting of each month; and (12) make rules and regulations for the internal management of the hospital.[36]

The executive committee exercised considerable control over patient admissions. Trustees were furnished with blank certificates of admission: "A" for the dispensary and "B" for the hospital.[37]

Form A read:

> I recommend ________________ living at ______________ and suffering from ________________ as a proper person to receive gratuitous dispensary relief, being unable to pay for advice and medicines.
>
> (signed)___________________________

Form B:

> I recommend ________________ living at ______________ and suffering from ________________ as a proper person to receive gratuitous hospital relief, being unable to pay for advice and medicines.
>
> (signed)___________________________

The trustees (later only the executive committee) were authorized to appoint agents in the different Island districts who could then recommend admissions of forms A or B. Their recommendations, however, had to be countersigned by a trustee. The reason for this procedure seemed to be finance-driven, because there was a limit to how many patients could be given "gratuitous" care. Yet the executive committee had to give its consent even when admitting paying patients. The committee of course fixed the charges.[38]

The "Rules and Regulations" also provided for visiting hours to be set by the physician, though in emergency cases any clergyman could be admitted at any hour. A visiting committee of trustees was to be appointed for each quarter and allowed at least weekly access to inspect the hospital.[39]

The Temporary Facility

On July 15 the trustees took over Thrum's "large and airy" building at the corner of Fort and King Streets, and during the next two weeks workmen put up partitions and installed furniture and fixtures. The temporary facility had a total of eighteen beds. Notices of the opening of *Hale Maʻi O Ka Wahine Aliʻi* were printed in Hawaiian and circulated. The *Pacific Commercial Advertiser* expressed the hope that "the natives will take advantage of this opportunity in preference to their ignorant and conjuring native doctors."[40]

The temporary hospital officially opened on August 1, 1859. Despite the talk in the community that Hawaiians would be too afraid to go to the hospital, in the first month over 100 patients came to be treated, along with ten "boarding inmates." From August 1 to October 10, there were 386 Hawaiian applicants and 965 consultations or fourteen a day. Twenty-five resident patients had been accepted, and fifteen dismissed, twelve of whom were listed as cured. Two of the resident patients were Caucasians, and a total of three patients had paid for their board and lodging. Also several destitute outpatients had been provided free meals.[41]

The trustees were pleased with these early results, especially the low operating costs: the entire expense for caring for the resident patients and for feeding the purveyor, attendants, steward, and cook for the two months of August and September was $97.00.

After inspecting the hospital in January 1860, the visiting committee reported that the number of applicants was increasing and that natives were coming from remote parts of Oʻahu, as well as from the other Islands, to seek treatment. It praised Dr. Hillebrand and his assistant for their hard work.[42]

At the time, the staff had no nurses. Instead, family members, relatives, or friends cared for the patients. They were called either *kōkua* (helper) or *makamaka* (close friend). In fact, the first trained nurse at Queen's, Mrs. Mary Adams, was not hired until 1886.[43]

The visiting committee's report also stated that the hospital had "secured the confidence of the native population in a most remarkable manner . . ." and that the hospital had "exerted a happy effect in checking the most pernicious influence and practices of native doctors."[44]

In his official report covering the first five months, Dr. Hillebrand stated that there were 765 applications at the dispensary, five or six daily consultations, and 2,160 prescriptions given out. There were fifty-four resident patients of whom forty-three were dismissed, four died, and seven were still in the hospital. Of the deaths, one was from tuberculosis, one from typhoid, one each from croup and from pulmonary apoplexy. All told, thirty-nine house patients had been cured, two were incurable, and two had run away. Applications averaged from eighteen to twenty per day, depending on the weather. On stormy days the number declined to six or eight, while in good weather it might increase to thirty-five or thirty-six. During December there was a considerable increase from the neighbor Islands.[45]

Despite these encouraging statistics, many native Hawaiians stayed away from the hospital out of fear. Even ten years later the board's secretary "was constrained to speak of the feeling of distrust, and even aversion, entertained by the larger part of the Hawaiian population towards the Queen's Hospital. . . ."[46] Many Hawaiians viewed the hospital as the place of last resort—only for those who were sick and did not expect to recover. Hawaiians sought out their own traditional doctors *(kāhuna lā'au lapa'au)* because they were familiar and comfortable with their methods and devices. But they were not very comfortable with *haole* doctors, their strange prescriptions, and especially some of their instruments such as the giant forceps and "automatic scarificator" used for bloodletting.

Perhaps no one understood these feelings better than Queen Emma herself. She had lived her entire life helping or observing her physician father treat sick natives. She, as well as the trustees, knew that Hawaiians would have to be educated and, in effect, sold on the benefits—call it marketing, if you will—of the hospital. But this process would take time.

Finding a Permanent Site

In the meantime, the board had appointed a site committee to find a permanent location for the hospital. Four sites were considered: the first was near the new prison on Iwilei Road, and the second was on Pālama Road next to a soap factory then in operation. These two sites were rejected out of fear that the strong winds of Nu'uanu would prove harmful to hospital patients.[47] The third site was at the "head" of Emma

Street (now the corner of Emma and School Streets) consisting of about one and a half acres, and the fourth was a nine-acre parcel in the lee of Punchbowl and on Beretania "road."

In January 1860 the trustees decided on the site where The Queen's Medical Center stands today. (In 1967 Queen's Hospital became The Queen's Medical Center.) Its grounds are now lush and green, but at that time the site was almost totally barren. There were no homes, fences, trees, or any "respectable undergrowth" from above Beretania right up the slopes of Punchbowl. Nor was there any water, which was the biggest drawback. The *Pacific Commercial Advertiser,* which campaigned for the site, wondered whether the new Honolulu waterworks would be able to supply that part of town; otherwise, water could be piped from Pauoa Valley around the base of Punchbowl.[48] (Today The Queen's Medical Center has its own well that supplies all of its current water needs.) Some thought the site had another advantage and claimed that the climate on Beretania was greatly superior to that some six or eight blocks away![49]

The land was the property of the high chief Kapa'akea, the progenitor of the Kalākaua dynasty, and his son David and daughter Lili'uokalani were born there. The place was called Manamana, meaning "branching" or "lots of *mana*" as in the name Kūmanamana or Kū Exceeding Great Mana.[50] When rendered as a verb or *ho'omanamana,* Manamana also means to impart *mana*—a fitting name for a place that could empower those who are in contact with it.

The trustees paid $2,000 for Manamana including the two-story frame building that stood on the site, which turned out to be a fine bonus.[51] More spacious than the temporary building on King Street and better ventilated, it was used as a temporary hospital until the permanent building could be built. It took five weeks to renovate the building to accommodate twenty-four beds. On March 10, 1860, Dr. Hillebrand with his staff and patients settled in the new Queen's Hospital building. This date marks the hospital's first occupation of Manamana. On June 21, three months after the move to its new campus, Dr. Hillebrand reported that 1,354 patients had applied at the dispensary since August 1, 1859: 835 males and 519 females. During this period around 4,000 consultations were held and a similar number of prescriptions filled, and a total of thirteen deaths occurred at the hospital. Since mid-April the hospital had been filled to capacity, and for some time even the dining room and the dispensary were used to bed the sick. At the same time Dr. Hillebrand reported twenty-one patients were being cared for.[52] The growing demands upon the hospital soon outstripped its resources, drawing the attention of the trustees to their perennial concern: money.

Hospital Finances

An important source of money came from the subscribers, some of whom still owed on their pledges; in fact, the unpaid amount exceeded $4,850. In January 1860 the trustees felt compelled to hire a collector to obtain the delinquent contributions.[53] A year later there was still $1,400 to collect, and the *Pacific Commercial Advertiser* threatened to publish the names of the delinquent subscribers.[54]

Still another source was the tax placed on seamen sailing under the Hawaiian flag, the proceeds of which were to be used for the care of the sick. In January 1860 the trustees and the minister of the interior signed a contract that stipulated that the government would pay quarterly to the hospital all amounts received and that the hospital would care for all sick and disabled Hawaiian seamen who might arrive in any port. The hospital would be responsible for paying the cost of their transportation from any other port to Honolulu.[55]

Potentially, the most promising source of cash income was the foreigners, both the seamen and the various consuls. In February 1860 a special committee was formed to pursue that market.[56]

Finally, there was the money from fund raising drives by the queen and her ladies. For example, in May the Amateur Musical Society put on a benefit concert for the "Hawaiian Hospital Fund" that realized $218.75.[57] Another musical concert featuring Prof. J. H. Anderson, the "Wizard of the North," was held in November 1859. Despite the boycott by American ship captains, the event generated nearly $400.[58] About a year later, Queen Emma sponsored a fair that netted over $1,600 for the hospital.[59] Many other fund-raising events would be held in subsequent years.[60]

By the end of September 1859, the hospital had a balance of $7,336.57, which included a $2,000 donation from the legislature. Curiously, the trustees permitted the treasurer to loan $7,000 on ninety days' call on security up to six months. A financial report of January 5, 1860, showed that $6,000 had been loaned to Janion, Green and Company.[61]

Construction of the New Queen's

Meanwhile, plans and specifications were being developed for the new hospital building. The trustee who spearheaded the design work was the architect Theodore Heuck, Hawai'i's first professional architect, who had arrived from his native Germany in 1850. Although he eventually designed the Royal Mausoleum, 'Iolani Barracks, and other structures, the Queen's Hospital would be his first important work in Hawai'i.

Never bashful about giving advice, the *Pacific Commercial Advertiser* recommended that there should be a modest-sized central building, capable of expansion, with "rows of thatched huts" in the rear. It said that nine out of ten natives would prefer to lie on a mat in a hut attended by their own *makamaka*.[62]

The trustees considered several plans before deciding on a two-story structure 100 feet long, 48 feet wide, and 35 feet high, with a wooden floor and a flat roof. (The plan did not include any thatched huts.) They also determined that the total cost should not exceed $13,500 (about the same sum that King Liholiho had raised).

The construction contract was signed on May 26, with the optimistic prediction that the hospital would "turn out the finest public building, as well as the most commodious for hospital purposes, that Honolulu will have to boast of for many years to come."[63] The contract called for completion by November 1, 1860.

The trustees thanked the architect Heuck for his work and promised him that his name, as architect, would be placed on the completed building.[64] But he did not receive any money for his work. The contractor was C. H. Lewers, and the subcontractors were G. Thomas, mason; C. W. Vincent, carpenter; and R. Gilliland, painter, who were paid.[65] Ground was broken on Wednesday, June 13.

The cornerstone laying ceremony was scheduled for July 14, 1860, but the king took sick, and the ceremony was postponed to the 17th.[66] When the day arrived, because of the short notice in the date change, many Hawaiians who would otherwise have attended were not present. But almost the entire foreign community, who had donated the lion's share of the subscription money, were there, seated under awnings set up on the hospital's treeless grounds to provide some shade. Also present was Queen Emma accompanied by her ladies.

At 11:00 a.m. the procession formed at Kawaiaha'o Church and marched to the hospital in the following order: William C. Parke, Marshal of the Kingdom, Mechanics' Benefit Union, Odd Fellows Lodge, Masonic Organizations, trustees of the hospital, His Majesty the King, Chancellor of the Kingdom, Justices of the Supreme Court, Ministers and other High Officers of the Kingdom, Commander of the U.S.S. *Levant* with Officers, U.S. Marines and Sailors, members of the House of Nobles, members of the House of Representatives, other officers of the Kingdom, subscribers to the Hospital Corporation, citizens, and the military forces of the Kingdom.

The program began with a prayer given in Hawaiian by the Reverend Armstrong, followed by two hymns sung in Hawaiian by the Reverend Lowell Smith's church choir. King Kamehameha then spoke briefly in Hawaiian. The cornerstone was laid according to the ceremonies of the Ancient Order of Free Masons, of which the king was an active member. A cachet or the official seal was placed in the cornerstone and the stone anointed and lowered. After the king's concluding remarks, trustee Reverend Samuel Damon offered the benediction.

The King Kamehameha gave one of his most eloquent speeches, which at times hushed the crowd so that one could hear a feather drop. He began:

> The Queen's Hospital, established for the relief and comfort of the indigent sick, has already taken its place among the prominent institutions of our country. Founded, as it mainly was, by individual charity, its existence bears honorable evidence to the feeling with which this community regards the necessities of humbler members at the time when they are least able to express their wants. Contributions towards the support of a hospital, are declarations of kindness aforethought, and of a long-sighted policy of love towards those who need other hands than their own to smooth their restless pillows. . . .
>
> Ignorant as some of [the people] are, and still more or less possessed of prejudices which they have inherited, they may fail, for the present, fully to appreciate the service that you have rendered them; but I feel assured that the time will soon arrive when those prejudices will cease to exist. Already we see passing away the misgivings of those who doubted that a hospital would ever be resorted to by pure Hawaiians. The trial has been made. It has succeeded, not perhaps to a wish, but beyond our expectations. . . .
>
> But let me remind you that so long as sickness shall exist, there will be a duty imposed upon us. Charities, like taxes for the commonwealth, have to be met from time to time. There is no commuting for a given sum and claiming exemption for all time to come. . . . I do not envy the man who could wish, if such a thing were possible, to pay at one installment all the claims of humanity. There is something wholesome in being called upon from time to time to acknowledge, however strong our own health may be, and however prosperous our fortunes, that after all, the destitute and the sick are our brothers and sisters—our lot happier for the time being, but our liability to want

> and suffering the same. This it is that makes us human and members of the human family. Society makes distinctions broad enough, but strip us of our artificial robes and we are one and all equally naked and equally exposed to the keen winds of want and torments of disease. . . .[67]

The cornerstone consisted of two blocks of Wai'anae sandstone, the lower block measuring twenty-four by thirty-eight inches and the upper twenty by thirty inches. The cachet held ambrotype likenesses of the king and queen; a Hawaiian Bible; a copy of the laws of the kingdom; copies of the *Pacific Commercial Advertiser, Polynesian, Ka Hae Hawaii,* and *The Friend;* a list of hospital officers and trustees; a copy of the hospital charter, bylaws, rules, and regulations; as well as a list of the subscribers.[68]

The completion of the building required an additional four and a half months and an extra $1,200, but in the opinion of most people, the

In 1855 King Kamehameha IV expressed his profound concerns to the legislature about the rapid decline of the native population. The king emphasized, "It is a subject in comparison with which all others sink into insignificance." The first hospital was finally built in 1860 (on the same site where The Queen's Medical Center stands today).

wait was well worth the time and the money. Hailed as one of the finest buildings in the kingdom, hewn coral stone formed the outside walls, and a ten-foot veranda ran all along the front. The first floor was about five feet above the ground by a basement. Through the center of this floor, from front to back, was a hall, and from the hall the main staircase rose to the second floor. On the left of the hall was the reception room and next to it an assistant physician's room, which adjoined the dispensary. To keep down the noise, dispensary patients would assemble on the veranda and leave the dispensary by a door at the end of the building. The first floor also accommodated three large wards, bathrooms, storerooms, and a dining room.

Folding doors were arranged so that the wards on both floors could be partitioned off into smaller spaces and even into private rooms. Ceilings were high—thirteen feet on the first floor and eleven on the second. To maintain cleanliness all inner walls and partitions were plastered. Double rows of ventilators, fitted with removable covers, ran along the walls near floors and ceilings. Additional fresh air was provided by a large raised skylight, surrounded by venetians in the center of the building.

The *Pacific Commercial Advertiser* declared that the "beautiful structure" was "perhaps the best evidence of the present civilized condition of the Hawaiian nation."[69] One of those most pleased with the new building was the architect Heuck, as revealed in this self-congratulatory letter: "There is the new hospital—Heuck is the architect and I have the satisfaction to have given essential service and to have met the requests from on top to down the scale. An architect has to be very cautious that no blame hits him especially with buildings for the government. I can well say I have succeeded; in a very cordial manner one has given me recognition publicly as well as privately to have created a lasting monument to myself, an ornament to the city and a very useful property to the people."[70]

The new hospital opened on December 6, 1860, nearly six years after King Kamehameha's first appeal to the legislature to establish a hospital for the sick and the destitute. In the arid and barren surroundings of Manamana, the new edifice stood as a tangible monument to the efforts of the king and queen and their supporters.

9

The Neilson Ordeal

In early September 1859, after the selection of Dr. Hillebrand and establishment of the temporary quarters for the hospital, the king and queen left Honolulu with the year-old prince to spend several weeks on Maui. Accompanied by a large party, they stopped first in Lahaina and then sailed on to Wailuku in a "cavalcade" of boats. Elizabeth K. Pratt described the spectacle: "You should have seen the cavalcade of boats plying on their way towards Maalaea Bay. His Majesty's boat took the lead with Pauahi Bishop and Lydia [Liliʻuokalani] as passengers; next followed Lunalilo with Her Majesty [Emma] and myself; then came the little Prince's boat, with his grandmother Kekelaokalani and his nurses, manned by a skillful steersman. Kalakaua and his particular friends joined the cavalcade and innumerable residents of Lahaina formed near the rear. . . ."[1]

The day after, the king and queen and company mounted their horses and ascended Haleakala. "Upon arrival at the summit," Pratt wrote, "we glanced around and beheld the whole multitude of people who had followed the King's party. . . . In those days there were no rest houses so we were obliged to seek shelter in tents with carpets laid on the bared ground. We found ourselves high above the clouds looking down on the Islands . . . mere specks on the blue ocean. The sights were marvelous. . . . As night approached we sought shelter in our tents—it was freezing cold but blazing bonfires somewhat lessened the temperature."[2]

When they returned to Wailuku, the excitement came to a worrisome halt as the king suddenly suffered another asthma attack. The party broke up, and the king and a small group, including his private secretary, Henry Neilson, went back to Lahaina. The king was still experiencing the suffocating pain of the asthmatic when his ordeal began.

The Shooting

The king had heard through idle or malicious gossip that Neilson had abused his confidence and that the queen had been involved.[3] While in Lahaina he brooded over the matter and then began to drink heavily. Suddenly he declared he was going on to Hawaiʻi, boarded his yacht, and sailed away with his captain and one attendant, without any of the royal party. The captain thought he was in "a state of false excitement" and would return in the morning; instead, they remained at sea the entire next day. Onboard was a fresh case of liquor, which the king consumed.

The king came ashore about 11:00 that night—it was September 11—and went directly to the governor's home, located in the same compound of dwellings as Neilson's quarters. The king was not only drunk but also delirious. He ordered his attendant to fetch a pistol, causing a slight but audible commotion at the house next door of Maui Governor Paul Nahaolelua.

At that moment Henry Neilson stepped out on the stairs of his quarters just before going to bed. As he stood breathing in Lahaina's night air, he noticed the commotion. He spied one of the king's men being taken away and heard something about his refusing to get the king's pistols, which were in the house he [Neilson] was occupying. Another retainer came to fetch them, but Neilson had no inkling as to why the pistols were needed. As he continued to stand on the steps, he suddenly saw the king rapidly advancing toward him.[4]

In Neilson's words, "When within three or four feet of me, without speaking, he fired from a dueling pistol straight at my body. The ball struck me fair on the lower part of the chest, just where the short ribs join the breastbone, and where there is a good deal of cartilage. It then passed towards the right side, struck a rib about midway, which it followed, and just managed to drop out a few inches below the right armpit. . . ."[5]

Crying in pain and bleeding profusely, Neilson managed to drag himself to Dr. McKibbin's room in the same quarters and received immediate care. It was a miracle, he was told, that the bullet had passed through his body without killing him.

No one was as shocked as Neilson, for he thought he and the king had long been on excellent terms. The night before the shooting he and others had dined with the king. As Neilson recalled later, "I never saw him more lively or in better spirits."[6] As far as he was concerned, the king's jealous suspicions of the queen were totally unfounded. Charles de Varigny, who knew all three of the principals intimately, agreed and wrote, "The name of the queen became involved, although quite unjustly, for she had nothing to do with the matter."[7]

Damage Control

News of the incident spread lightning fast across Maui and then all the Islands. Without any credible information—the newspapers were conspicuously silent—conjecture and unsubstantiated opinions circulated. Rumor mills worked overtime as hints spread that King Alexander Liholiho had acted out of jealousy. If the grounds had been justifiable, his loyal subjects would have willingly and heartily supported the king's act of revenge. Meanwhile, his detractors, relishing the moment to bring down the kingdom, turned into frenzied gossip mongers.

As soon as word reached Honolulu, Prince Lot immediately sailed to Lahaina to assist his brother and to assess the situation. There he found that doctors had been able to stabilize Neilson's condition and that his life was not in danger. But he found his brother in a state of complete physical and emotional exhaustion. He also learned that the king had made his own quick investigation (apparently by questioning some members of his party) and concluded that his suspicions of Neilson and the queen were without any merit. As a consequence, he was so filled with guilt and remorse that he decided to abdicate. That turned an already given crisis into an even greater crisis.

After assessing the aftermath of the shooting, Lot sent the king and queen, the little prince, Dr. McKibbin, and the royal entourage to the king's ranch at Kalua'aha on Moloka'i. There they would be insulated from the din of Lahaina.[8] Lot returned to Honolulu to meet with members of the privy council with instructions from the king.

These instructions requested that a public explanation be made immediately acknowledging his complete responsibility, that "the act of violence was committed from an extreme want of judgment as to the authenticity of facts," that all "the reparation possible" be made to Neilson, and that the ministers "express the sincere hope that the Royal explanation will prove satisfactory to the people."[9] He added that he would be awaiting their response with "intense anxiety."

The Threat of Abdication

The members of the privy council decided to release a statement to the *Polynesian* explaining the incident and stating their rejection of any consideration of the king's abdication. Wyllie immediately wrote to the king urging him "not to exaggerate the gravity of the affair" and suggested that after Neilson recovered, "the whole affair will die away as if it had never occurred."[10] The king wrote back saying, "I hope you will not, my friend Wyllie, attribute this to weakness on my part but simply from a sense of what is righteous and just."[11]

On September 24, 1859, the *Pacific Commercial Advertiser* mentioned the incident for the first time but only indirectly by reporting that "Mr. Neilson is as comfortable as could be expected—rests well, has no fever, and although not out of danger, is thought to be in a fair way of recovery."[12]

That same day, Wyllie, convinced that abdication would only compound the king's predicament, wrote a lengthy letter, remarkable for its passion and fealty, to dissuade the king from abdicating. "While the feelings expressed by you," he stated, "are highly honorable to your heart and conscience, permit me to say, with all loyal respect, that they originate in a judgment pronounced by you against yourself vastly beyond any just occasion and contrary to the feelings entertained . . . by all your Ministers, by all respectable foreigners here resident and I firmly believe by all Your people.

"Why persist in an idea of self-sacrifice beyond all just occasion in morality or necessity in State policy?" Wyllie asked. "The matter with Neilson would be best settled in my opinion by a public declaration from himself, and in what concerns a Personage almost coequal with yourself whose honor and purity remain, I assure you, as unsullied as ever." He insisted that the best action the king could take would be to return to Honolulu. Wyllie continued:

> Sincerely attached to Your Majesty's person as I have been since you were the laughing spirited boy at the Royal School, and having devoted all my energies to the Support of Hawaiian Sovereignty for fifteen years, I could never consent to the self-sacrifice which you are ready to make. So long as God spares me in life I shall stand by Your Majesty's Throne to the last—and if I cannot do so on two legs I shall do so on one. . . .
>
> If during my long public service I glory in any thing it is in having moved the admission of Yourself and Brother while Princes under

> age, into the Privy Council and House of Nobles where you both greatly distinguished yourselves, and having energetically pushed through the Privy Council the Proclamation of Your Accession to the Throne while faction was said to be brewing another result. It would therefore KILL me, were Your Majesty to descend from your High position, possessed as you are of such eminent talents. . . . I believe all my colleagues concur with me in a desire to dissuade you from your purpose of *self-immolation*. . . .
>
> I pray you, in God's name, for the sake of your pure and Virtuous Queen and Your hopeful son, the Prince of Hawaii, as well as Your whole people, to banish forever such an idea from your thoughts . . . to turn your mind to the business of State, to complete your Royal Progress as originally intended and to return to Your capital at Your own pleasure, happy in the enjoyment of domestic bliss and showing to the world that you are so.[13]

On September 27, 1859, the privy council unanimously adopted a resolution protesting the king's contemplated abdication. It read:

> The abdication of the king is a self-sacrifice that, however honorable its intention, would produce the most injurious consequences to the Sovereign and His people.
>
> It is without any adequate cause either in morality, Christian obligation, or Kingly duty.
>
> It would discredit the Hawaiian government and people to such a degree as to render the future government of the nation as an independent state extremely difficult if not impractical. . . . It is a measure which would be condemned by the sound part of the foreign community and by the Hawaiian people generally.
>
> The honor and duty of the King, the happiness of the Queen, the hopes of the young Prince of Hawaii, and the welfare and independence of the Hawaiian people require that His Majesty *not abdicate*.
>
> Therefore the undersigned respectfully protest against the idea of Abdication or its submission to the Privy Council.[14]

The resolution was signed by Prince Lot, Robert C. Wyllie, David L. Gregg, and Elisha H. Allen. Gregg was charged with taking the resolution to Moloka'i and delivering it directly to King Alexander Liholiho.

Two days later the privy council received the king's answer to "the momentous question of my abdication": he would not abdicate.[15] The next day a relieved Wyllie wrote to the king: "I wish to direct your mind from brooding over *one overpowering Idea*. Let that idea be gone for ever; let *"Richard be himself again"*. . . [let] the breaking up of the government never be again pronounced."[16]

The *Pacific Commercial Advertiser*'s Story

On September 28, the *Pacific Commercial Advertiser* detailed its opposition to abdication in a long editorial, which also told its readers about the shooting for the first time:

> A rumor has obtained currency, which we are forced to regard as well-founded, that it is the purpose of our King to abdicate his throne, and retire to private life. The reasons assigned for it emanate in the recent unfortunate event at Lahaina. The simple announcement of such a purpose will create a deep feeling of regret in the bosom of every one who cherishes the honor of our Sovereign Kamehameha, or desires the prosperity of his kingdom.
>
> It is unnecessary for us here to rehearse the details of the affair alluded to, which are familiar to each of our readers. At the time of its occurrence, His Majesty appears to have been excited by the false reports which he had heard, to a degree, which, had his suspicions been well grounded, public sentiment would have fully justified and acquitted him of evil intent. He believed he was acting on sufficient grounds—that his information was reliable—that his own personal honor, the honor of his throne, his family and his realm, were at stake—and that in shooting his secretary, he was simply meting out that justice which public sentiment, had these rumors been known to the public, would have imperiously demanded.[17] Subsequent investigation has shown that he was mis-informed, and that his informants had no valid grounds for the reports which had been communicated to him. On learning the facts as they existed—that he had acted rashly, and without justifiable cause, in taking the law thus hastily into his own hands—he has been overwhelmed with self-condemnation, and his feelings can better be imagined than described.
>
> Naturally of a quick temperament, he appears to have acted without that caution which should have been exercised in the matter, and without seeking the proof necessary to confirm his suspicions. Those who are personally acquainted with our King, know that his disposition is kind and amiable, more so than is generally found in persons holding the rank which he does: and this rash act has been followed, as we have full evidence before us, only by that poignancy of grief, which a person of the most refined feelings, might be expected to experience under the like circumstances. All the amends which it is possible for a person to make, he has been willing to make, and we are

> informed that the fullest reconciliation possible, has been made between all the parties concerned. . . . The recent tragedy at Lahaina is, in one sense, a private affair, and on that account some may say we have no right to comment on it. Yet at the same time . . . it is equally a public one, and must have a public influence; and it is in this light that we feel called on as public journalists to refer to it. Not being amenable to the law, what more can his people ask of their Sovereign than that he seek to repair, to the extent of his power, the injury which he has inflicted. This he has done—he has done all that they can ask. And the mere fact that he seeks thus thoroughly to repair the injury, and remove the stain, speaks more in his praise than anything else he could say or do. He has erred, so are we all liable to commit acts of error. But 'tis the course pursued, after such acts, and after the knowledge of our errors, which tend to elevate or degrade us in the sight of our fellow men. The course which His Majesty has pursued since this unfortunate affair, in seeking to make the utmost reparation in his power—the feelings of self-condemnation which have since possessed him—show him to be a man in every sense of the word—a man of refined and tender feelings, and worthy of the position he holds. . . . The conduct of His Majesty since the occurrence, needs but to be known to his subjects, to raise him in their esteem and endear him to them as their Sovereign. There is not a person in his realm who will not vehemently protest against his resigning his high and responsible position, or consent to his doing it, even if he feels himself bound so to act. They believe that he has done all that justice or reason calls for in this case. The interests of the kingdom—the interests of every subject or resident, demand that the King banish forever the idea from his mind, and maintain the position which the God of nations has decreed to him, and in which every subject will loyally support and defend him.

The *Pacific Commercial Advertiser* had been a critic of King Kamehameha IV, but in this instance there was no doubt about its loyalty.[18]

On September 30 Wyllie made public the following statement:

> The opinion of the King's ministers has been confirmed by public opinion, unmistakably pronounced. . . . His popularity and means of usefulness are not impaired by the late events. . . .
>
> The consequences of an abdication could not fail to be an agitation for Republicanism that would be fatal to the rights of the young Prince, the rank and file of all the Chiefs, to the institution of monarchy in the Hawaiian Islands and to the welfare of the Hawaiian people. . . . As a Minister of the King I will join my colleagues in stand-

> ing by the King and His Sovereign rights to the utmost extremity, so long as God gives me health and strength and soundness of mind to do so.[19]

That evening the king and queen, the little prince, and their suite, in accordance with the king's wish to avoid any public demonstration, slipped quietly into Honolulu harbor and returned to the palace.

On October 1 the government-supported newspaper, the *Polynesian,* published its first words on the "Lahaina occurrence" in which it too stated its opposition to abdication. The idea "has given rise to a unanimity of opposition almost without parallel in any country. . . . It is important to remark the estimate which public opinion has put upon the original act, which we all deplore for the sake of all concerned in it. The feeling is one of sympathy . . . towards all the parties to this great mistake there is evinced such a generous and benevolent feeling as could not have existed, were not the solution of the error evident upon the face of it."[20]

In the same editorial, the paper justified its nearly three-week blackout by stating that though the "public has a right to be kept informed in all matters of public interest, individuals have their rights also, as they have feelings, and to these some measure of deference is due." The major reason for the blackout was that both the *Pacific Commercial Advertiser* and the *Polynesian* had to wait for the government's official report, which was not released until September 27. After this date, the newspapers never again brought up the shooting. No legal notice of the event was ever taken. Had it been, the king would have been shielded from prosecution by virtue of his sovereign position.[21]

The morning of the 27th King Kamehameha IV attended his first meeting of the privy council in over a month. Coming in the aftermath of the shooting and the events described above, the moment was a poignant one for the humbled king and his ministers. Tired but uplifted by their support, the king explained why he had changed his mind about abdication. He then asked them to support his proclamation of the Prince of Hawaii as his heir and successor. He also requested that they authorize a cash settlement for Neilson as well as a guarantee of medical care as long as it was needed. A sum of $5,000 was authorized.[22]

On October 3 the House of Nobles unanimously resolved that it concurred with "His Majesty the King in appointing and proclaiming His Royal Highness the Prince of Hawaii, as the heir and successor of His Majesty to the Throne of the Hawaiian Kingdom."[23]

Making Amends

Although King Alexander Liholiho had weathered the storm caused by his threatened abdication, he still had to deal with the pain inflicted on his victim lying in a sickbed in Lahaina, as well as with his own unmitigated remorse. Since the shooting the king had visited Neilson on more than one occasion but had not made any formal amends. Neilson expected some public demonstration or explanation, but the king did not think it was either appropriate or necessary. Instead, he decided to write a letter, probably the most difficult letter he had ever written. Dated October 12, it read:

> My dear Nielson,[24]
> I hasten to avail myself of the permission granted by your physician to discharge a duty which your serious illness alone has prevented me from performing sooner. It is to express my thankfulness to an overruling Power that you have been spared from an end which none would have regretted as much as myself.
>
> My feelings upon the whole affair, in which you and myself are the principal actors, can better be imagined than expressed, and I am indeed grateful that an opportunity is afforded me by which I can, at least, make an attempt at some small amends for the great injury which you have suffered at my hands. I shall commence by an honest statement to you that the act committed by me was premeditated, founded upon suspicions long harrowed up and extending through a length of time. Though facts could not sustain me in my suspicions, I felt they were well founded, and consequently acted in the manner I did. How wisely, how justly I, of all parties interested need not now be told. I therefore have cause to consider it of the greatest importance as a duty to myself and for my own satisfaction, to render to you the necessary explanations and to offer such reparation as may be in my power to make.
>
> To say that I regret the sad occurrence were too little, that I sorrow sincerely for the injuries I have unrighteously conferred, would hardly be justice even; but believe, Sir, I would be thankful indeed if anything I may say in this letter could fully convey to your mind the feelings of self-reproach and sorrow which I assure you I feel night and day. These expressions, I know, are of no avail, as the injury is done, the act committed, but it would be some satisfaction, however, for me to know that you are aware of my feelings with reference to the whole affair and my sentiments towards one whom I have seriously injured. I know of no other mode of explanation more satisfactory in this matter than the voluntary unqualified acknowledgment to you of the wrong committed, a full exoneration from everything that suspicions

may have connected you with, which I do most heartily and, to repeat what I have already said, that words cannot express my own feelings of sorrow and regret at this great false act of my life.

I am aware that there are other means resorted to, in cases like the present one, with the view of completing any amend that may be offered, but as they are, to my mind, only of secondary importance, it is with some delicacy that I have alluded to them. Nothing, however, it seems to me, can exist in this world, that can indemnify the man who had been on the verge of the grave, through an act founded on unjustifiable suspicion, to say nothing of his character as a man and his reputation as a gentleman, which may have been in danger of being compromised.

My duty to you, as well as to myself, I should consider to be imperfectly discharged did I not here express my deep conviction of the great importance of this affair especially as bearing upon our future relations and the consequent complete separation which the unfortunate circumstances have rendered inevitable.

If I have disappointed you by any want of force in my language, attribute it rather to a want of capability of expressing my thought truly than to a want of sincerity or a lassitude of inclination.

If I have detained you too long with my views of our relations to each other and with self-reproaches, it is, at least, with the hope that my attempt to do what is just and right for an unjust and unrighteous act will be, in a measure, appreciated. I forbear to touch here of what I have considered to be my duty to others who are more or less interested; to them, I trust, I have done my duty as conscientiously as I am now doing to you. The public and the members of my own family, assure that my performance of that duty is satisfactory. My mind, therefore, with reference to them, is relieved. Hoping to be favored with an opportunity of being more explicit, if necessary as regards a subject already attended to, and that your health will be rapidly improving towards a speedy and complete recovery,

I remain very respectfully,
Yours,
Liholiho

The King's Mistress?

The king's confession raises many more questions, some very troublesome, than it answers. For example, he answers the question about whether he acted impulsively or premeditatively when he states that his suspicions had been "long harrowed up" and that the act "committed by me was premeditated." But how long did he entertain his suspicions?

Weeks? Months? How did he come by them? Did some eyewitness tell him? Or did he catch Neilson and the queen saying or doing something wrong?

The king must have been a master at concealing his feelings because not even Neilson suspected anything. Nor did any of his closest advisers including his brother Lot and sister Victoria, as well as Wyllie, Gregg, and Allen. And, apparently, neither did any of his occasional critics such as the *Pacific Commercial Advertiser, The Friend,* and even Lili'uokalani. No one ever suggested that King Alexander Liholiho had any reason to doubt the loyalty of his wife. The king, in the throes of anxiety and stress, could have been expected to seek the private counsel of Lot or Wyllie or some other confidante, but there is no such evidence.

Ironically, the king himself may have been guilty of what he accused Neilson of doing. According to Charles de Varigny, the king had his own mistress. He writes: "Now despite his marriage, the king had not entirely broken with the habits of his bachelor days; he had, in fact, continued a liaison with one of the ladies of the court, who after his marriage had even become a lady-in-waiting of the queen."[25]

How much stock should be placed in what de Varigny says? He was present and therefore presumably knew what was going on. He was also a supporter and friend of the king and hence would have had no reason to damage his reputation by deliberately fabricating a story. Moreover, as any reading of his book would suggest, de Varigny was also a fairly honest and accurate chronicler of the events of the time.

On the other hand, if the king had a mistress, Neilson would have surely known. Such a relationship could not be hidden easily from a secretary and personal friend. Moreover, Neilson, who had just been shot point blank, would have had every reason to tell of the affair in his private letter to his brother. But not once does the letter mention or even hint at it. Furthermore, even when the king's enemies, such as Gorham Gilman, attempted to persuade Neilson to incriminate the king, he never strayed from his story.

Lili'uokalani, who described the "Lahaina occurrence" in her book, did not mention a mistress either.[26] Given her somewhat critical perspective of the Kamehamehas, she would not have hesitated to tell about the king's mistress if she had known about it.

In any case, if de Varigny is correct, the question of who poisoned the king's mind against the queen is easily answered: it was the king's jealous mistress. According to de Varigny, the king's mistress had allegedly incited the jealousy of the king so that she could revenge herself on the queen who was beginning to suspect "the adulterous connection" with her husband. He wrote, "The truth was that the royal mistress was herself jealous of Neilson because the latter had urged his close friend the king to break with the lady and keep his marriage vow." De Varigny further contended that the king even accused Neilson of making amorous overtures to his mistress in the hopes of supplanting the king in her favors.[27]

Gilman the Troublemaker

In the meantime, the king continued to commute between Honolulu and Lahaina comforting the convalescing Neilson, while consoling his own heart. Emma wrote to him saying that she and "Baby" had come to the palace to hide from any "visitors that may come in during the day." It is not clear whether she was avoiding conversation about Neilson or whether she was just weary of seeing people. She wrote him that the little prince had a burning fever and was calling out "Papa dear," which, she said, was a new word he had learned on his own accord. She was probably trying to change the subject and to buoy his spirit when she told him how economical she was trying to be. "I have no doubt you will laugh when I say that I have not spent so much as $5 every day marketing since you've been gone."[28]

Another visitor to the convalescing Neilson was Gorham Gilman who was a prosperous Lahaina merchant and a known troublemaker. The king wrote to William Webster, a close friend and businessman, that he had heard from Neilson that "Gilman has repeatedly approached him upon the subject of some communication over Neilson's signature in the Advertiser. Whether this is meant to be friendly to me or otherwise, I cannot as yet surmise."[29] The king learned soon enough that Gilman was not a friend.

Gilman tried desperately to persuade Neilson to sign a statement denouncing the king and then to travel with him to Honolulu to make a public demonstration. Neilson's doctors suggested that Gilman's attempts to influence Neilson were setting back his recovery. In a letter to the king, the queen wrote that Dr. McKibbin was "enraged" that Gilman was allowed to visit Neilson again.[30]

Gilman had made a statement about the shooting that was clearly intended to embarrass the king and that *The Friend* had published: "It seems almost impossible to believe that the King could have any real distrust of the Queen . . . her whole life and character from childhood up was against any cause for such a thought . . . like Caesar's wife she was above reproach. Some evil demon, some devilish Iago must have distilled some damnable poison into the King's mind to have caused him to commit such an insane act!"[31]

Whereupon the king wrote to Webster: "The Hawaiians here say contemptuously of Gilman: *Kupaia-naha maoli no o Kilimana. No ka loha ana paha hoia ke 'lii. Ke kii koke ia ku nei no o ka wahine haole a hoihoi ia ae nei.* Strange about Gilman—first he tears a woman down, then he builds her up."[32]

The point is that had Neilson wanted to embarrass the king, he was presented with the perfect opportunity. However, he rejected each one of Gilman's blandishments and remained steadfast and loyal to the king.

In March 1860, King Alexander Liholiho went to Lahaina to personally attend to the moving of Neilson to Honolulu. He had a special bed made for the journey and reported to Emma: "Neilson likes the idea of going down to our house on the beach [at Waikīkī]. He says it will be more quiet and free from annoying visitors. . . . So if you will have your little room cleared out for his servants and my little room makai, as a sort of a stowaway place, I will send his bed and mosquito bars. If I think of anything else to add I will do so."[33]

Neilson made a faltering recovery but died two years later.

The Queen's Innocence

One absolutely clear fact in this entire sordid tale is the queen's innocence. Both Neilson and de Varigny, though they may have told different stories, agreed that there was no truth to the king's suspicions about the queen. Even the king came to that conclusion after his investigation as did Lot. Furthermore, none of the contemporary accounts of 1859 gives any indication that the queen had an affair with Neilson, or anyone else for that matter. Her detractors might have disputed the purity of her bloodline—but not her marital fidelity.

Why then did the king doubt her loyalty? Why was he so willing to believe that she was involved with Neilson? The key to understanding the king's irrational behavior may be found in his attempt to justify his own relationship with a mistress (that is, if one accepts de Varigny). To assuage his own deep-seated guilt, he was receptive to any suggestion that the queen might also be having an affair—"If I'm doing it, she's doing it too." This self-deception was a way to project his own guilt onto the queen. Thus, if he was jealous, it was not because the queen was having an affair but rather because down deep he knew she could never be as disloyal as he. The depth of his shame blinded him to the reality of his obsession.

Needless to say, the innocent Queen Emma felt hurt, disappointed, even rejected and betrayed, as she struggled with her own inner turmoil. She had to wonder how she had failed him for she had given him no cause to doubt her loyalty. It was of some comfort to know that she enjoyed the sympathy of her people and that she was deemed the "perfect" wife for the young king and now an excellent mother for his princely son, but forgiveness on the verge of tragedy is never easy. Yet, in the depths of her compassionate nature, she had little room for spite and little time for self-pity, especially when her kingdom hung in balance. Throughout the ordeal and for months thereafter, she stood by her "Alex," comforting him as he suffered the pangs of humiliation and remorse. Emma recognized his contrition and his efforts to make restitution, and her heart went out to his in the ultimate act of love—forgiveness.

The very psychological and spiritual trauma that King Alexander Liholiho experienced not only turned him to religion but also may have shortened his life. Meanwhile, a more immediate and even greater tragedy for both the king and queen was to follow.

10

The Flight of the Heavenly Chief

May 20, 1859, was the first anniversary of the birth of His Royal Highness *Ka Haku O Hawaiʻi.* It was proclaimed a public holiday—"a lovely day, a proper day for a national jubilee." The celebration occurred in the midst of efforts to found the hospital—the king had finished soliciting funds on the streets a week before and the queen was preparing for the hospital's benefit concert a week later. But this day was for "Baby" or Kauikeaouli, as his parents called him.

The national event was typical of the next three birthdays to follow: Diplomatic and consular offices, residences and private homes, and public buildings were decorated with flags and bunting. Bishop Maigret held a great mass in the Fort Street Catholic Church. School children attended a morning reception in the palace and joined representatives of official and private life in congratulating Their Majesties. The queen and the prince were present to receive the children. At noon a royal salute was fired from the Punchbowl battery. The morning reception ended with a well-executed drill by the Honolulu Rifles.

That afternoon more than 4,000 persons gathered at the harbor to see six whaleboats and five gigs [a light rowboat designed for speed] race in the first such regatta held in Honolulu. In the evening, while the little prince slept, his parents hosted a grand reception and ball at the palace.[1]

In more traditional times, they would have hosted an *ʻahaʻaina piha makahiki* or feast on a child's first birthday, with merry-making, gift-giving, and feasting, along with recitations of *mele inoa* (name chant) dedicated to the royal child. Even without the feast, however, their loyal subjects were still composing name chants for the prince. One of these, composed only a few months before his birthday, was entitled *Pūʻali inuwai* (literally "the water drinking host," which was also the name for the Temperance League).

Ke ʻoliʻoli nei kākou
I ka loaʻa ʻana mai
Ke aliʻi ʻōpiopio,
Haku o Hawaiʻi nei
I makua no mākou
Ka hoʻoilina o ke aupuni.
Pōmaikaʻi ai nā lehulehu
Nā keiki a kānaka,
Ka wai, ka wai! E inu, e inu nō!

E inu kākou a pau nā kamaliʻi
Nā wai kahe o kahawai,
Ke Pūʻali inuwai.

We are delighted
To have
The young chief
Prince of Hawaiʻi
Patriarch of ours
The heir of the kingdom.
Blessed are we,
The children and adults,
The fresh water, the fresh water!
Drink, drink!
Let us all, the youth drink,
The flowering waters of the stream
The Pūʻali inuwai.[2]

The year-old prince had already become the idol of the nation, and, like the composer of *mele inoa,* many Hawaiians invested their hopes and dreams in the future heir. His admiring and doting parents also wondered what the future would bring for their son.

Not a Well Child

Prince Albert was already a fine-looking, observant, bright, and lovable child but not a well child. Jane Smythe, one of the queen's ladies in waiting, described the little prince as a "delicate child, subject to spells of fever."[3] The first and earliest reference to the child being ill is found in Liliʻuokalani's autobiography entitled *Hawaii's Story.* She was a member of a party traveling with the king and queen on Maui in the early summer of 1859 "when word was received that the little Prince of Hawaii, then but a little more than a year old, was ill."[4] He took sick while the king and queen were away touring the island, one of the few times when the child was not with them. Dr. McKibbin had informed the king that the child had a slight fever and, although he did not consider it at all serious, the king insisted on returning to Lahaina at once and alone.[5]

Apparently, a disagreement had occurred between the king and queen. According to Liliʻuokalani, "The king was deaf to the entreaties of the queen to be allowed to go directly to her child, because he thought

Bishop Museum

To Queen Emma and King Kamehameha IV was born one child, Albert, the Prince of Hawai'i. Beloved throughout the Islands, the little prince was deeply mourned in 1862 when he died at the age of four.

it would delay his own departure and arrival at the bedside of his boy." The king rode all night at a gallop, changing horses frequently, and arrived in Lahaina late the following afternoon exhausted. By that time "the illness [had] passed away without serious consequences."[6]

The prince's health was of constant concern to his parents, as revealed in their correspondence. On November 14, 1859, the queen wrote the king, who was in Lahaina tending the convalescing Neilson, that "Baby is a little feverish this morning." The following day, in another letter, she wrote, "Baby had a burning fever on him all night." She continued with the report that their son was "running round the rooms crying and calling for Papa Papa dear which is a new word he learnst [sic] of his own accord for we did not teach it to him." In concluding the letter, she noted "this morning the fever has entirely passed off, the Doctor says it arose from a little disarrangement of the stomach only."[7] In still another letter to Alex, Emma wrote, "Baby continues little unwell he had a dose of castor oil last night and is looking very sunken in the eyes."[8] In a January 30, 1860, letter, the king wrote, "I am glad to hear that baby appears well. . . ."

Visit to the New Princeville

Queen Emma was anticipating the royal visit to Hanalei scheduled later in the summer of 1860, but she came dangerously close to missing it. Late one Saturday afternoon, the queen, together with the little prince and Princess Victoria, was riding on Beretania Street in the royal carriage, while the king, on horseback, had galloped on ahead. The horses took fright and sped away at full speed. While the royals held on for dear life, the driver tried desperately to bring the horses under control. Liholiho dashed back to help but was too late. The carriage had overturned and its occupants thrown to the side of the road. Both the queen and princess were injured slightly, but the baby prince was unharmed. The driver was seriously hurt. On the next Sabbath, the grateful but shaken king sent notices to each church, asking parishioners to give thanks for the providential escape of the royal family.

The queen and the prince, together with his high chiefess nurse, journeyed to Hanalei for a two-month vacation. (The king joined them in the second month.) The accompanying party consisted of Mrs. Gregg and her three children, Anna McKibbin, Laurie Paty, Peter Ka'eo, Fanny, John Welch, her manservant, and Robert Wyllie, plus the usual retinue of servants.

As the guests of Wyllie, they stayed at Kikiula, the name of what was then "the finest country seat" in the Islands, in the spacious home erected on a bluff overlooking the winding Hanalei river.[9] The nearby peak of Namolokama, towering over its sister mountains with their nineteen waterfalls that plunged down their precipitous slopes, formed a stupendous backdrop to Wyllie's plantation that covered much of Hanalei's 2,000 acres of mostly wetlands.[10]

Wyllie had brought George Hyatt, a black clarinet player, with him from Honolulu to play for his guests at dinner time and for dances in the evening. Their Majesties, always fond of dancing, delighted in doing the Tyrolese waltz, which Wyllie's plantation manager, Mr. G. F. Wundenberg, taught them.

Josephine Wundenberg (his daughter) wrote a number of vignettes about this particular royal visit from which the following were taken:[11]

The queen was particularly fond of playing with the children and loved to go upstairs to their room in the evening and have a romp or a pillow fight. It seemed so natural that no one thought her undignified.

At a picnic one day on the banks of the river, about a mile from its mouth, the queen accidentally slipped into the water and wet her shoes while crossing on some stones near where several families were catching fish. Unbeknownst to her, two of the children were sent racing home to fetch her some dry shoes. When they presented her with her new shoes, they were happy because the queen was grateful.

One day while the queen and her party lunched on the grass under a spreading kukui tree, she helped to organize the food baskets. As she divided the pieces of cold chicken with her fingers, she remarked to the children that fingers were made before "knives and forks" and that Queen Victoria also liked to eat chicken with her fingers.

The queen, an inveterate gardener, planted or exchanged slips and seeds wherever she visited. She had brought a number of fruit trees and planted them in the valley. One day she rode up to "Mount Rooke" (Makana) and planted a mango tree there. It may have been the same day when the two-and-a-half-year-old prince climbed to the top of the peak, 1,200 feet tall, entirely unassisted, but with Wyllie at his side.[12]

A strong swimmer, the queen was fond of "seabathing" in Hanalei Bay. On one visit she spent four days at nearby Wainīnī (now known as 'Anini Beach), a secluded place where many Hawaiians lived at the time. There she and other members of her party bathed in the sea, picked *'opihi* (limpets), and even tried to coax a few eels out of their tiny holes among the rocks.

As for the king, Josephine Wundenberg wrote that he was "a very entertaining man and loved to dress in disguises for the entertainment of us children. He dressed up as a ghost once and gave himself quite a shock when he peered into a looking glass in a partly darkened room."[13]

Alexander Liholiho also spent considerable time riding in the hills shooting birds. One day he shot a quail, which was prohibited by law. He was told by some over-zealous children that if caught, he would be arrested and forced to pay a fine of $50. They did not know who he was, but he pretended to be very alarmed and made them promise not to tell.

Both the king and the queen had their own boats (presumably canoes) with crews and spent a great deal of their time rowing and racing on the "waters of Punikaiwa" (the Hanalei River).[14]

After this royal visit, Wyllie, a confirmed bachelor who had become quite attached to the little prince, renamed his estate "Princeville" and rechristened his trading schooner *The Prince of Hawaii.* He had also intended to will his estate to the prince and to suggest to the king that the boy be given the title of "Baron de Princeville."[15]

The party returned to Honolulu in October 1860 with Queen Emma feeling that the two months in Hanalei were "perhaps the happiest" of her life.

Nurse Julia Kapiʻolani

The little prince's "high chiefess nurse" was Julia Kapiʻolani (who would later marry David Kalākaua). Two years older than the queen, she was the granddaughter of Kaumualiʻi, the last king of Kauaʻi and daughter of Kūhiō, a high chief of Hilo, which placed her status near that of the queen. Described as lovely, shy, and gracious, she spoke only Hawaiian, although she was educated in English and Hawaiian.[16] She had married the queen's uncle, the High Chief Benet Namakeha in 1852, when she was eighteen. Five years later they made a trip for his health to the Gilberts (now part of Kiribati) and other islands aboard the missionary vessel *Morning Star,* but her husband did not improve. Kapiʻolani was living in Honolulu helping him convalesce when she was engaged by Queen Emma.[17]

Josephine Wundenberg wrote of Kapiʻolani during the queen's visit to Hanalei, "She was a lovely sweet woman and we became great friends. She ate her meals with the Prince at the children's table, and was with us a great deal. She helped me to make a little Hawaiian flag out of white and blue cotton cloth and turkey red, which I flew on my own flag staff, and at the stern of our boat when we went rowing. I used to play tricks on her, too, such as putting sand in her private bowl of

Kapiʻolani served as the governess of the little Prince Albert. In 1863 she married David Kalākaua and was crowned with him in 1883 on the ninth anniversary of his accession to the throne.

pink poi and hiding her shoes up in a tree, where she could not get them until I was ready to give them to her, whereby gaining the name of *kaikamahine kolohe* [naughty girl] which title she was pleased to remember after she became Queen of Hawaii and tease me with."[18]

Mistaken Ancestry

The queen's twenty-fifth birthday was celebrated without much fanfare: a salute was fired from Punchbowl and was responded to by the guns of the British warship *Alert.* This fact scarcely deserves mention except for its amusing or embarrassing sidelight.

On board the warship was Dr. Leonard, the ship's surgeon, who had written a letter to a newspaper in his hometown of Ayershire, Scotland, in which he said that Queen Emma was the daughter of Robert Wyllie. The letter was published under the heading of "An Ayershire Queen" and was picked up and reprinted by several newspapers in England and even in the United States. The *Pacific Commercial Adver-*

tiser took pains to dismiss Dr. Leonard's report as "ridiculous." "Only the seeming impossibility that a naval officer of the education and character of Dr. Leonard could write . . . an untruth of the paternity of Queen Emma, can account for its being believed even in Mr. Wyllie's native parish of Dunlop, that she is . . . the daughter of R.C. Wyllie. . . ."[19]

The claim had absolutely no truth. But because Queen Emma had been very close to Wyllie, when he died she did say that he had been "almost a father" to her.

Operatic Roles

In these "happiest" of times, the king and queen took an active part in the first local operatic production in Honolulu on March 8, 1861. Together with other members of the Amateur Musical Society, they performed scenes from Verdi's *Il Trovatore* and Friedrich von Flotow's *Martha* at the Royal Hawaiian Theatre (which was located at the Waikīkī *ma uka* corner of Hotel and Alakea Streets). The crowd of invited guests filled almost half of the 500-seat theater. As a member of the chorus, directed by Eugene Hasslocher, Queen Emma must have enjoyed singing familiar songs such as Verdi's "Anvil Chorus" or von Flotow's "The Last Rose of Summer." In one scene Theo. H. Davies, an English merchant, who went on to establish one of the largest factors in the kingdom, took her hand and walked her across the stage. Because the performance had six rehearsals, he claimed that is how he became well-acquainted with the royal family.[20] As for the king, he acted as the stage manager for the productions and defrayed the expenses of the entertainment. Wyllie thought the performance was "admirable," and the king and queen agreed because they proposed repeating it annually.[21]

Victorian Visitors

In April 1861 the king and queen were visited by Lady Jane Franklin, the widow of the famous English explorer, Sir John Franklin, and her niece, Sophia Cracroft. On meeting the queen for the first time, Cracroft wrote: "She was evidently a little shy and nervous, but her manner was perfectly simple and she shook hands with us and welcomed us in a pleasant way. . . . She is rather good-looking and has fine eyes—brown complexion (a sort of chestnut colour), plenty of good hair, slightly wavy, a pretty nose and generally good features, with a stout and not very good figure."[22] Elsewhere she described Queen Emma as "a sweet-mannered person, beloved by everyone, with excellent sense and charming simplicity."[23] While visiting the Queen's Hospital a few days later, Cracroft wrote of the queen's manner as being "excessively pleasing. She recognized two or three of the patients and spoke to them (as she did also to some whom she did not know) with so much simple cordiality that it did some good to see her, though we did not know what she said."[24]

She described King Kamehameha "as the perfect gentleman, his manner very cordial and unaffected . . . with fine wavy hair and good features, rather tall and not stout." She added that the king was "certainly one of the most gifted and remarkable men to be met with anywhere, being perfectly fit to take his place among the Sovereigns of Europe."[25] She also thought that both the king and queen spoke English "perfectly," but that he was more than fluent—he had "complete command" of the language.[26] She noted that the king regularly received the *Times, Illustrated News, Punch, the Quarterly, Edinburgh, Blackwood,* and *Westminster Review,* and that he "reads them all."[27]

These two visitors also met Prince Albert whom Cracroft described as "a sweet little boy, with his mother's pretty eyes, but fairer in complexion than either parent, and dark silky curls."[28] They noted that the prince was well-mannered because Queen Emma was "very anxious that he should not be spoilt, nor learn to think much of himself."[29] They were also impressed by the fact that he spoke English as well as he spoke Hawaiian.

In their conversation, the king spoke of his "love for England" and the obligation he felt for the way he was treated there, and he expressed his wish to have his son educated at Eton or Rugby. He also mentioned the fact that he had written Queen Victoria asking for her help in establishing the Anglican church in Hawai'i and that he wished his son to be baptized in the church.[30]

Cracroft commented on how English both the king and queen were "in their habits of feeling and tastes," particularly the queen who was "English in the third degree."[31] The king, she said, had as "great a dislike for Americans and as strong a love for the English."[32]

Vacation at Kona Retreat

In late June of 1861, the prince accompanied the queen on a lengthy vacation, this time to the royal estate in Kailua, Kona. (The king was to join them in August.) Also invited were the Greggs and their three children, Chief Justice Elisha Hunt Allen, his wife Mary, and their two children, and Dr. Robert McKibbin, the assistant court physician. There was the usual small army of servants to take care of the royal family and their guests.

Part of the time was spent in the king's summer house in Wai'aha, located about 2,000 feet above Kailua, on the slopes of Hualālai. Originally built by Governor B. W. Kapeau, the king had purchased the property from the Reverend. T. E. Taylor who had enlarged the house and lived in it for several years. Situated among groves of coffee, orange, breadfruit, and other tropical trees, it was judged "one of the most delightful and healthy spots" in the Islands, "worthy of being made the [king's] Kona country seat."[33] The king eventually acquired the southern half of the 235-acre *ahupua'a* of Wai'aha that extended from the mountain to the sea.[34]

After a time, they moved down to Hulihe'e Palace, on the beach in Kailua town. There they were joined in September by Princess Victoria whose stay was cut short by an accident. She was thrown from her horse and suffered a broken rib requiring that she be evacuated to Lahaina for medical aid.[35]

According to Mary Allen, the Gregg and Allen families stayed in the main house, "a fine large house, with very large rooms, twelve or fourteen feet high, and great windows with wide window seats, where the air blows through in all directions." The king and queen and prince and the doctor occupied two grass thatched cottages in the garden.[36]

Prince Albert must have enjoyed the company of the children, especially Freddy Allen who, born just ten days after the prince, was his regular playmate. Mary Allen, who had formed an early and lasting friendship with Queen Emma, lived only a few blocks away. They visited each other frequently and, while they conversed or sewed, their sons played. When the king and queen established a second residence at Hānaiakamalama in Nu'uanu, the Allens also moved to a home nearby, and there the parents and their two little boys continued to see each other regularly.[37]

The vacation routine for the children was: breakfast at 7:00 a.m., mid-day dinner at 1:00 p.m., and supper at 6:00; for their elders, breakfast at 8:00 a.m., dinner at 2:00 p.m., and "tea" generally at 7:00 or 8:00 in the evening. The parents spent considerable time relaxing on the lounges or rocking in the hammocks, chatting or reading. "Occasionally someone would get up enough energy to play the piano or sing, but the pace was definitely leisurely."[38] Alexander Liholiho had a fine bass voice, and the queen often joined him in singing.

Queen Emma, who always enjoyed sewing, spent some of the time making clothes for the little prince as well as learning how to scale fish. She wrote to her Alex (who had returned to Honolulu) how proud she was of being able to clean her own fish.[39]

As for the prince and his friends, they spent their time playing games or playing on the beach, bathing in the sea, and collecting shells on the shore. The prince "revelled in his small companions."[40]

After the Allens left, the queen moved nearby to their "charming little cottage looking out upon the water [and] over the rose bordered avenues." "What happy creatures children are," she wrote to Mrs. Allen, telling her how "Baby" now "takes his place at the table and is the source of great amusement to us all."[41] Besides wonder, she also expressed how frightened she was over the little prince's fearlessness, jumping precariously from a stone wall into the water to swim every day.[42]

Queen Emma's interest in collecting Hawaiian valuables is revealed for the first time when she tells Mrs. Allen how she and Alexander Liholiho conducted a search for Hawaiian "curiosities" one day in an old dilapidated stone house once occupied by Dr. Seth L. Andrews. The house was filled with human skulls, electric batteries, books, old clothes, skeletons, a large collection of sea and land shells, and calabashes of all sizes and shapes, many of which were difficult to procure at the time.[43]

"I enjoy it much farming in the country," the queen wrote in her last letter to Mrs. Allen. She told of their work in clearing more land for coffee and cultivating her own "large piece of ground" for growing food for their table. She also vowed upon her return "to practice on my sewing machine, and perfect myself in the art of stitching so as to be able to turn off as many yards, as any of you can."[44]

After being away for nearly six months, the royal family returned to Honolulu in late December 1861 quite "healthy." Instead of resuming residence in the palace, they sojourned for a while at Rooke House with Emma's mother Grace who was not well.

Honorary Fireman

Shortly before Prince Albert's fourth birthday, the Honolulu Volunteer Fire Department had made him an honorary member. The *Pacific Commercial Advertiser* reported: "The Prince of Hawaii has joined the Honolulu Fire Department by becoming a member of Engine Company No. 4. The company feel highly honored by the acquisition of their royal brother, though he may not be able to man the brakes with them for many years yet."[45] He was allowed to take part in the gala celebrations marking the king's twenty-eighth birthday. Wearing his own bright red uniform jacket and carrying his miniature silver trumpet, he rode in the parade perched up beside his grinning fellow firemen on Engine No. 1. When they passed the reviewing stand where his parents waited, he stood up, swept off his hat, and made them a low bow. Then, just to be quite sure they had seen him, he shouted, "Look, Papa! We're here!"[46]

Another glimpse of the prince at this time is provided by Curtis Iaukea who acted as his junior retainer. He recalled the days when he "used to romp around the Palace Grounds, dancing attendance on royalty in the role of page and valet to His Royal Highness, the Prince of Hawaii . . . then, well on in his fourth year and in the full enjoyment of health and happy childhood.

"Up and down the broad driveways of Iolani Palace we would go; the Prince sitting pretty in his little barouche or baby carriage, drawn by a stalwart groom in livery; with two or three personal Kahus and retainers in attendance, taking turns at the Kahili, ever present and never missing when the Prince was in the grounds taking his recreation; whilst I, his embryo page and valet, played the part of a footman, and as the cavalcade came to a rest, run up and execute a heels-over-head turn, for the edification of his serene highness; landing on my head as often as not, much to my personal discomfort and embarrassment."[47]

First Attendance at Parliament

On May 2, 1862, Prince Albert attended the opening of parliament for the first time, and, surprisingly, it was also the first time for the queen. Because the event was the outstanding official function of the season, and was presented with all the available pomp and ceremony, it attracted crowds of people. Their Majesties arrived at the courthouse in an elegant English carriage drawn by four horses, accompanied by outriders in livery, at precisely 10:30 a.m. They were escorted by a company of cavalry, while cannons were fired and drums beaten. The king and queen, with the prince walking between them, led the procession of government officials and their aides and retainers into the courtroom. The king sat on his throne, with the queen and prince seated to his right, surrounded by the court retainers, each wearing striking red and yellow feathered capes and holding the royal *kāhili.* The large room, handsomely decorated with Hawaiian flags, was filled with foreign representatives and other guests.[48]

Mary Allen, in describing this scene in a letter to her mother, admitted that as a friend of the queen and as a fellow mother she was anxious about the prince, but the four-year-old heir to the throne sat through the lengthy ceremonies without "a single fidget."[49] It is said he was blessed with a "regal manner"—observant, disciplined, attentive, and centered, but this was more an outcome of careful education and training than genetics.

For all of his chiefly bearing, Prince Albert was particularly sensitive for his age. Late that summer his playmate Freddy Allen had fallen from a swing and bruised his collarbone. Mrs. Allen explained to her mother that the prince "came down frequently, tied onto his little pony, attended by his two boys, to see him and ask after him. His mother said it seemed to weigh on the little fellow's mind that 'poor Freddy' should be dressed in a wrapper, with one arm in a sling, and one sleeve hanging loose."

Having observed the prince from close quarters, she could describe him with some confidence "as an unusually sweet child, gentle and gentlemanly in his manners, bright and precocious and of a most happy, serene temperament."[50]

The Last Illness

Shortly after Freddy's accident in August, Prince Albert was taken ill. On August 19, 1862, the queen and prince went to Waikīkī to spend the night with Princess Bernice Pauahi Bishop and her husband Charles. That evening the prince was so restless that the queen called in a doctor, and the next morning she drove the sick boy to the palace and sent for the king who was out fishing.

Chief Justice Allen saw the prince that day and said the child was very restless and kept "putting his hands where his bowels were as if in pain." It was obvious to the chief justice that something was wrong, but the doctors could not make a diagnosis and speculated that the cause might have been the heat or something that his attendants allowed him to eat. Or both. King Kamehameha insisted it was sunstroke and kept worrying about the effect it might have on the youngster.

The next day Prince Albert suffered a series of spasms or fits and cried out in pain. According to Mary Allen, the king and queen were beside themselves, helpless and despairing. Queen Emma was in a dreadful state, for she had not eaten a mouthful since the prince fell ill and slept only through exhaustion and then at the foot of her son's bed.[51]

On Saturday morning, as she stood at the foot of the child's bed, Mary Allen wrote "my tears fell fast." The bright little boy, full of life and fun, who had played daily with her precious Freddy, was obviously very, very sick. His eyes were turned up, his tongue working from side to side of his mouth, and from time to time he twitched convulsively.

Emma was seated beside him on the bed, the tears rolling down her cheeks.[52]

The local newspapers reported that the prince was suffering from an inflammation of the brain or water on the brain, and they tried to comfort the public by saying the disease was common among children.[53]

Mary Allen wrote: "From time to time the Prince regained consciousness and seemed to be better, but often he was restless and excited, thrashing about the bed. . . . It became necessary to give him some medicine. When the King took him up in his arms to administer it, kissing him, he softly whispered, 'Baby, kiss me?' The little fellow at once leaned towards his father and kissed him."[54]

Too Late for the Baptism

Previously, the king and queen had made a successful appeal to Queen Victoria and the Anglican Church in England to establish a mission in Hawai'i. (See Chapter 11 for the complete story of the founding of the church.) When the prince fell ill they were awaiting the arrival of Bishop Staley whom they had asked to baptize and christen their son. They were particularly happy that Queen Victoria had agreed to be the prince's godmother. Because she could not attend the event herself, she had designated as her proxy William W. F. Synge who had just been appointed the new British Commissioner in Hawai'i. Synge arrived on August 22 only to learn of the prince's condition. He immediately went to the palace to meet the distressed parents and their dying son. In his moving official report he wrote:

> The king asked me whom the Queen had appointed to be her Co-sponsors for the child. I told her that my Sovereign had not, I believed, understood that it was His Majesty's wish that the Godfathers should be chosen by Her. He then said, Do you think the Prince of Wales would consent to be Godfather, and will you act as proxy? At such a moment I thought I could not answer otherwise than I did, namely that I had little doubt that His Royal Highness would be glad to be associated with His Mother in the Sponsorship of a Prince in whom Her Majesty took so lively an interest, and that I would venture to act as His proxy, subject to his future approval. The King then asked his brother Prince Kamehameha to be the other Godfather, and the Baptismal Service was at once proceeded with in the antechamber. . . . It was a most affecting Ceremony. . . ."[55]

The king had asked the Congregational pastor of Kawaiaha'o Church, the Reverend Ephraim W. Clark, to perform the Anglican rites. The service was held at 10:00 on the morning of August 23 in the queen's parlor, which opened out to her bedroom where the prince lay. All the officers of the household and the cabinet were gathered. As Mary Allen wrote, "When the prayers were read all present fell on their knees, as if by a simultaneous impulse, and if sincere praying for his recovery could have saved him he would have recovered."[56] When the Reverend Clark made the sign of the cross on his forehead and formally baptized him, the little prince was quiet.

After the ceremony was over, the exhausted and shattered queen became drowsy and stretched out beside her "Baby" on the bed and fell into a deep sleep. The bed was the same one she had used from the time she was a child, sleeping in it until the day she was married.

"My Baby, My Baby"

Throughout the next few days everyone in Honolulu watched the flag flying over the palace, fearful that at any moment it might be lowered. On Sunday Mary Allen and Princess Bernice Pauahi Bishop spent the entire day with Emma and her gravely ill son. They were able to persuade Prince Albert to sip a little tea, but little else could be done. By Monday, even the queen had resigned herself to the fact that the impending death was only a matter of time. When the prince died on August 23, 1862, the queen took him in her arms and weeping over him, said, "My baby, my own baby, and you did not know me!"[57]

Was It the King's Fault?

In her biography, Queen Lili'uokalani claims that the cause of the prince's death was the "temper of the Kamehamehas." She wrote that the prince had become dissatisfied with a pair of boots and had "burst into an ungovernable fit of passion. His father sought to cool him off by putting the boy under an open faucet of cold, running water. The little one appeared to be unharmed, but later in the day broke down with nervous weeping, and could not be comforted. Then it was discovered that the cold douche and shock had brought on an attack of brain fever. From this he did not recover. . . ."[58]

Lili'uokalani's story has been challenged by modern medical historians. For example, writing in the *Queen's Hospital Bulletin,* C. R. Bennett stated that it is "medically impossible" for the shock of the cold douche to have caused brain fever.[59] Dr. Alfred D. Morris, a Honolulu physician, analyzed the possible causes of the prince's death. In describing the progressive stages of the illness, he noted how on the fourth day the physicians tried to cause the bowels to act after which the prince suffered fits and spasms and cried out in pain, all suggestive of bowel obstruction. On the fifth day, the child felt better, but on the sixth day he again went through severe spasms, perhaps even convulsions from fever and approaching coma.

Dr. Morris concluded that the most likely cause of death was not sunstroke or brain fever (meningitis) but rather appendicitis. One of its symptoms is an upset stomach, which after a few hours localizes in the lower right abdomen; this explains why the child kept putting his hand "where his bowels were." Usually the bowel movement stops because of paralysis of the gut or blockage due to swelling and irritation followed by cramps, spasm, and vomiting. But when the appendix ruptures into the abdomen the irritation is relieved and the patient appears to improve, as the prince did on the fifth day. However, soon infection develops in the abdomen with fever and most often progression to coma and then death in a few days if antibiotics and surgery are not available.

The king had placed the blame for his child's death upon himself, but Dr. Morris absolves him completely by stating, "If indeed Kamehameha IV died because of remorse over his part in this affair, there is no medical information to incriminate him."[60] C. R. Bennett also agreed: "Whatever he [the little prince] died of we know now it was not brought on by the King, in spite of popular belief."[61]

The Funeral

The Hawaiian flag over the palace was lowered to half-mast and its staff was draped with black crepe, while the minute guns sounded. No longer would those outside the palace walls look forward to his growth and yearn for his eventual assumption to the throne. As one newspaper stated, "The death of no other person could have been so severe a blow to the King and his people."[62]

The funeral was delayed for several days while carpenters built a temporary mausoleum in the shade of a large tamarind tree in front of the palace. In the meantime, he lay in a metallic coffin in the state room where the heartbroken queen remained, even sleeping there at night.

Mary Allen, who saw the queen twice during this period, wrote that "I never saw a more woe stricken face, a strange absent look, for she neither ate nor talked and, in fact, they said scarcely slept and could not weep."[63]

The funeral service took place at 11:00 a.m. on Sunday morning, September 7, in the drawing room of the palace. Beginning at sunrise guns were fired every five minutes. The mourners crowded outside, including members of the Fire Department's engine house No. 4. Soon there were the heartrending sounds of *uē*, the traditional wailing and weeping.

Inside two or three hundred people, including members of the court, were dressed in white, the traditional Hawaiian mourning color, and in the foreigners' customary black. At the head of the table on which the coffin lay was a small table covered with a black velvet cloth on which stood on its ebony stand, a large silver vase, the christening cup commissioned by his godmother, Queen Victoria. The Reverend Samuel Damon preached the funeral sermon reminding everyone that life is too short, that there is always danger in setting our affections too strongly on earthly things, and that death does not discriminate against high or low, rich or poor.[64] After his sermon, the choir sang "Go To Thy Rest Fair Child."

Mary Allen closed her description of the funeral as follows: "As soon as the service was ended the King and Queen left the room and we accompanied them to their house again. I did not say good-bye to the Queen for she at once entered her room and threw herself down by the side of the little one's crib and I heard such a profound sigh as made my heart ache."[65]

In the evening the coffin was placed in its temporary tomb below the tamarind tree. But before the coffin lid was closed, King Liholiho removed from his breast the star of diamonds he wore and laid it on the bosom of his son. For the next four days and nights Queen Emma never stirred from the little grave beneath the tamarind tree.

Following the Hawaiian custom of bestowing a new name on a person in commemoration of a momentous event, the king gave the queen the name of *Kaleleokalani* or "the Flight of the Heavenly Chief."[66]

A Mother's Lament

Shortly after her son's passing, Queen Emma composed the following *kanikau* or lament:

E ka lei, e ka lei, *E Kaleiopapa—e,* *Auhea o—e,*	O Kalei, Kalei Ka-lei-o-papa, O where are you?
O ka leo paha ia o kuʻu keiki, *E pae nei i ke Kualono,* *Me he ula-ʻai-hawane la,*	Is it the voice of my son that strikes the mountains Faint call of the *ʻula-ʻai-hawane* bird
Iu-ka	in the uplands?
I ka uka kamalahi a ka wahine *Ku ka pihe ka ikuwa iluna,* *Paepae ana i ka leo o ka ahiahi—a*	In the uplands is a frail child of woman; The din of wailing arises Striking through the evening sounds
E hoo—hihi	twisting through
E hoohihi ana paha i ka ua Haao,	Twisting through the cherished rain of Haao
Ke noho pu la me ka ua kuahine, *E hilinai ana i ke Kamakahala,* *Ua hala aku la oe,* *Aia ke kaha o Haleloa,*	Sitting in the rain of Kuahine Leaning on the *kamakahala* But you have gone To the sands that span Haleloa, distant home
Aia oe la i Paia, *I ke ala Kahinihini ʻula* *Hinihini lei—a,*	You are in the bower of Paia In the fragrance of *kahinihini* Red moss lei of *hinihini,*
Kuu le—i.	My lei.
He lei kuu keiki, *He hoa no ka ua me ka la,* *No ke anu me ke koekoe,* *Me ka hale a makou e nonoho ai,*	My child is a lei Companion in the rain and sun In the cold and chill In the house where we lived,
Hanai a ka malama—a	Hanaiakamalama,
Anua—nu.	in cold Nuuanu.
Anuanu mai nei ke aloha *Kolokolonahe ana i ka houpo,* *Wawahi ana i ka pili,* *O kuu manawa—a,*	Cold is the pity of love Fluttering in the breast Breaking through the bonds Of my innermost heart
Auhea o—e.	Where are you?
Auhea ana oe e Kalani li lau pua *O ke kahulihuli,* *Ke huli wale nei au ia oe,*	Are you listening, *Ka-lani-li-lau-pua,* Chief among so many blossoms, O the uncertainty of seeking you everywhere
Aia la oe ihea, ihea i nalo iho nei—a	That I shall only be seeking you wherever love put you soaring in the clouds
Ua na—lo.	Where you are gone—

Nalo, nalo, nalo peepee aku la i ka poiu o lani,	Gone, gone, gone—hidden in the sacred zenith of the sky
I ke kau kaha eaea a ke aloha	In the clouds billowing into air the beloved
Aloha ʻino kakou i ka la nui o Kona,	Alas that we regret the sunlight of Kona
O kona ia o ke kai malino a Ehu—la.	Kona of the calm sea of Ehu there
Eu o—le.	that rises not—
Eu ole ke kai, hanu olu i ka pohu	The sea rises not, yet a cold breath in the stillness—
Malie iho iho la ke Kona a ke Kailua,	Still like the currents of Kona and Kailua
Lai aku la, ha ka pokii a Umi—a,	In the calm lies the youngest scion of ʻUmi,
U—mi.	Breathless—
Uumi wale iho i ke aloha o ke keiki	Breathless is my love for the child
I ka ne a ke keiki makua,	For the fretting of a son maturing
E ne ana i ka ia o Makaula,	Fretting for the red-eyed fish of Makaula
I inai no na kalo Uluwehiwa	The garnish of dark *uluwehiwa* taro
O pele kei—a,	Because they were made sacred by law,
Auhea o—e.	Where are you?
Auhea oe e Kapuialani kapu o Mehekaea.	Where are you, Sacred Chief of Mehekaea?
Kaulana lani manu i kahi ano,	Famous scion of the birds of revered sanctuaries
Ka mana nana i kaha paoa ka lani,	Whose was the power over Paoa-ka-lani;
E laanau ana i ka wai o Halumi,	Adrift in the crushing flood of Halumi,
Ke lulumi nei no loko ia oe—la,	My insides are crushed with grief for you,
I lulumi au a waiho,	I am overwhelmed and left
I lanaau ae i ka manawa,	drifting through time
Ike wau i ka haka lewa i manao iho nei—a	When I see the emptiness of space afar I think
O ka lipo i Hauailiki,	Of the darkness of Hauailiki where the cold pinches
O ka uka o Lonokaiuiu,	Of the uplands of Lonokaiuiu to the farthest ridges
O ke aumoe lei i Hanalei ke aloha,	When at midnight was the love that wreathed Hanalei
Aloha wale kuu milimili i ka nalowale—la	Love for my playmate who has gone—[67]

11

Establishment of the Anglican Church in Hawai'i

The two tragedies—the death of his son and the shooting of Neilson—plunged the king into a state of profound despair. In the matter of Neilson, his despair was compounded by an unforgiving sense of personal guilt, shame, and remorse. He was, after all, the constitutional monarch of a law-abiding and Christianized nation, and his act of vengeance could have been judged attempted murder. Given this state of mind, the king sought redemption by dedicating himself to the building of the kingdom of God. His God, however, was not a Congregationalist but rather an Anglican.

Partial to the Anglican Faith

His decision was made easier by the fact that, although schooled by the missionary Cookes, preached to by the Reverends Samuel Damon, Benjamin Parker, and other Congregationalists, and lectured to by Dr. Judd in New England morality, King Kamehameha was a passive, even indifferent, adherent of the Congregational faith and somewhat antagonistic toward the Roman Catholic church. His partiality to the Anglican faith may have started when he visited England as a teenager. Kuykendall wrote that "he had been impressed by the services of the Episcopal [Anglican] Church as he had witnessed them in England."[1] It is said that the king also "admired the liturgy of the Church of England, which he observed firsthand . . . at Westminster Abbey and St. Paul's Cathedral in London, and at St. George's Chapel, Windsor."[2]

His temperament leaned toward the ceremony and ritual that were largely absent in Puritan New England churches. But the fact is, however, he never actually saw much of the services or heard any of the liturgy in the London churches he attended. The then prince had written in his journal that they were "too late" for the service at St. Paul's;[3] at Westminster Abbey they were seated so high up in the stalls that they "heard nothing of the sermon";[4] and at St. George's Chapel they found just the "Organ player who favored us with some music."[5] Ironically, the only complete Anglican service the king may have witnessed was in Philadelphia when, on his way home from Europe, he "attended church at an Episcopalian and heard a begging sermon for Contributions for the Slavery Cause."[6] Based on the number of words he wrote, King Alexander Liholiho was far more impressed by the art and architecture of England's great cathedrals and chapels (as well as by the castles and royal residences).

In contrast, Queen Emma had been raised from childhood in an enclave of Anglicans. In fact, the queen appeared to be so thoroughly Anglican that Sophia Cracroft assumed that the queen "was brought up as a member of our church."[7] Both her mothers had been exposed to the faith through their English father, John Young. Her *hānai* father, Dr. Rooke, was a devout Anglican who gave his daughter a strong intellectual and spiritual grounding in the faith. Many of the family friends and acquaintances, such as the Janions and the Skinners residing in Honolulu at the time, were Anglicans. Sarah Von Pfister, Emma's tutor who played such an important role in her growing-up, was also an Anglican.

By the time Alexander Liholiho and Emma married, the missionaries and everyone else knew that they were Anglicans at heart. The couple declared this choice rather dramatically when they used the Anglican ceremony for their wedding even though it had to be performed by a Protestant minister in the Congregational citadel of Kawaiahaʻo.

Establishing the Church

The idea of establishing an Anglican church in Hawaiʻi was not new, although the king's ardor was. A number of Anglicans, both English and American, resided in Hawaiʻi. In 1841 it was reported that about forty of these families desired Anglican services. In the absence of a church, chaplains on British warships passing through Honolulu conducted services using the Prayer Book, preaching on Sunday evenings, and occasionally even performing baptisms. In 1844 King Kamehameha III had sought to find out from the foreign community whether there were people who wanted an Anglican church and were willing to subscribe to its support, but nothing came of this effort.[8] In the late 1850s, Dr. Rufus Anderson, who was foreign secretary of the American Board of Commissioners for Foreign Missions and who was closely associated with the American missionaries in Hawai'i, stated that he had advised one of the bishops of the Anglican church in America "to procure the sending of an evangelical presbyter" to Hawai'i; he added "that the right man would strengthen the influence of religion" there.[9] In 1858 King Liholiho and Queen Emma reportedly headed up a subscription list to pay for an ordained Anglican clergyman to establish and conduct services for an Anglican church in Honolulu.[10]

Interestingly, the American missionary group did not oppose the king's and queen's efforts to set up an Anglican church at this time. In fact, the *Pacific Commercial Advertiser*, whose editor often spoke for the missionaries, editorialized that the need for an Anglican church had "long been felt" and thus encouraged its establishment.[11]

The king had two formidable supporters: the queen and his loyal minister of foreign affairs, Robert C. Wyllie. As in the founding of the hospital, Emma remained in the background. Hence, the details of her actions are unknown, but clearly she played a major role because her name is mentioned in every important public statement and event pertaining to the establishment of the church.

As for Wyllie, he was in a receptive mood when the king delegated to him many of the details of promoting the church.[12] Although still a Protestant, Wyllie had just recovered from a dangerous fever that had left him partially paralyzed in his right leg. Believing at one point that he was going to die, he seriously thought of becoming a Catholic and making his confession to his friend, Bishop Louis Maigret. The illness had chastened him in spirit, and he, like the king, turned to faith.

On December 5, 1859, Wyllie, at the behest of the king, wrote to Manley Hopkins, Hawaiian consul general in London, informing him of the earnest desire of both the king and queen "to promote the establishment of an Episcopal Chapel or Church" in Honolulu. The king offered to donate a site for the church, and on behalf of his own family and of foreigners in the community he engaged to pay a properly qualified clergyman $1,000 annually and to provide a parsonage. Hopkins was directed to confer with the Archbishop of Canterbury, the Bishop of London, or the directors of the Church Missionary

Society in the hope that some assistance would be given to the proposed effort.[13]

On that same day Wyllie wrote a private letter to Hopkins stating: "The King desires me to make known to you, confidentially, that He and the Queen would prefer that the Episcopal Clergyman, for the proposed Chapel or Church, should have a family of his own, and be eminently liberal in all his principles and ideas."[14] The reason for this statement was that though the king was initiating the enterprise, he did not intend it to be a state religion. The constitution provided everyone, including the sovereign and family, the freedom of religion. The king and queen wanted services to be performed with "all the rites and ceremonies sanctioned by the Church, for which purpose, the proper vestments, Baptismal Font, Sacramental Cup, a Bell and an organ will be requisite."[15]

Several evenings later a small group of those interested in the establishment of the Anglican church met in the courthouse. They were informed that the king and queen were "specially desirous" of organizing such a church and that the king had offered a lot located on Emma Place for the erection of the church. A subscription paper was prepared, and a committee of three members, one English, one American, and one German, was appointed to raise the money to build the church. The *Pacific Commercial Advertiser* predicted that sufficient funds could be collected "within sixty days."[16]

Unlike the founding of the hospital, neither King Liholiho nor Queen Emma took a visible or active part in raising funds for the church. Had they done so, perhaps the newspaper's prediction of sixty days would have been fulfilled. But, as later events will show, the queen would eventually lead a fund-drive that would collect thousands of dollars for an even larger church.

Meanwhile, in England, Manley Hopkins responded to the king's request as spelled out by Wyllie with energy and enthusiasm, "rising before daylight . . . all through the winter." He considered it a great honor to be invited to spread the faith to "the distant islands of the ocean" so that "the craggy heights of far Hawaii might now 'stand up and take the morning.' "[17] For much of the year 1860 he devoted his time to the task, consulting with church authorities and prominent laymen and with their support organizing a "Committee for Promoting the English Church in Hawaii," whose intent was to raise money for and to create interest in the church's establishment. He also obtained the crucial assistance of the Bishop of Oxford (Dr. Samuel Wilberforce), and together they sought approvals and funds. Hopkins even appealed to Queen Victoria, but to no avail.

Then, in November 1860, the king wrote directly to the English monarch: "I approach Your Majesty with this letter for the purpose of requesting Your Majesty's approval of the establishment of the Anglican Episcopal Church within my Dominions. . . .

"I therefore presume upon the well known graciousness which Your Majesty has always extended to me, my Predecessor and my people, and for which we have always been thankful, to ask for such countenance to this pious undertaking as may seem most meet to Your Majesty, and to whatever degree that may be extended, I and my people will ever be thankful."[18]

Queen Victoria's response, as written by her foreign minister Lord John Russell, was that she would "watch with the greatest interest" the king's efforts to establish a church but that she by law would not be able to contribute in any way except her good wishes.[19]

At the same time that King Kamehameha IV was writing to Queen Victoria, Wyllie wrote to the Archbishop of Canterbury about the proposed mission: "I take the liberty, by command of the King, to address Your Grace, upon a subject in which He and Her Majesty the Queen take great interest, which is the establishment of Episcopacy in this Kingdom, after the form of and in connexion with the Episcopal Church of England."

Wyllie comments on the Congregational and Roman Catholic churches in the Hawaiian kingdom and then goes on: "But their Majesties the King and Queen, preferring the Episcopal form of Worship, were married according to the rites prescribed in the English liturgy; and they desire, both for themselves and for all others who have the same preference, that there should be churches in which they can worship God according to their consciences. . . .

"After these explanations, the King hopes that Your Grace will deign to countenance favorably His Majesty's and His Queen's desire to have Episcopacy regularly established within His Kingdom, in spiritual relation with the Church of England of which you are Primate."[20]

It is not known whether Wyllie ever received a reply, but the king and queen must have made a favorable impression, as future events would indicate.

In the spring of 1861, a debate took place among high officials of the Church of England on the subject of missionary bishops, in the course of which the Bishop of Oxford said that "the King of the Sandwich Islands was most anxious to see a Bishop of the English Church established in his dominions. . . . He proposes to make the Bishop preceptor to the Crown Prince. . . . I think it most important that we should at once consider the question."[21]

Within a month the Bishop of Oxford made a speech in convocation advocating the measure and stating that the king would on his own behalf give a site for a church and 200 pounds yearly, together with land to support the mission.

In August the Reverend Thomas Nettleship Staley, a one-time fellow of Queen's College, Cambridge, was designated as the new bishop of the missionary diocese in Hawai'i. On December 15, 1861, he was consecrated as the first Anglican Bishop of Honolulu.

With the news of Staley's consecration, the new year seemed a harbinger of more promising times for the king. The proof seemed to come when the kingdom celebrated his twenty-eighth birthday in a way that "surpassed all previous" celebrations. But the respite proved to be brief, for within a week he was burdened with the news that Henry Neilson, who seemed in fit condition when he visited him the day before, had died quietly in his sleep on February 11. The death cast a pall over his life that not even the coming of Bishop Staley and the Anglican church could totally overcome.

The Bishop's Coming

Considerable feeling was aroused among the missionary group at the bishop's coming, "this intrusion upon the comity of missions," as Laura Judd put it.[22] Dr. Rufus Anderson had written earlier in a letter of protest to the Archbishop of Canterbury that he feared "the introduction of a branch of the Church of England" would lead to the "possible extension of British dominion" in Hawai'i and the Pacific. The Archbishop replied that he would be "truly sorry if any circumstances [should] occur calculated to create jealousy between parties who have the same great end in view."[23] Among the leaders of the opposition were Dr. Judd and the Reverend Eli S. Corwin, pastor of the Fort Street (Congregational) church. Of their opposition the king wrote: "I am sorry to hear that Judd Corwin & Co. are so inimical to the establishment of Episcopacy here. I wonder if they really are in earnest in objecting to peoples getting in to heaven by any way they please? I am sure I have none, and it is just as well that they get in at the back door if it suits them, and if they find it open."[24]

Many in the community waited for Bishop Staley's arrival with interest, but none with greater personal interest than the king and queen. As mentioned earlier, they had looked forward to the baptism of their son, his christening, and the bishop's supervision of his education. They had been particularly excited that Queen Victoria had agreed to be the godmother of their son, an eventuality that they had hoped for even before the prince was born but a favor that the king had long hesitated to request.[25]

Sophia Cracroft describes a two-hour conversation in the palace on June 17, 1861, when "the King kindly read us the letter he wrote about two years back to the Queen [Victoria], asking her to be sponsor to the Prince, which letter has lain ever since in his desk for want of courage to send it. Even *we* were astonished at the beauty of the letter, so charmingly expressed, with mingled modesty and dignity. My Aunt [Lady Franklin] was for sending it (with necessary alterations) even now. But the King dreads (and of course would not risk) a personal refusal."[26] He did, of course, finally send the letter and was ecstatic to receive her positive reply.

According to the previous plan, the first important act of Bishop Staley was to be the baptism of the Prince of Hawai'i. But, according to Lady Franklin, even before the bishop had left England, he had "declared that the baptism of Queen Emma should come first; and that it could not be too private—indeed he wished it to be kept a secret and should never make it known to anyone she had ever been baptized, lest needless talk be aroused over the fact that the Queen had never been baptized before." Lady Franklin thought the little prince's baptism might be put off until Christmas by which time the special font that she had ordered made out of Caen stone would have arrived.[27]

Bishop Staley and his party of fourteen arrived in Honolulu on Saturday, October 11, 1862. Though the bishop's party was shocked to learn of the prince's death, they were grateful for the welcome from Wyllie and Gregg on behalf of Their Majesties. Apparently, Wyllie and Gregg were surprised to see the bishop accompanied by an entourage consisting of his wife, their six children, a nurse, a governess, the Reverend George Mason with his wife and daughter, and the Reverend Edmund Ibbotson.[28] The king's carriage took the party to a temporary residence on the grounds of the palace. In the meantime, handbills announced the services on Sunday for which Wyllie secured an abandoned Methodist church building on the corner of Kukui Street and Nu'uanu Avenue. Here the first Holy Communion was celebrated and the first sermon given by the Reverend Mason.

Queen Emma and King Kamehameha IV were baptized in 1862 in the Anglican (Episcopalian) church.

On Sunday, October 19 Bishop Staley preached his inaugural sermon when the king and queen were present. Though the sermon was in English, the king had insisted on singing the hymn in Hawaiian. Within a month there were two congregations, one in the Hawaiian language and one in English.

Two days later, on October 21, a large number of chiefs and prominent foreigners assembled to witness the baptism of Queen Emma—one that was intended for her son. She was overjoyed yet saddened that she rather than her son would be the first person named in the cathedral parish register of baptisms. Her registered name appears as "Emma Alexandrina Francis Agnes Lowder Byde Rooke Young Kaleleokalani."

On October 23 a meeting was held in the courthouse with King Kamehameha in attendance. The group adopted resolutions that welcomed the mission, pledged support, and applied for a charter of incorporation under the name of the "Hawaiian Reformed Catholic Church." The charter was granted by the privy council at its next November meeting.[29] And with its approval, the king's gift became official: the land where St. Andrew's Cathedral stands today.

Another step was required to gain full membership in the new Episcopacy. On November 28, the queen—dressed in a plain white muslin dress, high at the throat, with long sleeves, and a long white crepe veil on her head held in place by a lei of *pīkake* (white jasmine, her favorite flower lei)—and the king, attired in full uniform, came to the church to be confirmed in the presence of the members of the House of Nobles, the royal court, and the consular corps. If the king had missed the full impact of Anglican ritualism in London, he was now about to experience the full measure of it: The service began with the Litany chanted in Hawaiian, the choir responding, followed by a procession led by Major Hoapili Kaauwai, the king's aide-de-camp, who carried the bishop's banner, the all-male choristers, clergy, Archdeacon Mason, and the bishop, all chanting the Nineteenth Psalm, "The Earth Is the Lord's and the Fullness Thereof." The king and queen then stepped before the altar, and as the bishop asked the requisite questions, they responded in clear, audible voices, exactly as they had rehearsed. The congregation was asked to spend a few moments in silent prayer and then rose and sang the "Veni Creator" (an ancient hymn invoking the presence of the Holy Spirit) over Their Majesties, who remained kneeling. The bishop confirmed the first royal couple and delivered an impressive address that "deeply affected" the king and queen. The service closed with the singing of the 100th Psalm and the benediction. One elderly chief is said to have remarked to his son that "if a man did not know English, or even if he were quite deaf, still he might understand all that was passing before him from what he saw."[30]

The following Sunday, the first in Advent, Their Majesties took their first communion, thus completing their initiatory passage in a spiritual union with the body of Christ.

The King's Translation of the Prayer Book

As part of his redemptive process, the king had begun to translate the *English Book of Common Prayer* into Hawaiian. Following the death of the prince he had retired to Hānaiakamalama where he consoled himself by laboring on the translation with even more intensity. When the bishop called on the king and queen after their return to the palace, the king told him that he had already completed his translation of the *Morning and Evening Prayers* and *Litany* into Hawaiian and that it was in the hands of the printer.[31] This section of the *Prayer Book*, a hand-sewn pamphlet of thirty-five pages, was distributed on November 9, 1862, when "the King's Morning Prayer was used for the first time at a purely native service."[32]

The king added a lengthy preface of his own explaining the new faith. He had it set in type and then submitted it to Bishop Staley who declined to make any changes, thinking it better that "so remarkable a production should go forth as the unprompted and untouched work of the king."[33]

Manley Hopkins made the following statement about the king's translation:

> [It is] in every respect a very remarkable work. It is remarkable in its origin . . . that he should of his own mere notion have designed such a labour . . . and without help and without fearfully weighing the difficulties of transfusing into his own language, deficient in words, and more deficient in abstract ideas, the moral and theological conception of the Church, should have proceeded at once to his successful accomplishment. . . .
>
> The execution of the book is also remarkable. The King took extreme pains in the translation; and persons well acquainted with the Hawaiian language and competent to judge, inform us that the work has a right to be entitled a good translation, and that they are satisfied with the general truth and beauty of it. As an instance of the good taste with which Kamehameha proceeded, it may be mentioned that no foreign words are employed, except a few Latin titles to psalms.
>
> The book is remarkable also for what it omits. The name of '*Halelu Davida*' appears on its title-page, but the King's hand was cold in death before this part of his task was completed. The other omission to notice is that of the Athanasian Creed. Its absence is to be accounted for, in the first place, from the insuperable difficulties which would have encountered the King in trying to give expression and meaning to its language. The King knew his people well, and what the native mind was capable of apprehending. . . . So the King, with thoughtful regard to the present condition of those who were to use the prayer-book, left the Athanasian Creed untouched.[34]

Manley Hopkins wondered how the king found time to do the translation while tending to the cares of the kingdom. He attributed this accomplishment partly to the fact that the king was "a very early riser" and then related this story: "One of the clergy of the English mission mentions that before six one morning, and ere he was up, the King and the Queen came to him requesting him to see a poor dying native whom they had themselves visited that day already. Most other nations rise earlier than the English, or, what is more true, the English do not rise so early as other nations; and at 5:30 A.M. the generality of Englishmen are, and without reproach, still asleep."[35]

King Kamehameha IV was not finished. The following year he, with help from the clergy, produced a hymnal containing thirty-nine hymns in the Hawaiian language and advised them on pronunciations and meanings.[36] This would not be the king's last act of restitution.

The Beginnings of the Anglican Schools

In his initial discussions with Bishop Staley, the king emphasized the need for an Anglican school for Hawaiian boys and girls. "From the first of our private interviews, the King, assuring me that great superstition and witchcraft were rampant in every island, stressed the immediate need of boarding schools for both boys and girls, to remove the children early from such influences, and promised help in every way possible with his small income. Needless to say I heartily agreed with him, and I promised the Queen to write to Pusey about his Sisterhood of the Holy Trinity. They would be able to train the girls in nursing and minister to the sick also, who at present are afraid to go to the little hospital [Queen's] lately opened."[37]

The bishop and his commissioners lost no time in opening separate schools for both boys and girls. On November 8, less than one month after their arrival in Hawai'i, the *Polynesian* gave notice of the opening of a College for Hawaiian Girls, also called the "Female Industrial Seminary," to be taught by Mrs. George Mason under the patronage of Queen Emma, and a Grammar School for Boys under the Reverend George Mason. The king contributed $4,000 of his own money for the erection of a building for the girls' school at the entrance of Pauoa Valley. The girls' school was a family boarding and industrial school, with a curriculum emphasizing the domestic arts. The tuition was 25 cents a week. But if a student wanted to study French, German, music, dancing, and embroidery, the cost was $25 a term for girls under twelve.[38] By mid-April the school was flourishing with day students and more than forty boarders, many of whom were financed by the king and queen.[39]

In the meantime, an English school, known as the Cathedral Grammar School for "poor outcast Hawaiian boys" was also started under the tutorship of the Reverend Ibbotson. In early 1863 the Masons were transferred to Lahaina, and this school became St. Alban's, commemorating the first martyr-saint of the ancient English church. Mrs. Mason's boarding school for girls was also turned over to another director, but it did not last and its buildings were given to St. Alban's, the forerunner of today's 'Iolani School, named after the king. The school started with twenty boarders and several day pupils and offered Latin, Greek, Euclid, and algebra, among other subjects, all of which were taught in English.[40] Unlike other schools, both missionary and government, which were taught in Hawaiian, the Anglican schools were strictly English-speaking.[41]

The Reverend Scott, a recent arrival, had gone to Lahaina to set up another parsonage and the school for girls first known as the Female Industrial Seminary. Bishop Staley wrote: "These Hawaiian girls under Mrs. Scott's care in Lahaina are getting splendid training to fit them to be wiser mothers and wives. We are trying to catch them young. . . . The king's father [Kekūanaoʻa] . . . urges more Church boarding schools for boys and girls. He says infanticide is rife, superstitions, sorceries, praying to death by kahunas, vile incantations and idolatries, and other crimes are common."[42] After the Masons moved to Lahaina, Mrs. Mason directed the girls' school until late 1864 when the Sisters of the Society of the Most Holy Trinity under the Reverend Mother Lydia Sellon arrived to take charge. By then the school had twenty-five boarders and about forty day girls. It was renamed St. Cross School.[43]

Thus, by the time of his death, King Alexander Liholiho had contributed to the beginnings of three Anglican schools: St. Cross in Lahaina, which no longer exists, ʻIolani, now a non-boarding coed institution, and St. Andrew's Priory, still a girls' school.

12

Celebrations Amidst the Sick

Less than a month after their confirmation as members of the Church of England in 1862, King Kamehameha IV and Queen Emma officially celebrated Christmas for the first time. It was one of the unintended consequences of their conversion to the Anglican faith. In 1856 the king had set aside December 25 as a national day of Thanksgiving, though subsequently he named the last day of the year as Thanksgiving Day. In either case, the decision was left to the people as to how they wanted to celebrate Christmas. Now, as a confirmed member of a church that celebrated the Birthday of Christ as a holy festival, King Kamehameha IV gave public notice that Christmas would be formally observed on December 25th. It was the first attempt to popularize Christmas on a large scale in Hawai'i.

A Hawaiian Christmas

Acting with the enthusiasm of new converts, the king and queen threw themselves into preparing for the holiday celebrations. They learned the hymns and the carols especially and helped the twenty-member choir in its practices. They sent people to the mountains to gather boughs of *kileka* (cypress) to decorate the temporary Anglican chapel, and from the palace gardens they provided other plants and flowers. "I never saw in England a church so beautifully decorated," wrote Archdeacon Mason. "The natives have great taste in these matters. Here too we have all the advantage . . . in being able to get all kinds of flowers at this season."[1] The king and queen also lent all of their silver candelabra to the church.

Not to be outdone, the members of both the "Stone Church" (Kawaiahaʻo) and the Cathedral of Our Lady of Peace decorated their own premises with wreaths of foliage and lights. The ships in the harbor and the town itself were decorated with flags.

On Christmas eve the streets, churches, and homes were ablaze with lights whose display was "the most magnificent ever witnessed" in Honolulu. The cathedral was illuminated from pavement to dome with an "astonishing" array of lights as if "announcing to mankind that a child was born," while inside more than 1,000 candles cast their flaming shadows.[2] In the vestry stood a Christmas tree that carried over 200 lights, and on its branches were strewn the gifts for the church's seventy school children.[3]

The *Pacific Commercial Advertiser* listed other Christmas trees at the Wickes, the de Varignys, the Lowell Smiths, Dr. and Mrs. Judd, Judge and Mrs. Robertson, the Damons, and the Brewsters; it made special mention of the tree belonging to Mrs. Dominis (Washington Place) who was credited with starting the Christmas tree tradition in Hawaiʻi. The newspaper also described Santa as someone who was always "courted and coaxed" in Honolulu but who was "severely taxed for his favors" this particular year. Curiously, no mention was made of either a tree or Santa Claus being at the palace.[4]

On December 24 at 11:30 p.m., the king and queen joined other Anglicans at the church in their first Christmas eve service held in Hawaiʻi. Archdeacon Mason describes the scene: "The Litany was first softly chanted in native. Then the bishop and clergy put on their best robes, and with a choir of twenty in surplices we walked in procession round the church singing 'Adeste Fideles.' The Holy Communion service commenced—choral throughout. About thirty received. After the consecration of the elements we sang, on our knees, the beautiful hymn 'Thus we adore a hidden Saviour.' "[5]

When the service ended at one a.m., the battery on Punchbowl fired a Christmas salute, while barrels of tar were lighted and rolled down its barren slopes leaving trails of fire (none of which, fortunately, hit the new hospital situated at the very foot of Punchbowl). Outside the church the congregation formed a procession, with the king and queen at the head, followed by the bishop and clergy and Mr. Synge, the choir, and twenty royal torch bearers, each of whom carried an eight-foot long torch made out of the kukui tree and coconut fiber dipped in tar. Others in the procession carried "an innumerable number of blue lights." While they walked through the streets of Honolulu, they sang Christmas carols and stopped at several places to call out greetings. They proceeded to the palace where, as Mason wrote, "The torches and blue lights were ranged round the small circular piece of water in the middle of the palace courtyard. The fountains played grandly, and the reflection of the torch lights, together with the clear brilliant moonlight of these latitudes on the water, and on the dark excited faces of the people, was very remarkable."[6]

The procession gathered in the courtyard, "some really good fireworks were let off, and rockets shot up into the air amidst deafening shouts from a thousand voices for the king and queen." They all sang "Good King Wenceslaus," toasted the festivities with a glass of champagne punch, and made the air ring with the National Anthem. After another round of "protracted Hurrahs," the crowd dispersed and Their Majesties retired.[7]

That evening the king and queen attended the German Club's grand Christmas party at which they were toasted again, this time by its physician-president, Dr. E. Hoffman, who praised Their Majesties for providing foreigners "a freedom unparalleled elsewhere" and for being "the patrons and partakers of every liberal sentiment, of every onward movement that looked to the happiness of others."[8] Immediately after Christmas and New Year's Day the kingdom celebrated another national holiday on January 2, the queen's birthday. The town and harbor were dressed in their brightest colors, royal salutes were fired at noon and sunset, and "many and warm were the prayers from loyal lips that God would bless their beloved Queen."[9]

Given the situation in 1857, the queen herself would certainly have prayed for the health of the king—and of her people.

Hospitals Not Enough

Five days after her birthday she was sharply reminded of the needs of the sick by a strident editorial in the *Pacific Commercial Advertiser.* Prompted by the appointment of a new Board of Health and by a desire to remind its members of the "position and duties expected of them," the paper editorialized on the "depth of misery and degradation" to which the people had plunged, especially those living in Honolulu. "The physical life of the nation is calling loudly for help! It has been long suffering and needs as skillful and faithful physicians to save the bodies of the people as ever were needed for their souls. Each day brings to light fresh details of the heaped-up horrors endured by the helpless poverty of Bethnal Green. Coroners' inquests show to our shuddering gaze, with kaleidoscopic rapidity and variety, scenes of misery, pestilence, and neglect, which make the blood creep with pity and disgust, and the mind wonder that such things can exist in a Christian metropolis." The editorial pointed to the squalor in what is now "Chinatown" with its "dilapidated huts, densely over populated by the worst classes of natives, male and female." In one block inhabited by sixty families with 850 children among them, one resident complained that almost none of the houses had any water, that their "water closets" were "cesspools," and that their water tanks, when they did have water, were filthy.

The pro-missionary newspaper railed against the inadequate measures of the government, particularly the act of the legislature that denied missionaries the right to prescribe and furnish medicines to natives. It argued that the law prevented missionaries on the other Islands, in stations far removed from physicians, from helping the sick. For years the American Board of Commissioners for Foreign Missions had sent annually to Hawai'i between $500 and $1,000 worth of medicine, which the missionaries furnished to native Hawaiians, making only those pay who were able to do so, while the poor and needy received the medicine gratuitously. The newspaper blamed this law in part for doubling the ratio of deaths to births, 2,496 deaths to 1,483 births, in the previous year.

Suggestions for establishing hospitals in Hilo and Lahaina were sound, but the newspaper saw little hope for this plan because Queen's Hospital itself was "barely supported." After receiving $6,761.13 in revenues and spending $6,424.74 in 1862, the hospital's operating balance was $336.39. Of the total receipts, $4,423.94 came from the public treasury, $1,574.94 from private contributions, and $740.60 from paying patients. Thus about two-thirds of Queen's annual cost was met by the government.[10]

What was needed even more than hospitals, according to the editorial, were men with "a thorough knowledge of the native language and peculiarities of the people" that would enable them to win their confidence. "Of what use," it asked, "would a Hospital be with a physician installed who had no sympathies in common with the people; who by his haughty conceited bearing towards them would tend to make the institution worse than useless?" The paper did commend the "present efficient and worthy physician [Dr. Hillebrand] of the Queen's Hospital" as "one in ten thousand."[11]

The editorial concluded with a question: "Could not such of our physicians as are conversant with the language receive into their employ smart, capable young Hawaiians, and in the course of time make them valuable assistants in the treatment of the minor ills which flesh is heir to?"

"The health of the Hawaiian people," according to *Ka Hōkū o Ka Pākipika*, "is a hot topic at this time." In an oblique criticism of the missionaries, the newspaper stated, "Too often the people are first taught how to take care of the spirit, but not taught how to take of the physical body. Church members can tell you all about the scriptures and other things about the Bible, but they don't know how to take care of themselves. . . . When people get sick, they go outside in the wind or swim in streams to cool their fevers. . . . As a result, they become sicker until they have to go to the doctor, but they are afraid of the doctor bill, and then they become even sicker." It concluded that the "reason for all this is that we haven't been taught how to live properly so that we may be healthy."[12]

The Queen Heads the District Visiting Society

The conditions described by the two newspapers no doubt influenced the action by Bishop Staley and Queen Emma in February 1863 to organize the Cathedral District Visiting Society or *Ko Hawaii Cathedral ʻAhahui Hoʻolauna*. The purpose of the society was "to encourage good health and proper living" among all residents in the Islands, particularly among the needy sick. Only married women and members of the Anglican faith were eligible for membership unless approved by the bishop. Members were required to go out in teams of no less than two women, one of whom had to be Hawaiian or at least speak the language.[13]

Ka Nūpepa Kūʻokoʻa praised the queen for forming the society and urged its readers to "follow her noble example and go out and help others. . . . The Queen started this, but it should be everyone who continues it."[14] The *Hōkū O Ka Pākipika* also hailed the queen's initiative: "We are blessed by the Queen's forming this hui. . . . She built the hospital at Mana [or Manamana] for the poor people, and now she is going door to door among our houses to hear our problems and to guard us and to give us as much help as she can. Just as she treats us with so much love, so should we treat others."[15]

The queen served as the society's first president. She was also its patroness contributing moral and financial support to its work. Not surprisingly, the society worked closely with the Queen's Hospital.[16] The queen instructed its members accordingly: "Be always ready to note any sickness in the family you are visiting, and offer help for any and all of their needs. Especially advise that serious cases should be taken to the new Hawaiian hospital, where all food and treatments are free. In Honolulu the Sisters of our Church, who are trained nurses, are always glad to go and visit such cases. We too are to visit them when they are in the hospital, and to help them on their discharge, when often there are family needs and difficulties."[17]

They were also instructed to inform the bishop of the sick who were unbaptized so that "they would not be taken by another religion."[18] The queen told her charges: "You go out to my people as God's messengers. . . . Our beloved Church regards her children as having bodies as well as souls to be cared for, and sanctions the consecration of these and all that is beautiful in nature and art to the service of God. . . . Baptism should be urged for infants as early as possible. . . . But tell the parents they have their part to play in it; bringing the little ones in faith to Christ, and renouncing for them the world, flesh, devil, so setting an example, and training them to do this as they grow."[19]

The *Pacific Commercial Advertiser* praised the goals of this new society, which it called the "Cathedral Sanitary Association" and wished its members success, but did so begrudgingly. After reminding its readers that for many years the missionary wives had been doing what the society intended to do, it said, "We can not see how it will be possible for them to carry out their philanthropic views without coming in contact with the regulations of the Board of Health or of the statutes of the kingdom. We hope that no restrictions or threats will be thrown in their way as they have been in the way of others." The paper added, "We hope that the druggists and physicians of Honolulu will be ready gratuitously to second by advice and medicines the benevolent views of the ladies."[20]

Through her work with the society, Queen Emma would become, as the contemporary historian James Jarves observed, "the most constant and devoted visitor in the homes of the poor and afflicted natives."[21] And, he might have added, in Queen's Hospital whose patients she visited almost daily.

Hillebrand's Report

In April the queen received Dr. Hillebrand's report to the trustees on the hospital's activities. She must have been impressed with the results: from August 1, 1859, to April 1, 1863, the hospital treated 7,500 patients and issued 16,496 prescriptions or about twelve per day. On average thirteen persons applied to the dispensary for relief; sometimes the number reached from twenty-five to thirty. In the first quarter of 1863, of the 612 patients admitted, ninety-one were foreigners. Of the total patients, eighty-six had died, most from "incurable diseases such as consumption, dropsy and paralysis."

Dr. Hillebrand and his colleagues had performed 141 surgical operations, the most prominent of which included twenty exarticulations and amputations of fingers, toes, metacarpal, and metatarsal bones, nine for club-foot, sixteen removals of tumors, eighty for cataracts, twenty for phimosis and paraphimosis, and thirty fistula in ano. In addition, he had set broken limbs, removed diseased bones, and opened fistulas and deep-seated abscesses, which he deemed were "some of the most hazardous, but at the same time most successful."

He then enumerated some difficulties faced by the hospital. One was the character and habits of the natives:

> Ignorant and superstitious, accustomed by his ancient kahunas to view only a supernatural agency in disease and remedy, he cannot easily reconcile himself to the sober unpretentious working of a scientific method in curing disease. Jealousy of the foreigner, who has far distanced him in the unequal competition for wealth and influence, makes him distrustful of the foreigners' institutions. It has taken a considerable time before people could comprehend that the Hospital was a dispenser of unreserved charity; they feared that, after having received its benefits, they would be held to pay in some shape or another for the aid received. This prejudice has worn off by this time. . . . Their faith in the old kahunas has not been demolished yet, but faith in the foreign kahunas seems to have sensibly increased, and what the final result will be, it is not difficult to guess. I have not seen a native yet, who, once having been an inmate of the Hospital, was not anxious to avail himself of its benefits again.

The most serious problems had to do with the "straightened circumstances" due to the lack of finances and personnel. Dr. Hillebrand said the building was fine but the furniture was "most rudimentary." The washstands had to serve as a dining table, a wardrobe, a medicine cabinet, dressing container, and sundry other uses, and there was not even a chair for each patient. The facilities for cooking and heating water for warm baths and the other equipment were "very defective."

Dr. Hillebrand's entire staff consisted of an assistant who served as steward, an apothecary, a nurse, a cook, and two native helpers "who have never served in a foreign family." He went on to complain:

> If you take into consideration that we generally have from thirty to fifty house-patients, and these mostly of a class which never has learnt habits of regularity and cleanliness, it will strike you how inadequate such a labor force is for the service required. It is impossible to impose upon the native strict discipline, with a rigid observance of fixed rules, and at the same time make him feel easy and at home. But unless we can do the latter, he will not enter the House. We are often obliged, if a wife is sick, to allow the husband to stay with her, and vice-versa. A sick mother must carry with her the youngest children, because there would be no one at home to tend them, and a sick child takes with it generally both parents. All these persons will take their meals in the House (not, however, at its expense) and in many instances, spread their mats on the floor during night. Then again, we have not the means of furnishing new suits of clothes to the many ragged wretches who are received.

Some people charged that the hospital had not been kept sufficiently clean. Dr. Hillebrand contended that "There is a short time in the day when it always is neat, but, how it can be kept so during the whole day, under existing circumstances, I cannot see. To keep the house always neat would require the employment of an intelligent white servant for this sole purpose, and the frequent summons of the painter and white-washer."

Dr. Hillebrand warned the trustees about the dangerous spread of leprosy and added that he had used the former temporary hospital building to isolate those affected with the disease. He also urged the trustees to erect "an asylum for the insane" to accommodate the "many applications" for admission received by the hospital.

He ended his report by acknowledging "the beneficial influence" of the "Ladies Sanitary Association" and especially "the unremitting exertions of Her Majesty our noble Queen" who came almost daily to "convey sick people to the dispensary, or to visit the inmates of the hospital." He concluded, "If such energetic sympathy for the objects of our charitable institution were more generally diffused, its efficiency would be greatly increased."[22]

Dr. Hillebrand's observations concerning Hawaiian superstitions and *kāhuna* were typical but mild compared to the aspersions of the

Pacific Commercial Advertiser's editor. He wrote: "It is a peculiarity of Hawaiians that they are exceedingly superstitious," which has been "part and parcel of their being for centuries past." The most frightening of the superstitions was being prayed to death by a dreaded *kahuna,* a practice that the missionaries had been able to almost eradicate. He claimed, however, that the practice, together with hula and idolatry, had been revived within the "past four or five years." The hula was implicated because it was viewed as "a part of the sorcerer's avocation. He teaches and presides over the dance one day, and the next may be employed to pray a person to death. Consequently, if hulas are encouraged, sorcery and praying to death are encouraged also." Hence, it was easy to blame the hula masters for the upswing in sorcery and idolatry.[23] The newspaper's recommendation was typically uncompromising: destroy every form of sorcery and idolatry (and much of the hula as well).

In contrast, the *Polynesian* recommended that the *kahuna* system should be left alone. It said, "We do not believe in the violent suppression of an ingrained evil. But with a better education and ampler facilities of enlightened medical attendance, the Kahuna practice in Hawaii will dwindle down . . . and finally only be remembered as a horrible dream, an ancient superstition."[24]

Interestingly, *Ka Nūpepa Kū'oko'a* sided with the *Pacific Commercial Advertiser*'s unsympathetic view of the *kahuna.* In commenting on Dr. Hillebrand's report, the *Kū'oko'a* castigated the *kāhuna ho'opunipuni* or fake and lying *kāhuna* and the "ignorant and unenlightened" people who still believed in their "old falsehoods." It described one such "crazy" woman who "prophesied that on May 1 an epidemic would kill the whole Hawaiian race except for those who brought her gifts." The newspaper chided its Hawaiian readers for giving money to these *kāhuna* instead of to the hospital, which was in great need of money to cover its growing debt.[25]

Four months later the *Kū'oko'a* reiterated the need for Hawaiians to support the hospital. "We shouldn't be indolent and wait for the foreigners to start everything for us. The rich, healthy people [among us] should give some of their money. . . . The poor can give taro, sweet potatoes, or chickens instead. . . ." It then reminded its readers that when Kamehameha IV went around asking for donations for the hospital, "*ali'i,* some Hawaiians, and many *haole* agreed to give certain amounts. . . . Some have given what they promised, and others haven't. . . . Isn't it a shame that these people who can afford to give and promised to do so by signing their names have not, while the *haole* are continuously giving their money to heal the sick Hawaiians? Can a true *ali'i* really give his word but not keep it?"[26]

What did the king or queen think about these matters? There are no articulated reflections from either, but they both had a sympathetic understanding of and great hopes for their people.

13

Oh, My Husband

In the aftermath of Prince Albert's death, the king and queen began to search for a site for a new royal mausoleum. They had had to build a temporary tomb for the prince because the palace vault was full. They selected a three-and-one-half-acre site that was nearly opposite the home of Judge Lorrin Andrews in Nuʻuanu. Together with Theodore Heuck, the same architect who designed the hospital, the king and queen began drawing up the plan for a new royal mausoleum. No one knew then that the king would be its first occupant.

Last Birthday

On the king's twenty-ninth birthday in 1863 the press reported the usual scene: the town and shipping decked out with colors, flags, and pennants; salutes fired at sunrise, noon, and sunset; a parade by the Fire Department and military companies; parties, picnics, and so on. However, this birthday celebration differed from all others in two respects. First, a special service of thanksgiving was performed at the Anglican pro-cathedral, where the National Anthem was sung at the entry of Their Majesties, followed by "Te Deum" music, prayer, and communion.[1] The second difference is that for first time the king did not receive visitors.[2] Although no explanation was given, it can be safely assumed he did not feel well. In the past, such events had sapped his strength even when he was in good health. Hoping to find some relief on Hawaiʻi, the king departed Honolulu in late February for his summer residence in Kailua-Kona.

First Sermon

Among those accompanying him were Bishop Staley and Major Hoapili, who was about to resign his appointments as an officer in the military and as a district judge to become the first native Anglican clergyman. The king had always been careful to separate his personal religious preference from his official nondenominational position as head of state. However, on this trip he was clearly assisting the bishop in spreading the Anglican faith.

The last time King Alexander Liholiho had visited Kona was when his young prince was still alive and when he himself was in better health. While wandering through the house, the memories of that happier time greatly affected his moods. When he chanced upon a box containing playthings of his son, he could not hold back his grief.

Near his summer residence was a Congregational church, and when Sunday arrived, feeling sad and alone (the queen had remained in Honolulu), he decided to attend church services. (Bishop Staley was holding services at another Kona church some fifteen miles away.) The sermon he heard presented such an alarming and terrifying picture of a vengeful Christian God delivering eternal punishment on the wicked on the Day of Judgment that the king announced that he himself would hold a second service that afternoon and deliver a different kind of sermon.

The church building was crowded with his eager but respectful subjects. Major Hoapili, wearing a white surplice, opened the service by reading from the king's translated version of the *Prayer Book*. Then the king, also wearing a surplice to symbolize the religious office he now assumed, gave his sermon using as his text the passage from the Gospel of John, "Jesus wept." He described a God of sympathy and mercy rather than one of fear and recommended that abounding love and beneficence and long suffering be the reason for holiness and hope. The congregation was held spellbound not only by the power of his words but also by his *mana*. For here was their *ali'i nui*, a Kamehameha, suffering from his own deep pain and uttering words of compassion and solace.[3] Perhaps this was his defining moment as a Christian king.

The excitement of his agitated feelings must have been too much for him, for when he finished his sermon, a numbness seized one of his hands causing a slight paralysis. A doctor was called but the attack passed. He felt that the situation was more serious than it appeared, however, and immediately sent for Queen Emma.[4] Although she had already made plans to join him, she left immediately on the next steamer with a party that included Lady Staley and Mrs. Hoapili. One measure of her popularity was the "immense crowd" that went to the harbor to see her off and to "convey their aloha to the good Queen Emma."[5] With the queen's arrival the king seemed to regain his cheerfulness and some measure of his health. But Emma probably knew that under his external cheer, there throbbed a broken heart that could not be easily mended.

A Loving Exchange with Kapiʻolani

While in Kona the queen exchanged letters with Kapiʻolani, the prince's former nurse, who at the time was staying at Hānaiakamalama with Grace, the queen's mother. In a letter dated March 19, Kapiʻolani wrote:

> Seen are the places where your child would walk, bathe and tarry. They are too numerous to count. . . . Dear Kaleleokalani [Flight of the Heavenly Chief] . . . you would say, 'Greetings, Kapiʻolani, my companion sharing the care of the child, wearied from work.' I did not think tribulation would lie between that caring and this present sorrow. Kaleleokalani, what grief for my chief who is not far or lost to you. Pity, what pity for my lord, the sight of whom stirs grief in me. What pity for my traveling companion about these islands surrounded by ocean.
> God's mercy is eternal,
> Kapiʻolani[6]

The queen replied:

> "Dear Kapiʻolani, my companion in the caring of my son. You were my son's favorite, your chest must be filled with hurt. You were our third companion in the sun, on the rough ʻāʻā lava, in the wind, on the sea, at meals and in hunger. Beloved are the plains, beloved is this place, our seas, everywhere. Oh, my son, my child, alas!
> Kaleleokalani.

This loving exchange merits special mention here because of a story by Helena Allen, the biographer of King Kalākaua, that Queen Emma "blamed Kapiolani for having 'allowed the king near the child' to douse him with cold water" and that Kapiʻolani also "took the blame with great grief."[7] How does one reconcile the story and the letters? It could be argued that, if the story were true, neither woman would have expressed such sentiments of mutual love and respect and that Kapiʻolani would not have been welcome at Hānaiakamalama either by the queen or by her mother. However, it could also be argued that the story is true and that the two had forgiven each other and that the exchange of letters is evidence of their reconciliation.

Ups and Downs

After the royal couple returned to Honolulu in early April, 1863, the king fell sick again. The *Polynesian* said he was "considerably indisposed."[8] He had to be operated on but recovered nicely. Prince Lot, in a letter to Governor Paul Nahaolelua on Maui, wrote that the king promised him that he would "be better in the future."[9] For the next few months the king did improve and took a more active part in the business of state, as evidenced by his attending and presiding at all of the privy council meetings.

Although in the interest of his health the king avoided most ceremonial functions, he quickly made an exception in May for the birthday of his son's intended godmother, Queen Victoria. The royal party attended an early choral celebration of the Blessed Sacrament at the temporary cathedral to offer up special prayers for England and its queen. They later called in person on Mr. Synge, the British commissioner, and that same evening attended a dinner in honor of the event. In addition to his personal participation, the king provided a 21-gun salute (using his own artillery), ordered government to fly flags at the palace, the governor's residence, and Punchbowl, among other places, and generally encouraged his subjects to make the day an auspicious one. Apparently all the foreign dignitaries followed suit except for the American commissioner who failed to render proper diplomatic courtesies.[10]

While most of his subjects respected the king's spending less time on his social and ceremonial functions, some complained that he was spending too much time on his church activities. For example, he helped the bishop arrange a building contract for a new Anglican procathedral at a cost of $6,500 on the lot that he had donated.[11] He assisted the bishop in establishing a new Anglican mission in Lahaina. He and the queen attended Sunday services regularly, frequently attending the early morning six o'clock worship. On Sunday mornings he breakfasted with the queen and others on the palace verandah and always concluded with prayers from the Hawaiian liturgy. He often brought little children to the church to be baptized, which required spending some time in instructing them. They both also sought and brought couples to the altar to be sealed in marriage. Indeed, to the dismay of some Protestants, the royal couple were the most effective missionaries of the Anglican church.

Taro and Rice Cultivating

In June 1863 the king ordered the work of cleaning out the weeds and bulrushes and the planting of "taro tops" to begin in his *lo'i* (taro patch) at Keokea in Waikīkī. These fields were the ones that he and other chiefs had already begun cultivating in 1856, partly as a demonstration of the government's commitment to support the traditional taro culture.[12] It is not clear whether this time he actually stepped in the *lo'i* and did some physical labor as he had done in previous years; for if he did, his health had greatly improved.

Queen Emma was also growing taro on her own lands. A letter from her mother Grace to Emma describes the work in her taro patches at Hānaiakamalama and other properties. She wrote: "Kauhola is working on the upland irrigated patches. The ones seaward have not been worked. Those and the ones at Pu'unui and Pauoa were left for Kalaikau folks to do because they did not come to cook the taro. Twice they were called and they didn't come. . . . When the chiefs return, then it will be done. They are just sitting around now, not farming." And in another passage Grace stated: "Lapaula's men are working on the patch Kalalaha had told you was a rice patch. The work is done except for the planting of the taro tops, then it'll be finished. . . . The men came to cook the taro. They just came to get the taro tops for the patch at Niolopa. Kauhola folks are presently turning over the soil and at the same time planting the taro tops."[13]

The mention of "a rice patch" suggests that the queen may have ventured into cultivating rice as well. If so, she was planting what many other landowners were at the time. "Rice fever" had swept the islands and "everybody and his wife" were into planting rice as a cash crop. In fact, so many taro patches had been converted into rice fields that the *Pacific Commercial Advertiser* was prompted to ask: "Where is our taro to come from?"[14] This was no doubt one reason why the king had promoted the taro project in Waikīkī. Ironically, the king had supported the initial experiments in growing rice as an economic measure to replace the lost revenues due to the collapse of the once prosperous whaling industry. In fact, Prince Lot himself had planted a large tract of land in rice at his Moanalua estate and "even went so far as to pull up and destroy large patches of growing taro to plant rice." By 1863 rice was being grown everywhere, including Nu'uanu Valley where the queen's farm lands were located.[15]

"Emmaville"

One of the kingdom's largest rice-growing areas was in Hanalei where Robert Wyllie had renamed his estate "Princeville" in honor of *Ka Haku O Hawai'i*. In August he decided to name the land of the former Titcomb estate, which he had just purchased, after the queen. He described the setting and the moment of his inspiration in a letter to her dated August 2, 1863:

> Madam:
> While sitting in my verandah along with Monsieur de Varigny and M. Bourgoyne on the evening of the 31st and while talking about Titcomb's Estate, I said to him that it was no longer to be so called, but to be known by the name of 'Emmaville.' The word was scarcely out of my mouth when up blazed a high bright light, seemingly in the very centre of the houses. M. de Varigny thought that as I had ordered the old sugar houses on the brink of the river to be illuminated with lamps, that they had taken fire; but I replied that I believed it to be a Bonfire volunteered by Captain Morse; and so it turned out to be.[16]

Because this offer came from a man who was absolutely devoted to the royal family, the queen was no doubt appreciative. But nothing seemed to have come of the idea—perhaps "Princeville" stood better alone.

The Second Flight

As they approached the month that marked the first anniversary of the death of *Ka Haku O Hawai'i,* the king and queen had been considering how best to memorialize their lost prince. In the evening of the day of the prince's passing, they called on Archdeacon Mason; they were accompanied by six native children including the "foster-brother" of the prince. They informed him that the children should be educated at their expense in commemoration of their son.[17] It was a poignant and loving gesture, but it did not seem to diminish the king's grief. As one who saw him daily put it, "If ever I saw a broken-hearted man, it's the King."[18]

A short while later, King Alexander Liholiho and Queen Emma missed serious injury in another carriage accident. Their horses ran away and were heading for a steep bank when the carriage was upended, and they were thrown to the ground. Luckily, they suffered only a few bruises and sprained ankles. Thankful for their narrow escape, the king said, "When we have received signal mercies, there is no higher form by which we can express our gratitude than the sacrifice of praise and thanksgiving."[19] They requested the bishop to include them in his evening service and the next morning received the holy communion at his hands.[20] Whether the shock of the accident had any effect on the king's already delicate health is uncertain.

Although King Liholiho did not appear well, he continued to perform some ceremonial duties, such as receiving a new diplomatic agent or the commander and officers of a newly arrived warship. On November 2, for example, he received the new French commissioner, accompanied by de Varigny, in a palace audience, although he had been suffering for several days from one of his attacks of chronic asthma.[21] The king told de Varigny he planned to give a banquet on November 28 in honor of the 20th anniversary of the restoration of Hawaiian independence and then leave afterward for Hawai'i where he hoped to recuperate.

According to Bishop Staley, on Sunday, November 15, 1863, he was called to give the Holy Communion to Their Majesties in the palace because the king was "too unwell to be at church." But he was sufficiently well to attend the evening Litany at the church the next Sunday evening. The bishop stated, "I was struck with the earnest and devout manner in which he joined in the responses."[22] Earlier that day, the king had told one of his attendants that "he could not live long," but apparently others did not share his premonitions.[23]

The king had been suffering from diarrhea for several days and was quite weak, but he insisted that the "Independence Day" reception and banquet proceed as scheduled. On the appointed evening the palace, colorfully decorated and brightly lit, was filled with a large crowd of local and foreign dignitaries. No one was surprised to see that the king was not present, for everyone knew that he was ailing. Instead the queen received the presentations of official and private guests and spoke kind words to all who approached her. But after an hour, she disappeared to the bedside of her ailing husband. That is where she spent the next two days.

On the morning of the 30th, alone with the king, Emma watched his face as he spoke to her in a low voice. Because the court physicians had not detected any life-threatening symptoms, she had no cause for alarm. But suddenly he began to have difficulty breathing. She thought that a spasm might have caused him to lose his breath or that he had fainted. Instantly she placed her lips on his and with her breath tried to restore his breathing. She summoned for help but it was too late. At 9:00 a.m. on November 30, 1863, King Kamehameha IV died in her arms.[24] It was St. Andrew's Day in the Anglican faith.

Bishop Staley, who was one of those summoned, wrote: "I arrived a few minutes too late. . . . When she saw all her efforts were of no avail, she begged me to pray. Most of the members of the Royal Family were present, and we all knelt down and implored our Heavenly Father to grant us resignation to His will, and strength to endure with meekness the sudden and unexpected chastisement. We were all overwhelmed with grief."[25]

Prince Lot was out of town and unaware that his brother's life was in danger. Wyllie, who was the only minister present, immediately sent word to Lot and summoned his other ministerial colleagues. Lot hastened to the palace, complaining bitterly about the physicians who did not know enough to foresee his brother's demise.

Later that day Lot met with the privy council whose first action was to query the queen as to whether she was pregnant. The question was awkward but necessary because it was reasonable to expect that the queen would have wanted another child, and as long as that expectation existed, no decision on succession could be made. In the absence of a direct heir, Prince Lot was the rightful successor to the throne. When the disconsolate queen said she was not pregnant, the council was free to announce a successor.[26] At 3:00 p.m. on November 30, 1863, Prince Lot was proclaimed King Kamehameha V in what was the quickest act of succession in the history of the Hawaiian monarchy.

The body of King Kamehameha IV was placed in the throne room for public viewing. Several thousand mourners from all over the Island came hour after hour crowding into the palace. De Varigny described the scene: "Both night and day the lamentations and the chanting continued, sometimes monotonously plaintive, sometimes piercing and shrill. It is impossible to describe the bizarre spectacle enacted all night long . . . [as] natives filed past, row after surging row, while others rested themselves outside, scattered about and squatting on the grass . . . fantastically illuminated by the hundreds of flaming torches held aloft by retainers of the royal household."[27]

All the while Emma remained at her dead husband's side, bowed down in silent disbelief that the man she so passionately loved had been taken away in his prime, not yet even thirty.

On December 3, the privy council met and appropriated $10,000 for the funeral; at the same time it approved the construction of a new royal mausoleum. The decision was made to postpone the funeral until the mausoleum was completed.[28] Construction started immediately and was based on the plans for a chapel-like structure in the shape of a cross drawn by architect Theodore Heuck with the assistance of Queen Emma and Bishop Staley. With the use of prison labor to mine coral blocks in Kaka'ako, the west wing was built first. When it was completed on February 1, 1864, Kamehameha V issued a proclamation dedicating the plot of ground, known as Mauna'ala and the mausoleum to be "forever set apart from all common and profane uses" for the royal dead.

Throughout this entire time of nearly sixty days the casket remained in the throne room and the queen beside it. Staley states: "The Queen sits almost incessantly by the coffin. She has prayers in the room night and morning, in the Hawaiian language, so that all present may understand, taken from the Book of Common Prayer; and I read to her from the Psalms or other consolatory passages of Holy Scriptures every day. It is beautiful to see how she seeks for consolation only in God. . . . Among all the classes of people there is one common feeling of sympathy with her in this hour of her anguish. For by her works of charity and mercy, she had endeared herself to the hearts of all."[29]

At Mauna'ala

The funeral took place on Wednesday morning, February 3, 1864, in the small temporary cathedral, which was packed with members of the royal family, officials, clergy, dignitaries, and fifty-two choristers. The bier was raised six feet from the floor, surrounded on all sides by steps; at its head knelt the widowed queen. With the exception of the Anglican Creed (Gloria In Excelsis and Agnus Dei), the entire ceremony was in Hawaiian, from the opening chant to the Lesson, the Holy Communion, the two chorales, and the prayers.

At the conclusion of the service, a procession was formed to accompany the body to the new mausoleum, one mile away. It had rained heavily the night before, but on this day the sun shone brightly. The streets were lined with anxious spectators, observing the funeral cortege as it wended its way to Nu'uanu in almost absolute silence except for the guns on Punchbowl, which were fired every five minutes. The funeral procession was the longest the town had ever witnessed. It included 800 children, who, with their teachers, had walked into Honolulu that morning, many from a long distance "to testify their love and regret, and their gratitude to the memory of a prince to whose heart their cause was ever the nearest."[30] Behind the hearse riding in a crepe-draped carriage were Emma and her mother Grace. At Mauna'ala, in a brief ceremony, King Kamehameha IV's body was laid to rest.

At midnight the next evening, the queen went through the experience again as the small casket of the little prince was taken from its temporary tomb and placed upon a bier borne by six pall bearers. Then, followed by the royal family, friends, and retainers, and with the prince's own Artillery Corps serving as torchbearers, the queen led the mournful

At the age of twenty-seven Queen Emma was left a childless widow. In 1863—barely one year after the death of their son—King Kamehameha IV passed away after a brief life characterized by significant accomplishments as well as by profound tragedies. He was not yet thirty.

cortege to Mauna'ala one more time. And there the tiny casket was placed beside the larger one.[31] For days the grief-stricken Emma slept in the damp and badly ventilated vault beside the bodies of her husband Liholiho and her son Albert. During the day she remained in a tent erected near the entrance to the mausoleum. Lot, his father Kekūanao'a, Bishop Staley, and Wyllie, concerned for her health, entreated her to stay at Rosebank (the name of Wyllie's home) nearby, but she declined, saying "she must remain night and day near the tomb for at least a fortnight."[32] Eventually Emma did accept his invitation and stayed at Rosebank for a time in a "castellated chamber" overlooking the valley. It had been built especially for her.[33]

For the second time, the queen took on a new name. Instead of Kaleleokalani, the Flight of the Heavenly Chief, she would henceforth be known as Kaleleonālani. The singular form *ka* or "the" was replaced by the plural form *nā* to signify the flight of the two heavenly chiefs, her son and her husband.

A Queen's Lament

The eulogy written by Abraham Fornander about King Kamehameha IV was a deeply felt and poignant farewell to "the brightest and most intelligent among a bright and intelligent people—the readiest thinker in the country—the leader in every council—the promoter of every good work—the true friend—the Prince given to hospitality—the lover of literature—the fosterer of manly exercises—the graceful and admired in society. . . . That his talents were brilliant, that his feelings were keen, his appearance elegant, his conversation sparkling and bright, and his sorrows unfathomable, we all know."[34]

King Kamehameha IV's accomplishments were many: maintaining the independence of the kingdom, spurring the remarkable growth of rice, sugar, coffee, and other products, and improving public education and interisland transportation services. However, the one act, according to the *Pacific Commercial Advertiser,* "which will place his name and that of his noble Queen Emma in the letters of gold on the pages of his country's history" was the founding of Queen's Hospital. "Well do we remember seeing him in 1859 going alone and unattended through our streets, from house to house, and from store to store, with his memorandum book and how the addition of $50 or $100 to his subscription list brightened up his countenance and cheered him on . . . you [may] remember his quiet, earnest bearing, as he asked you to 'allow him the honor of setting your name down for any amount you might choose to give,' accompanying his request by a genial smile or by some lively remark. As long as that coral building stands and serves as a hospital, so long will the names of Kamehameha IV and Queen Emma be cherished and venerated by all their people."[35]

The most poignant goodbye was Queen Emma's own *kanikau* (lament), which she composed in December 1863 and entitled "He Kanikau no ka Mōʻi ʻIolani Kamehameha IV" or "A Lament for King Kamehameha IV."

Kuu kane—e kuu kane hoi,	My husband—O my husband,
Kuu kane i ke kehau anu o Kaala,	My husband in the cold dew of Kaala,
Hoolue iho la ilalo o Haleauau,	Dripping down upon Haleauau,
Ke kini ka kehau anu o uka o Kanehoa—e!	Countless drops of dew upland of Kanehoa—O!
Kuu hoa, he hea noʻu i ka makani kilihau, kiliopu;	My companion, mine is a call to the cold winds carrying the fine misty rain
Ka pue, ke wai o ka mauna,	Crouching in the cold of mountain streams,
Ka *mauna pali makai o Pueohulunui—e—huli,*	Mountainous cliffs on the seaward side of Pueohulunui that turns
Ke huli wale nei au ia oe—e.	I turn to you, searching—O
Oia wahi aloha ia,	This love.
Na—wai hoi ka ole o ke aloha—?	For whom shall this love not be?
Na—na no—e.	For him.
Kuu kane—e kuu kane hoi,	My husband—O my husband,
Kuu kane mai ka wa heu ole o maua	My husband from the time of his beardless youth
Mai ka ua popo kapa o Nuuanu,	From the popo kapa rain of Nuuanu when one rolls his clothing under his armpits into a ball to keep it dry,
E ahai ana ma ke kua o pulu i ka ua haao—e,	Following the ridge-back (trail) drenched in the rain of Haao—O
Ke lele ae la maluna o Leleaanae,	That leaps upon Leleaanae,
Lele ka ua lele pu no me ka makani;	The rain that leaps together with the wind when it flies,
E lele poo ana ka wai o Kahookane,	When the waterfall of Kahookane leaps headfirst,
Kuu Haku mai ka wai noho pu iloko o ka hale,	My lord who valued the streams of his household,
Oia wahi aloha ia	This love,
Na—wai hoi ka ole o ke aloha—e	For whom shall this love not be?
Na—na no—e.	For him.
Kuu kane—e kuu Kane hoi,	My husband—O my husband,
Kuu kane mai ka makani hoeu o ka aina,	My husband from the wind stirring up the land,

E ahe mai ana i ka ili o ke kai,
Halialia aloha mai ana ia'u ka maka
o ka Opua—e

Kuhi no au o oe ia,

He kane auanei he hoa pili no ke anu,

He hoa ukali no ke alanui

A maua e alo ai i ka ehukai—a!
Oia wahi aloha ia,
Na—wai hoi ka ole o ke aloha—e,
Na—na no—e.

Kuu kane—e kuu kane hoi,
Kuu kane mai ka la lailai o Kona,

Mai ka makani ka lehua o Lehuakona,

O Kona ia o ke kai malino a
Ehu—e!
Ke ala a Ehu, ke ala a kaua i hele ai

I ke ao i ka po, powehiwehi i ka ua na
ulu a weli,

He weliweli he maluhia i ke aloha ia oe;
Ia oe, ia oe e Kalopelekei i
ka la—e!
Oia wahi aloha ia,
Na—wai hoi ke ole o ke aloha—e?
Na—na no—e.

Kuu kane—e kuu kane hoi,
Kuu kane mai ka ua Kipuupuu anu o
Waimea,
E nanahu ana i ka ili o ke kanaka,
He ahi ke kapa a mehameha ai ko laila
kini—e;
He kini Peepakaiaulu pa makani,

Kuu kane mai ka ua malanalana,
Lana kuu aloha, lana me he wai la,
Ka waiwai nui no ia e noho nei o ke
aloha ia oe.
Oia wahi aloha ia,
Na—wai hoi ka ole o ke aloha—e?
Na—na no—e.

Blowing over the surface of the sea,
Bringing the fond memory of love
conjured in the eyes of the
clouds—O
That gesture to me as though they
were you,
You were just a husband, one to
cling to in the cold
A companion for me to follow
on the pathway
Where we faced the fine sea spray—
This love,
For whom shall this love not be?
For him.

My husband—O my husband,
My husband from the calm days
of Kona,
From the wind of the lehua season
of Lehuakona in the Milky Way
O Kona of the calm sea of
Ehu the king!
The path of Ehu, the path that
we both travelled
In the day, in the night, when
the sudden showers obscured
our vision and I was afraid
Fear that was assuaged by love of you;
(Love) of you, chief prized in
the sun—O!
This love,
For whom shall this love not be?
For him.

My husband—O my husband,
My husband from the pummeling
rain of Waimea,
Biting the skin of man.
Tapa is kindling for fire when
people there are alone
The many who hide from the cold
touch of the wind,
My husband from the light rain
My love flows, flows with the streams,
The streams of love for you that made
life worth living here
This love,
For whom shall this love not be?
For him.

Kuu kane—e kuu kane hoi,	My husband—O my husband,
Kuu kane mai ka makani o Kamaaa,	My husband of the Kamaaa wind
E wehe aku ana i ka lau o ka ulu o Lele	Opening the leaves of the breadfruit trees of Lele
Lele aku la oe i ka aina kuahiwi lau o Wailuku,	You have flown to the land of mountain ridges in Wailuku,
Ke hoomalumalumai la ke aloha oia wahi iaʻu,	The love of this place overwhelms me,
Iaʻu ka u, me ka minamina ia e noho	For me is the grief, for me is regret that remains,
E apaia nei au e ke aloha me he wai liula la,	Love that appears to be the mirage of a stream there detains me,
Me he wailiula—la ke ahi o kula—e!	That heat of Kula glittering like a mirage of water—O
Oia wahi aloha ia,	This love,
Na—wai hoi ka ole o ke aloha—e?	For whom shall this love not be?
Na—na no—e	For him.
Kuu kane—e kuu kane hoi,	My husband—O my husband,
Kuu kane mai ka wai ula Iliahi o Waimea,	My husband of the streams of fiery red surface in Waimea,
Wai nonoula a ka ua Kapaahoa,	Streams colored red by the Kapaahoa rain
He hoa aina ke aloha no ke kanaka—a;	Love is the country companion of a man,
He kanaka ka hala ai a ke Kinau,	Man is the fruit of the hala to be eaten by the kinaʻu eel when it falls,
I kiina ʻku ka Lauae e ka Lehuamakanoe,	He is the lauaʻe fern sought by the lehua-in-the-mist,
Noenoe me he uwahi la i kuu waimaka,	It is misting like smoke through my tears,
Ka waimaka e hanini aku nei—la,	Tears outpouring.
Oia wahi aloha ia,	This love
Na—wai hoi ka ole o ke aloha—e?	For whom shall this love not be?
Na—na no—e.[36]	For him.

14

New Love, Old Grief

The accession of Kamehameha V to the throne seemed almost perfunctory because of the speed with which it took place. Even after the long-delayed funeral, there was none of the pageantry of investiture that occurred in 1855 when his brother was enthroned. A few celebrations took place, of which the most spectacular was in Hanalei where a large bonfire was lit on top of Mount Rooke (Makana); instead of the traditional lighted embers being thrown to the winds, twenty-five immense rockets were fired.[1] But, all in all, the beginning was sober and unfestive, which appeared to be in keeping with the character of Lot Kamehameha.

The New King

Seemingly imperturbable, stony, and impersonal, Lot's attitude was partly forged by the lifelong campaign to which he dedicated himself: the preservation of the cultural identity and political sovereignty of his kingdom. His brother had championed the same causes, but Lot was far more blunt and uncompromising. It is said he was more Hawaiian in nature, as displayed in his active promotion of the ancient hula and chanting, his acceptance of certain beliefs and practices of the *kāhuna*, and his outspoken insistence on practicing traditional values. Though passionate about values such as hard work, Lot, together with his brother Liholiho, was especially frank in pointing out the faults of the common people such as indolence and excessive fondness for riding horseback and attending hula as dancers or spectators.[2] When he and Liholiho addressed the Royal Hawaiian Agricultural Society in 1856, he spoke bluntly to a native crowd:

> I hope you will remember what I say, that you must not think great numbers make great wealth; that is the first point, and the second is that if you want to make money by keeping fowls or pigs, or goats, or sheep, or cattle, you must work and look after them every day, from the 1st of January to the 31st of December.
>
> See what a large work there is before us. The Hawaiians have got to conquer the enemy which of all others is most difficult to subdue. They have got to conquer themselves. They must say we have got the land and climate, government and everything in our favor, but they are all rendered useless and unprofitable by our laziness. A lazy man is no better than without any arms.
>
> Some of you are so caught up with laziness that there is nothing to hope for; you will never be better than you are; you will never be richer or more important in the eyes of other people. If you ever get any money, it will be left you by somebody in his will—you will not make it.

Reiterating what his younger brother had said at that same meeting, he went on: "Suppose you have been working in your kalo patch from morning till night and when you go home to supper some good-for-nothing fellow comes and sits down to eat up what you have labored for to fill the stomach of your wife and children? Why can't you say to him, 'When I was sweating in the sun and bending my back till it ached, or carrying hulis [taro plantings] on my shoulder till it swelled up, where were you? Excuse me, but you had better go somewhere else to eat'."[3]

King Kamehameha V, however, reserved most of his energy to fight his worst enemies, which he labeled the "power-hungry" and "greedy foreigners," the "self-righteous hypocrites" who hid behind the thin veneer of religion, the anti-monarchist republicans, and the annexationists. Thus the skirmishing began even before he settled into the palace. Some challenged his right to the throne, while others opposed his ministerial appointments, particularly Wyllie and de Varigny who were less than sympathetic toward American interests.

His enemies reserved most of their ammunition, however, for their attack on the king's first major move—amending the Constitution of 1852. In fact, as king, Lot refused to swear an oath to uphold it. He objected to many of its provisions such as universal suffrage, which he thought was beyond the political capacity of the Hawaiian people at that point in their development; he also objected to the office of *kuhina nui* or co-ruler (more powerful than a premier), which diluted the power of the sovereign. When he issued a proclamation in May calling for the election of members to a Constitutional Convention, the *Pacific Commercial Advertiser* denounced it as an "imbecilic attempt" at a "coup d'état."[4] When the convention met and failed to produce a suitable document after two months of feuding, King Lot abrogated the old Constitution and announced: "I will give you a Constitution."

Queen Emma was a supporter of the Hawaiian cause and admired Lot's fierce devotion to it, but she saw clearly the differences in personalities and styles of the two brothers. Her Alex was like a hawk: smooth and trim, nimble and quick, creative, brilliant, and impulsive, while Lot was a bull: massive, plodding but powerful, shrewd, decisive and ruthless, relentless and coldly passionate. She always preferred the soaring *'io.*

The Solicitous Lot

As king, Lot was genuinely solicitous of his brother's attractive widow. One of his first actions upon his succession in 1863 was to invite the grieving queen to continue to reside in the palace.[5] With the assurance of his sympathy and affection, he also placed the royal residence at Hulihe'e in Kona at her disposal. Before the year was over he enacted a law giving the queen an annual stipend of $6,000 to enable her "to maintain a style of living suitable to her station and dignity."[6] It was more than a kind gesture: Alexander Liholiho died intestate and in debt to the tune of $42,000. Wyllie worried that Queen Emma would be left in circumstances of extreme poverty.[7] He had also given her the additional title of "Countess of Halawa," which the privy council subsequently Hawaiianized to *Wahine Ali'i o Hālawa.*[8] (At the time Hālawa was owned by her mother Grace.)

For her part, Emma was understanding of and sensitive to Lot's feelings. She was well aware of his aborted betrothal in 1850 to Bernice Pauahi whom he had loved from childhood and for whom his devotion continued, even after her marriage to the banker Charles R. Bishop. She still remembered the hurt and embarrassment he suffered in February 1863 when he was prevented from adopting the newly born child of Princess Ruth, which he had desperately wanted because of its Kamehameha blood.[9]

Now as king the need for an heir was even greater, as was his need for a queen. His subjects urged him to marry in order to guarantee an undisturbed line of succession to the throne. De Varigny, serving as his minister of finance, had often talked with Lot about the importance of marriage particularly from a dynastic point of view; he wrote: "He did not positively reject the idea, but simply dismissed it with a laugh, urging me to find him a wife who combined the attributes necessary for his happiness, asserting his preference meanwhile for a bachelor's style of life."[10]

As a bachelor he had had a mistress for years, the chiefess Kamaipuupaa from Moloka'i. She was a powerful *kahuna* or healer highly esteemed by the people. Although branded as a "sorceress" by his missionary detractors who spoke contemptuously of her as the "King's mistress," she was described by one American observer as "magnetic, intelligent, and adept to a wonderful degree." The fact was, however, that Lot had taken her to love but not to wed.[11]

Given his extremely limited choices, if Lot truly wanted a queen, who would have been a natural choice? The young, handsome, intelligent widow of his brother, the Dowager Queen Emma—who was still capable of bearing children—was his only real choice. He had not yet asked her, but in time he would.

Emma Shares Her Grief with Queen Victoria

Queen Emma's profound grief is revealed in a letter she wrote on February 14, 1864, to Queen Victoria:

> Madam,
>
> My heart is very, very heavy while I make known to Your Majesty that God has visited me with that great trouble which in your kind and consoling letter you said you hoped I might be spared. On the 30th November my Husband, of whose danger I had never entertained one thought, expired suddenly, almost while in the act of speaking to me, and it was a long while before they could make me believe that what I saw was death and that he had really left me alone for the remainder of my life. This blow has been very hard on me. It seems truly as yesterday that we lost our beautiful boy Albert, Your Majesty's Godson, of whom I am afraid we were too fond and proud, and from whom we looked for such great things, flattering ourselves that his very name gave an assurance of his becoming as he grew up, every thing that is good and true and Prince-like. Madame, I know you will feel for me, for you have undergone this terrible ordeal, but you have children to remind you of their illustrious Father and in their talents and virtues you must seem to have some thing of him left to you still.

> While thinking of your grief, long before this grief came upon me, I have often thanked God that you have that alleviation. It is not so with me, I am desolate altogether, with nothing left but the hope of a meeting hereafter.

Six months later (it took at least three months for a letter to travel from London to Honolulu or six months for an exchange of letters) Emma received a heartfelt reply from Queen Victoria.

> Windsor Castle
> June 14, 1864
>
> My dear Friend,
>
> Your kind letter has deeply affected me, and I thank you much for the volume which accompanied it.
>
> My bleeding heart can truly sympathize with you in your terrible desolation. A dear & promising only Child and a beloved Husband have been taken from you within two Years! Time does not heal the really stricken heart! The only consolation I have found in a sorrow which seems only to encrease is in living on in spirit with the beloved ones whom God took in love to a better World, in the certainty of an everlasting Union hereafter!
>
> Till then we can but bear & submit & strive to fit ourselves for that blessed future, by following the example of our beloved ones.
>
> May God give you strength to bear up under your heavy affliction.
>
> I remain,
> Your Majesty's affectionate & unhappy friend,
> Victoria R.

(The phrase "unhappy friend" was often used by Queen Victoria after the death of her husband and consort Prince Albert.)[12]

Plans for Travel Abroad

Minister de Varigny, who was an eyewitness to the events of this time, wrote that "For many months Queen Emma had suffered from nervous depression, so severe that her physical health was threatened."[13] Her physicians urged that she rest and travel, and Wyllie and Bishop Staley specifically recommended England and Europe.[14] The idea was not new; Emma and Alexander Liholiho had already planned such a trip. In her letter to Queen Victoria, she wrote that "It was the purpose of my husband to visit with me England, and several portions of the Continent during the summer of this year, when we hoped to have had an opportunity to thank Your Majesty in person for all the kindness and sympathy you have extended to us—but that was not to be."[15]

Coincidentally, while Queen Emma was writing to Queen Victoria, Lady Franklin was writing to Queen Emma urging her to visit England for the sake of assisting the Anglican mission.[16] Before Emma could answer her invitation, Wyllie had written Lady Franklin and informed her that Queen Emma was showing evidence of improved spirits. He wrote: "She inquired if the Bishop had read to me a letter from his Commissary naming Lady Franklin as the best friend of the Mission in all London. I said he had. She was greatly pleased with that intelligence, for she is heart and soul in all the good the Bishop is doing upon which she believes that the salvation of the Hawaiian people depends. And it is my belief that if she could only persuade herself that her presence in London would induce the nobility to subscribe, so as to raise a fund adequate to the wants of the Mission, she would undertake the voyage perhaps under the Bishop's care. But this step I could not advise, until it be ascertained what pecuniary provision is to be made for her."[17]

Wyllie tells us in a letter he penned to Lady Franklin in late May that Emma was still in "morbid" grief. He related how he was about to leave with the king for Princeville to begin the "Royal Progress," that is, Lot's island-wide tour to win popular support for amending the Constitution of 1852, and he had hoped the queen would accompany them. "I wished the Queen to go with us, but she cannot yet be weaned from the morbid desire of being always near to the mausoleum so as to make frequent visits to it."[18]

In any event, Queen Emma was quite ready to accept Lady Franklin's invitation to visit England and to be her houseguest. She wrote:

> My dear and good friend Lady Franklin,
>
> I thank you from the bottom of my soul for your kind letter of Feb. 15th which I received ten days ago. I cannot say enough for your many kindness to me. Having great respect to your opinion, that my visit to England would benefit the Episcopal Mission, the King and I are concerting together seriously in what way to accomplish it; but as yet nothing has been finally decided.
>
> Mr. Wyllie would gladly accompany me, but at present the King cannot spare him. Perhaps his Lordship Bishop Staley would go with me, I look upon him as the best conductor that I could have. My motives in visiting London are not for display or enjoyment; they are with your kind assistance and the blessing of God to save if possible my dying people. From the great good already done by the Episcopal

> Mission, I believe that to support that mission is one of the best means to save and render virtuous the Hawaiian people. It would be cruel and ungenerous in me to accept your kind and romantic offer to come out from England with Miss Cracroft merely to accompany me to England—for that offer words cannot express the gratitude of my heart.
>
> This is all I can say to you at present, for there are many points connected with my visit that require serious consultations and the King and I have not yet fully made up our own minds, but whenever my voyage is fully determined upon I shall take care to apprise you, repeating my warmest gratitude to you and with my love to Miss Cracroft.
>
> I remain my dear Lady Franklin, yours ever affectionately, Emma[19]

Her letter omitted two important points: One is that the queen did not mention the Queen's Hospital when she stated that the purpose of her mission was "to save if possible my dying people." She must have believed that she could improve the lot of her people through religious faith and Christian morality as well as by medicine. The second point not mentioned is that she was going to England specifically to raise money to build a cathedral, which was intended to be a memorial to her late husband.

The king and his advisers agreed that the queen should accept Lady Franklin's invitation, but when Wyllie informed Earl Russell, the British foreign minister, of Queen Emma's wish to visit England, Russell, speaking for Queen Victoria, advised strongly against the visit because of the "great risk" of being exposed to the harsh climate that "has been proved to be fatally injurious to natives of the Sandwich Islands."[20] When Queen Emma persisted in her decision to make the journey, the British government relented.

Wyllie then asked the British to allow Mr. Synge to accompany the queen on the voyage and to send a British warship to convey the queen and her party to Panama and then on to London. The British agreed and became, in effect, sponsors of the queen's trip. What began as a private matter by a former queen for her own well-being and for the Anglican mission became an affair of state.

Concern over the Queen's Visit

By November 1864 the queen's planned visit to England was public news. It did not sit well with certain American missionary and commercial interests who saw it as yet another event leading to the erosion and eventual destruction of American influence in Hawai'i. They were still seething with anger that the Constitution of 1852 was abrogated in August, even though none of the *Pacific Commercial Advertiser*'s predictions of "popular outbreaks, buildings burned, murders . . . civil war" had materialized. The bold and strong-willed Kamehameha V had won his first battle, and the defeated foreigners could only bide their time and wait.

On November 1, the king and many other notables attended the twenty-sixth birthday of Victoria Kamāmalu; the event had been declared a national holiday. A great feast was held at the residence of Prince William Lunalilo for 800 guests, most of whom were members of the *'Ahahui Ka'ahumanu* or Ka'ahumanu Society, which Victoria had organized to nurse the victims of the smallpox epidemic and to help bury the dead. The women were "all gaily dressed in the height of European fashion. It was a sight not often witnessed," reported the *Pacific Commercial Advertiser.*[21] In the evening the customary ball was held at Victoria's residence.

Among the notables was the American Minister James McBride who regarded the government of Kamehameha V as anti-American. He was opposed to the growing British influence of what he described as the two "English parasites": Commissioner Synge and Bishop Staley. In fact, he thought that Kamehameha IV had died "from the effects of most depraved appetites, stimulated and kept to their full tension" by Synge and Staley. McBride also believed that his thirty-five-year-old brother Lot, in following the same course, was liable at any time to die as suddenly as his predecessor. When that happened, he hoped to see as queen the heir presumptive, Princess Victoria, whom he viewed as a woman of "considerable mind" and as definitely pro-American; he viewed Queen Emma as definitely pro-British.[22] McBride's hopes and schemes turned to nothing, however, as Lot would reign for nine more years and Victoria would die within the year.

As 1864 came to an end, King Kamehameha V enjoyed the overwhelming support of his people who were caught in a fervor of patriotism that was probably unmatched since the restoration of Hawaiian sovereignty by the British in 1843. This year-end should have been one to celebrate. When the king's birthday occurred in December, Governor John Dominis and his wife Lili'uokalani hosted a ball that was attended by the queen and many others despite a prevailing hurricane—perhaps a portent for the kingdom of the times to come.[23]

15

Travels Abroad

A "concourse of spectators" gathered at the Honolulu harbor on May 6, 1865, to say goodbye to the queen and her party. Some Hawaiian spectators, remembering the fate of King Kamehameha II and his queen while in London, wailed pitifully thinking she might never return.[1]

Accompanying Queen Emma were William Synge, appointed by the British Foreign Office to act as Emma's escort; Charles G. Hopkins, the kingdom's minister of interior, who happened to be a bachelor, appointed by Kamehameha V to be her secretary and aide; her loyal manservant John Welsh, a Canadian; and the Reverend William Hoapili Kaauwai, the first Episcopal deacon ordained in Hawai'i, to be her chaplain, and his wife, Mary Ann Kiliwehi, to be her lady in waiting. Also traveling with the queen were two young school girls, Kealakai and Palema, daughters of chiefs, whom the queen was taking to England to be educated.[2] In addition, there was the English Sister Catherine Chambers who helped to establish St. Cross School for girls in Lahaina.[3]

En route to England the queen stopped in Acapulco where she was welcomed by the governor, "a nice old gentleman, exceedingly courteous, but rather infirm," she wrote. Acapulco, according to her description, was dilapidated and dirty, with "thin looking people not unlike our poorest examples."[4] They also spent a short time in Panama City where the *Panama Star and Herald* described the queen as being "very interesting, not to say handsome in personal appearance, and . . . exceedingly popular with all classes and nationalities, for she delights in exercising a quiet, unassuming benevolence."[5] There they took a train to cross the isthmus from whence they boarded the Royal Mail Steamer, the *Tasmanian,* which took them to England.

On the way they stopped at St. Thomas where the queen was royally welcomed by its Danish Governor. She described the scene in her letter to Kamehameha V: "The Governor waited on me, and kindly asked us on shore to his mansion . . . he sent his boat off for us . . . on landing, there was a guard of honor placed on the pier, their band playing the Danish national air, amidst deafening shouts of the people who crowded to the water's edge. We found the Governor's carriages waiting to take us up [to his hilltop residence] . . . where we were welcomed most warmly by his lady, a most charming person . . . a most agreeable hostess & reminded me a little of Mrs. Gregg. We lunched there on all things nice and tastey, then drove off to see more of the town. This is the prettiest of all the places we have been to yet, and the men and women are so joyous and happy. . . . The Houses are clean as well as handsome, their streets and roads fine."[6]

Once the girls were back onboard, living in the cramped quarters began to take its toll. Emma wrote in her diary: "This morning woke and dressed myself only in a black muslin holoku. Mary [Kiliwehi] came into my room and asked how she should dress for the day. We spent the day in the front cabin, sleeping principly, breakfasted there, on fish, potatoe & coffee. Kealakai has been very sick, & Palemo, very cross & noisy, most annoying when one has headaches. Sister Catherine slept on the floor in the front cabin, & Mary on the floor in her room. Hoapili sent to ask for permission by the steward as to see me which was granted. He brought a book of photographs for me to look over of Limalian ladies belonging to one of the passengers."[7]

They arrived in Southhampton on July 13, 1865. The only item the queen recorded in her diary about the event was her "utter amazement" to find out when she awoke in the morning that "I had not undressed the night, & there I was as I laid down in the evening, in my dress, shoes, and cloak (crimson violet)."

Her arrival in England was a quiet affair with little pomp and ceremony. A reporter from the London *Times* was at the dock. The paper gave its readers their first glimpse of "the Queen of the Sandwich Islands" who was visiting England as a guest of the British government and who had "expressed herself highly gratified with the attention she had received during the whole of her long and protracted voyage"—almost ten weeks had passed since she had left Honolulu.[8] The queen and her party were placed in waiting carriages and whisked off to London. There they were welcomed by Lady Franklin and Miss Cracroft who were happy to see the queen but surprised at the presence of Rev. Hoapili and Kiliwehi and at the absence of a maid. This was the first of several surprises that would cause some tension between the queen and her hostess.

New Encounters

On seeing Queen Emma for the first time after four years, Miss Cracroft wrote that she was "distinctly altered." Although she still had a "very sweet face" and a sweet, musical voice, she was now quite thin instead of stout and was "disfigured by blotches of pimples" caused by the voyage. She seemed to have lost the "excellent sense and charming simplicity" that they had experienced in Honolulu. When Lady Franklin welcomed the queen to Upper Gore Lodge, as she called her residence, and apologized for its smallness, the queen answered with "a very little tiny laugh but not a single word." She immediately went up to her room and disappointed her hostess by choosing not to make a round of social calls that afternoon. When dinner was ready, they had to wait an hour for Emma to come down despite repeated requests. Miss Cracroft conceded that on this first day the queen was quite tired and "evidently has the habit of making no reply when she is uncertain what to say."[9] Miss Cracroft would continue to be somewhat critical of the queen throughout her stay with Lady Franklin.

The queen, as well, was not entirely happy with the situation. Three days into her stay, she wrote in her diary: "This morning Mr. C. Hopkins was called to get his orders for the day, and I told him of Mr. Synge's arrangements about the dress or livery for my servants, & I told him also that I did not like this place, from various causes, some of which were the previous engagements made for one by our hostess & maiden (old) niece, without my knowing of it." The observant queen also noted in her diary that "Miss Cracroft has the neuralgia [acute twitching of one or more nerves] in her face today."[10]

Even before she was able to recover fully from the long voyage, Queen Emma was busily involved in a seemingly unending agenda of official and social engagements. On July 17 she wrote that she had seen "many visitors" including her old friend Miss Miller (now Mrs. Williams) and a group of officers who had been on the expedition searching for Admiral Franklin. She wrote in some detail how one of the officers recalled his visit to Captain Cook's burial place in Ka'awaloa "telling of their landing on the identicle spot where he fell, of their having taken away pieces of the rocks where he died, of seeing the cocoanut stump which through the canon ball was fired, & of having the very spear (as he thought) given to their Captain by Kinau, which is now in the British Museum."[11] The next day she told of another visit from a Mrs. Newmans who "welcomed me with tears of affection which was pleasent to a stranger in a strange land among strangers. She embraced me in her little arms & kissed me repeatedly on my cheeks and head, her tears flowing the while, she was very much agitated from returning recollections of old days, & walked here & there in her usual mincing, quick steps, exclaiming oh! oh! oh dear! that you. . . ."[12]

On another occasion the queen received Hopkins's sister-in-law Kate whom she described as "nothing very remarkable, on the contrary, rather ordinary." She impishly wrote, "We joked together a great deal about our being use[d] very queerly by the old ladies of the house."[13] A few days later when Queen Emma sallied forth "incognito with Mrs. Dixon in her carriage for a 2 hours sightseeing in the cheep shops of London, & a delightful time we had, the very fact of losing sight of *My Aunt & My Niece* & going from them was a very great pleasure, one felt as if a load had quite been taken from our back, there was no restraint, but instantly felt merry. Mrs. Dixon added much to our merryment by her emphatic twangy voice being put to use in the funniest manner possible. We passed three or four herds of sheep & she exclaimed oh! those wretched creatures they are all going to be killed and hung out in the butcher shops."[14]

Possessing a passion for clothes, the queen indulged in mini-buying sprees such as the time she invited to her room a dressmaker, "a tall fine looking young woman" from whom she purchased some veils, bonnets, canzoozs [*canezou,* a shawl-like blouse], basquines, circulars, handkerchiefs, sashes, gloves, shoes, jett ornaments, and fans.[15] She demonstrated her keen eye for fashion by describing in detail the clothes women wore such as the dressmaker's "plane spotted muslin dress, a rich but plain basquine with little lace on, & a neat white tall bonnet" or the fat woman's "purple colored dress, silk trimmed round the bottom of the skirt with purple velvet ribbon edged with white lace."[16]

Lady Franklin commented on her royal guest's powers for "spontaneous observations." For example, when she arrived in London, "She found the Needles smaller than she had expected, was disappointed not to see Hurst Castle at all, and to find Netley Abbey concealed from view by the trees surrounding it." On catching a glimpse of the Houses of Parliament, she had felt she had seen them before—so exactly did they fit their description. Lady Franklin concluded that "These are all indications of ready perception and retentive memory."[17]

She was also intrigued by Queen Emma's fascination with the extreme forms of the weather, "the frost, the snow, ice, thaw, & fog, and especially the latter being, she declares, the things of all others she wishes to become acquainted with."[18] On her first Sunday service at the Chapel Royal at St. James Place, the queen wrote: "It was raining a little & there was a great mist, the clouds were dark . . . there seemed nothing but a curved leaden cover thrown over the pretty blue & white clouds . . . the air has not been particularly sharp & there has been a . . . *ua noe* [misty rain] very very fine & drizzling through a fog which was not very thick, but enough to make the building misty in the mist."[19]

The queen went on countless sight-seeing expeditions in and outside London, visiting the Royal Academy of Paintings in Trafalgar Square, the Charterhouse School, the Fleet, Guildhall, the colleges of Cambridge and Oxford, the Tower of London, and so on. She saw some of the same places her late husband had seen fifteen years before. Significantly, among the places she visited was Chelsea Hospital.[20] However, no mention is made of her visiting any other hospital in England or in Europe.

Over the following days, weeks, and months the motley parade of callers included dressmakers and peddlers of sundry items, emissaries of the Bishop of Oxford and other clerics, an East Indian Parsee, Miss Cracroft's sister and other relatives, writers and journalists, Foreign Office officials, the Bishop of Jamaica, the Bishop of London, Mr. and Mrs. Jannion, Lady Charlotte Lockes, Lady Stanley, Lady Strangford, and numerous others of various rank and title, friends of friends of friends or outright strangers, all drawn to her out of friendship or sympathetic interest in her mission or frequently out of basic curiosity.

Media Coverage

The public's interest was partly stimulated by the wide coverage Queen Emma received in the press. The *Illustrated London News* described the purpose of her visit as "interesting the friends of English Church missions in the welfare of the Christians among her own people." The article included details of the founding of the church by Kamehameha IV, the queen's family, the makeup of the government, and the nature of its leaders.[21]

The extent of the English people's enthusiastic, if not wild, response to the queen is shown by the author of a pamphlet that was published some time after her arrival. He stated: "There is a royal lady now on our shores coming and going amongst us, and learning daily more and more what English people are, about whom very little is known to the majority of the people who seem to welcome her so gladly. It is therefore the object of this little book to give some account of Queen Emma, and of what has induced her to leave her island home in the South Pacific and brave the perils of this long voyage, and to try and enlist the sympathies and interests of some of the thousands who throng to catch a sight of her." After making a passionate plea for helping the queen in her mission, the pamphlet's author stated: "Our own gracious Queen has welcomed and honored in every way the visit of her sister in affliction to these shores, and from the highest and noblest in the land she has, and will continue to receive, every consideration and honor that her exalted position and yet simply borne state can command. . . . It is no mere wish to stare at a royal personage that impels such crowds of Queen Victoria's subjects to go and see this other Queen; but, let us venture to hope a higher and worthier motive—to attest by their presence how deeply their sympathies and interests are roused, and how desirous they are of helping forward the good work so ably begun and so touchingly pleaded."[22]

Back in Hawai'i, David Kalākaua expressed the sentiments of the people when he wrote to Bishop Staley: "We have very flattering accounts, in quite a number of the English papers, of the handsome reception of our beloved Queen. God grant her a safe return to her sunny Island home. It will give us all great happiness to have her here among us once more."[23]

Missionary Cause

Because her main purpose was to gain support for the Anglican cause in Hawai'i, many of her activities and contacts were connected with the Anglican church. One of the first and most important people was Bishop Wilberforce of Oxford who acted as her adviser and guide throughout her sojourn in England. The bishop remarked that "her energetic efforts and activities taxed his physical endurance."[24]

One of the remarkable fund-raising events graced by Queen Emma's presence took place in the small town of Wells in Somerset County. Local dignitaries, an honorary company of guardsmen, and a large number of townspeople assembled at the railway station to greet Her Majesty. The Dean of Wells, the Bishop of London, and an overflow crowd of parishioners filled the nave of the cathedral for a special service. The queen, who was enthroned on a raised dais, heard the Reverend Canon Boyd preach on behalf of the Honolulu mission. He praised King Kamehameha IV for establishing the Anglican church in Hawai'i and mentioned the king's intention to visit England, but by "the inscrutable Providence of God her Majesty Queen Emma has come alone, and I feel sure that the nobility, gentry and clergy of this great county are prepared to give her a most hearty welcome (loud cheers). . . ." He praised the queen for making the voyage at great cost and self-sacrifice and for coming as a "Missionary" to collect money for the benefit of the mission and erection of a cathedral; he urged his listeners to give generously.[25]

Another fund-raising meeting was held in the afternoon where there was an overflowing audience, with hundreds unable to gain admission. A raised seat was provided for the queen who was dressed in deep mourning, still wearing a small white border encircling her "pleasing face." The Bishop of London, who had spent several days with the queen, spoke of how much he admired her "Christian courtesy" and her great zeal for the missionary cause. He too pleaded for support not only for the building of a cathedral but also for a school for girls. When the meeting ended, the money collected totaled over 180 pounds, which amounted to the largest collection ever made in the Wells Cathedral.[26] In fact, by the time the queen had finished her fund-raising in England, she had helped to raise 6,000 pounds (about $30,000) for the mission and construction of the cathedral.[27]

Although no mention is found in her diary, one of her important visits in London was to the office of the architectural firm of Carpenter and Slater. She had studied various plans for the cathedral in Honolulu and was impressed with the grandeur and beauty of the great Gothic cathedrals she had seen in London. She chose a design by B. F. Ingelow, one of the firm's architects, for a "pointed Gothic" cathedral.[28] Before leaving England, she and her Anglican sponsors had purchased the cut stone arches, windows, and pillars and arranged to have them shipped to Hawai'i.

Another important Anglican visit of the queen was to the headquarters of the Society of the Most Holy Trinity where she met the Reverend Mother Lydia Sellon and requested that more sisters be sent to the Islands to establish a formal school for girls. Mother Sellon, who had already sent three sisters directly to Lahaina to establish St. Cross School for girls, agreed to the queen's request, thereby initiating a remarkably productive, albeit brief, relationship that would lead to the establishment of St. Andrew's Priory in Honolulu.[29]

On one occasion Queen Emma spent several hours visiting Westminster Abbey with the writer Augustus Hare who was so impressed with her knowledge of the place that he wrote: "She went over Westminster Abbey with far more knowledge of the tombs and persons they commemorate than I have seen in European royalties with whom I have visited the Abbey in later years. . . ."[30] He was also impressed in other ways, with her "gentle and pleasing" manner, her "copper-coloured" complexion, and her "good-looking" features. He observed that "She had greatly looked forward to the fogs of England, having been used to nothing but the blue or copper-coloured sky of the Pacific, and was dreadfully disappointed when she saw the resplendent blue sky of the glorious day on which she arrived at Southhampton. "Why, I might just as well have been in the Sandwich Islands."[31]

The queen showed another aspect of her personality when she displayed her annoyance at ill-behaved parishioners attending the Sabbath services at St. Paul's. She wrote about the "well dressed and fashionably dressed young ladies and gentlemen, who annoyed me much with their irreverent behavior in that holy abode of the Most Holy One who was present even looking into their hearts and seeing their frivolity. I allude particularly to two young creatures, pretty looking girls . . . [who] were continually looking round to a young man at their back, of whom be it said he never encouraged their ill timed flirting . . . the men choresters also I was sorrey to see, paid no attention to the object of their gathering, but was laughing, whispering passing notes from one to another, & casting glances up forwards . . . to see old men doing such things, is to say the least, most disgusting, & my thoughts reverted back to my own native land, on such a day, & thought of the reverent devout, & sincere behaviour of my own countrymen at such a time, my dear own home & service, our good Bishop and priests, how I long to enjoy you once again."[32]

Troubles Flare

A few days after their arrival in England, Synge and Hopkins disagreed over their roles and duties. Synge complained to Lady Franklin about Queen Emma because she seemed to have no use for his services and placed too much confidence in Hopkins. He needed to speak to her directly and at once because he had to inform the Foreign Office about his activities. Lady Franklin managed to bring the two together, and after relating his feelings, he asked if she wished for him to serve her or not. As Lady Franklin described the incident, "Queen Emma frowned and looked angry. Mr. Synge got more and more excited . . . the more so as the Queen remained silent. At last, when the question had been urged upon her in all sorts of forms, she said: 'What am I to do with Mr. Hopkins?' "

Synge was not blameless. Hopkins had told the queen that he had heard that Synge wanted nothing to do with him and that he had been spreading scandals and tales about him to the Foreign Office. The queen clearly sided with Hopkins because, despite Lady Franklin's low opinion of him as "a loose unmarried man addicted to drunkenness," she had known Hopkins to be one of her late husband's closest and most trusted friends. In fact, the queen had insisted on him accompanying her on the trip, even though Wyllie had tried to discourage it.

This incident demonstrates an important facet of Emma's character that Amos and Julliette Cooke knew all too well: she could be stubborn. She could also hide her feelings and thoughts. When she was not ready to speak, she could remain quiet. Observers in England were sometimes disappointed by Emma's "reserve, extreme impassivity, even a dullness in the royal countenance." Her face could be masklike and noncommittal, like a "bronze statue."[33]

The queen could also feel indignant and spiteful when she felt she was being unfairly treated, as illustrated in the following passage from her diary:

> Wednesday, July 26
> While at the breakfast table this morning Miss Cracroft asked me to answer the Bishop's letters to me as soon as possible today—either through herself, or Aunt, or do it myself. I told her that I had made a rough draught [draft] of one but will copy it soon—she was exceedingly fidgety & I, divining her intentions, prolonged as long as possible the completion of the copying act.
>
> Last night the last thing I did was to write to C. Hopkins asking him to frame me replys to the Bishop of Oxford's notes which was inclosed, & this morning early they were sent me, which was very nice, & being copied in my own hand I sent them as I wished by Mr. C. Hopkins, but Miss Cracroft snatched them from Mrs. Hoapili's hand & rushed up to tell me she would send them by post right off—but they first had to be shewen to My Aunt. I suspect they want to fish for an invitation, & want to have a look at my note first, so as to frame theirs to correspond—and that was the reason I wished to send them

> through Hopkins, so as they might not see it or have anything to do with the Bishop but they have been so pertinatious & impudent about [it] they actually have gained their point, and consequently we were later than we aught to have been, for Lady Franklin was only in her nightdress, busy writing these mysterious dispatches of theirs, so when I found it so, I thought they could well afford to wait half an hour for me, so laying aside my bonnet laid on the sofa for a while till Miss Cracroft rushed up to tell me her Aunt had been half an hour waiting, & was most hurried & anoyed about it, which pleased me exceedingly not thinking at all of the anoyence & mortification she caused me yesterday by leaving me in the street to wait an hour & half while she was having a tooth pulled."[34]

On another occasion Queen Emma wrote about Miss Cracroft: "Mrs. Hoapili got a note from Hoapili, written from Isle of Wright, & which Miss Cracroft was most anxious to hear, so insisted upon having the letter fetched down & I read it at the breakfast table. Mrs. Hoapili received an invitation from the bishop of Oxford to go to Cuddeston with me, which thing excited great vent of anger on Miss Cracroft's part —says she, the Bishop has acted most strangely in this matter, instead of writting to my Aunt, like Sir Chas. Harvey, & all the sensible people do to ask her to arrange matters, so that the Queen may not be trouble[d] about it, he never says anything about it, & never asks Hoapili to go."[35]

By the end of the summer Lady Franklin's and Miss Cracroft's attitude toward the queen betrayed more than a bit of sarcasm. When someone remarked that Emma was "more a saint than a queen," as Miss Cracroft replied to Mrs. Dixon, "You can understand that something different from the reality is looked for. People are startled and a little shocked by the appetite for *all sorts* of novelty and that the Mission is not at the surface." Lady Franklin agreed with this estimate of the queen's delight in "trivialities." "She wishes to see everything and know everything." (One of these "trivialities" was the first lawn mower she saw, which she was determined to take back to Honolulu.) And [she] "is by no means, though I say it without disrespect, the 'saint' which Mr. Keble [the poet] expected to find."[36] (The reference to "saint" was probably prompted by statements such as that made by the Archbishop of Canterbury: that his interest in the queen was piqued by "her deep rooted piety, her almost saintly piety.")[37]

By now Queen Emma's attitude had changed toward her hosts, especially Miss Cracroft. She wrote that they were attending a tea party where "the odious Miss Cracroft persisted to shew her dislike of the sett of people we were in by trying hard to sleep at supper table."[38] As for Lady Franklin, sometimes the queen thought she was a bit overprotective, if not controlling, but she remained deferential and friendly to her.

As for Kiliwehi Hoapili, although intelligent and capable—fluent in both speaking and writing English—she too became the object of the queen's displeasure. Emma wrote that she was irked at "her stupidity & arrogance & ignorant management of listening to anyone's conversation when they are speaking to her is most disgusting, & it mortifies me not a little—she never does her duty as lady in waiting, never opens the door for one, never going out of her way to get one a chair—& not trying or even studying others' pleasures or comforts by understand[ing] their frame of mind & framing her conduct towards them accordingly—but in the most uncouth, unladylike manner thrust home the subject most painful to them—horrible, horrible. . . ."[39] Apart from this one episode, harmony between the queen and Mrs. Hoapili seemed to have prevailed throughout the remainder of her travels, although this was not the case with Mr. Hoapili.

Audience with Queen Victoria

The highlight of Emma's visit was her audience with her son's godmother and the ruler of the most powerful nation in the world and hence the most powerful woman in the world, Queen Victoria. She had looked forward to the meeting since her first letter recounting her son's death. But so had Queen Victoria who, according to Prime Minister Lord John Russell, was "anxious to show her every attention & civility, & will be much interested in seeing her."[40]

For their meeting on September 9, 1865, Queen Emma was appropriately dressed in her widow's weeds. She was aware of the intricacies of Victorian etiquette that dictated widows were to exhibit their status with specific clothes and accessories. And she knew that Queen Victoria remained in mourning although more than five years had passed since her Consort Prince Albert had died and that she would be dressed accordingly.[41]

Their meeting took place in the afternoon of September 9, in the white drawing room of Windsor Castle. Queen Victoria recorded the event in her journal: "After luncheon I received Queen Emma, the widowed Queen of the Sandwich Islands or Hawaii, met her in the Corridor & nothing could be nicer or more dignified than her manner. She is dark, but not more so than an Indian, with fine feathers [features?] & splendid soft eyes. She was dressed in just the same widow's weeds as I wear. I took her into the White Drawing room, where I asked her to sit down next to me on the sofa. She was much moved when I spoke to her of her great misfortune in losing her only child. She was very discreet & would only remain a few minutes. She presented her lady, whose husband is her Chaplain, both being Hawaiians. . . ."[42]

Although Lady Franklin had not been invited to Windsor Castle, she made notes of the meeting based on reports from Emma and the Hoapilis. When Queen Victoria met Emma, she took both of her hands and kissed her and then, as Emma spoke, turned to her daughter and said: "How beautifully you speak English! does not she?" When Queen Victoria spoke of Kamehameha IV and of her godson, Emma was quite "overcome"—and, in Emma's words, "behaved badly." And when Emma rose anxiously as if to go, Victoria insisted that she sit down again and asked several questions about Hawaiian customs.

Victoria: "How do your people dress?"

Emma: "Like common people in England."

Victoria: "But before that?"

Emma: "Very little dress indeed—cloth round body and neck covered with leaves and flowers."

Victoria "laughed."

Curiously, Emma did not record anything in her diary about the meeting. However, her short note to King Kamehameha V indicated her feelings about the meeting: "I have this moment returned from Windsor Castle where the Queen received me *most* affectionately, most sisterly. Now that I have given you the greatest news I beg your forgiveness before I go on any further for being so negligent and ungrateful for not before letting you hear from me. It was not at all from forgetfulness that such happened but absolutely from want of time."[43]

This first meeting went so well that Queen Victoria invited Emma back, this time to stay overnight at Windsor Castle. Queen Victoria recorded the second meeting with "good Queen Emma" in two entries in her diary:

> November 27, 1865
> Went with Vicky & Fritz [the future Emperor Frederick III of Germany, and his wife, the Princess Royal of England] to see Queen Emma, who has come for the night. She is not looking well, & coughs, poor thing, for which reason she is ordered to go to the South of France, to Hyeres. She, her lady, Mrs. Hoopile [sic], L[ad]y Waterpark & L[or]d Methuen dined. The Queen sat between Vicky & me.

> She was amiable, clever & nice, in all she said, speaking of her own country, which she said had originally been very mountainous. There were no animals, but small dogs & pigs, & these only since they had been imported in the time of Van Couvers[sic], the same with flowers. The people were now always dressed like Europeans & were all *nominally* Christians, but not very fervently so. The lady *looks* rather like an uncivilised savage, but is, on the contrary, peculiarly civilised & well mannered, very pleasing & clever. Took the Queen to her room, remaining a little while with her.

Queen Victoria's second entry was made on November 28: "A wet morning.—Directly after breakfast, we went to wish good Queen Emma goodbye, & I gave her a bracelet with my miniature & hair. She thanked me much for my kindness, & for consenting to be godmother to her poor little child. . . ."[44]

What could have drawn together these two women, so unlike in so many ways? They differed vastly in terms of their civilizations, their age (Victoria was nineteen years older), the number of children (Victoria had nine), the length of their reigns (Victoria ruled for fifty-four years), and the size and power of their realms. While Queen Emma could gain politically, economically, and religiously, neither Queen Victoria nor Great Britain stood to gain much from Emma's visit. Ultimately, the bond was a spiritual and emotional one derived from their shared experiences of losing loved ones (Victoria lost her beloved husband Albert in 1861). Their life-long correspondence reveals that they continued to maintain sympathy and affection for one another.

Visit to the Tennysons

An avid reader, Queen Emma had looked forward to meeting Alfred Lord Tennyson, Alexander Liholiho's favorite English author. He lived far away from the hustle and bustle of London on the Isle of Wight, a two-day journey from Kensington Gore. In late September the queen and her party, along with Lady Franklin, visited Lord and Lady Tennyson who left this record of the visit:

> Sept. 28th. Farringford. Queen Emma of the Sandwich Islands, arrived, Major Hopkins and a huge native, Mr. Hoapili, in attendance. Aunt Franklin came. . . . We had a throne chair made out of our Ilex wood. It was first used by the Queen. She, poor lady, wanted to stay quietly here, but she had to go to banquets, etc. about the Island. I collected money for the projected cathedral in Honolulu.

> Lady Franklin went with the Queen up the Down. John Welsh, the Queen's servant, said nothing would induce him to leave her, she was so good . . . endless guests came in to tea. A. [Alfred] took her out that she might read her letters; and hid her from the guests in the summer-house in the kitchen garden ("among the cabbages" she said). A. and I were pleased with her sweet dignity of manner, and a calmness that made one think of an Egyptian statue; her voice was musical. Mr. and Mrs. Hoapili sang Hawaiian songs. They sat on the ground and acted the song while they sang. They then chanted an ode to the young Prince, a wild monotonous chant. All great people's children in Hawaii have odes made to them on the day of their birth, a kind of foreshadowing of their lives. When a bard meets the hero of any ode so made he has to sing it to him.
>
> Oct. 2nd. A. gave her two large magnolia blossoms on her leaving. She has a sweet nature; something very pathetic about her."[45]

It was said that "in the evenings Mr. and Mrs. Hoapili would sing Hawaiian songs, sitting on the ground, their hair wreathed with briony berries, and the Queen would tell stories and legends of her native land."[46]

After her visit to the Tennysons, Queen Emma sent them a copy of Alexander Liholiho's Prayer Book and Preface. She wrote to Lady Franklin as follows: "It is a great satisfaction and pride to me to send my Husband's translation and productions to the greatest men of the age, that they may see and know him to have been their equals in tallent and genius—how much Mr. Tennyson would have appreciated him!"[47]

On to France

In October Emma and her party left Lady Franklin's home and moved to the fashionable Claridge's Hotel as a guest of the British government. She was not an ordinary guest but, as Charles F. Adams, the United States minister in London, observed, equal to "a sovereign guest." (As he also noted in his dispatch, Adams did not think Queen Emma's visit had any political significance for the United States.)[48] The earlier misunderstandings between Queen Emma, Miss Cracroft, and Lady Franklin notwithstanding, the parting was quite amicable. (Part of the reason for the move was Lady Franklin's plan to spend the coming winter months in the warmer climes of southern France.) Lady Franklin had in fact contributed significantly to the success of her stay.

From London Manley Hopkins wrote to Wyllie: "The Queen's reception in England surpasses in success anything that could have been anticipated by the most sanguine of Her well-wishers. . . . Through all, it is perfectly understood that Queen Emma's visit is quite a private one, unconnected with politics, and which should not give umbrage to any other power. Her dignified and gentle bearing win all hearts, and secure Her a place in the memory of all who have the good fortune to meet Her Majesty."[49]

Hopkins' reference to the queen's visit being a "private one, unconnected with politics" indicates that he was well aware of the outcry in the United States against the queen's tour of England and the simultaneous American tour by Bishop Staley. The purposes of the bishop's trip were to attend the General Convention of the American Protestant Episcopal Church in Philadelphia and to seek cooperation between the English and American churches, which had been a feature of the original plan for the Hawaiian mission. However, suspicious Americans linked together the twin tours as two phases of a single scheme to destroy American influence in Hawai'i and tie the kingdom to the British empire. The U.S. Secretary of State William Seward advised Adams to "prevent any intervention by Great Britain in the affairs of the Hawaiian kingdom." Adams reported to Seward that he had met Queen Emma on various occasions and that he had "no reason to suspect any political significance in her presence in England."[50]

With the onset of winter, concern over Emma's health grew among her English hosts. She had caught a severe sore throat, which developed into a case of persistent bronchitis. To get well, her physician urged her to leave England for the warmer and healthier climate of southern France. Lady Franklin agreed (and may have recommended Hyères on the French Riviera). Manley Hopkins did not agree and instead recommended that the queen abandon her travels and return to Hawai'i. Although homesick, Emma was not about to miss seeing the continent that Alexander Liholiho had described to her and decided to depart for France. When the Bishop of Oxford heard of this plan, he worried about her "touring the Continent with the two Hoapilis and with no other guardian than the appalling Mr. Hopkins."[51]

Emma was concerned about her finances. She had used her own money to pay for part of the trip, but she did not have sufficient resources to cover the sojourn in southern France. Previously she had asked King Kamehameha V for assistance; when no remittances arrived, however, the British government through Lord Clarendon came to her rescue.

Sad News

On the eve of her departure from Claridge's Hotel, Emma learned of the death of Robert C. Wyllie whom she regarded as a "Father almost." She penned a sad letter to King Kamehameha V:

> Your Majesty
> It is with a very heavy heart that I write this letter. The news of Mr. Wyllies loss, by the telegram sent from Home on the 19th of Oct has just arrived, and we are all sad, and mourning the misfortune that has befallen us. I feel it very much, for I had quite looked upon him as a Father almost. How little did I dream when I saw him last on the day we left the Islands, that that was to be our last meeting. Everyone who has had any acquaintance with him here speaks of his disinterested devotion to our Kingdom and its Dynasty as something most unusual, and his thorough allegiance to his new country, very remarkable. Men such as Lord Clarendon, Sir John Bowring, Earl Russell and many others say the same. The first impulse of the moment was to return to the Islands immediately, but on longer thought I have concluded to proceed on my journey to Hiere tomorrow according to our arrangements, which was all attended by Lord Clarendon, as I last wrote on Saturday when he called especially for that purpose.[52]

The queen's sorrow was profound; Wyllie had played a part in almost every important event in her life from her courtship and marriage to the establishment of Queen's Hospital and the Anglican mission. He was at her side in her happiest times in Hanalei and her saddest times at the untimely deaths of her Prince Albert and her Liholiho. But if he was devoted to the queen, he was equally devoted to Hawai'i, which he served conscientiously for twenty-one years. As a leader of the cabinet of two sovereigns, no one had done as much in establishing a constitutional and parliamentary government and, more important, in preserving and protecting the rights and privileges of the kingdom as an independent and sovereign nation. As a mark of the high esteem in which he was held, he was buried at Mauna'ala (the Royal Mausoleum) near Kamehameha III and Kamehameha IV whom he had loyally served.

Passing Scenes

On December 5, 1866, Queen Emma left London by train with her entourage, which now included Chevalier, a Swiss maid acquired in England. They arrived at the harbor of Boulogne where Queen Emma was greeted by the British Consul who had received instructions "personally hand written" by Prime Minister Russell.[53] They reached Paris just before midnight and after a night's rest, she wrote:

> When we woke the next morning . . . we threw open the long windows and shutters, and slipping out into the little balcony whiled away 15 minutes before breakfast was announced, in looking down upon the rue Marenge [Marengo] at the pretty variegated sights in the street, of the bright dresses of both men and women, market vans, light phaetons, bright shops opposite the road, young demoiselles that trip along with blooming cheeks, and a bundle of sewing for the day's work under their arm, Zouaves [members of a French army unit noted for the precision of their close-order drill and colorful uniforms] who jostle along with all their medals on their breasts, old women in sabots, white caps, short petticotes and a rainbowie handkerchief folded over their chest and shoulders—now all this was an early morning sight at the end of the street. . . . We sat down to a light breakfast of sweet toast, bautiful coffee sweetened with square lumps of white sugar in large light green cups."[54]

She left Paris that day but would return a few months later. On her railway journey south, she described the scenes that reminded her of home:

> The country we passed on our journey hither is like our Island scenery along the South of Hawaii and Oahu, and the soil and rocks [are] like the nature of that of Leahi [Diamond Head] in Waikiki, yellow and brown color, wild in some spots. . . . The sights all along is extremely beautiful and varied, and . . . every ten or five minutes whisked us pass quiet rustic little towns on an open plane, with its pretty little old looking church raising its head above the other housese from its midst, or passing immediately under frowning ruins of old Castles, whose battlemented walls brought to mind old songs such as 'Gaily the Troubadore,' 'The Minstrells return from the war,' and the distant high hills on whose sides were pretty villages with grape & olive plantations and on whose tops stood out prominently some towering tower in the clear atmosphere of 'La France.' I could not help thanking inwardly Him who orders our goings out and our comings in, that he should have given me such opportunity to see these parts of the world. Most picturesque are the old buildings, houses, and dress of the people of this land, just precisely what one sees in prints and pictures of them.[55]

They then stopped at Lyon where she saw her first confessional and the model of the cathedral she dreamed about building in Honolulu:

> At Lyon, I saw the first actual confession, such as one reads about, in the Cathedral du Lyon, a building as large as the Roman Catholic Church in Honolulu, & one which I wished our new Cathedral would be like, it is just the size, & I rather liked the style of architecture, ornamental Gothic. . . . On both sides of the nave are a series of chapels formed underneath the arches (8 in number) in one of which I saw the confessional act, as performed in the Church of Rome. . . .
>
> One of the penitents was a beautiful girl, kneeling in the repentant's open recess, where is a crucifix or picture of our Lord hung before her in the queer arrangement of the Confessional box, which is like a low wardrobe with the two ends not enclosed & the center only so, the door of which when the priest enters is shut upon him, & he listens & absolves all the sinner's faults which is made known to him through a finely grated opening in one side—it is precisely like the sentry boxes at the Palace gates at home, just put three of them together side by side & you have it, only a little more elaborate—there were many of them in the Church. Various services were being performed at the same moment, thus we saw confessionals, christenings, private devotions, mass &c in this one Cathedral.[56]

She was not impressed with the men in Lyon, as she wrote: "The main thing about the men in France is they do not put their hands in the sleeves of a warm coat, but just let them hang and button up their coats up to the neck, they have a cigar in the mouth, or keep their hands in the pockets of their pants. And when they go about they spit anywhere, whether in a room, on the floor, in the street. A filthy habit."[57]

Emma and her party overnighted in Marseille at the Grand Hôtel du Louvre et de la Paix, which she noted as the "grandest hotel" on La Canebière (the main street of the port city) where "all crowned heads & illustrious visitors go." Viewing the street scene from her balcony, she took a verbal photograph:

> I never thought that the colored prints & pictures of street scene could be so true. Why! it is to the reality! It was a most animated scene all day long, & the variety of costumes is something very gay—the bright dress of Zouave soldiers, each regiment differing in brightness—the sedate looking French proprietarie in plane clothes with overcoats buttoned at the throat, & sleeves not used but dangling about, both hands being buried in the trowsers pockets—the narrow waggons or

> carts drawn by a tandem team of animals, foremost is the small donkey then a large mule, & a poor horse all with the queer head gear that looks like [a] yoke on their necks with a horn in the top of it covered with tiny globular bells on them that jingle through the streets—the Arabs in their white burnoose enveloping head & all, thrown over one shoulder—the young girls that swarm the streets passing up & down, their hairs so prettily & stylishly made, & who dresses in the most becoming of latest Móde de Paris—Americans in their usual quick businesslike walk—Priests in long robes & shovel hats shuffling through the crowd—the women of the lower order dotting the mass with white caps—the English discernable through that mottled crowd by their tall black hats, excessive simplicity of dress & dignified ladylike & gentlemanlike bearing—Turks with red fezzes & full trowsers, gay broad sashes wound round the waist—Sisters of Mercy of many orders & odd dresses, sailors, shabby cabs & drivers run about them, & once in a while a fast looking young gentleman dashes through this crowd in his Phaeton managing two beautiful bays with his footman in livery & folded arms as stiff as you please behind him. . . . This was at our feet. The tall houses whose ornimental fronts & windows draped with bright sunshades, shop windows glittering with all kinds of purse temptations was opposite to us, piano music coming from our next door neighbours in the adjoining rooms. Now with all this live scene utterly new to me you must not be surprised that I sat out on that balcony a very long time, taking advantage of our being unknown in that place—sat exposed without being known. . . .[58]

In another letter she described "men and women on the wharf eating the ʻina, hawaʻe and haʻukeʻuke types of sea urchins which gave us the cravings."[59] Among the sights she saw that struck her the most were the "crowds of people," which she compared to "our holidays [in Honolulu] when the streets are all filled," and the soldiers who seemed to be everywhere in France but whom she did not see at all in England. After reminding Kapo "to pray sincerely," she closed her letter with the words: "There is no need of anything when there is love."[60]

The Côte d'Azur

Queen Emma and her party reached Hyères on the famed Côte d'Azur (the French Riviera) about 4:00 p.m. on December 9, 1865. The once-isolated fishing village, located in what Emma called "*kuaʻāina* (back-country) parts of France," was already the winter resort for the English upper-class, for here it was as warm in December as it was in London in May. Still, for the queen, it was a "queer little town, small & rather interesting," but had filthy streets and dreadful smells. She could walk the length of the town in about fifteen minutes, and wrote about its beautiful climate and surroundings where "The mountainous character of the scenery, & always keeping the Mediterranean in view, makes it very home like to me, where always the sea & mountain go together."[61]

The queen and her attendants stayed in Hyères at the Hôtel du Parc, from December 1865 to March 1866. Hyères was warm, relaxing, and peaceful, the ideal place to regain her health. During December she did little except rest, walk for exercise, entertain a few callers, and catch up with some long-overdue correspondence. The regimen was exactly what the doctor ordered, so to speak, because in January she informed Lady Devon in England that "The beautiful climate [of Hyères] is doing wonders for us all, already we are almost ourselves again."[62]

While she was happily regaining her health in Hyères, people in Hawai'i were receiving weeks-old reports from England that she was in extremely poor health. The *Pacific Commercial Advertiser* stated that her health had been very much impaired not only by the cold London weather but also by "the unusual and severe labor to which she has been called by the Bishop of Oxford, in compelling her to make the tour of England, and to be exhibited as a public curiosity." The missionary mouthpiece seemed more intent on widening the rift between Anglicans and Hawaiians than on being accurate. It raised the specter of Kamehameha II's tragic death on an earlier visit and stated, "Human nature cannot stand long continued abuse. Her medical advisers have strictly forbidden her appearance before the public; and if she obeys, she may be spared to return to her country and her people."[63]

Money Crisis

By January 1866 her funds were running dangerously low; she had yet to receive any money from Hawai'i. She wrote to King Kamehameha V again in January: "We have only 700 pounds. It cannot support a party of 7 for 3 months as our expenses are 60 pounds a week—that is the lowest we can live."[64] The king replied: "By Manley Hopkins letter of the 9th instant of December, I regret to hear that your physician thought it necessary to change your residence to the South of France. I think it would have been wiser to have returned at once home, than to have incurred additional expenses. I wished you had taken Mr. Manley Hopkins advice. The British Government through Lord Clarendon behaved very generously which it will be hard to repay and more still, to thank through the proper channel. I regret that clearer heads were not near you, when you determined to go to France. It is an awkward position to be under an obligation, when we know it cannot be repaid."

Ever solicitous of her feelings, the king added, "But since you have gone I hope you will enjoy the trip, and that the fine climate of the South of France will do your health good as well as the rest of the party. " Even if Queen Emma had known in December of the king's wishes that she return to Hawai'i, it is doubtful that she would have listened to him.[65]

In any event, as each week passed, so did another sixty pounds. At one point she was sufficiently desperate to consider borrowing 3,000 pounds from a Mr. Stephen Spencer in England. But the king had written to her in May saying that several remittances had been sent to her and that the money would last her only until July. He reminded her that she had already drawn on her annual annuity (which was 6,000 pounds) up to January of 1867 and that she should not try to draw any more because it would only be a "source of annoyance to the Legislature."[66] However, in June the legislature approved a resolution giving her an additional $3,000.[67]

Life in Hyères

Her financial plight notwithstanding, by January the queen's health had improved considerably. She plunged into a schedule of activities that at times kept her as busy as she had been in England. She began the New Year by attending services at the English chapel, along with "12 communicants all mostly English" and by receiving a visit by the town mayor.[68] On her thirtieth birthday she went shopping and bought a few presents for her landlord, took an afternoon drive into the nearby town of Le Grau, and celebrated her birthday that evening with a little party.[69] Like Alexander and Lot earlier in Paris, she took French lessons, along with the Hoapilis. According to her teacher Monsieur Denis, she had made "a favourable progress."[70] She visited the town casino at least once, not to gamble but to listen to "a pair of needy" violinists.[71] She also visited the local orphanage with its thirty-seven young inmates, run by the Sisters of the Order of St. Vincent de Paul, and noted in her diary that she visited "the dormitorys, Chapel, Kitchen, Apothecary room, & saw the distribution of food to the poor."[72]

Of special interest was a Hawaiian-style picnic that Queen Emma and her party held on the beach. In a long letter to King Kamehameha V, she wrote:

February 14, 1866

Your Majesty
Kiliwehi, Hoapili, John and I walked for a day's outing to an old Roman ruin called Pomponianna [Pomponiana], the remains of a very old Roman town destroyed by Earthquake—it is about 3 miles from our hotel—we enjoyed it immensely because free from etiquett & restraint & for once quite to ourselves.

The courier followed an hour after, with our lunch of rare beef, cold potatoes, pickels, bread, butter, oranges & wine. On our way back we met a boy who carried in a mat bag on head some fishes which we bought, a plump little Aku & some Hinaleas [wrasses], for 3 francs & a sous. John carried them on an olive twig strung by the gills to the beach. I scaled a fish entirely myself, which is a thing I had never done before. . . .

At noon Hoapili & John built a fire right on the water's edge & broiled our fish & beef, in the course of which I & Kiliwehi, the Courier & Maid gathered greens & strewed our little recess in the cliffs where we were to eat, & spread our lunch on it, the hot part of which no sooner was placed in the midst then we, servants & all, sat round it & ate the greatest meal we have ever eaten since we have been abroad. It was a regular Hawaiian feast, barring the poi, but the sweet potatoes filled its place in a measure. What do you think we had for supper that night? Why we had some very nice rare Aku [tuna], it tasted so good,—we all enjoyed it going to bed that night really maona [full, satisfied].[73]

In the same letter, she described an excursion during which she demonstrated her royal leadership.

Yesterday we made an excursion to one of the Islands which lie in front of the town & connected with the main land by a narrow strip of long sand. I had asked two English ladies, invalides, whose acquaintance we made here, one a widow from Ireland & the other a young Londoner only 17. . . . They are very pleasant, full of fun, quick & appreciates good jokes. My doctor & the clergyman of the place are the other members of our picnic party.

At 9 in the morning we went in 3 carriages to the Island, which is something like Molokai but not half so large—a ridge runs through it just like that of the former, in the middle adjoining which is a long low strange looking house, which proved to be the church & Cure's lodgings in one. We crossed over & down to the other side of the Island, which only took 10 minutes & had our picnic under the trees near the shore, the fire & cooking close by. I kept the party from mis-

> chief by giving them occupation, some of the ladies to pick ferns & greens. The clergyman, who is a very agreeable man in spite of his low church views, had to scrape radish roots, pare onions, manufacture paper dishes, &c. &c. Mr. Hopkins & one of the ladies dressed the salad into a saucepan which served as a deep dish for it. Our Muleteers, coachman, servants & my maid gathered firewood. They were all in the highest glee being sett to doing such queer things, & liked very much Hoapili's stripps of broiled beef & beautiful spatchcocked fowls.
>
> The ladies looked at him with surprise as he rubbed the salt, pepper and onions into the meat. Everyone sat down pleased with himself & everything they (the haoles) ate was a real pleasure to see, even to the fruit cake—the gentlemen devoured it declaring they never saw any in Hyeres before. The ladies grew merry over the Burgundy—as the hot pieces of meat came from the close fire they all scrambled & snatched for it, enjoying it amazingly, not waiting for knives or forks but tearing it with fingers. After lunch we sat on the rocks over the sea & watched the breakers dash up under our feet, while we strung some scarlet berries & wild flowers into garlands & necklaces.
>
> About half an hour after, we mounted our donkeys, the gentlemen leading them, & took a long ride & ramble to one end of the Island. At 5 we left, the good Cure taking leave of me with the hope that we may meet in Heaven. . . .
>
> Our coachman, like knowing Frenchman that he is, took us out of the straight way home, to the other end of the town, so that he had the satisfaction of making a sensation by dashing through the Route Imperial (the principle street) & landed us safe at our hotel portals, our guests having enjoyed their day's excursion very much. Everything was new to them, & has proved quite an incident in Hyere. This little place is very like Honolulu with regard to the spreading of storys, scandals, & the existence of cliques. . . .[74]

Emma recounted this epicurean event in a letter to her cousin Peter Kaʻeo: "All enjoyed the day's excursion, but my guests especially so. It was something so entirely new to them, the cooking one's meal in the woods & eating it hot from the fire each & everyone contributing towards the getting up of it, that they declared they will always imitate it hereafter. They say that such a party has never been done in Hyere before. I assure you they enjoyed it so much that they are still talking of it, & now it is the talk of the town. . . ."[75]

Queen Emma thought the beaches were "strange" because they were covered with pebbles rather than sand. She also observed that some plants resembled the Hawaiian *laua'e* (fern) and *koali* (morning glory) and taro. She described another sight as "a very big kind of grey lizzard here that is scary."[76]

Throughout her stay in Hyères the queen attracted visitors of all classes: Lady Victoria Scott and the granddaughter of the writer Sir Walter Scott; Dr. and Mrs. Griffith; Rev. John Robinson and his wife and daughter ("stupid people," she called them); the Countess of Semeiesville de Pritsbuer; the Sisters of St. Vincent de Paul; Sir Henry Bulwer, and many others. Even if the queen had wanted a bit more privacy—and at no time did she seem to discourage callers—she could not escape the fact that people seemed to seek her out.

Even as she reveled in the excitement and novelty of Hyères, she worried about her ailing mother Grace back home whom she "cared for more than anyone in the world." In a rare letter to "Taffy" (David Kalākaua), she wrote: "What shall I say about the King's kindness to me and mine of his care for my dear dear Mother, in taking upon him to perform the duties of her child to her in my absence. I owe him a life long debt of gratitude. I have cause indeed to thank our Heavenly Father for all his merciful kindness to one in sparing my Mother, and in protecting me while this far from friends and all I love." She reveals again her homesickness when she closes her letter with "I have one thing only left to say, I wish I was on my way home."[77]

Reverend Hoapili's Trysts

In mid-March the queen left Hyères venturing on to the resort towns of Nice and Menton. While her diary is silent about the few days there, they were anxious days marred by a scandal and the near breakup of the Hoapilis. It seemed that the tall and good-looking Reverend Hoapili had become romantically involved with a French lady in Hyères. The affair had progressed to the point where the woman expected that he would take her with him back to Hawai'i. The matter came to a head in Nice when Kiliwehi attempted a "runaway"—the word is Queen Emma's. The Hoapilis managed to patch up their differences, but the queen made the painful decision that the couple should return to Honolulu, without any unseemly publicity.[78] They did not leave immediately but continued to travel with the queen for several more weeks.

From Menton, located on the French-Italian border, the queen continued her odyssey by carriage to Genoa, Italy, traveling all the way seated on the seat outside, while her servants followed in another carriage piled high with luggage. She delighted in the scenery along the road that hugged the seacoast. Writing to her mother Fanny in Hawaiian, she made comparisons with scenes back home: "The view of the land was good and resembled very much Kahakuloa [Maui], but Kahakuloa many times over: that was how lovely the land was, and the road was like Nuuanu Street—it was so beautiful and such fun for the people to ride horseback on. . . . The flowers were very charming, all varieties of them at the top of the cliffs, along the plains, on the banks of the streams, by the beaches, and in the gardens surrounding the villas and everywhere else."[79]

Of all the towns and places she experienced from Nice to Genoa the queen preferred the small fishing village of Cogoleto near Genoa. She wrote, "This noon 'we staid our wheels at Cogoleto,' as Tennyson says of it. . . . It is a quaint little town, in fact it seemed nothing but a fishing village with the highroad running through it as its only street. The people are of the poorest sort but healthy looking. There was nothing save the fact of its being Columbus's native village that can arrest the passers by—no monument no nothing to give it any importance. Yet of all the pretty towns we have come through . . . I like this fishing village best of all. There is something so true, simple & natural looking in the houses, people, dress & impliments belonging to it, that it was pleasant to think that we are looking at just exactly the sights which the great discoverer did years ago. It was enjoyable to me—none of the brief & new improvements of the age."[80]

Once in Genoa, she compared Genoans to her own people. "The men and the women and the way they behave I compare to our people, the shouting and singing that are so like Tahitian song, as they stroll along the highway. But they do not wear bonnets. On the heads of the women are men's hats, woven of the finest of white straw. The elegant ones wear the [Leghorn hats?], but the peasants wear figured and flowered calico, like the curtains used by Kalalaha [one of Emma's retainers] and others."[81]

From Genoa the queen went by train to Bologna, Italy, where she overnighted at the Hotel Pension Swiss. Only one item worthy of mention in her diary is the great cathedral, which she described as "stupendous wide & light inside, the pillars are very large, the alter is under a sort of Grecian temple in the choir. . . ."[82] She left that day for Florence, stopping for a night at Praechia, a small station in the middle of the Apennines, "bitterly cold, Ice and snow close at hand."

She stayed in Florence for a few days to attend to the departure of the Hoapilis, among other matters. The couple did not leave together, for Queen Emma simply wrote in her diary without a word of explanation that Rev. Hoapili "left for Hawaii" on Friday, April 6, and Kiliwehi on Saturday.

The story has a strange sequel. Queen Emma assumed, of course, that they would be returning to Hawai'i by way of the United States. On the same day Hoapili left Florence, the queen wrote to Bishop Staley stating "You will have seen Hoapili and been surprised at his sudden appearance before you can read this." She also explained why Hoapili was returning, none of which hinted at his romantic affair in Hyères or the near breakup with his wife. The only hint of wrongdoing was her statement that "His trials and failings overcome him at times and he says it is because he is idling, and has nothing to occupy him so is very strong in desiring to be at home and in its bosom (the Church's) again."[83]

In the meantime, the Hoapilis had traveled to London where he wrote to Charles C. Harris, the Minister of Finance in Honolulu as follows: "My Dear Sir: You will be surprised to learn that the Queen has consented not only to me coming home, but my wife also; and further to learn that instead of coming home by the same way we came out, we are taking a rather long round-about, and slow way toward home, that we may be able to see all we possibly can of different countries. I am not sure I shall have another favorable opportunity to write you, as we are about to leave England for the East day after tomorrow (April 25, Wednesday)."[84]

In actuality, he headed for one country only, New Zealand, where he and his wife Kiliwehi remained for nearly a year. There, without any instructions from his government, he tried to encourage the emigration to Hawai'i of Maoris who were fighting a long and bloody war against the British. He got back to Hawai'i many months after the queen's own return. And when he did return the king refused to receive him because he considered that Hoapili's conduct toward the queen was "despicable."[85]

The day before Hoapili's departure from Florence, Queen Emma had telegraphed Mrs. Charlotte Hasslocher, the wife of the Hawaiian consul in the Duchy of Baden in southern Germany, "to come and travel with me."[86] Charlotte was a Hawaiian friend who had been married and then widowed before she met Hasslocher, the maestro of the Amateur Musical Society and instructor of the army under King Kamehameha IV. They married and moved to Germany in 1863.[87] Charlotte readily agreed to the queen's request, met her in Florence [or possibly Turin], and accompanied her to Venice, Milan, and Geneva, then to Karlsruhe, Germany, and back to Paris.

Of her visits to Venice and Milan, the queen's diary is silent, although she probably spent many days there. (This assumption is based on the fact that between April 7, when she was in Florence, and May 15 or thereabout, when she arrived in Geneva, Switzerland, about thirty-two days are unaccounted for in her diary. Because these were the only two places, besides Switzerland, she visited during this period, she must have spent considerable time in the two Italian cities.) She looked forward to romantic Venice with gondola rides on the Grand Canal, the Piazza of St. Mark and its pigeons, the magnificent churches of Santa Maria della Salute and the Frari, and the historic *palazzi* that lined the Grand Canal. Nor does her diary mention why she visited Milan. Was it perhaps for its great opera house? Interestingly, nowhere in her diary or letters about her travels in England or Europe did Queen Emma ever mention attending an opera or a concert, events that she enjoyed in Honolulu.

From Italy the queen went to Geneva, where the *Neue Zuercher Zeitung* reported that "the black-curled Queen Emma of the Sandwich Islands" was staying at the Hôtel des Berques, one of the city's deluxe hotels.[88] Revealing her interest in astronomy, the queen visited the observatory of Dr. Pitschner, a distinguished astronomer, and spent two hours observing the constellations.[89]

On Monday, May 21, 1866, they "left Basel at 9 by fast train" for Karlsruhe, Germany, the home of the Hasslochers. She told her diary they were "welcomed by Mr. Hasslocher at the station, & his son Louis & Mrs. Hasslocher's children at the house [where] the Hawaiian flag [was] at the staff. . . ."[90] Queen Emma spent ten days in Karlsruhe meeting new and a few old friends. One of the latter was Augustus Hare who wrote, "I saw again, and for the last time, the very pleasing Queen Emma of the Sandwich Islands, and presented the Bunsens to her."[91] She also purchased a grand piano by Emil Ascherberg in Dresden, which she had shipped to Rooke House.

Before departing Karlsruhe, she wrote on June 1: "The Grand Duchess sent her state carriages for me & I went to make my adieus. We all walked through her hot houses & drove in the park. . . . She was most affectionate & wept at my leaving her." On the day she left, the grand duke came to the station to see her off and placed at her disposal his private railway car.[92] Mrs. Hasslocher continued on with the queen to her next and final stop in Europe, Paris.

Death of Victoria Kamāmalu

Unbeknownst to the queen, as she was about to leave for Paris, Victoria Kamāmalu had died in Honolulu (on May 29, 1866). Because she was the heir apparent, her death raised the issue of succession. Though he was still a bachelor, some reasonable hope existed that King Kamehameha V could produce an heir. But the *Pacific Commercial Advertiser,* fearing the worst—the king dying without a successor—urged a thorough airing of the issue. It listed the names of those *ali'i* who would be eligible: the males, Lunalilo, Kalākaua, Kekūanao'a, Kapa'akea, Peter Ka'eo, and Albert Kūnuiākea, and the females, Bernice Pauahi Bishop, Lili'uokalani, Queen Dowager Kalama, Princess Ruth, and Queen Emma. For the first time, but not the last, Queen Emma was prominently mentioned in the press as a successor to the throne.[93]

Meanwhile, the queen had received a letter from the Governor of Maui, Paul Nahaolelua. He wrote how glad he was when he heard that she had refused "the request of a certain young man of England to have intimate relations with you. I say to you, stand firm and do not comply with any request of that nature, lest your enemies here say that it is true, those who said that you shouldn't go to England. Perhaps your enemies will hear and say, 'She went to seek a husband.' "[94]

The Emperor and Empress

Had the decision been hers, Queen Emma might have chosen to return to Hawai'i. Instead, she was now heading for Paris at the urging of King Kamehameha V. Despite his previous regrets about her not returning to Hawai'i, the king had written to her while she was still at Claridge's Hotel that it was "imperative" for her to go to Paris to visit with the Emperor and Empress. He stated that "They will take it as a slight if you do not; more especially as I understand you are going to visit the Queen at Windsor Castle."[95]

In addition to promoting the kingdom's diplomacy, he thought the visit would have personal benefits. "I think you will be pleased with Paris, and the Court, and your visit there will no doubt . . . do you vast deal of good," he wrote, "and some of these days you will no doubt narrate to us savages your reminiscences of your visit to Paris. Pray keep a sharp eye on the purse. Money goes rapidly in the fashionable and elegant City."[96]

Clearly, King Kamehameha V could not have begrudged the queen's travel expenses when he charged her with carrying out important diplomatic responsibilities. He wrote in June that calling on the Emperor and Empress in Paris "is a very important point in your journey, and demands . . . a most careful handling on your part that a most favorable impression might be left by you on the mind of that most acute Sovereign and his government. England and her publicmen knows us pretty well thanks to our late friend Mr. Wyllie's friends. But France [does] not, she thinks and feels that we are prejudiced against her interests and particularly to their Church . . . your visit will bring up again that knowledge of us, and I can only hope, that your presence and tact will do us some permanent good. I feel that you understand the importance of your visits to Europe, undoubtedly it will be a great gain for our Country. I can only thank Providence that those great interests of State is in your able hands."[97]

She arrived in Paris on June 3, 1866, and had her audience with the Emperor Napoleon III and Empress Eugenie six days later at nine o'clock in the evening. When she returned to her hotel room, although "very tiard," she described what happened in a lengthy letter to the king.

> Hotel du Louvre
> Paris June 9
>
> This morning, in returning from a visit with Mr. M. [Martin, the Hawaiian Consul] to that part of the Louvre where are shewn the 1st Napoleon's dresses & travelling things he used to use in his campagnes, Mr. Martin found a note to him from the 1st Grand Master of Ceremonies of the Emperor, conveying his Majestys wish to receive me at 9 at the Tuilleries this evening. I was a little surprised at the shortness of the time given, as we were not quite ready for an evening reception. Mrs. Hasslocher & I started off instantly with Mrs. Martin to hurry up our dressmakers,—at the same time ordered an evening dress, in case of another such short notice. We got home at 5, very much tiard from the shopping bother & heat (intense). Mrs. Hasslocher & I in full evening toilets, Mr. Martin & Mr. Hopkins in black evening dress, knee breeches & silk stockings & pumps—all black.
>
> Mr. Martins carriage drove off at 9 precisely entering the small court of the Tuilleries, adjoining the Place du Carusal. On alighting at the foot of the grand stair case, we were met & shewn up by two Chamberlains, between two rows of liveried footmen that stood on each step, as far as the second flight of stairs, where the Countess de [Lancy?], Dame d'Honour to the Empress awaited us,—passing through 2 beautiful large rooms, splendidly illuminated & lined on either side of our way with Cent guards [Cent Gardes] in armour & lance, as motionless as statues. For a moment all seemed like old days of the french court in my imagination.

> At the door of the reception room were their Majesties the Prince Imperial & Court. The Emperor came out & met me & then the Empress greeted me kissing & the Emperor presented his son Louis. The Empress shewed me into a small room that led from the large reception room, where the Emperor, Empress & the little Prince remained with me—the court & my suite remained in the large room.
>
> Their Majesties were full of inquiries about the Islands, the exports, the climate, food, character & capabilities of the people & soil. The Emperor was so surprised when I told him Your Majesty had been to Paris once. He asked what year that was, [and I] told him in the beginning of 1850 & that the late King & yourself were presented to him at one of his soirees when president, at the Eleasee Palace. He had forgotten the circumstance but was much pleased about it when I brought it to his recollection. The Emperor asked if Your Majesty was married. I said no but we all hope you will soon & he asked what your age is & what relation I am to you & if you had brothers & sisters. The Empress asked whether you spoke french. Of course, said I, & learnt it in Paris.
>
> She laughed very much when I told her that her hot house plant which she was rearing with care in the room we were sitting in on a beautiful little table in a vause of Severence was a forest nuisance. It was nothing less than our Ki plant, from which okolehao [distilled liquour] is made. I told her we feed our cattle on it, used it instead of paper for cooking fish & cutlets, & never for one instant would we think of putting a valuable Severe vause on our table for such a plant then they would to put a cabbage plant.
>
> After a pleasant conversation of 3/4 of an hour, we went into the other room and mixed with the court, the Empress presenting her ladies, & the Emperor all the gentlemen present. He went to one of the windows & brought a stereoscopic instrument for looking at views & carried it himself to the centre of the room for me to look at. He brought me a chair & turned the views himself, while I looked at it. Then he insisted upon giving it to me, & asked me to keep it as a little souvenire of this visit to him & the Empress. I thanked his Majesty very much. I must finish my letter in the morning because I am so sleepy now. . . .[98]

While in Paris Queen Emma also visited the Palaces of Versailles and Trianon and posed for a photosculpture statuette to be made of herself. ("Photosculpture" was a new method by which a picture was taken from different viewpoints by several cameras all in the same instant, and the sculpture was then modeled from this picture.) One of the statuettes was a bust, six inches in diameter, that looked like it was chiseled out of the purest white marble, with the brow encircled by a wreath of fern leaves. (Mrs. Hasslocher described the studio as having been lined with mirrors so that the "photosculptor" could see his model from all sides without moving.)[99]

The *Hawaiian Gazette* reported that "Her reception in Paris has been of the most friendly nature, and everything that French politeness and French taste could do has been done. . . . Our readers and all friends of Hawaii will be gratified by these marks of interest and sympathy towards our Queen. They constitute a new proof of the friendly feelings entertained by His Imperial Majesty's Government towards our King, Government, and people."[100]

Return to London

By the end of June 1866 Queen Emma had returned to London for a second sojourn of sightseeing, socializing, and more fund-raising. It was a varied and crowded three or four weeks. On July 2, for example, she wrote: "We lunched at Marlborough House with the Prince & Princess of Wales . . . they seemed to be nothing more than a big boy & girl, no conversation. . . ."[101] The next evening she dined with Lady Devon. The following day, having been asked to be the godmother, she attended the christening of Mrs. Cutts' child named Alexander Albert Francis.[102] A week later she stood as godmother for another child, "the Fitz Roy's little girl."[103] On another day she had lunch at the home of Lord Houghton where she met the African travelers Mr. and Mrs. Baker and the young Lord Milton who had crossed Canada on foot.[104] On July 16 she wrote, "Mrs. Williams went with me to . . . St. Georges Hanover Sqr Church, it was the worst service I have heard in England." Besides the terrible service, she thought the church building was "very ugely."[105] The following day she attended a large meeting presided over by the Archbishop of Canterbury.[106] A week later she lunched with a deputation of ladies from Boston who were collecting money for the cathedral in Honolulu.[107]

In the meantime, Lady Franklin and Miss Cracroft had returned from India via southern France to London and Upper Gore Lodge where the queen was once more installed. On the evening of the 18th the twosome accompanied Queen Emma to a "souiree of the S.P.G. [Society for the Propagation of the Gospel] at London House"; earlier in the day she went shopping for friends at Harvey & Co. The Bishop of Oxford also called to bid the queen goodbye, and during the next few days a steady parade of notables came to do the same: Lady Clarendon, Lady Victoria

Hope Scott, Mrs. Gladstone and daughters, Lady Augusta Stanley, and the Dean of Westminster, among others. The number of people who came to bid her aloha was far more numerous than the number who came to welcome her arrival at Southhampton the previous year.

In total, the six months that Queen Emma had spent in England were a remarkable success, surpassing the expectations of even the most sanguine of her Anglican sponsors. Not only did she manage to raise the considerable sum of 6,000 pounds for a cathedral but also she acquired the architectural drawings and arranged for the first shipment of finished stone to Honolulu.[108] By any account, the sojourn was also an immense personal triumph for Emma. She had struck a chord in the hearts of the British with her faith, integrity, compassion, and courage that resonated in the cheers and tributes that they rarely paid to other monarchs or even their consorts.

Ireland

On the morning of July 24 the queen, Charles Hopkins, John Welsh, and Chevalier, accompanied by Lady Franklin and Miss Cracroft, left London's Paddington Station for Ireland. En route they stopped in Stratford-on-Avon to tour the birthplace of William Shakespeare whom Alexander Liholiho was so fond of quoting. In addition to his home, Queen Emma also visited his grave at the Church of the Holy Trinity and the cottage of his wife Ann Hathaway. They caught glimpses of Warwick and Kenilworth Castles as they traveled to Birmingham to spend the night.[109] The next morning they proceeded to the ferry port of Holyhead where they boarded a steamer for the three-hour trip to the harbor of Kingstown, from where they traveled to Dublin.[110]

Why did the queen travel to Ireland? There was no obvious political or diplomatic reason. Nor did she have any special friends living there, although, as in so many other places she visited, many people called. They included the Mayoress of Dublin and her daughter, Mr. and Mrs. Fortesque, a Sir R. Shaw, a Mrs. Blackburn, and the Chancellor's wife and daughter. Furthermore, she does not appear to have done any fund-raising because during her four days in Ireland she met only once with members of the Society for the Propagation of the Gospel headed by the Dean of St. Patrick's. This meeting took place on the morning of June 27 and was quite brief because she and her party left early that afternoon for Killarney. Based on the amount of sightseeing, she came to Ireland to be a tourist.

Queen Emma spent her one full day in Dublin visiting Phoenix

Park, the Roman Catholic Cemetery, the Exhibition Palace, St. Patrick's Cathedral (where Jonathan Swift spent his last years as dean, a fact that the well-read queen undoubtedly knew), and Dublin Castle. She also stopped at some shops, particularly those selling the lace for which the Irish were famous. The lace may have reminded her of her son's christening robe, which was made out of the same material.[111]

She spent what must have been one of the more physically taxing days of her travels when she toured Killarney Park, a thirty-seven-square-mile area comprising a magnificent string of forested mountains and lakes. She wrote in her diary: "Mrs. Williams, I & John [Hopkins had missed the train at Limerick and was left behind] drove to the Gap of Dunloe—took poneys over the Gap to the lakes, then by boat home, landed on one of the little Islands & Tom Murphy & boats crew christened it after me. Visited Ross Castle and Muckross Abbey."[112]

From the top of the Gap (a mountain pass), which offered views of some of the finest scenery in the park, they rode their "poneys" down a seven-mile trail to the bottom and then to the lakes that cover most of the park. A little island was christened after her and was probably in Middle Lake where the Muckross Abbey is located.

On July 30 the queen and her party left Killarney for the City of Cork where they were received by the Hawaiian Consul, from whence they were escorted to Queenstown harbor by a detachment of mounted military police. There they boarded a tender, which took them to the waiting Cunard steamship *Java* that would take them to New York.[113]

"We Are Off for America"

Queen Emma had already planned to stop in the United States on her return to Hawai'i, but King Kamehameha V gave her another incentive. He had written a letter to the queen while she was still in Karlsruhe, Germany, urging her to visit America. He wrote, "If you receive an invitation from the President of the United States of America, then I would advise you by all means to take advantage of that invitation." He said that she would thus "be enabled to see more of the world but at the same time show that your visit to Europe was not of any political purpose, but for private purposes. They [the Americans] are a very sensitive people, your visiting them will disarm all the lies and insinuations directed against our family from what they say of our dislikes of that Country."[114]

After nine days of an extremely rough Atlantic crossing—the queen described each and every sickening day in her Diary—the *Java* arrived in New York early on the morning of August 8. As it sailed up the Hudson River, it announced the queen's presence on board by displaying the Hawaiian Royal standard. The Customs Collector of the Port had received instructions from the Secretary of the Treasury to meet the queen and her party and to welcome her with a gun salute from the customs steamer *Jasmine.* A telegraph operator was supposed to have relayed word at first sighting of the *Java* to the *Jasmine,* but for some reason he did not and it lay innocently at its moorings awaiting the signal. The gaffe proved fortunate because, according to *The New York Times,* if the gun salute had occurred, it would have roused the queen and New Yorkers alike from sleep at the unpleasant hour of 5:00 a.m.[115]

About 10:30 a.m. the *Jasmine* did wake up and pulled alongside the *Java* and welcomed the queen with a thirteen-gun salute. Onboard was the official welcoming party. The queen recognized two members of the party: the Hawaiian Consul General, S. U. F. Odell and Brig. Gen. James F. B. Marshall, who had served Kamehameha III some twenty-three years before as his ambassador to England at the time of the restoration of the kingdom's sovereignty.[116] When he was in the Islands, he had been a frequent guest of Dr. Rooke. The queen and her retinue (now consisting of Charles, John, Chevalier, and the two young ladies, Miss Torbert, who was Hawaiian, and Miss Spurgeon) were received on board the *Jasmine,* which ferried them across the river to their waiting carriages. When Queen Emma stepped on the wharf, she became the first queen to visit America.

From the waterfront, carriages carried the queen and her party to Brevoort House, where a luxurious suite of apartments had been readied for her use. There she was greeted by R. S. Chilton, a special envoy from Washington who carried a letter of welcome from the United States government in the handwriting of the Secretary of State William Seward. She acknowledged the welcome by the government and its secretary and expressed herself as being "much pleased with her European tour." When asked about her plans, she replied she had not yet formed them.[117]

The newspaper described the queen as "well formed and graceful in her movements. Her features are quite regular, her eyes dark, large and lustrous, and the expression of her face when in repose is rather sad than otherwise. . . . When interested in conversation her expression is extremely pleasing, and she is eminently distinguished by the easy grace which marks the accomplished lady, which no doubt she is."[118]

The New York Times went on to say that America did not need

England's example of hospitality to know how to treat Queen Emma. "The presence of this Royal lady in her widow's weeds, with the knowledge of her Christian life, and our sympathy for its sorrows, awaken sufficient interest in us to secure her a reception befitting her many virtues and her rank."[119]

While in New York, she attended Anglican services at Trinity Church whose immense auditorium was completely jammed with the curious and the devout. When she was escorted to her pews the audience rose and remained standing until she had taken her seat, which was the same that had been placed at the disposal of the Prince of Wales a few years before. In his sermon the Reverend Dr. Francis H. Vinton presented Her Majesty with a handsomely embossed prayer book "as a memorial of Christian regard and personal esteem." He then compared the character and work of the queen to the biblical Queen Esther in risking reputation and life in her final and successful effort to obtain from King Artaxerxes the recognition, protection, and rebuilding of God's chosen people. For the final prayer, the grateful queen asked that a special blessing be pronounced for those who have "escaped the perils of the sea" as a token of thanksgiving for her safe crossing of the Atlantic. Informed of the queen's mission to secure aid for the Anglican cause in Hawai'i, the audience contributed funds in excess of $2,500.[120]

From New York, Queen Emma traveled to Washington, D. C., on August 13 by special train provided by the United States government, for her meeting with President Andrew Johnson.[121] That evening the president received in the Red Room the first queen to grace the White House in the history of the United States. In his welcoming remarks, the president said: "In according you this earnest welcome permit me to assure you that it is not because you bear the title of a Queen—it is induced solely by the prestige that has preceded you that has assured us of your virtues as a woman, and especially of your efforts in the cause of Christianity, civilization and education among the people of your country. . . . If I were disposed to be facetious on this occasion, I might say that, while none of the people of these United States wear crowns, while no man is acknowledged as a King and no woman as Queen, yet while you are here in these United States you will have none but Queens to associate with. None of our citizens wear crowns, but all are sovereigns."[122]

According to *The New York Times* reporter who was at the reception, the queen responded to the president in an "inaudible tone," so we cannot know whether she appreciated the President's remarks on

American egalitarianism. However, he reported that she did enter into an "animated conversation" with members of the cabinet.

Thomas Lately, the biographer of Andrew Johnson, wrote that although besieged by the problems of the post-bellum Civil War period, the president was thrilled to meet the queen. In fact, the president had urged the full cabinet to attend the reception, and members vied for the honor of escorting her. It is said that when he was not selected, Secretary of War Edwin McMasters Stanton stayed away in pique. First Lady Eliza Johnson, who was an invalid and normally did not attend such functions, decided that the occasion was too important and intriguing not to attend. It was only the second time during her years in the White House that she made such an appearance.

Secretary of the Navy Gideon Welles was quite fascinated by Queen Emma, whom he judged to be "well developed," with fine bust and figure, a roguishly roving, "round, full eye," and complexion "a shade darker perhaps than a brunette." Lately wrote, "Reporters found the Queen full of animation and mirthfulness, while the President seemed in a happier mood than he had been for a long time. Graciously attentive to all, he presided with animation and courtesy."[123]

After her singular appearance in the White House, the queen visited Niagara Falls and then Montreal on August 20th. From Canada she was scheduled to visit Boston where General Marshall was serving on the Massachusetts governor's staff, but before she could depart for Boston, Emma received word that her mother Grace had died on July 26. Grace had been an invalid for years, so her death was not a surprise. But the news was extremely sad; as she had once written to Kamehameha V, there was no one in the world whom she loved as much as her mother. Emma immediately went into mourning, canceled her trip to Boston, and made plans to return home.

Meanwhile, General Marshall and the members of the Hawaiian Club of Boston, established earlier in January, had made elaborate plans for her reception by the governor of the state and the mayor of the city. Interestingly, according to the *Pacific Commercial Advertiser*, the club, which had as one of its purposes "to advance the interests of the United States at the Hawaiian Islands and the welfare of the Hawaiian Nation," took the initiative to call the attention of the U.S. government and New York City officials to the queen's visit, which resulted in the State Department's reception for the queen. It is difficult to believe, however, that the Hawaiian government had not taken similar initiatives on its own. The club's thirty or so members included such distinguished former

Hawai'i residents as the businessmen Charles Brewer and James Hunnewell, Gorham D. Gilman, Benjamin Pitman, Dr. R. W. Wood, Edward Bond, and Gen. Marshall.[124] Pitman later wrote to the queen to say everyone was sorely disappointed when she canceled her visit to the city.[125]

Queen Emma returned to New York and on September 1 departed for San Francisco via Panama as a guest of the Pacific Mail Steamship Company. In the meantime, California's governor, who appreciated the fact that she was a potential future ruler of the Hawaiian kingdom, sent a telegram to Washington authorities requesting that the U.S. warship *Vanderbilt* be detailed to return the queen and her party to Honolulu. Upon her arrival in San Francisco, she was received as cordially as she had been in New York and Washington. One newspaper in a laudatory article described her as "truly gracing the position she appears well entitled to."[126] Rear Admiral H. K. Thatcher, commander of the North Pacific Squadron and the *Vanderbilt,* said that his intention was to take the queen back to the islands "as a queen *should go.*" He added: "I have no doubt but that a friendly and conciliatory course with the Government of those Islands will be better than a bluster."[127] The queen left San Francisco on October 13 on the *Vanderbilt* as a guest of the United States government. Together with the admiral's wife and daughter whom she had persuaded to accompany her, Queen Emma arrived back in Honolulu on October 22, 1866.

Home at Last

The *Hawaiian Gazette*'s extra edition described her reception as follows: "The town became alive with excitement immediately [upon the news of her arrival]—the streets thronged with people wending their way to the Esplanade. . . . Almost every house hung out its welcome-banner to attest the joy felt by the event of the Queen's arrival. . . . The crowd was immense—thronging the wharf up to the Custom-house—and all the tops of buildings covered with spectators.

> Echo guns, from hill to hill;
> Man your yawls from truck to still,
> Mighty cheers from mount and plain,
> And welcome Emma home again."[128]

16

The Anglican Visionary

Awaiting Queen Emma on her return was a letter from Lot, King Kamehameha V, who had written: "I regret exceedingly that I cannot in person welcome you home. This letter is intended to be handed to you on your arrival. . . . I promise myself a feast, on my return and hear all the incidents of your travels."[1] She replied, "I am well & glad to be again on our own soil although my house is a very sad one to me. I loved my mother above everything on this side of the grave & perhaps it was very erring in making too much of any earthly thing that she has been taken from me. It is only through the severest trials that we can ever lift our eyes & see our Savior's beaming face & outstretched arm." She added that she was deeply grateful for the kindness he had extended to her mother and that she looked forward to seeing him.[2] Lot wrote back complaining about the various ailments afflicting him and regretting losing so much precious time "as I am wanted at home and more particularly to see you."[3]

In Love with Emma

Emma had been on the king's mind constantly. He had talked at length about her with de Varigny who wrote that the king's feelings were "more pronounced than brotherly affection." In fact, the king acknowledged that "he loved the queen" (*"il aimait la reine,"* in de Varigny's original French version) and that he wanted to marry her. However, knowing her religious faith and the opposition of the Anglican clergy to marriages between a brother-in-law and sister-in-law, he strongly doubted that she would consent to marry him. Afraid to ask her himself, he had authorized de Varigny to talk to the queen on her return and "to convey to her his assurances that he would know how to respect her refusal and to beg of her to retain her affection as a sister to him if her religious scruples or her true sentiments did not permit her to accept him as a husband."[4]

When the king returned to O'ahu on January 12, he proceeded immediately to the palace to tend to some official business and met the queen there for the first time since she left Honolulu 20 months earlier.[5] It must have been a joyful, if not tender, reunion. Although de Varigny had not yet spoken to the queen about the king's love for her, she may have sensed his feelings.

When de Varigny did speak with the queen about the king's affection and desire to marry, he was told what both he and the king expected: her religious scruples and the memory of Alexander were insurmountable obstacles. But did she love the king? De Varigny hints at the answer in the following statement: "I believe that under different circumstances and a lesser exposure she would have listened more closely to her personal sentiments and that the esteem and the affection she had for him would have triumphed over her hesitation."[6] Despite the various speculations, the fact is that Emma and Lot remained very close friends until he died.

Building the Cathedral

Queen Emma witnessed the first tangible result attributable to her travels abroad—the start of the building of the cathedral. Bishop Staley's original plan had called for a cathedral to be built of lava and coral rock and plastered inside and out with a highly decorated interior like other churches in Hawai'i. However, the plan was abandoned in favor of the design that the queen had acquired in London. It was to be a cathedral in the French gothic style of the twelfth century and of a size that could accommodate 600 to 800 worshipers. It was to have arches and windows of cut stone, iron grills for the choir, clerestory windows of stained glass, a tiled roof with a spirelet, and a tower mounted by a spire.[7]

The queen must have been especially gratified to view, from her place near the king, the laying of the cathedral cornerstone on the morning of March 5, 1867, less than six months after her return from England. The ceremony took place under an open tent surrounded by a large crowd of dignitaries, lay members, students, and the king's entire military establishment, which consisted of the Hawaiian Cavalry, the Artillery Company, the Household Troops, and the Hulumanu (the court favorites of Kamehameha III) in Zouave dress—white leggings, scarlet trousers tucked at the knees, blue shirts, and scarlet caps.[8]

As King Kamehameha V laid the cornerstone, he declared, "In the faith of Jesus Christ we place this stone of the Cathedral of Saint Andrew, to the honor of Almighty God, and to the pious memory of our Royal Brother, ʻIolani, deceased (King Kamehameha IV), in the name of the Father, and of the Son, and of the Holy Ghost." Although he was not an active Episcopalian, the king spoke these words with emotion and respect for the church. The cornerstone has a brass plate inscribed in Latin. Above it is a marble plaque containing the English translation, which reads:

> TO THE HONOR OF ALMIGHTY GOD, FATHER, SON AND HOLY SPIRIT, AND IN MEMORY OF THE MOST PIOUS KING OF THE HAWAIIAN ISLANDS, KING KAMEHAMEHA IV, WHO DIED ON THE FEAST OF ST. ANDREW THE APOSTLE A.D. 1863. HIS BROTHER, THE MOST HONORABLE KING KAMEHAMEHA V, LAID THIS CORNERSTONE ON THE 5TH DAY OF MARCH A.D. 1867.[9]

The queen must have been moved by these words, which culminated in Alexander Liholiho's efforts to make restitution.

Work started at once on the foundation of the choir and tower but stopped after only forty-five feet had been laid. The money that the queen had raised was simply not sufficient. Thus, when Bishop Staley left for London shortly thereafter, one of the main purposes of his trip was to raise additional funds. The cut stones for the choir that the queen had ordered in London had arrived months before but they still remained in their crates. These unopened crates became a painful symbol of the ensuing disagreement among Anglicans about the design and size of the cathedral.[10]

Instead of the grand cathedral, a "pro-cathedral"—a temporary building containing the cathedra or bishop's seat that is used until the cathedral itself is built—had been constructed the year before. This temporary wooden church would serve as the congregation's and the queen's "cathedral" for the next twenty years. Bishop Staley had divided the church into Hawaiian and English congregations, and the queen regularly attended the Hawaiian services, which were held at 9:30 a.m.

and 4 p.m. (English services were at 11 a.m. and 7:30 p.m., which she occasionally attended.)[11]

Founding of St. Andrew's Priory

If the queen was disappointed in the progress of the building of the cathedral, she was pleased and satisfied with the development of the Anglican schools. While in England, she had met with the Reverend Mother Lydia Sellon of the Society of the Most Holy Trinity to express her desire that a school for girls be established and to request that more Sisters be sent to Hawai'i. Mother Sellon, who always had an interest in the Islands, agreed not only to send three more Sisters but also to establish a school for girls of a higher social class than those at Lahaina. She also decided to make the trip to the Islands herself.

The Sisters landed in Honolulu in March 1867 and were welcomed by Queen Emma, David Kalākaua, Bishop Staley, and others. They stayed in Rooke House with their royal hostess for several weeks, while Mother Sellon arranged for the property and the building of the school. In May, Mother Sellon visited the Anglican schools for boys and girls in Lahaina. She was accompanied by the queen, Kalākaua and his wife, Kapi'olani, Bishop Staley, and other *ali'i.* The queen wrote to Kamehameha V about how much she enjoyed attending the students' "examination," which was actually a public presentation of the skills the students had acquired in reading, arithmetic, music, and other subjects.[12] Before leaving Lahaina, Mother Sellon gave a "loo'au" with prizes for the students and gifts for the queen. The Sisters were impressed by the "incessant stream of presents," mostly food, the queen received from her native people.[13]

In the meantime, in Honolulu the work went forward on the new school buildings planned by Mother Sellon. Kamehameha IV had previously donated a large piece of property to be used for the cathedral. On a tiny portion of this land a small structure had been built and was used for a girls' day school, but it was far too small for what Mother Sellon was proposing. She had several more buildings constructed; these included a two-story dormitory, a schoolroom, a refectory (dining hall), and a chapel, which were connected by an arched cloister, a covered walkway of about 150 feet. Mother Sellon expended $7,000 of her society's funds to build the school, which she called St. Andrew's Priory School for Girls.[14]

Mother Sellon proved to be a very efficient and forceful taskmaster —the buildings were completed in less than two months, and on Ascension Day, May 30, 1867, the school was dedicated by Bishop Staley. After a short service in the pro-cathedral, a procession was formed consisting of the choir, priests, the bishop, the Reverend Mother and Sisters, the children of the school, and Queen Emma. As the procession moved from the church through the priory gate and along the cloister, it stopped at each building where the bishop said a prayer. A feast, described as "English style," followed with ice cream as the only item of food mentioned.[15]

Prior to this event, the queen had been admitted into the "Companions of the Love of Jesus," a devotional group organized by Mother Sellon in 1855 to "engage in continuous intercession for the conversion of sinners and the succour of the dying." It was divided into nine "choirs," with each choir responsible for a fixed period of prayer every day. As a member of one of the choirs, she held the title of "Companion Associate." Each companion also undertook to do some work for the society, and Mother Sellon subsequently assigned to the queen the task of making a garden out of part of the playground area, which the queen did at her own expense.[16]

Four days after the school's dedication the Reverend Mother left Honolulu for England. On the day of her departure, Hawaiians brought *ho'okupu* or farewell tokens of respect, such as pigs, chickens, and other items that were given to *ali'i* on special occasions. Queen Emma, who had developed a strong bond with Mother Sellon, was very pleased with the gesture and told her it was usually not done for a foreigner.[17]

Mother Sellon took with her Ella Dudoit to be a "nursery governess" and four Hawaiian girls, including Manoanoa Shaw and Keomailani Crowningburg, to be educated by the Sisters in England. The queen noted in a letter to Kamehameha V that little Keomailani "was jumping with glee at the prospects of going to England."[18]

St. Andrew's Priory School for Girls opened with eleven boarders and a few day students, and by the end of 1867, seventeen boarders had been registered. Because the queen had requested a school for Hawaiian girls, the majority of the girls were Hawaiian, most of whom were *ali'i* or of prominent Hawaiian families. In fact, the priory was known as a school for *ali'i,* due no doubt to the queen's influence. But from the beginning a few *maka'āinana* (commoners) and white girls attended as day students.[19] The girls ranged in age from four and one-half to sixteen; most were ten years old or younger at the time of entrance.

They received a "solid English" education including reading, writing, arithmetic, geography, deportment, and, most important, biblical principles.[20] Both Queen Emma and the Sisters intended to establish a Christian family environment where high moral and religious principles would be instilled, where a sound education would enable them to take their place in the increasingly modernized life of the Islands, and where they would learn to be wise and capable wives and mothers.[21]

The queen believed that the girls should also be trained in nursing, particularly as children's nurses. With the hospital in mind, she once expressed the hope that in time to come "girls trained in nursing by our Sisterhood will save many suffering lives."[22] Although the Sisters were experienced nurses and qualified to give such instruction, the curriculum did not reflect the queen's hope. It was not until 1910 that the first priory graduates entered the nursing profession.[23]

The girls learned sewing, embroidery, drawing, and music—the first piano was loaned to the school by Queen Emma.[24] The boarders were also expected to help with the housework by sweeping, making beds, and setting tables every day. Because most of the girls were *ali'i* who by tradition thought housework was below their dignity and status, the Sisters at first found it difficult to persuade the girls to do these tasks. They solved the problem by showing that they themselves, although white and friends of the queen (who had learned to do the same as a boarder at the Chiefs' Children's School), were not ashamed of such work.[25]

Although the priory was intended mainly for Hawaiians, neither the queen nor the Sisters intended it to be free. The annual tuition for boarders was $100 (at a time when beef was five cents a pound), with music, drawing, and French available at an additional fee. (The $100 tuition was to remain the same for the next forty years.) Day students paid 50 cents a week for tuition plus an additional 50 cents a week for dinner daily and for tea on school days. The policy was never to turn away a child for lack of money, but the lack of money was a genuine problem. Although the Sisters did not want to rely on the government, they sought and accepted grants from the Board of Education. They also accepted scholarship aid from private donors such as Queen Emma and King Kamehameha V who personally gave several hundred dollars out of his own pocket to Anglican schools every year.[26]

Revisiting St. Cross School

In 1862, when St. Cross School was founded in Lahaina, the queen was only peripherally involved. This situation changed in early 1867 when she visited the school with Mother Sellon to find conditions deplorable.

The school building (which was the former American Seaman's Hospital) was dilapidated; the dining room was only partially roofed and had no floor; there were only a few books that had come from England; and the diet included bread, meat, and potatoes but little milk and no butter.[27] Together with Mother Sellon, Emma immediately took action to improve living and educational conditions, beginning with the purchase of the lease on the property that allowed the Sisters to make sorely needed improvements. By 1868 the conditions at the school were so improved that Bishop Staley reported that it was "filled to overflowing, and applications for admission have to be refused" and that it was receiving substantial capitation grants from the government.[28]

When Miss Isabella Bird, who spent six months in the Islands in 1873, visited the school, she found a very pleasant place. She described a large house of plastered stone or adobe, which contained dormitories, a visitor's room, an oratory or chapel, and three houses at the back that were used as a schoolroom, cookhouse, laundry, and refectory. A visitor's room and a playground were located under some "fine tamarind trees." She also described the cheerful and loving atmosphere of the school:

> I never saw such a mirthful-looking set of girls. Some were cooking, some ironing, some reading aloud, but each occupation seemed a pastime. When they spoke to the Sisters, they clung to them as if they were their mothers. I heard them read, play the piano, and sing, and their legible handwriting I envied. Their accent and intonation were pleasing, and there was a briskness and emulation about their style of answering questions, rarely found in country schools with us, significant of intelligence and good teaching. All but the younger girls spoke English as fluently as Hawaiian. . . . It was a family manner rather than a school manner, and the rule is obviously one of love. . . . Strict obedience is, of course, required, but the rules are few and lenient, and there is no more pressure of discipline than in a well-ordered family.[29]

Bird had noted that the Sisters had initially encountered some hostility but had won the hearts of the people of Lahaina by their ministrations to the sick. They were willing and able to care for anyone who needed their help, even those afflicted with leprosy. They opened a free dispensary for the poor and soon gained a reputation for doctoring the sick and the lame.[30] On one occasion Sister Catherine wrote to Queen Emma telling her how she prescribed medicine for the ailing Governor of Maui, a very close friend and relative of the queen.[31]

Although Bird had no special fondness for Anglicans, she had only praise for the Sisters. She wrote: "One Sister sleeps in each dormitory, and these highly educated and refined women have no place of retirement except a very plain oratory; and having taken the vow of poverty, they have of course no possessions, none of the books, pictures, and knick-knacks wherewith others adorn their surroundings. Their whole lives, with the exception of the time passed in the oratory, are spent with the girls, and in visiting the afflicted at their homes."[32]

Despite the dedication of the Sisters and the support of the queen, St. Cross was forced to close its doors in 1884 for lack of students.

A Deep Attachment

As an unfailing friend of students and the Sisters everywhere, Queen Emma wrote Bishop Staley: "How can I tell you, dear Bishop, what these dear Sisters are to me, my greatest comfort in this world. They attend to the beauty and order of our solemn and dignified services, and are helping the mothers of my people to realize the love of God and that His Kingdom is coming to them, now and here in His Church on earth. Oh, how I wish above all that every child in my country could receive this firm grounding in the Faith of Christ and so be armed against all temptations."[33]

In turn, the Reverend Mother Lydia wrote of the queen in a letter to Bishop Staley:

> The perfectly restored health of the Queen was to me great encouragement. She, so beloved by the people, and so loving them, is a centre on which one's thoughts fix, under God, with reference to the work of the Church in the Islands. God has apparently given her so entire a submission to His Will, that the cup of anguish . . . has never embittered to her life or its affections. Living amidst her people, ever ready to give cheerful attention with that peculiar fresh sweetness so exclusively her own, one cannot but feel that to her the time of her deepest sorrow has arrived, because, to all human eyes, her deepest sorrow is past. This very powerfully struck me, in one whose young life of an almost singular happiness has been so suddenly and so irremediably stricken. She is the joy of her people's heart.[34]

Apart from her respect and love for the queen, Mother Sellon's commitment to educating Hawaiians was based on the conviction that education could improve their health and "longevity." After her return to England, she wrote to Bishop Staley:

> It is said that the natives must perish; but I do not see why this is to be assumed as a reason for apathy . . . or why energy in attempting to avert so great a catastrophe as the extinction of this fine people is to be damped, as though we had been told on irrefragable evidence that the hour is at hand.
>
> More reasonably might we say that, man being born to die, we should treat with indifference the warnings of some illness, which nothing but our own carelessness need render mortal.
>
> People assume as a fact that the Hawaiian race must die out. They may as well, first of all, try (as the King is doing) whether it is the will of Heaven that it should survive.

"Careful education," Mother Sellon argued, could improve the health of Hawaiians and extend their life span as well. She offered as partial evidence the excellent health of the children of the mission boarding schools. "There is a reasonable hope," she concluded, "that by careful cultivation and by attention to the sanitary measures the King is adopting, the longevity of the people may in the course of generations be equal to our own."[35]

The bishop concurred when he praised the work of the Anglican mission "especially in the education and training of those on whom, more than in the case of any previous generation, depends, the question, whether the Hawaiian, at least as an unmixed race, is or is not doomed to extinction."[36]

Queen Emma must have been buoyed by Mother Sellon's hopeful views on Hawaiian health coming at a time when Queen's Hospital was under criticism. According to *Ke Au ʻOkoʻa,* people were saying "*Hale Maʻi O Ka Wahine Aliʻi* (Queen's) was "no longer a place for poor people to go to for treatment . . . they are being turned away without proper treatment. And that . . . it is for rich people as well as the poor." However, this same newspaper responded in an editorial, stating that there was no truth to these complaints and that "the hospital was built for the poor and it is still for the poor."[37]

Helping the Missions

The queen's services to her church did not end with building the cathedral or supporting the mission schools. She also supported the work of the Anglican mission stations on the other Islands. In May 1867 she paid a visit to the Reverend G. B. Whipple, who had opened a station in Wailuku the year before on land donated by the king. He too had succeeded in starting a school for boys and one for girls, which the queen visited. Mrs. Whipple described how the queen received the students who came to pay their respects and make their offerings. "The youngest of all—a pretty child of four years—as soon as one of the older boys had made his little speech introducing the others, evidently thinking it was time for him to be doing something, walked directly up to the Queen, and with a most confiding, yet timid air, gave the bunch of flowers which he had brought, and received a kind greeting from Her Majesty, whose simple dignity of manners is combined with the most winning graciousness towards her people."[38]

During the ensuing days she visited the different departments of the mission's day schools and voiced how pleased she was that a pure Hawaiian boy excelled in his class of several "half-caste" boys. One evening, after the English service, she visited the free evening school for adult natives who were learning English. At another meeting with native parishioners, Col. Kalākaua spoke to them about the posture they assumed in prayer. He remarked that he had seen many of them approach the king to ask a favor by kneeling or even crawling. "And yet," said he, "can you think it proper to ask a favour of the King of kings, without any outward mark of respect, sitting upright when you are praying to Him?"[39]

One Saturday evening the queen dined with Governor Paul Nahaolelua, Col. Kalākaua, and Judge Kahalewai, all of whom were staunch supporters of the church. On Sunday, at the mission's Church of the Good Shepherd, she attended all the services, including the 4:00 p.m. Hawaiian service at which she stood as sponsor for the baptism of three infants. On the final morning, she was present at an early celebration of the Holy Eucharist and "gave her parting aloha" to her people as she left Wailuku.

In early 1867, the Reverend Charles G. Williamson arrived from England. He may have felt destined for Hawai'i since his days at St. Augustine's Missionary College in Canterbury where he was put in charge of the red and yellow feather cloak that Queen Emma had gifted the college during her visit to England. Williamson once reported that he noticed that the cloak was "being attacked by moths, so I got some cyanide of potassium and placed it in a basin containing sulfuric acid and placed it in the wardrobe so as to fumigate the cloak.[40]

He was assigned to open a mission at Kealakekua on the slopes of Mauna Loa on the Island of Hawai'i.[41] Unable to raise money from local parishioners, he had collected funds from friends in England to build a church. (It still stands and is known today as "Christ Church," the oldest Episcopal church in Hawai'i.) He then built a school as a memorial to "the Great Navigatory" or Captain Cook who was killed on the edge of the famous bay four miles below.[42] Despite the opposition of Calvinist missionaries, by the end of 1867 Williamson had at least sixty foreigners attending a morning service and twenty-five natives attending a separate afternoon service.[43]

Such was the state of things on the third Sunday of 1868 when Queen Emma decided to call on the Reverend Williamson. From Hulihe'e Palace where she was staying, the queen rode fifteen miles on horseback ascending approximately 1,500 feet *ma uka* to visit the mission. When she left the confines of the palace the area was in rebellion staged by the religious fanatic Kaona and his small band of followers who had threatened the lives of anyone denying his prophecies or authority.[44] Nonetheless, she arrived safely and attended services at "Williamson's church," attracting many of the loyal and the curious natives to the church. She wrote to King Kamehameha V about her visit saying that her prayers were more "carefully said" as she asked God to ease the adversities facing him and the kingdom.[45]

A few months later, in March, a severe earthquake and a tidal wave as "high as the tops of coconut trees" (or forty feet) devastated the area.[46] Amoe Ha'alelea wrote to the queen describing how "The ocean boiled like hot water and was very red like red dirt. When it was feverishly boiling, the water covered the land."[47] The tsunami killed at least thirty-one people. The earthquake, which measured 6.5 on the Richter Scale (the one in Hilo four days later measured 7.5), caused considerable property damage, but the mission was saved. The queen, always involved in disaster aid campaigns, put out an immediate appeal for help in Honolulu and collected several thousand dollars from churches and others for the people of the area (Ka'u).[48]

By 1868 there were Anglican missions on each major Island, and an effort was being made to establish a mission on Moloka'i where the king spent considerable time on his cattle and sheep ranch. In time, other missions would be established in Honolulu as well, all of which the queen supported and visited. Queen Emma was a tireless missionary for the church and personally accounted for hundreds of baptisms, including 150 children, many of whom she had met while visiting the poorer districts of Honolulu and whom she embraced as her godchildren.[49]

Annexation versus Reciprocity

On the day Mother Sellon departed for England, the queen wrote to King Kamehameha V that the Reverend Mother had requested that his portrait be in the schoolroom at the priory to "help teach the children Loyalty."[50] From the beginning, the Sisters sought to instill in their students allegiance both to the Hawaiian monarchy and to Hawai'i's independence—a teaching supported by the Anglican mission itself. King Kamehameha V, after all, regarded the church as a "sacred legacy" bequeathed to him by his brother, and frequently he appeared to be the "Protector of the Mission" despite his advocacy of the separation of state and religion. Thus, predictably, from the bishop down, the Anglicans opposed annexation by the United States. At the same time, however, their Congregationalist enemies accused them of trying to persuade England to annex Hawai'i.

Even before the queen had returned from England in the fall of 1866, an acrimonious debate raged over annexation versus reciprocity. The issue was whether a reciprocity treaty with the United States that would admit Hawai'i's products, mainly sugar, with little or no duty, was preferable to annexation. The sugar planters wanted the reciprocity treaty not only to make them richer but also to lead them to annexation. Many Hawaiians, stirred up by the native press and politicians, such as the fiery part-Hawaiian William Ragsdale, opposed the reciprocity treaty for the same reasons that the planters favored it. The two diametrically opposed positions were both proposed as solutions for the kingdom's dire economic situation. In the end, the king was forced to decide on the lesser of two evils, which of course was not annexation. Most American residents and even some English residents were in favor of annexation, but the vast majority of Hawaiians were not. This point was made clear to British Commissioner James H. Wodehouse by Queen Emma who assured him "that with a few exceptions, all the natives were opposed to annexation."[51]

Determined to fight any annexation attempt, King Kamehameha V wrote to Queen Emma in Kona (December 1867) and condemned those who advocated annexation as "hellish conspirators."[52] The queen replied: "There are many who say that our weakness & isolated position is our greatest safeguard, but I certainly cannot see the logic of such a belief. Our beautiful situation, climate & resources make us the sovereign Isles of the Pacific & those are the temptations that have made the larger powers of Earth covit your Majesty's possessions. . . . I must confess my ignorance as to how this Reciprocity Treaty is going to benefit us or no, notwithstanding all that has been said on it. . . . If it is going to be a commencement to our annihilation, it *surely cannot of course be for our good.*"[53]

She lamented the fact that the efforts of the few remaining chiefs of the realm were ineffectual. On an uncharacteristically self-effacing note, she ended her letter: "I wish I knew how to make myself serviceable to you but alas I am the most good for nothing of all."[54]

Troubles in the Church

When Bishop Staley had first arrived five years before, he had every reason to be hopeful of success. The church enjoyed the support of King Kamehameha IV and Queen Emma, as well as the leading government officials. But when Staley left Honolulu for London in the summer of 1867, he was less than hopeful. Raising funds in Hawai'i and England for the mission had been difficult. The clergymen did not remain in Hawai'i long enough to make an impact. Serious disagreement occurred between the clergy and the parishioners over church rituals, the relationships of the separate congregations, and even the cathedral design. In addition, he personally found that with his large family the cost of living exceeded the combined income from the church and his private means. And finally the majority of members did not like his style of "Churchmanship," which was called "popish."[55]

During his stay in England, he published his report, *Five Years' Church Work in the Kingdom of Hawaii,* in which he described the "difficulties and perils" that the mission had to face. One was being caught between the Congregational and Catholic missions that had staked out their influence and memberships. Staley tried to steer a middle course. He did not want to appear overtly competitive or aggressive and spoke of the danger of proselytizing for more members because the great object was not "the numbers we can count as members" but rather the salvation of souls.[56] But by now both he and his church were being attacked by the "malignant writing" in the Congregational organs (referring to the *Pacific Commercial Advertiser*) and by the Roman Catholics who discredited them as "heretics and schismatics" and who tried to prevent them from establishing mission sites.[57] Staley also wrote about the unmitigated jealousy of his opponents who pointed to the lack of funding from England, the unfinished cathedral, and the constant shifting of clergy as evidence that the support of the Anglican church would be "withdrawn speedily from the Islands."[58]

Bishop Staley acknowledged the problem of retaining clergy in the mission field and readily pointed to the Roman Catholics as the model. He praised their approach to missionary work in which a priest was sent out to live and die among his flock and never considered returning to his native land except in his old age and rarely even then. But he criticized his own church's practice of allowing missionaries to have outside jobs to supplement their meager income.[59]

Bishop Staley remained away for about two years. As far as Queen Emma was concerned, the main purpose of his trip was to raise funds for the cathedral. When the bishop wrote about returning to Hawai'i, the queen made it clear that he should "not return till money is raised to complete the Cathedral."[60] She herself was raising funds by "begging of the people for the poor natives" and had raised $3,000 during a four-day period.[61] She told Bishop Staley that the new dean was "working splendidly" and had "thoroughly roused the Church from its lethargy," which may have been an unintended criticism of what the bishop had left behind. She also reported that Lili'uokalani had "quite forsaken" the church and "attends regularly the Kawaiahao meetings to show off her new dresses and finery, which she has new every Sunday. But pray," she added, "don't expose me in this bit of scandal."[62]

In the meantime, the problems of the church did not disappear; they multiplied. The Sisters who chronicled the events at the time wrote that Bishop Staley "returned to a stormy See, so stormy that it obliged him to resign in May, 1870."[63] Not the least of the causes for his resignation was the queen's disapproval of his attitude and policies.

His resignation prompted the *Pacific Commercial Advertiser* to report in January 1870: "Thus after seven years of trial the experiment of building up an expensive ecclesiastical establishment unsuited to the wants of the place and repugnant to the tastes of the people, has proved a failure and will be abandoned.

"The establishment here of the Reformed Catholic Church was one of the visionary schemes of the late R. C. Wyllie and never met with the cordial support of English or American Episcopalians for the main object appeared transparent from the first to be political rather than religious."[64] The newspaper was being careful but not totally honest because the establishment of the Anglican Church was not just Wyllie's scheme, of course, but the wishes of King Kamehameha IV and Queen Emma.

The queen was greatly concerned because Staley had precipitated a crisis that threatened the very existence of the mission, not to mention her own work. Both she and King Kamehameha V were fearful that the English would be so discouraged that the mission would be turned over to the American Episcopal Church.[65] The queen wrote to the king expressing her complete opposition to any such attempt and accused Bishop Staley of trying to effect the change "to cover his own disgrace as it were [his] expulsion from this Diocese . . . he had said as much to me two or three times during some threatening conversations before he left here." The queen said that he threatened to tell the Church in England that Hawaiians did not want English support, that it was "utterly useless," and that they preferred American clergy. "It is very funny," she wrote, "how suddenly rich the American Church has grown of late so much so that it assumes a material responsibility towards us as our Mother, which when Bishop Staley was here recently they were altogether too poor to help." She offered to help the king in any way she could.[66]

The crisis was partly resolved when the Anglican Church in England dispatched the Right Reverend Alfred Willis. He arrived in Honolulu in June 1872, but by then the prospects looked bleak for the Hawaiian Anglican church.

The Duke of Edinburgh

Despite the trials of her church, life went on for the queen. She still wore her widow's weeds, but she was scarcely a social recluse. She still favored handsome clothes, and once wrote to Kamehameha V about a ship's captain in Honolulu who was "very good looking, tall & graceful" and someone "everyone is raving about."[67] She continued to attend dinners, receptions, and balls, often as a partner to or in the company of the king.[68] She occasionally acted as the king's official emissary in greeting visiting ships and hosting their officers.[69] And she regularly visited her residences in Nuʻuanu, Hālawa, Rooke House, Waikīkī and Waiʻaha in Kona.

The highlight of her social life in the years following her return from Europe was the visit of Queen Victoria's second son, Alfred Ernest Albert, the Duke of Edinburgh, whom she had not met in London. The duke was captain of the *Galatea,* a ship-of-war, which arrived in Honolulu on July 21, 1869. The *Pacific Commercial Advertiser* effusively opined that the duke would "win . . . golden opinions of not only his country men but others, and show to all that Queen VICTORIA has brought up persons in a manner as to reflect honor to an empire on which the sun never sets."[70]

The queen, the entire royal court, and the community had eagerly anticipated the first visit of a prince of the British royal family to Honolulu. The duke was welcomed by the Hawaiian military and other dignitaries amid a boisterous crowd at the wharf. He was then taken by royal carriage through the streets draped in bunting and flags and containing "throngs of cheering natives," to the Queen Street residence of the king's late father, Kekūanaoʻa (who died on November 24, 1868). The duke was next escorted to the palace to call on His Majesty, his cabinet, and members of the privy council. It was high protocol but also a mark of his respect for the duke that King Kamehameha V called on him at his temporary residence that afternoon. The esteem in which he was held is revealed in a passage of a letter by Queen Emma to Lucy Peabody: "One of the Duke's pillows which he used at Mokuahua was sold yesterday at the sale for $13. What do you think of such veneration & admiration for Royalty (English, ehem)."[71]

The queen attended every social event for the duke either as a partner or guest of the king. At the ball held by the king at the palace in the duke's honor, it was the duke who took the queen's arm (while the king took the arm of Mrs. Wodehouse) and escorted her to the dinner table "always marching to the sound of the bagpipes." After the midnight dinner the dancing began with 100 ladies representing the "youth and beauty" of Honolulu and about 150 gentlemen. Queen Emma would not have missed the opportunity to dance with the duke, and probably stayed till the last grand reel at dawn.[72]

The duke wanted to meet native Hawaiians in an authentic cultural environment. At the king's request, Princess Liliʻuokalani issued invitations for a lavish *lūʻau,* starting at 11:00 a.m. at her residence in Hamohamo (a district in Waikīkī). The duke had an opportunity to taste each kind of Hawaiian delicacy and to appreciate various native dances, chants, and games. A violent rainstorm put a stop to the party at five o'clock, which otherwise might have continued much longer. However, the storm seemed not to bother Princess Keʻelikōlani because Emma noted that "Ruth went out to Waikiki . . . Tuesday & is there still. . . ." (almost two weeks later).[73]

Liliʻuokalani considered the party "one of the grandest occasions in the history of those days," but not everyone agreed.[74] The *Hawaiian Gazette* presented the critics' views: "We have heard it stated that . . . several half-caste ladies, who have married foreigners, were invited and their husbands omitted . . . certainly a very singular and questionable procedure, and one not calculated to engender good feeling. We regret to have to chronicle the fact that the disgraceful Hula-dance was a part of the programme, and trust for the sake of common decency that it may be the last time that this relic of heathenism may be performed. . . ."[75]

The day after the *lūʻau* the people brought *hoʻokupu* sufficient to provision the duke's ship with fowl, pigs, taro, sugar cane, pineapples, maize, tapa, and more. It took two large scows to haul the goods on to the *Galatea.* On the day of his departure, the duke reciprocated with gifts of his own. Queen Emma wrote, "I went up to the Palace to show the King my bracelet from the Prince. . . . His Majesty showed me a set of gold studs . . . Mr. Prendergast received a scarf pin. . . . Taffy got a ring with 2 pearls & a pink stone. . . ."[76] Liliʻuokalani received a solid gold chain with an anchor-link and copies of two of the duke's own musical compositions.[77]

17

Lāwaʻi Adventures

By 1870 Queen Emma was already a major landlord with title to the *ahupuaʻa* or land division of Kawaihae; to Hānaiakamalama, which she had inherited from her uncle Keoni Ana in 1857; to the *ahupuaʻa* of Waiʻaha in Kona, which she claimed from her husband's estate in 1865; and to her father's lands in Nuʻuanu Valley and in downtown Honolulu, which she received from her mother in 1866, making a total of approximately 12,700 acres.[1] When she received the *ahupuaʻa* of Lāwaʻi, Kauaʻi, another 4,200 acres were added to her estate. It was a gift worth celebrating.

Lāwaʻi

Lāwaʻi had been awarded to Emma's uncle, James Young Kanehoa, in the Mahele of 1848, except for six small parcels of land containing a total of sixteen *loʻi* or taro patches.[2] Upon his demise in 1851, his land was bequeathed to his widow Hikoni.[3] In 1871, fourteen years before Hikoni died, she deeded the land to Emma for "love and affection and for the sum of one dollar" with the proviso that the dowager queen would assume responsibility for her care.[4] Eager to see her new property, Emma journeyed to Lāwaʻi with nearly 100 people six months before the deed was officially registered on June 24, 1871.

Situated between the *ahupuaʻa* of Kalāheo and Kōloa, Lāwaʻi was divided into three areas: the seashore area or Lāwaʻi Kai fronting a large bay, the gulch-like valley fed by Lāwaʻi Stream and several large springs, and the extensive upper lands or bluffs that rise a hundred feet above the valley floor. Lāwa'i Kai consisted of taro fields that reached back into the end of the valley, a fishpond, and the stream that emptied into the small bay. A wide crescent beach lined the head of the bay between two rocky points. This was by far the most beautiful part of the *ahupua'a,* although the entire valley floor had an idyllic charm of its own. In contrast, the upper lands were uninvitingly dry, almost treeless, and pitted with rocks.

When Emma and her entourage, which included her cousin Peter Ka'eo, Mrs. Sarah Weed, and Lucy Peabody, plus retainers, servants, and "wards," arrived in Lāwa'i on December 21, 1870, they went to the upper lands where Hikoni awaited them in a house that seemed isolated and forlorn. In a letter to Kamehameha V, Emma described their arrival: "We arrived [at Kōloa] late in the afternoon last Thursday & had to ride over two miles before we reached this place. . . . The house we are in is one by itself for couple of miles round, rather lonesome I fear for some."[5] In contrast to the hubbub of activity at the thriving sugar port of Kōloa, it was indeed a lonesome spot.

The house was actually a *kauhale* or compound consisting of a large square frame dwelling with a thatched roof and several smaller dwellings enclosed by a low stone wall. There were a few struggling shade trees around the compound, but the surrounding area was a desolate and rocky expanse. The place was hardly a garden, but that is what it was to become with Emma's nurturing.

The compound seemed hard-pressed to accommodate a hundred people, and over the next few weeks the queen asked her mother Fanny to send a long list of supplies: five lined bed covers, five spreads, twelve hand towels, twelve small towels, four bolts of calico, one bolt of muslin, four men's stockings, cloth, brocades, fish nets, fish hooks, pens, quills, pencils, a holder, unground coffee beans, a grinding mill, two bread, men's flannel shirts, thick trousers, cases of beer, one barrel of fat, salmon, two dozen pants and shirts for the men and two dozen for the women, cases of small cans of fish, one barrel kerosene, bundles of necklaces, a flower pan, and several pairs of shoes, among other items.

For the people of the region the presence of the dowager queen was a singular and exciting event. Almost everyone desired to see the queen. On Christmas day alone approximately one hundred people came to Lāwa'i to celebrate "the birthday of God," as she put it. She wrote to the king to say that they had celebrated a typical Christmas by dancing, playing games, and enjoying other amusements of the season.[6]

A few days later, on the queen's birthday, people continued to come to pay their respects. The Reverend Daniel Dole in a letter to Dr. Baldwin, wrote: "Queen Emma is sojourning on Kauai for a season. This is her birthday, & many natives have gone to see her, carrying some little present, as a boquet, some kind of fruit, a few eggs &c. &c. It has rained moderately all day, but the rain does not prevent the natives from riding 3 or 4 miles to visit the Queen."[7]

Alaka'i Swamp

While visiting Lāwa'i Queen Emma engaged in an astonishing array of activities. The most spectacular of these took place in January when she hiked through the prehistorically beautiful but scary Alaka'i Swamp, covering ten square miles in the cloud land of Mt. Waialeale. King Kamehameha V himself may have suggested the hike, as he had been on a pig hunt there twenty years before.[8] However, the fearless queen, with little or no hesitation, decided to make the trek.[9]

She needed a guide because the swamp was almost trailless. Its very name, *alaka'i,* means "to lead," thereby suggesting the need to be guided. It was easy to become lost especially when a heavy rainfall covered the landscape with a thick mist called *noe* (the same word the queen used to describe the fog in London). When a guide was found—an old man called Kaluahi who had hiked the trail long ago—and told of her plans, he thought carefully before he agreed. Even when the reluctant guide did agree, he tried to dissuade the queen. Eric Knudsen (his father Valdemar of Waimea had recommended Kaluahi), in his account of the hike, wrote that "no amount of talk would change the mind of the queen. . . . She was pakiki [stubborn] and refused to be frightened out of her trip."[10]

The queen's party was small in the beginning, but by the time the group reached Waimea it had swelled to 100 men, women, children, hula dancers, musicians, and retainers, all mounted on horseback. As they climbed the bridle path up to Kōke'e, the company stretched along the trail for nearly half a mile. They finally reached the end of the trail at the edge of the deep valley of Kauaikananā. Too steep for horses, they dismounted and started down on foot. The slippery trail led down a long narrow hogback. The chant composed for the event tells of this particular spot:

Ka nahele o Haua'iliki lā *I laila o Kapukaohele lā* *He ihona Kauaikananā lā* *He kahana koke aku nō ia lā*	In the forest of Haua'iliki The traveller comes upon Puka'oleho, But the descent of Kauaikananā Is not easy, even though downstream all the way.[11]

A few hundred feet from the top is a flat spot of about thirty feet square with a 200-foot *pali* (cliff) guarding the south side. There the queen stopped. Entranced by the beauty of the scenery, she called for the hula dancers and musicians to sing and dance. Worried about losing valuable daylight, Kaluahi protested, but the entertainment went on for more than two hours.

They resumed their hike down into the valley and up the other side and down again into Kawaikōi Stream. They waded the narrow but deep-running stream and climbed the slippery slope, with water spurting from the ground springs at every level, up to the ridge. Inching upward with hands, knees, and elbows and grabbing onto whatever they could, they finally reached the swamp plateau (which is 4,000 feet above sea level) where "The land undulates like the waves of the sea, little lines of stunted lehua trees run hither and thither, long open glades lie between and all are dotted with water holes of all shapes and sizes . . . deep enough to drown a person and if you fall in and try to climb out the turf breaks like rotten ice and you cannot pull yourself out. . . . All is wet, the turf you walk on is soggy. . . . To step on a seemingly solid piece of earth and sink to your knees instead is a bit disconcerting and if you do it too often you become exhausted."[12]

In a letter describing the hike, the queen later told the king in what must have been an understatement: "The walking was rather fatiguing & almost took my breath away."[13] The queen may have been helped across one portion of the swamp, where it is only two miles wide. It had an old trail (which ancient Hawaiians may have used as a shortcut from Waimea to Wainiha) made up of sections of tree ferns that were dropped horizontally over the bogs to provide a floating foothold that her retainers had restored for her use.[14] Even with the "corduroy road," the trail was still hazardous because with one misstep on either side of the logs, a traveler could sink chest-deep or even deeper in muck.

Darkness had fallen by the time they crossed the swamp, and the party spent the night in ʻAipōnui forest. According to Knudsen, as people tried to warm their wet and chilled bodies, Queen Emma, relaxed and unperturbed, called to them "to cheer up and to help, [while] she chanted some of the ancient meles to their great delight. . . ."[15] The chant tells of this night:

Kūnihi mai ʻAipōiki lā	To one side stood ʻAipōiki,
Lawelawe nā lima o ke anu lā	Where the cold gripped with fierce hands.

Kipū paʻa mai e ka noe lā	The fog hung motionless,
Hālana wai aʻe ko lalo lā	And water flowed below.
Moe ʻole ia pō a ao lā	All night there was no sleep
Nā hoa i ka heu kalakala lā	For the companions miserable with their gooseflesh,
Hoʻolale i ke ahi lala poli lā	Even when they tried to warm their chests by building a fire
Pulupulu i ka pua limu lā	With bunches of moss for tinder.
Ua noho pōhai a puni lā	All sat about in a circle
Leʻa ai kūlou a "Emma" lā	Where Emma lay bowed down,
Aia ka pono o ke ao lā. . . .	Eagerly awaiting the daylight. . . .[16]

The next morning they walked the final few hundred feet through a thick growth of shrubs to the edge of the Wainiha cliff that marked the abrupt end of their adventure: Kilohana (lookout point). The following excerpt from the same chant tells of the sight 4,000 feet below:

Okipau ka hana a ka Wahine lā	Wondrous indeed was the lady
Kau pono iho i kai wekiu lā	Standing on the heights,
Ka pane poʻo Maunahina lā	On the summit of Mauna-Hina
ʻIke i nā pali Koʻolau lā	Looking toward the Koʻolau side
Ka waiho nani a Hanalei lā	At Hanalei's beauty spread before her,
One haliʻi o Mahamoku lā	The sandy stretch of Mahamoku
Oni ana ʻo Naue i ke kai lā	Naue moves in the sea
O ka wai o Lumahaʻi lā. . . .	The waters of Lumahaʻi. . . .[17]

The return trip to Waimea was relatively easy, and as they rode back, the queen was happy that despite some of the roughest terrain imaginable, no one was hurt, not even the few people who fell off their horses.[18]

She summed up her experience in a letter to Kamehameha V: "Oh the scenery, mosses, Lehua, ferns, wild flowers &c are perfectly beautiful. Kahaaanamahuna, Puu Kapele, Waineki, & Waikoi were pointed out as your various camping grounds on a boar hunt in '51. The large stone with Mr. Brenchly & Mr. Remy's names & others marked on it has rolled off from the top a little way with its face down so I did not see the names, but our guide told us thence. . . . It must not be ascended in the wet months, for then the Lehua is not in its perfection."[19] She enjoyed the hike so much that she told the king that she wanted "to go up again in the autumn." Although the king's reply is not known, he did tell Fanny that he admired the queen's "nimbleness" in climbing the storm-drenched slopes.[20]

An over-solicitous Governor Nahaolelua wrote her that he thought the trip was an unnecessary risk. He compared the cold and damp chill of the hike to the "Prussian soldiers now fighting who have to bear the cold and discomfort" and chided her for abusing her health.[21]

As far as Emma was concerned, the expedition was worth celebrating. On January 29, 1871, a grand *lūʻau* was held with all Waimea present, and the commemorative mele and chants composed in honor of the trip up were recited. One such chant was entitled *I Waimea o Kalani:*

A i Waimea o kalani	The Queen was in Waimea
I ka uka o Waiahulu,	In the upland of Waiahulu,
O ka Halau-a-Ola	At Halau-a-Ola
Malu i ka hale lau koa	She was sheltered by koa trees.
Hoʻonohonoho Waineki,	At Waineki was arranged,
Kauhale a Limaloa.	Shelters like Lima-loa's.
Hoʻokahi puʻu hulahula,	On an unstable mound,
Ka nohona a Emalani,	Sat Emalani the Queen.
I ka-ua-i-kanana,	At Kauaikananā,
Paheʻeheʻe i ka ihona.	The trail was slippery.
Naue ana i ke loa,	On the long trail we moved,
Kū ana i ke kualono.	Till the mountain top was reached.
Puʻili hua ʻohelo,	ʻOhelo berries were gathered,
Mea ʻaina ka wahine.	For the lady to eat.
ʻAlo anu o ka mauna,	She endured the mountain cold,
Mauna anu a Alakaʻi.	The cold mountain of Alakaʻi.
Haʻina mai ka puana,	This concludes my praise,
O Emalani no he inoa.	Of the name of Queen Emma.[22]

According to the queen, Judge Lilikalani, who was a member of the expedition, told the assembled people about "the pleasure of being together in the uplands & how they had to bear the cold, something to brag about for all the people who were on the trip to the mountains with their beloved queen."[23]

In addition to the chants, the people presented other *hoʻokupu* to their queen. She noted that when the people were told not to shake hands with her (presumably out of respect for her royal presence), they complained and insisted on shaking hands. So she obliged.[24]

Significantly, while in Waimea the queen also called on the Honorable J. Kauaʻi, the popular legislative assemblyman. He would play an important role in the queen's later political activities.[25] In keeping with the oral tradition of giving names to people or things to commemorate a significant event, she gave her Lāwaʻi homestead a new name in memory of the trip: Lookout Mountain or Maunakilohana.

One week later she returned to Waimea with her "scholars" to stage a tableau featuring Hawaiian children wearing Chinese costumes portraying English and American characters.[26] She wrote to Elizabeth Pratt:

"Our dance came off on the 9th at Waimea & the scholars made their debut on that occasion very creditably. The Tableaux were most successful & pleased the audience greatly. We actually attempted the Court of Queen Elizabeth with Lucy as her Majesty & [it] looked very well too. Lizzie Hart took Pocahontas in the rescue & marriage of Capt. Smith. There was one very pretty scene from Byron's Corsair, which Lily Richards . . . & a young fellow here took, & we sang Juanita to it. After the performance everything was removed & the tent left clear for dancing, which was carried on with vigor till early morning."[27]

The Ditch

After the Waimea festivities, she planned to visit Niʻihau. According to Fanny, however, when the king heard about this plan, he expressed great concern. "Why is she sailing when the storm season is returning? She's seen Niihau and Kaula. This is stormy weather for boats to sail there." Fanny feared for Emma's safety and declared, somewhat melodramatically, that if she were going to die, she wanted to be her "death companion." She closed, "None of us would want this, only your [dead] husband."[28]

Eventually, Queen Emma postponed her visit to Niʻihau because of another urgent matter: the construction of a two-mile ditch or *ʻauwai* to bring water down to Maunakilohana. On February 14, she wrote: "Today I went with Willie Smith, the Sheriff here on Kauai, who is the son of Dr. Smith, the missionary in Koloa, and George Wilcox, another missionary child. We went to look at the water source so that our ditch can be dug. The haoles made specific measurements and told me that if ten men worked on it, then the digging will take thirty days to the stream, then 3 more weeks of digging to reach the house. The ditch will be only a foot deep and foot wide."[29]

She wrote to Fanny to send ten picks and ten shovels, clothes, blasting powder, and cases of beer, "the cheaper kind," as she put it, "to warm them [the workers]."[30] When they were in the middle of digging the ditch, she received a letter from King Kamehameha V inquiring about her return and offering to send a ship for her. She replied, "When we're finished we will return as it would be a waste of labor and not end up with water if we leave [now]."[31] They finished the first portion of the ditch by March 6, 1871, providing the house with its first running water, but more than two-thirds of the ditch above the highway leading to Wahiawa remained to be finished. The ditch was finally completed on the 18th of April 1871.

The Horticulturist

Once the ditch was completed, she proceeded to build the stone walls to protect the garden from grazing horses so that she could make Maunakilohana blossom. She wrote to Fanny and other family members with numerous requests for plant slips such as *kamani,* mango, rose apple, bamboo, banana, *haole lehua, laua'e, pīkake* (her favorite flower), and white spider lily (which grew profusely at Hānaiakamalama). (It is interesting to note that in Fanny's correspondence with Emma only Dr. McKibbin is mentioned as helping with her plants and not Dr. Hillebrand at Queen's, who was one of Hawai'i's outstanding horticulturists.) Not all the plants shipped from Honolulu arrived safely. Once boxes of plants were lost at Kōloa when the cargo canoe overturned scattering its contents.[32] Other plants grew from the slips of tamarind, thornless kiawe, and magenta bougainvillea given her by the same Dr. Smith from Kōloa.[33]

Queen Emma personally planted the *kawowo* (seedling) of the *hau, ki,* banana, sugarcane, taro, and *pia* (arrowroot) at Maunakilohana, all of which were intended for sale on the local market.[34] She planted the first bougainvillea at Maunakilohana and the white spider lily *(crinum augustum)* (also known as the Queen Emma Lily).[35] She created a shady driveway by having mango and monkey pod trees planted on both sides.[36] Down in Lāwa'i Kai along the stream near its mouth she also planted the tamarind and thornless kiawe.[37]

A story tells of the queen, who was dressed in gardening clothes, hat, veil, and gloves, sitting on the banks of the taro patches and cutting grass while the farmers worked their taro.[38] Perhaps she also hoped to instill the idea that manual labor was not demeaning.

Hawaiian Collectibles

The queen was an avid collector of Hawaiian valuables such as calabashes, *kāhili, kapa,* mats, water gourds, coconut bowls, and shell leis. Much of this traditional craftwork in Hawai'i was either dying out or disappearing. Two years before, she had lamented this loss in a letter to Mrs. Williamson: "Our beautiful as well as old and original articles of native manufacture such as dress ornaments, tools, impliments of husbandry, warfare, etc. etc. have become so scarce by the universal adoption of foreign habits that nearly all purely Hawaiian things have quite disappeared from disuse."[39] Queen Emma, as one modern writer put it, "more than any other member of the Hawaiian royalty had a great appreciation for the traditional Hawaiian crafts."[40]

If she was unable to hunt for the precious objects herself, she sent others to search. For example, she wrote to Fanny that she tried to get Hikoni "to look for wooden calabashes, kahili, kapa or other Hawaiian things. . . ." Though reluctant, her aunt did manage to get a small *kahili,* a calabash, and a carrying pole in Kekaha.[41] On another occasion, the queen wrote: "I am considering giving Mele $40. or $50. to get everything and so the calabashes will belong to us. The grain of the wood is beautifully dark."[42]

Displaying her ire against greedy, insensitive collectors, she wrote indignantly: "Why not do a thorough sweep like Pooloku folks? They stay behind, ask around, buy, plunder. The success is in the gains."[43] She criticized Kawai's wife for seeing only the external "lustre and value" of the bowls: "She doesn't see *the maker's soul inside. . . . That is why I want to procure them.*" (Emphasis added.)[44]

The queen also knew the value of the richly grained *kou* wood that was once used to make the great calabashes of the *ali'i.* These by now were rare because the trees had been almost eradicated by the red spider, an introduced insect.[45] By 1870 both chiefs and wealthy residents were storing (and hoarding) quantities of *kou* to be carved into bowls and furniture.

Emma wrote to Fanny on February 13: "Kapo is taking back two pieces of kou wood on this steamer. One has been hewn on the outside, but the inside was not dug into. The other has not been cut at all."[46] And the next day she wrote again: "If you have $25.00, send it now to buy a kou log to be made into calabashes. It is growing up at Wailua, a big tree. Wikani intends to go and look at it and if it is any good to cut it for us. It may not be good because of its growing in the mountains."[47]

While in Lāwa'i, Emma mentioned in a letter to Fanny that Queen Pomare IV of Tahiti told her that she was sending a box of coconut shell containers. Although she felt it was "unusual to have the Queen of Tahiti write to me," she was interested in the coconut shells because Hawaiian craftsmen had started making polished coconut-shell cups attached to wooden bases.[48] The "polished coconut opihi [limpets] container" she sent to Fanny was probably one of these types of polished coconut shells.[49]

In another letter to Fanny she wrote: "Don't give any patterned water gourds to Kilikiliula as I gave one to her. . . . As for Kahaawelani's patterned water gourd and place mat, send them to Malaea, her mother."[50] Emma was referring to the decorated *ipu* (gourd) that had been traditionally made on Niʻihau and parts of Kauaʻi but not on any other island.[51] Apparently, she had found or purchased some *ipu* on Kauaʻi and sent them as gifts to several friends in Honolulu.

The queen had a particular fascination for Niʻihau shell leis, as evidenced by several references to them in her letters. For instance, she had written Fanny to "set aside a small package of my small, white Niihau shells and give it to Kekaʻanīʻau [Elizabeth Pratt]. . . ."[52] She wrote to "Lizzy," as she called her cousin Elizabeth, with instructions as to how to sew the shells: "they are rather troublesome to string because they have got to be pierced with a very large needle, but don't draw it through as it breaks them, string with thread only—no needle to it."[53] In another letter she wrote to Sarah Weed: "Enclosed is a small necklace of shells, the latest novelty in that ornament from Niihau. I have only just got two strings of them & have cut it up for you folks in Honolulu."[54] In fact, one of her prime reasons for wanting to go to Niʻihau was to acquire more shell leis as well as other craft objects.

Once the ditch construction was resolved, Queen Emma began to think again of visiting Niʻihau, and Fanny resumed trying to dissuade her.[55] She warned her daughter that Niʻihau is "a road without branches" and that it would be said of her that "you are a woman who asks for too much."[56] When Emma learned that Fanny was crying over her plans, she gave her some strong advice of her own: "Don't be listless. Go and visit [people]. . . . If you merely stay at home all the time, people will forget and neglect you. Then you will feel comfortable only around me."[57] In a subsequent letter, Emma again reminded her mother: "Don't just sit at home. Go and visit the homes of those people friendly and loyal to us."[58]

The queen may have finally decided against visiting Niʻihau because of the frequent backbiting and jealousies that seemed to sour relationships within her party, as well as with the local people. After three weeks of togetherness at Lāwaʻi, for example, she wrote: "Our staying together has not been successful . . . the people in our group would not give freely what they had. They only thought of their own interests, taking things and concealing them."[59] She observed jealousy among her people in Waimea who felt she was not paying them sufficient attention.[60] Moreover, some of her suite from Honolulu were jealous of Kauaʻi people because they thought the queen preferred to stay with them. In their pique, they refused to honor the late king's birthday and

Queen Emma's cottage in Lāwaʻi-kai. In 1916 the cottage was moved from its original site on the bluff above, and in 1992 it was restored after Hurricane Iniki.

would not contribute food to the birthday feast.[61] The queen must have been annoyed at this petty behavior. When her Alexander was alive, she had depended on him to keep the peace on their island tours. Now she had to assume that role herself.

Other Pursuits

While at Lāwaʻi she entertained herself by reading. She wrote that she had borrowed three books from the Smith family, had read one, and was reading another entitled *Beulah,* which she did not like because "she [Beulah] is too strong minded."[62] She also acquired books from a private library in Kōloa started by friends who contributed a yearly amount to the purchase of reading material. It was located in a place the queen thought was "the last place one would look for literature"—the lumber room of a cooper shop [where wooden casks or tubs were repaired].[63]

The queen's hands were also busy sewing. She spent many hours doing piecework with the sewing circle seated under the trees. Among those sending in orders was her neighbor, Mrs. Duncan McBryde. The McBrydes were planning a trip to Honolulu, and Mrs. McBryde evidently needed new undergarments in a hurry. The queen did not seem happy when she described the situation to Sarah Weed, her close friend who had left Lāwaʻi earlier. "Yesterday Mrs. McBryde sent for her sewing which were all finished save three of the long drawers & the fourth only the tuck wanting to complete it. She seems to be cross with the delay as if fifteen drawers could be finished in four or five days by half a dozen Hui members."[64]

Peter's Birthday

Queen Emma did not come to Lāwaʻi to mourn.[65] She was finished with her period of dejection and now wanted to enjoy herself. Indeed, Lāwaʻi may have marked the return of her normal cheerfulness and zest for life.

On Lāwaʻi one of several events she and her party celebrated was the birthday of her cousin, Peter Kaʻeo. Although the two had been close since their childhood, Emma had seen little of Peter in the past few years and so was happy to have him with her. As for Peter, he must have been thrilled for he loved and admired her and considered himself to be like both a brother and a dutiful servant. He was at the time still a member of the House of Nobles and an aide to the king and thus brought an added degree of the royal mystique to the queen's entourage. The queen described the event in a letter to Sarah Weed:

> It was great fun on Peter's birthday [March 4]. We attended an auction sale of a chinamans shop mauka of the post office. Mr. William Smith was auctioneer & did it splendidly. He was really very good and facitious at it. The things were old, but the bids ran high, natives grew excited & ran each other up $1.50 for 5 years old cotton print. We were amongst the bidders & bought a variety of things to the ruinous extent

> of $9. in black beads, necklaces, knitting & crochet needles, needles, silk ribbands, wollen [sic] shirts, fish hooks, pins, needles &c. Lucy bought the glass ware. I enjoyed it immensely. From there we drove up the mountain above where Mr. Wilcox & Smith surveyed the water lead & hunted for turkeys. didn't get any. We had a little ride on the mountains . . . & in the evening Peter had a dance. To my surprise at dinner there was some custard. Oh Mr. Wright was one of the invited & danced. A shoe maker was here also who was called the dance & such funny figures. Every other call was balance all.[66]

She also wrote to Fanny describing the Hawaiian segment of the entertainment: "Kawai folks had a name chant [for him]. And I encouraged Makaaiau folks to hula Pehea ka ua o Nuuanu. . . . The hula dancers were Wikani, Kamaka, Panau, Aikoe, Kipola, Kekoa, Mamaina, Keoneloa. Kamaka took delight that night in chanting *Kīko'o au e oni a pau ku'u loa.* The hand gestures and body movements were delightful."[67]

News from the City

After a few months in the country, Queen Emma longed for news about "city life." She wrote to her cousin "Lizzy" Pratt, asking shamelessly for details of a recent ball, such as what she had worn, how she had her hair done, who was there, who was the best dressed, and so on. She added: "I wonder if you made use of your husband's permission to flirt with naval buttons as much as you like. do tell me something about these new parties. do you know any officers from the Syclla?" In excusing her *nīele* attitude (inquisitiveness), the queen added: "You forget perhaps that we kuaainas [country folk] have had once [up] on a time just sufficient taste of city life to make us long for particulars, scarsely being satisfied with generalities. pray do not think me inconsiderate."[68]

In one of her many letters, Emma asked Fanny pointedly about the king's will. "What inheritance will come to me, the throne perhaps or maybe his personal lands? Which of these two?" The queen rather ominously asked, "Who are the people lying in wait for me there?"[69] Although she did not receive an answer to these questions while she was in Lāwa'i, in time she would.

Sometimes Emma received bad news. When she did it usually concerned her wayward cousin, Albert Kūnuiākea. He progressed through an unending series of escapades and scandals from drunkenness to forgery to assault. Fanny wrote that he had lied again and that the king had told him "not to go wandering about lest he be seen by foreigners who will then bad-mouth him"[70] Governor Nahaolelua, who was trying to administer Albert's estate, also wrote to complain about his refusal to follow his advice. He begged Emma to return to Honolulu because he thought she would have more influence over Albert than he did. Albert's finances were desperate: Nahaolelua had over 200 of his bills with no money to pay them. He feared that he would have to sell off some of Albert's property to pay his debts.[71] Though her cousin Albert was a constant embarrassment, Emma always held out some hope that he was redeemable.

Other unwelcome information concerned the negative reaction of some people to her "journey and deeds." Fanny wrote: "There was some resentment when your name was heard [being] praised. . . . Some people here were angry over the fame given your journey and deeds."[72] Another item of sad news concerned one of her tamed birds, which had died.[73]

Farewell Lāwa'i

In early April of 1871 the queen received a letter from Fanny with instructions from King Kamehameha to "come home when the ditch is completed." It was the second such message from the king.[74] Fanny added a personal plea that she should return, warning her that "if your brother-in-law tells you to return, do so. As he can be a bitter person."[75] Emma informed the king that she would be returning around the 20th and bringing him ten head of cattle.[76] Boosted by the beer the queen had provided, the workers finished the ditch on time. On the 19th the queen and her party left Lāwa'i for Līhu'e and, after a few days there, departed for Honolulu on the *Pauahi,* on April 25, 1871.

She left with deep feelings for Lāwa'i. She wrote to Sarah Weed:

> I feel bound to defend the country sounds & sights of horses neighing, bellowing of cattle from the sight you cast on them because they have so often played music to my ears on the slopes & hills around Lawai, particularly in the evenings when driving about there. It is perfectly charming to see the pretty groups & attitudes those dumb animals put themselves into & it is then that the lowing comes so sweetly on the air when the calf is called back to its supper of sweet milk at twilight. I have many times gone home from Koloa & found them scattered about sleeping on the plains, the rumbling of my carriage startling the cows into an erect posture [and they] would give gentle moans of warning to each other that a great black object is approaching.[77]

Queen Emma in riding habit in the 1870s.

She had felt comfortable in Lāwa'i and thus had every intention of returning. She wrote to Keli'imoewai about the need for making additions and repairs to Maunakilohana. In January 1872 she hired a carpenter named Rathburn to do the work. Later in the year she had Keoni Kamaki (John Dominis) make a complete survey of the boundaries of Lāwa'i.[78] When some problems occurred with the ditch being blocked and some of the tree plantings dying, she told Keli'imoewai to wait until she could be there in person. However, she did not return until eight years later.

Readjusting to the Old Rhythms

In returning to Honolulu, Queen Emma was consoled by the knowledge that those who truly cared for her wanted her to come back: the king, who desired her companionship; Fanny, who had feared for her safety and health on Lāwa'i; her retainers, who depended on her management; Nahaolelua, who needed her sterner hand in guiding Albert; her scholarly beneficiaries and the Sisters at the Priory, who missed her attendance; the staff and patients at Queen's Hospital, who looked forward to her regular visits; and her "society" friends, who enjoyed their ritual tea times and conversations.

Shortly after her return she learned of plans for the King's Band to perform public concerts at Emma Square, located in front of St. Andrew's Priory.[79] The king, who preferred the Germanic cadence in band music, had asked the Prussian government to dispatch a suitable bandmaster. Henry Berger, an assistant bandmaster in the Prussian military, arrived in Honolulu in June 1872. He quickly turned the band into one of the most popular of all government institutions. In fact, one-third of the kingdom's entire military budget was appropriated for the band alone.[80]

Under Berger's baton, the renamed Royal Hawaiian Band performed its first concert at Emma Square on Kamehameha Day, June 11, 1872, and then held a concert every Saturday afternoon thereafter. A typical scene at the Saturday afternoon concert was described by the writer Isobel Strong during a lengthy stay in Hawai'i: There were "girls in gay *holokūs* garlanded in wreaths; beautiful large-eyed half-whites, the colour of golden cream; young men in duck, with *cummerbunds* and hat-bands of coloured silk; Chinese merchants; Japanese nurse maids in *kimonos* leading small befrilled, besashed, bare-kneed children. The benches were filled, as people walked back and forth or gathered in groups under the trees. Small boys frolicked on the paths . . . [with the] streets crowded with carriages, some drawn in the shade by the side of the road, others slowly driving round and round."[81] The band concluded each concert with "a march around Emma Square" led by Captain Berger.[82]

With the musical renditions of the band resonating in Emma Square, the queen seemed quite content with Honolulu in 1871–1872, but events were about to drastically change her life.

18

The Battles of Succession

In June 1871 Queen Emma received a disturbing bit of intelligence from her mother Fanny who was in Lahaina with King Kamehameha V. They had heard that a group of conspirators were plotting to shoot him and that one of the leaders was none other than the Reverend William Hoapili Kaauwai, who had accompanied the queen to England and the continent only to be sent home because of unseemly conduct. In fact, the king had termed Hoapili's conduct toward the queen "despicable." Moreover, after Hoapili and his wife had finally returned to Honolulu, the king had been forced to place him under bond for disturbing the peace because he had pointed a gun at his wife's head and had threatened to shoot her.[1]

Even though Hoapili had subsequently won election in Maui to the legislative assembly and had distinguished himself as one of its leaders, nothing would change the king's opinion of him.[2] Thus the king's refusal "to see him at all" drove Hoapili to plot the assassination.[3] The plot was treated seriously because, according to Fanny, the king did not leave his quarters, and a "secret" investigation was launched in anticipation of making an arrest. However, the potentially newsworthy incident seemed to have mysteriously evaporated because no reference to the incident can be found either in the queen's correspondence or in the news sources of the time.

At Lot's Deathbed

An even greater threat to the king's mortality was not assassination but illness. By 1871 he had become a sick man, with a heart weakened by excessive weight (nearly 400 pounds) and other complications. Though forced to spend increasing time at his residence in Waikīkī or on his ranch on Moloka'i, he continued to conduct the affairs of state. His physicians recommended that he distance himself from his office and take a vacation for his health. He thus decided to go to Europe and with Emma's help began planning the trip. The United States government even offered the services of a warship to convey him to San Francisco.

But in the autumn of 1872 he was in the advanced stages of "dropsy on the chest" (edema), though he concealed the severity of his condition from the public, partly by issuing regular bulletins that declared he was "in excellent health."[4] Insiders like Governor Nahaolelua, however, knew as early as November that the king was near death.[5] On the night of the 10th of December 1872, his condition had deteriorated drastically, and several officials, chiefs, and trusted friends were hastily summoned to Ho'iho'ikeea, his residence. They spent the entire night at his bedside "watching in silence" as he lay in a stupor.

The next morning was the king's forty-second birthday. Flags fluttered in the trade winds, offices were closed, the streets were crowded with people from the country eager to join in celebrating the national holiday. But while they were celebrating, King Kamehameha V was dying. Acknowledging the supreme irony of the moment, he is reported to have said, "It is hard to die on my birthday, but God's will be done."[6] One physician who called in the early morning, Dr. George Trousseau, gave him no hope. He advised that if Lot had "any business to settle he had better do it at once, as he would not live through the day."[7]

The most pressing business at that moment was the naming of his successor. In the king's bedroom anxiously awaiting his decision were queen dowager Emma and her mother Fanny, Princesses Ruth Ke'elikōlani, Bernice Pauahi Bishop, and Lili'uokalani, Governor Paul Nahaolelua, Elizabeth Pratt, Mrs. Brickwood, Kamaipuupaa, the Attorney General Stephen Philips, Prince William Lunalilo, and Col. David Kalākaua. Governor John Dominis was also present at the king's behest to take notes of his last words and acts.[8]

It was not an accident that among those present were the six candidates for the throne and the attorney general. Not only had Kamehameha V failed to name a successor but also he had not made a will.

Philips tried to draft a will for him then and there and again urged him to name a successor. Irritated by Philips's insistence, the king told him that "he wanted time to consider so important a subject and that he had been taken by surprise at the statement of the physicians, and was naturally nervous and under a great state of excitement."[9]

Strangely enough, the king began by asking Nahaolelua, who was kneeling by his head, to name his successor. *"O wai kou ali'i?"* ("Who of the *ali'i* is your choice?") After a moment's hesitation, the governor replied, *"He mau ali'i wale no lakou apau."* ("They are all *ali'i.*")[10]

To Elizabeth Pratt, the governor's neutral response came as a complete surprise. She stated that "Had the Governor but said the word which all those present knew was on his mind, Queen Emma would have been named." He was one of her ardent supporters, and everyone expected him to name her.[11]

That Emma was the king's first choice is confirmed by the British Commissioner James Wodehouse to whom the king had previously explained: "His choice . . . would naturally fall on his sister-in-law Queen Emma . . . but unfortunately said his Majesty, 'my cousin William [Lunalilo], however unworthy, still to the Natives, represents the ancient line of Kings, and as such would command their suffrages.'"[12] In a series of letters that Queen Emma wrote to Mrs. Wodehouse in January 1873, she stated that the king had offered to appoint her as his successor but that she had refused the offer.[13]

The king must have known that Emma did not want to succeed him because she shared his view on Lunalilo's primogeniture right to succeed him, but not his negative view of Lunalilo's competence and character. If so, the king may well have asked the governor the question, knowing what he would say, as a pro-forma gesture of support for Emma. Otherwise, it is difficult to explain why the king chose to ask the question of the Maui governor, who was a chief of lesser rank than any of the candidates, placing him in an awkward if not untenable position.

Pratt's view, as discussed above, differs from Governor Dominis's account. To provide the proper context, the verbatim responses of that account are presented below:

After the governor declined, saying that they were all his *ali'i,* King Kamehameha V turned to Mrs. Bishop, who was sitting at his bedside, and declared: "I wish you to take my place, to be my successor."

She replied, "No, no, not me; don't think of me, I do not need it."

The king said, "I do not wish you to think I do this from motives of friendship, but I think it best for my people and my nation."

Mrs. Bishop said, "Oh, no, do not think of me, there are others; there is your sister, it is hers by right." [She was referring to his half-sister, Princess Ruth.]

The king answered, "She is not fitted for the position."

"But we will all help her; I, my husband, your ministers; we will all kokua (help) and advise her."

The king replied, "No, she would not answer."

Mrs. Bishop then said, "There is the Queen, Emma; she has been a Queen once, and is therefore fitted for the position."

The king said, *"She was merely Queen by courtesy, having been the wife of a King."* (Emphasis added.)[14]

According to Dominis's account, at this point the king rose from his bed, and everyone left the room. No more was said of the matter, and about an hour later the king died.

At issue is the statement "She was merely Queen by courtesy, having been the wife of a King." Did he really utter those words? Given the king's deep feelings of love and admiration for his sister-in-law, such words seem so unfeeling and even callous as to be totally out of character. Furthermore, any objective assessment of her accomplishments in founding and raising funds for the Queen's Hospital, the Anglican church, St. Andrew's Priory, and the cathedral would clearly demonstrate that she and her late husband had formed an active and productive partnership, not merely a marriage of courtesy. Moreover, how could the king have dismissed the queen's candidacy in such a perfunctory manner when he knew that Governor Nahaolelua was an ardent supporter of her queenship just as he was?

How can this discrepancy be explained? Dominis may have deliberately distorted the king's words. According to Governor Nahaolelua, Dominis was one of the dowager queen's "worst enemies," quite capable of twisting words.[15] If the conversation was in Hawaiian—which most likely it was—Dominis may have translated the king's words to fit his own perceptions of the queen. After all, he saw Queen Emma to be the chief rival and threat to the ambitions of his brother-in-law Kalākaua and his wife Liliʻuokalani.

This motive would also explain why Dominis omitted Emma's name from his list of those present at Lot's death and why Liliʻuokalani did the same in her account of the incident in her biography in which she is harshly critical of Queen Emma. In Hawaiʻi's nineteenth century dynastic rivalries, no love was lost between the triumphant Kamehamehas and the ambitious Kalākauas.

Of Lot's death, the queen wrote to a group of his grieving subjects on Moloka'i, "My heart is filled with hurt from this sad burden God has placed upon us all, but only he knows his own wishes and we must bow before him courageously without complaint."[16]

Letters to Moloka'i

During the period 1873–1876 Emma and her cousin Peter Ka'eo engaged in a loving and historically rich correspondence that provides an intimate and extraordinary perspective on events during this time.

Unfortunately, this correspondence was made necessary by a tragedy that had befallen Peter. In mid-1873 he was diagnosed with leprosy and moved to the segregation facility on Moloka'i called Kalaupapa. Of its 400 patients he was the only *ali'i* and lived apart with his servants in his own cottage, which he called "Honolulu" to remind him of what he had left behind. Isolated by geography, by his disease, and by his own aristocracy, Peter was a lonely man except for the letters he exchanged with his cousin Kaleleonālani.

Over the next three years, or until Peter was released in May 1876, their letters captured a highly personal but graphic picture of both their lives. Peter was not hesitant to write in some detail about his swelling feet and crooked fingers, recurring fits of depression, longings to return home, dreams of *mo'o* (dragon), black coffins, and other demonic symbols, his need for *kalo* (taro), poi, and other foods tastier than the "disgusting" stuff he had to eat, and of course royal politics. For her part, Emma filled her letters with advice and counsel, many words of practical and spiritual wisdom and of encouragement, but most of all with news and gossip about social and political events, including her own involvement in the succession battles to come.

Because these letters, 122 of them, were never intended for public scrutiny or scholarly analysis, they constitute a compellingly authentic and open record and reveal their writers' most intimate thoughts and feelings. The queen's actions and motives during this harrowing period of political warfare cannot be truly understood without access to these letters.[17]

Election of Lunalilo

Following the death of King Kamehameha V, the atmosphere was one of confusion and fear for, in the absence of a successor, no institutionalized method existed for the transfer of power. The cabinet immediately put out a call for an unprecedented election of a new sovereign. The candidates were William C. Lunalilo, Ruth Ke'elikōlani, David Kalākaua, and Bernice Pauahi Bishop. There was widespread anxiety over the possibility of civil unrest as the different factions maneuvered for power. The situation was sufficiently serious for both the British and American commissioners to request that naval warships be dispatched to Honolulu.[18]

The race was quickly reduced to two, Lunalilo and Kalākaua, with the former clearly being the popular favorite. Queen Emma did not wish to be, nor did she make any effort to be, a candidate.[19] She supported Lunalilo because she genuinely liked him as a person and because he was a Kamehameha, despite claims by Kalākaua's genealogists that he was not.[20]

The election was to be decided by members of the legislative assembly at noon on January 8, 1873, but a popular vote taken a few days before had spectacular results: 3,049 votes were cast, all for Lunalilo![21] Yet still uncertainty persisted as to how the vote would proceed in the legislature. Actual physical fighting was regarded as inevitable if the vote went to Kalākaua who had lobbied hard to win the support of the legislators. Lunalilo threatened to proclaim himself king even if the assembly did not vote for him. According to Queen Emma, "thousands of natives stood in one dense mass round the Court House prepared to defy the voice of parliament if they decided contrary to the wish of the nation and quite readily to proclaim Lunalilo King in spite of it, hundreds awaited to tear to pieces [members] who were suspected of opposing Lunalilo."[22] Many in the crowd were in fact armed with stones and cudgels and some with revolvers. This menacing show outside must have had an effect inside because the vote was unanimous for Lunalilo —*ke ali'i lokomaika'i* or the kind chief, as he came to be popularly known.[23]

The Matchmakers

Queen Emma's friendship with William Lunalilo went back to their days at the Chiefs' Children's School where the Cookes had often paired the two as they marched the children from school to church. Because they grew up in the same royal milieu, they saw each other frequently. Emma was fond of Lunalilo and admired his superior intelligence, education, wit, his love of reading, especially English literature, and his good looks. In temperament he was sociable, romantic, poetic, and sensitive but also impulsive and reckless. And, like Alexander Liholiho, he had his demons, the worst of which was his insatiable appetite for liquor.

As for Lunalilo, no one doubted that he had feelings for the eligible Emma. According to Judge Alfred Stedman Hartwell, the king's attorney general, he was in fact "very fond of her."[24] Lunalilo must have been attracted to Emma for many of the same reasons as other men, including Kamehameha V.

Even before Lunalilo's election to the throne, people had talked about a marriage between him and Emma. As Governor Nahaolelua wrote to the queen in late December, "the people are saying W. C. Lunalilo is King and Emma is to be his wife. Only the people are saying this. . . ."[25] Whether the two were compatible or whether they were in love did not really matter. What the people wanted was what they had wanted earlier for Kamehameha V: a wife who could bear children and provide a successor. The governor continued, "[They are saying] that we won't benefit from Keelikolani or Pauahi, because they can't bear children. The people's main concern is that the two of you have children so that the Kamehameha dynasty continues to rule. That's your greatest purpose."[26] Although Emma had other thoughts on the matter, efforts to promote a marriage continued for weeks and months.

In another letter dated February 14, 1873, the governor complained: "The King succeeded due to the wishes of the people. But the people have not gotten their due. He hasn't married nor begotten a child . . . the people are raising their grandchildren. [But] Where are the children of the chiefs and the King to equal that of the common people? The chiefs have nothing. They haven't any children. Why aren't the chiefs thinking about the welfare of the Kingdom and the people?"[27]

The governor wrote to Emma again, this time about reports he had heard concerning her possible marriage to Lunalilo. One report was that Peter [Ka'eo] had said that "you denied that you will not marry the King" and that "you cried when Pauahi and the others said that the King will not marry you. That the wife for the King is in Borabora [French Polynesia]." Nahaolelua wanted to know whether what Peter said was true because he had heard otherwise. He recalled that she did not cry at "the refusal of the chiefs to have him marry Emma."[28]

Unfortunately, it is impossible to know what the queen did or said because none of her letters to Nahaolelua exists. The governor informed the queen that he had torn up her letters and destroyed them. He explained: "I couldn't keep them as I don't know when I might die and then they [will] be found later and all our secrets [will] be read."[29] The "chiefs" who were opposed to her marriage with Lunalilo included all her rivals to the throne, especially Liliʻuokalani and Kalākaua.

Stories and rumors about Emma's relationship with King Lunalilo continued to flourish. The queen wrote to Peter of an encounter at Hanauma between Hanaiole, one of her female retainers, and ʻĪʻī, the king's boy-servant, who asked her if there was anything the matter with the queen. When she said no, he asked, "Isn't there any trouble in her *opu* (belly)?" When she asked whether he was insinuating that the queen was with the king's child, he said yes because that was the report coming out of the *Aloaliʻi* or royal court.[30]

Emma heard another report from Hiram, one of her male retainers, that the cabinet ministers "have done and said" their utmost to persuade the king not to marry the queen. They had several objections, one of which was her church.[31]

The whole affair became such an embarrassment that Queen Emma decided she would prefer not to visit the king at all. Thus, when Col. Prendergast, from the king's staff, called on Emma to tell her of the king's illness and urged her to visit him, she wrote to Peter: "my hilahila [shyness or embarrassment] overpowered my loyalty—feeling people will be uncharitable and say I wished to . . . try my last chans of marriage. . . ."[32]

Was Emma willing to marry Lunalilo? It is certain that they talked about it, but whether she consented is highly problematic. She may have been fond of him but not fond enough to marry him—and his addictions. The truth is she was still in love with the ghost of her husband. She told Peter: "With all his faults, he is my husband and I love him still, he is ever with me I know, for my prayer book and bible says so, and as I believe in ministering spirits and Guardian Angels, why should not one naturally think that their loved ones are given a charge or work in the world? They live over those [left] behind in this place of trial, and you do not know what comfort I take in the knowledge that Alex and Baby are being used by our Heavenly Jesus . . . to guard me from harm and sin."[33] Her belief in the hereafter sustained her throughout her life.

Ceding Pearl Harbor

The thorniest problem faced by King Lunalilo during his short reign grew out of the depression of 1872, which was caused in part by a meager sugar crop and the consequent loss of government revenues. The proposed solution was to revive efforts to effect a reciprocity treaty with the United States but one with a new twist: the government would cede Puʻuloa or Pearl Harbor in return for duty-free access to the American sugar market. When the king and his new foreign minister, Charles R. Bishop, issued a joint public statement in July 1873 confirming that they had in fact made such a proposal, Hawaiians erupted with the fury of *Pele.*

They protested vehemently at public rallies in the streets and churches. At Kaumakapili Church, the site of many political meetings, a crowd of 1,500 cheering natives met to hear Judge Kapena assail the cession of Puʻuloa.[34] The *Nuhou* editorialized: "We can confidently say that the whole of the native people of these Islands . . . if tested by ballot, have indicated a decided determination to oppose the cession of Pearl Harbor or the alienation of one foot of Hawaiian territory to a foreign power."[35]

Emma wrote to Peter at Kalaupapa: "I like the *excessive* impudance of that race. What people possessed of any love of country, patriotism, identity and loyalty can calmly and passively sit and allow foreigners to their soil arrogating to themselves the right of proposing cession of the native borns' soil, in spite of their unanimous protests? My blood boils with resentment against this insult."[36] She wrote to Keliʻimoewai in Lāwaʻi: "There is a feeling of bitterness against these rude people who dwell on our land and have high handed ideas of giving away somebody else's property as if it was theirs."[37]

The king had earlier endorsed the proposal against his better judgment, but in the end he refused to sign a treaty ceding Pearl Harbor. Emma rose to Lunalilo's defense as she told Peter that "the Ministers are wickedly desperate to almost force the King to sign his name to the treaty. . . . I am so heavy of heart about this that I can scarse write."[38] She also criticized Kalākaua for "filling the natives' minds with public sentiments of the day—on cession of territory—and tells them to suggest at the coming Legislature displacing or dethroning the King for ignorance, drunkeness, utter incompetancy, for by [these failings] he jeopardizes the country's fate. . . . He held a drill last night I believe at the Armory—I do not know what troops. This is all for public display and [to] play on the people's credulity and ignorance."[39]

"Great Care and Nursing"

The stresses and strains of office did not help King Lunalilo's tuberculosis-ridden body, made worse by, in Emma's words, his "repeated intoxication." In August 1873 she wrote to Peter: "The King's conduct sometimes certainly gives us great anxiety for our future of these Islands. He does not seem to feel the weight of his responsibility, and who knows what may happen when he is not sober."[40] Revealing her knowledge of medicine, she described in detail the progressive deterioration of his health until one morning when Dr. McKibbin found him "on the point of death—pulseless, no circulation over the man, and all but breathing his last."[41]

During the next five and a half months of the king's living and dying, Queen Emma was at his bedside caring for and nursing him. She detailed these visits in her letters to Peter.

On a Sunday afternoon in late August she wrote: "He talked with me incessently for 2 hours or more and did not wish me to leave so soon. When I returned to his bed and wished him goodby, he said Oh, that is too long—as if you will not come again—say good day instead. Poor man, he was very weak . . . and appeared extremely ill."[42]

The next day, Emma, a firm believer in the power of the healing word, wrote to Peter: "I was exceedingly low at heart about him . . . silently praying for [his] recovery and an altered good Life hereafter by becoming a member of God's own church."[43] When she asked him to pray for the king, Peter wrote back: " I will on my bended knee beseach the Almighty to spare our young King from danger and all harm. Your being near him will I know releav him, for your presence and kind words to the poor Invalids is a Consolation as well as help."[44] And when, in response to her urging, Lunalilo promised that he was firmly resolved to quit drinking and perhaps to "join one of the Temperance societies" named after her, she wrote: "It is not [a] very dignified course to take, still perhaps better so than fall again. I advised him to make a resolve to himself and keep it. [It] would be the best way of breaking this fatal habit."[45]

When King Lunalilo's doctor told him if he did not eat well, he would die, Emma wrote:

> They all said (likewise the Doctor) [that] he becomes cross and stubborn when they urge him to eat, but each day I have been there he takes food—the arrowroot and milk and his brandy punch with egg, milk, sugar and nutmeg. . . . Once when I persuaded him to eat his arrowroot he asked me to have some with him. When we are all away he won't take it from his folks and they are afraid of him. Once after a doze I cut up 4 or 5 mouthfuls of watermelon and made Eliza [the King's mistress] give [it] to him to moisten his lips. He could not see

> me for I was back of his head. He would not take it [and] finally asked who gave it him to eat and she said the Queen, so he took them quietly, but of course it was all forced. When we left in the evening he held out his hot hand and wished me good evening. Horace asked me to go again the next day which I did, remaining till night, and the doctors said he was a great deal better from the quantity of food he took the day before. Actually the inflammation of lungs and setting in of pneumonia had been arrested by strength gaining the ascendancy, so death was escaped from but danger is still not free. Great care and nursing is required now to bring him round.[46]

What the queen meant by "Great care and nursing" was the kind of medicine practiced by western physicians such as Drs. McKibbin and Trousseau at Queen's Hospital, not the medicine of the native shamans. She said he did not need "superstitious Kahunas. That most decidely would have been wrong and offensive to our God. . . ."[47] She had little respect for their magical powers, for good or bad. Emma related to Peter, for example, how the king's enemies had placed "an ana ana [black magic] bundle done up in Ape leaf and containing Kumini, crabbs, and other stuffs—some burnt to ashes—stupid Hawaiians use for preying one to death." To prove it, she had driven over the very spot where the bundle had been placed and nothing had happened to her.[48] Earlier she told Peter who had consulted Hua, a healer and prophetess, "I have no faith in any one like her and believe not her prophesies."[49]

Even in King Lunalilo's periods of recovery, Queen Emma visited him for hours at a time. One of these visits took place on Sunday, September 7, when she, along with Princess Ruth, stayed the entire day at his residence in Waikīkī (where she often went for "seabathing"). It also happened to be the same day when the king's household troops mutinied and the day that "Taffy" or David Kalākaua paid a brief visit. The queen commented that Taffy "never went near" the king when he was ill and that he had come calling just after the mutiny began, which aroused the queen's suspicions about Kalākaua's involvement in the palace revolt.[50] The queen believed Dominis, whom she once labeled "a mean coward and a cur," was also involved.[51]

On another Sunday in late September 1873, the queen visited the king when he had one of his coughing fits that lasted ten minutes. She wrote that he was stronger and that he "repeatedly hinted that since I made him eat so heartily . . . it was my company [that] made him do wonders, and said if he only had that company he would probably eat more, but I would not respond to the hint, as I saw he was doing very well and growing better, in spite of all he says about not eating without me."[52] She confided in Peter that the king was very kind to her and offered "horses, carriages, and anything I wish from his stables at all times."[53]

Queen Emma was seldom, if ever, alone with the king because he was in the constant presence of his attendants, one in particular—his mistress Eliza Meek, who was the part-Hawaiian daughter of Captain John Meek, the harbor master.[54] Emma was amused because every time she visited the king, the green-eyed Eliza "growls and scolds" and watched her like a hawk. Even when the king tried to send Eliza away "with various messages to get rid of her presence," she would have none of it—"she knew better than to leave us alone together."[55] Emma related to Peter an incident when in a fit of anger he threw a chair and a spittoon at Eliza's head. "It seems the King told her to come to bed—she replied what right has a dog or a bitch there, which instantly gave vent to his ill temper that he had been brooding some days, and used a word of four letters belonging to Waterclosets. She retorted, 'Oh, I suppose that is what you eat to exist on.' This brought the King's rage to an instant climax and [he] threw the articles at her head."[56]

By mid-November 1873, thanks in part to the queen's nursing, the king felt well enough to sail to Kona for Christmas and New Year's. He invited the queen to join his suite, which numbered about thirty persons. The royal party represented an interesting assortment of people including Eliza Meek, Ruth Keʻelikōlani, Liliʻuokalani, her sister Likelike, the king's father Kanaʻina, Dr. Trousseau, Horace Crabbe, the king's chamberlain, Col. Charles H. Judd, the adjutant general, Lucy Peabody, and Judge and Mrs. John Kapena. The king seemed to have improved; as Emma wrote: "The King is much better already, eats well, and has danced each evening. He is getting better and the Doctor hopes to see him continue to improve."[57]

The improvement was short-lived. Dr. Trousseau examined the king on January 16, 1874, and was convinced that he could live only a short time. Forced to return to Honolulu, King Lunalilo stepped off the *Kilauea* "very much broken down and very feeble," and proceeded to Haʻimoeipo, his home adjoining the palace. The talk that day in Honolulu concerned only one subject: how long the king could live.

Royal Skirmishes

What everyone feared had happened again: a king was about to die without appointing a successor. Like Kamehameha V, Lunalilo refused to name a successor, despite the repeated urgings by his chiefs, the newspapers, the people, and Emma herself. When his ministers raised the subject, he said "that his mind was not made up . . . that he would not do anything about it until he was well, and could not say when he would do it. In fact, he gave very little encouragement that he would do it at all."[58]

Meanwhile, the ambitious David Kalākaua, who had lost the first election, was not about to lose the next. Even before Lunalilo had been throned, Kalākaua was actively organizing his supporters and drilling his own small army, the Young Hawaiians. Emma opined that he had sought to recruit three to four hundred to "secure their tickets at the next election for members opposing cession or annexation. The object given out thus is good if only that, but I cannot help thinking more is at the bottom."[59] No one knew for certain whether the Young Hawaiians were a revolutionary force or a political band, but at the time Emma felt it was "all for public display and [to] play on the people's credulity and ignorance."[60] Later in September Emma told Peter that

David Kalākaua first became a candidate for the crown after the death of King Kamehameha V in 1872 but lost to William Lunalilo. Lunalilo also died in office after a short reign, and in 1874 Kalākaua next ran against Dowager Queen Emma.

she had heard that Kalākaua had ordered several hundred firearms to supply his volunteers.[61]

Queen Emma also wrote that Kalākaua was "playing a deep game for himself to let no chanse slip for the family. Mrs. Dominis has written for Keelikolani to come down, hoping she may persuade the King to have herself appointed. Then naturally it will fall on Kalahoolewa [Prince Leleiōhoku, his younger brother] and all of their family of course will rise to the first place now."[62] The queen told Peter of another rumor. When Kalākaua had heard King Lunalilo was dying, he met with members of his family and staff about who would get which property after he became king. Mrs. Dominis, for example, was to get Kīnaʻu Hale, the former home of Emma's uncle Keoni Ana. "Thus," Emma wrote, "you can judge how high disloyal speculations were going on, and the man not dead."[63]

The queen was appalled to learn that the Kalākauas had met and agreed that Prince Leleiōhoku should seek Emma's hand in marriage and have "offsprings [who] will be tremendous alii" and then "ascend the Throne." Emma added, with exquisite sarcasm, "If Taffy should succeed to the Throne he is going to discard his wife and—who knows?—perhaps he will presume for the same honor as his baby brother. They certainly are very impudent—their ambition knows no bounds."[64]

Emma clearly disliked Kalākaua's methods, but she could not begrudge his persistence and perseverance. She turned the situation into a moral lesson for Peter:

> With Taffy's faults we must give him credit for a great ambition. He has worked and exerted himself both lawfully, and to be sure unlawfully, as well as right and wrong, to obtain his desire. But there is the fact—he has exerted himself, tried ways and means to secure his coveted object, the Throne. All these efforts too are made against strong dislike from the whole country, who are unanimous against him. Still he has not faltered, but keeps on trying for the end. This is a good point in him which we must copy. He is not idle. He has stumbled and blundered before the public till actually he really has gained courage amongst them, and can both speak out and write boldly. Now practice makes perfect. He has done the practicing and it is to be infered [that he] will be perfect consequent on it.

The queen's final point for Peter was that no matter what his passion may be, he must carry it out in "an honorable straightforward way" and not resort to Kalākaua's "base wickedness."[65]

Although Kalākaua was the queen's principal opponent, she told Peter that both Mrs. Bishop and Mrs. Dominis were also seeking the throne: "I think myself Mrs. Bishop will be the one whom the Ministers will ask the King's acceptance to appoint as successor to Throne for the great objection to me is my American antipathy and the dear dear church which I never will resign or place to one side for public favour. My God sees me from his Throne. . . ."[66] Emma reported that Mrs. Bishop had told several ladies that "she only regretted not accepting the late King's offer of [the] throne" and, hence, she was not about to let another opportunity slip by her. The queen said that the missionaries would of course side with Mrs. Bishop because of her pro-American sympathies and Calvinistic beliefs.[67]

In her attempt to be a somewhat objective reporter of events for Peter's sake, Emma tried to give both sides of the story regarding Mrs. Bishop. The queen wrote that some Americans, including Dr. Trousseau, tried to persuade Mrs. Bishop to seek the throne but that Mrs. Bishop would not accept the throne, even if offered, because she desired to protect her marriage. Thus she would "use her influence on my behalf, as being the most capable person to fill the place." However, the other version of the story, according to the queen, was that Mrs. Bishop had asked Princess Ruth to speak to King Lunalilo about succession and to offer either one of them as candidates for his approval, and that, if the matter was left entirely up to the King, "there isn't the least doubt he will appoint the Queen—Everyone knows that. . . . It will never do for her to reign Queen over us, and the King must not be allowed to choose her."[68] As an active participant in these events, Queen Emma could not resist giving her own opinion; in this instance, she told Peter that the latter version was the "more natural and authentic."[69]

In the heat of the fray, the queen may not have seen the battle lines clearly. As it turned out, Mrs. Bishop was never a serious contender for the throne. For her to be one, at least two conditions had to exist: the first was the approval of her husband and the second was the assurance of support by a majority of the legislators. Neither of those conditions obtained. In fact, Mr. Bishop favored Kalākaua but acknowledged that Queen Emma was the king's choice.[70]

Of Mrs. Dominis as a rival, the queen is noticeably silent. Except for one matter-of-fact statement that "Mrs. Dominis has a new love, a native boy of Waikiki," Emma says almost nothing, good or bad, about her in any of her letters to Peter.[71]

The rivalry with the Kalākauas was a theme used constantly by

Queen Emma to encourage Peter to greater effort and aspirations. "Albert, you and I are decended from a line of ancestors the men and women of which have acted their parts well and shewn that upward and onward was evidently the motto they acted on as their illustrious deeds tell. They have always kept their stations high as well as renowned, and it becomes us their decendants to do likewise . . . be ambitious and bold to hold our ancestral renown ever in its place high. Let not inferiors step into our places. . . . Still never be discouraged. Have perseverence. Make a name to yourself and consequently add another laurel to the ancestral tree."[72]

On another occasion she wrote: "Ultimate recovery is worth years of patient, happy working to hasten that, and our country will need [and] does need your services. Prepare yourself for her by reading the newspapers of the day." Emma encouraged him to practice public speaking and debating as "it sharpens one's thoughts." As for "reading aloud to oneself," she said that she often read aloud interesting passages slowly and sometimes even tried to act them out.[73] She asked Peter if he was keeping a daily journal because it was a way "to keep one in the habit of writing and you know practice makes perfect." She reminded him frequently of that truism.[74] She ended this lesson with: "But never despond or slacken—'Excelsior' be our motto. Then we will take our ancestors' places with worth."[75]

Emma's Pursuit of the Throne

That Queen Emma saw herself as a suitable, if not the most worthy, candidate and that she actively sought the throne there can be no doubt. As early as September 1873, she wrote to Peter: "The general report downtown for the week past has been the supposition that [the] King intends appointing me his successor—not from anything he has said, but his evident pleasure when I visit him and from things he has from time to time said of me since his accession."[76]

In her biography, the former Queen Lili'uokalani wrote of the royal visit to Kailua-Kona: "I suppose it is no secret, but really a matter of history, that the person most ambitious to succeed him in the rule of the Hawaiian nation was Emma. . . ." (Lili'u conveniently forgot that her brother Kalākaua was no less ambitious to succeed the king.) She wrote that while they took turns watching the ailing king, Emma "urged him in plain language to nominate her to assume the reigns of government at his decease. . . . Even when I was by his bedside, doing my duty as one of those chosen by birth to stand near during his dying hours, Queen

Emma did not cease from her persistency, but again broached the subject of succession, and spoke to the king of the great importance to his people of naming an heir to the throne. The indelicacy of this persuasion from a Hawaiian point of view will be understood by those who have studied our national customs."[77]

On January 19, 1874, Queen Emma wrote to her lady-in-waiting Lucy Peabody: "There is a great move to get Kalakaua appointed successor and it is represented that it is the wish of the people but it is not the truth. Only his party thinks so and talk to stir the people up in favour of it. The King is firm to have me appointed. This is a secret, he told me so himself just now, never breathe it to anyone but send word to Kewiki and to Simon for me, to work openly in my favour for they need fear nobody. I shall be chosen. The King says come what may, no one but me shall sit on the throne."[78]

Charles Alfred Castle, son of Samuel N. Castle (who together with Amos Cooke founded Castle & Cooke), wrote to his wife on January 20 that a strong English faction was trying to persuade King Lunalilo to place Queen Emma on the throne. He had little doubt that the king would have been glad to do it. But in his view it was too late. Had the king done so at the beginning, his subjects would have readily accepted the appointment of a queen. But after months of refusing to announce a successor, the king was now on the verge of death, and the people no longer talked about "who shall succeed" but rather *"who shall we choose."*[79]

On the same day, Charles Bishop, the king's minister of foreign affairs, described Queen Emma's situation in a letter to Judge Elisha Allen:

> Of course we are very anxious that [Lunalilo] should appoint a successor so as to avoid the damaging effects, trouble and expense of another election; and though we have used every argument and entreaty we have not succeeded. The public mind seems to be settled upon Kalakaua as the coming man, and as it is very doubtful if a majority of the Nobles would approve of any other, we have tried our best to have the King appoint him. Queen Emma, Ruth Keelikolani and Mrs. Bishop have each given him the same advice [Bishop was obviously mistaken in having included Emma]. Kalakaua has behaved in such a way towards the King as to offend him grievously, and it seems impossible to appoint him—he has indicated a preference for Queen Emma though he has not said he wants to appoint her. He has not named anyone. Some would prefer the young man, brother of Kalakaua, William Pitt Leleiohoku, but there are strong objections both to

> Emma and to him; and Kalakaua, under the circumstances, will probably be the next King either by appointment or election, and most likely by the latter mode.
>
> I think Kalakaua has been a good deal misrepresented. Should he have the responsibilities of a Sovereign put upon him, I trust that he will be reasonable, impartial and careful. You and I are aware of his weaknesses and faults, but what can we do, except to make the best of our position. There are strong fears that Queen Emma would be partial to a clique. Perhaps they do her injustice. The people would prefer a King to a Queen, and yet a Queen who would be impartial, select the best advisers to be had, and trust fully in them, would be better than a stupid and conceited King.[80]

On January 20, 1874, *Ka Nūhou Hawaiʻi,* which had been the first newspaper to champion Kalākaua as the "preeminent" heir to the throne on December 30, 1873, came out full-square for Kalākaua again. Its editor Walter Murray Gibson wrote: "There is only one individual who . . . meets the awakened passion of patriotism among Hawaiians,—who is the High Chief David Kalakaua." He opposed Queen Emma's candidacy but underscored the high esteem in which she was held by all.

> This distinguished and excellent lady commands our highest consideration and esteem; she is identified with those associations in which we are most interested; and we should be most happy to be her champion and partisan; but in this instance we feel that we would, by so doing ignore the wishes of the Hawaiian People. . . . The political hopes of the native people are now concentrated upon his [Kalākaua's] person, whereas Her Majesty Queen Emma, whom we esteem a most noble woman and devoted to her native country and People, and who we are sure takes no part in any political intrigue; and whose name is put forward by a cabal, or ring of foreign interests, does not satisfy the national hope as a Successor to King Lunalilo.[81]

During the next eleven days, supporters of both Kalākaua and Emma worked furiously to secure victory for their party leaders. The strategy of the former, who seemed better financed and organized, was to concentrate on winning over the representatives because their votes were the ones that counted the most. For example, they would await the arrival of the representatives at the pier with carriages, take them to the residence of fellow-representative Major Moehonua, and there provide them breakfast and other amenities they might need.[82] Meanwhile,

Emma's party seemed content to win over the popular vote but then shifted to the representatives. On January 31, 1874, Charles Castle reported that they had obtained the votes of six Nobles and were trying desperately to secure two more, which would have given them a majority. He felt that the longer the king lived, the better the chance the queen's supporters had of securing the other two votes.

Castle predicted Queen Emma's defeat and declared that her accession would be "a great disaster." He predicted that it would be a reign of extravagance and a waste of public money that would bankrupt the nation, lead to higher taxation, and ultimately cause unification of church and state.[83] As far as he was concerned, the choice was between the lesser of two evils, and he—along with the vast majority of Americans—preferred Kalākaua. The vast majority of Britishers of course favored Queen Emma.

It was the morning of February 3, 1874, about ten to nine, when King Lunalilo, having suffered through the pain of several hemorrhages, died peacefully without pain—and without naming a successor. Those present in his bedchamber were Mrs. Bishop, Princess Keʻelikōlani, and Fanny.[84] Surprisingly, Queen Emma was not present. It had been her fondest hope that he would name her as his successor.

So, why did King Lunalilo not follow his heart and announce Queen Emma as his successor? Even those unsympathetic to her aspirations, such as the *Pacific Commercial Advertiser* and the *Polynesian,* admitted that in his heart Lunalilo would have preferred Emma as his successor. Alfons Korn, the perceptive editor of the letters between Emma and Peter, concluded: "True, Lunalilo wanted Queen Emma as his successor, but he didn't want to make the legal decision."[85]

Emma or Kalākaua?

At ten o'clock that night the cabinet met and called a special meeting of the legislative assembly on February 12 to elect a new sovereign. That date would give time for the legislators, who had been elected only the day before, to reassemble in Honolulu but scarcely time for the candidates to mount a campaign. However, Kalākaua and Emma had been campaigning all along—now the pace intensified.

The next afternoon, February 4, about 3,000 Honolulu residents congregated at Kawaiahaʻo Church ostensibly to mourn King Lunalilo, but Kalākaua's lieutenants deliberately turned the occasion into a political rally on behalf of his succession to the throne. One of Kalākaua's spokesmen, Major Moehonua, asked for a resolution calling for the unanimous approval of David Kalākaua. It was a foregone conclusion because he had no intention of asking for an opposing vote. Well aware of the volatile atmosphere in the capital, he assured the crowd that his candidate wanted all matters to be conducted peacefully and in accordance with the constitution and the laws of the land.[86]

Following the meeting Kalākaua issued a proclamation addressed "To the People":

> The President of the public meeting held at Kawaiahao on Wednesday, the 4th of February 1874, has communicated to me the unanimous sentiment of that meeting as expressed in the Resolutions adopted, in which you have declared your wish that I should be chosen as King of our beloved country. . . .
>
> I sincerely thank you citizens, [na maka'ainana] for the expression of your confidence in naming me as the Successor to the Throne, and knowing myself to be in sympathy, with you, I shall study to carry out your wishes.
>
> His late Majesty died without nominating or proclaiming a Successor to the Throne, and it therefore devolves upon the Legislative Assembly, under the Constitution to elect a sovereign.
>
> I accept your nomination of myself to this high and responsible position of Guardian of the Government, with the earnest hopes that that Government may be conducted wisely, and so as to secure and perpetuate our national independence and the preservation and prosperity of our race.
>
> God Preserve Hawaii.[87]

The same day the *Hawaiian Gazette* gave a ringing endorsement to Kalākaua, declaring that among all the candidates to the throne "there is no one to whom the people look with more unanimity than to Col. DAVID KALAKAUA, who promises to be a just King, a kind Father and faithful Protector of the People. . . . Therefore . . . we recommend the Legislative Assembly to choose him as the successor of LUNALILO." Fearing a contested election would lead to civil disorder, the newspaper tried to persuade all other candidates to "waive" their claims to the throne for the sake of national harmony.[88]

All the talk about a unanimous vote for Kalākaua, however, was just that, for Queen Emma had her supporters on every Island. They were already organizing district committees, holding public rallies, writing letters of support, distributing handbills, and journeying to Honolulu to meet with her.

The day after Kalākaua issued his proclamation, Queen Emma issued hers, which was addressed "To the Hawaiian People":

> WHEREAS, His late lamented Majesty LUNALILO died on the 3rd of February 1874, without having publicly proclaimed a Successor to the Throne; and whereas,
>
> His late Majesty did before his final sickness declare his wish and intention that the undersigned should be his Successor on the Throne of the Hawaiian Islands, and enjoined upon me not to decline the same under any circumstances; and whereas,
>
> Many of the Hawaiian people have since the death of His Majesty urged me to place myself in nomination at the coming session of the Legislature;
>
> Therefore, in view of the foregoing considerations and my duty to the people and to the memory of the late King, I do hereby announce and declare that I am a Candidate for the Throne of these Hawaiian Islands, and I request my beloved people throughout the group, to assemble peaceably and orderly in their districts, and to give formal expression to their views on this important subject, and to instruct their Representatives in the coming session of the Legislature.
>
> God Protect Hawaii![89]

The queen's assertion that King Lunalilo had named her as his successor was challenged by Charles Bishop in his speech on February 6 before the privy council. He eulogized the late king but asserted that at no time did the king name a successor, despite having been urged on more than one occasion to appoint one. He maintained that they did not pretend to know what the king may have said to others, but that their duty was now to treat all candidates with impartiality.[90]

After the queen's proclamation was posted on a public bulletin board, one of Kalākaua's supporters scribbled above it: "*Aole makou makemake e ike i ka palekoki e hookomo ana i ka lolewawae*" or "We do not wish to see the petticoat putting on breeches." Some onlookers said, "*Pono, ko makou manaʻo no ia*" or "Right, this is also our thought." But one of the queen's supporters, Curtis J. Lyons, a former editor of *Ka Nūpepa Kūʻokoʻa* and member of the legislature, saw the offending notice, smashed in the glass door, and tore the paper to pieces. His action immediately drew a crowd and sparked several hours of partisan speeches. David Malo (not the Lahainaluna scholar) came forward touting the virtues of Kalākaua, while casting aspersions on the queen, when some drunken sailors ventured by looking for a fight.

He pointed to them as an example of *"haole ho'ohaunaele"* or brawling foreigners.[91]

At this point, one of the queen's supporters responded by reciting Kalākaua's undistinguished career as a government official. He said that Kalākaua had been Postmaster General once, but on account of his "incapacity" he had been replaced by a foreigner and that he had been appointed Chamberlain, but because of his incompetence he had been again replaced by a foreigner. And now, the speaker said, Kalākaua "wants to be elected to fill the throne, and if he is, he will have to be turned out and a foreigner put in his place."[92]

A few days later, a huge crowd of Queen Emma's supporters held a rally of their own at Rooke House, where, according to Sanford Dole, an attorney and writer at the time, who was a particular favorite of the queen, "much shouting took place."[93] A poll was taken and more than 3,000 votes were cast for the queen, including the votes of a group of sailors attending the rally from the British man-of-war anchored in the harbor. Although men, women, and children were allowed to vote indiscriminately, Castle was certain that a majority of the natives in Honolulu would vote for the queen. The shift in public sentiment in the last week of the campaign was in his view "astonishing."[94]

One of the queen's spokesmen, W. S. Pahukula, called for another cheering endorsement of the queen and her proclamation. Then, at her request, he read a letter from Charles Kana'ina, the late king's father, affirming that his son while at Kailua had expressed his intention to name the queen as his successor, but unable to obtain the approval of his cabinet there, he returned to Honolulu fully intending to name her before he died.

After the reading of the letter, Queen Emma addressed the audience: "I am much gratified with the unanimity which you have shown in supporting my claim to the vacant Throne. Love to you all." When she sat down, the audience cheered heartily and shouted, "Let us vote for her to be our Queen." She came forward a second time and said: "If your wish shall be carried out by the Legislature on the day of election, and I am chosen to be your Queen, I will select natives to fill the offices, with the exception of those which natives cannot fill. In those offices I will place foreigners."[95]

In addition, according to Marshal William Parke, Queen Emma had promised her supporters that if elected, she would take no salary, and repeal the horse, road, and any other taxes they wanted, as well as free all prisoners in the Honolulu jail.[96] Mrs. Sanford Dole, who knew the queen well, wrote that the queen also declared that she would release the lepers and that she would not marry a white man. And then she added: "It looks as if her [the Queen's] desires were running away with her. She is a good woman and I am sorry that she allows herself to be brought before the public so compromisingly for nothing."[97] For those who truly knew the queen, however, too many foolish promises were being made not by the queen but by a manipulative group of self-interested advisers.

Curtis J. Lyons, a former member of the legislative assembly and a supporter of Queen Emma, wrote that it "impressed one painfully that she had no persons of influence to stand by her." Of those openly supporting the queen there were Samuel Kamakau, the aging journalist and historian, Governor Nahaolelua, Charles Kanaʻina, Lunalilo's father, Frank S. Pratt, Lizzy's husband, the Reverend George W. Pilipo of Kaumakapili Church, Dr. Robert McKibbin, a physician at Queen's Hospital, Charles H. Judd, Bill Stephens, Horace G. Crabbe, and Reverend Alfred Willis, the Anglican Bishop.[98] With the exception of Nahaolelua, none of these men was a powerhouse.

One of her strategists was her private secretary Kepelino Kahoāliʻi, a former Catholic lay teacher and a skilled and impassioned writer, who had just joined the queen.[99] It is said she relied heavily on his services and advice.[100] Another possible strategist was one of her chief spokesmen, Pahukula (whom Lyons called a "scamp"). Unlike Kalākaua, who was able to muster the help of his large and influential family, Queen Emma had no family except for her mother Fanny and her cousins Peter, who was confined to the leper colony at Kalaupapa, and Albert, who seemed both helpless and hopeless. Nor could she rely on her family by marriage; the remaining Kamehamehas such as Bernice Pauahi Bishop and Ruth Keʻelikōlani favored David Kalākaua.

The queen's support came largely from the common people, mostly in Honolulu and Oʻahu, but also on the other Islands. Her harshest and, most biased critic, Liliʻuokalani, admitted as much when she wrote: "She naturally had about her a considerable personal following, scheming for office, and a large body of retainers, all within the city and environs; and hence could there make a formidable showing. She had also, of course, partisans here and there throughout the Islands. Her canvass was, however, limited almost exclusively to intrigue within the city, while Kalakaua and his friends sought the suffrages of the country people and their representatives."[101] That Queen Emma also enjoyed "the suffrages of the country people" may be gleaned from the reports sent by the partisan committees that had been set up from North Kohala to Koʻolau. One report was from J. Kaiʻiaikawaha in Waialua, Oʻahu, about a meeting attended by forty-six people of whom thirty were for Kalākaua and sixteen for the queen. "If all the people had come then just you would have been victorious. I protested the resolution because it was not from all the people here in Waialua, just a minority."[102] The committees in ʻEwa and Waiʻanae reported that the people were "estatic" in their support of Queen Emma.[103] "Even the school children yelp for Queen Emma," commented one of her non-admirers.[104]

Worried about the queen's accelerating support, the *Hawaiian Gazette* announced its opposition to her candidacy the day before the election:

> For her personal charms, and for her many worthy deeds and charities, we in common with all our fellow citizens entertain the highest admiration. Hawaiians mention her name only with affectionate reverence at home; while abroad the fame of her tour through America and Europe is still fresh. Many in foreign lands know the name and admire the virtues of QUEEN EMMA OF HAWAII. Hers is a wide-world fame; which no new royal honors can add to; and her name will always be one of the brightest jewels in the diadem of Hawaii. But while admiring her for her personal good qualities, in common with all who know her, we cannot consent to be a party to bring her into a political strife . . . [and] . . . endorse her nomination as a candidate to the throne, so long as there remains a Prince of at least equal rank qualified for the position, and for whom the people are so unanimous. That she would have been the first choice of the late King, had he made a nomination there can be little doubt; but his failure to publicly nominate her as his successor, leaves her without paramount claims to the throne.[105]

Meanwhile both Queen Emma and Kalākaua, together with their partisans, filled the air with claims and counter claims. For example, Charles Bishop urged the nomination of Kalākaua because as "the eldest male representative of a Princely Hawaiian family, which is undoubtedly next to the House of Kamehameha," he had a stronger genealogical claim.[106] The queen's backers retorted with a pamphlet entitled "To the Public," which declared that her genealogy was superior to "any other person." It also reminded people that she had established Queen's Hospital and that she was also a "person of wealth and extensive lands." It had been reported that Lunalilo had made the queen the heir to his large estate (of several hundred thousand acres); if so, it meant "she would save a government money . . . by living on her own private income, and dispensing with any allowance from the Treasury."[107]

In this war of words, *Ka Nūhou Hawaiʻi* fired a rebuttal: "The unwise friends of Queen Emma have again published a very foolish paper," referring to the above-mentioned pamphlet. "They say she built the Queen's Hospital. But this is not true. It was built with the money of the people—native and foreign. Her Majesty's name is given to it, because it was built during the reign of her husband.

"They speak of Queen Emma's benevolence to her servants, and to many children whom she educates, which is true and is true of all chiefs, but it must be remembered that she receives six thousand dollars a year from the representatives of the people which enables her to perform her good deeds."

Gibson warned: "If it were possible that there should be any other issue to this contest than the one of which we have the most assured conviction, and that is the elevation of Prince Kalakaua to the Throne of this Kingdom; still Her Majesty's name must suffer, and she who was once revered by all, can henceforth only hope for the love of but a portion of the people."[108]

How did Queen Emma feel about her chances on the eve of the election? She must have been hopeful, if not confident, of winning. She clearly enjoyed the backing of the popular majority. In addition, her party leaders felt that she had a solid chance of gaining three or four more votes in the legislature to win a majority there as well.[109] Her confidence also came from her belief that she was far more worthy of the honor than her opponent, that she had demonstrated her leadership abilities at home and abroad, that she had a thorough knowledge of how government did or did not work, and that she knew Providence was on her side. Liliʻuokalani said as much when she wrote that Emma never seemed to have doubted that "she must be the chosen sovereign."[110]

That evening the authorities prepared for the worst: the word was out that the Queen's party was intent on sending a crowd to "overawe" the legislature; orders had been given to disarm the Artillery Company (the majority of whom were part-whites) because of the fear that if they were summoned to face a disturbance, they would side with the mob; the report on the police was that they could not be trusted in case of a riot; and guards were posted at the armory to prevent excited natives from stealing any guns. Castle, who was one of the guards, wrote his wife: "It is a miserable feverish state of excitement which damages the country tremendously—and for which there is no compensating good. Well, I must go to bed and get a good nights sleep for I do not know when or where I may have to sleep tomorrow night—or indeed whether I shall sleep at all."[111]

At the same time far away in Hilo, as the "Emmaite" or "Queenite" Curtis P. Iaukea told the story, a group of people were wagering on who would win the election when someone said, "Oh, here comes the old wiseacre," who was an old and familiar man in the town.

He waltzed up to the group and said, "I see you are all Queenites."

"And what are you?" someone asked, while offering a wager that he could not predict the next sovereign.

"Oh," answered the old man, "I am for Kaleleonālani, but mark what I say. Kalākaua will be king, and his will be a troublesome reign. The very name Kalākaua spells it." *Ka* means "the," *lā* means "day" and *kaua* means "battle" or "war."[112]

The Riot of February 12

On February 12, 1874, several hundred Emmaites gathered at Rooke House to receive instructions and encouragement before marching to the courthouse where the election was to take place. In addition to the city folk, many people had come by foot or on horseback from the outlying districts of ʻEwa, Waialua, and Koʻolauloa in particular. Marching in squads of a hundred or more to the sound of a fife and drum and led by a man on horseback, they approached the courthouse slightly before noon. At the same time, Kalākaua's partisans had arrived, though not in the same numbers or with as much fanfare. Other spectators had also assembled at the courthouse so that by noon nearly a thousand people were milling about.

Unlike the election of Lunalilo, when his supporters came to the courthouse armed with clubs, cudgels, and even revolvers, none of Emma's people came armed. They did come with threats, however, deadly ones at that. "*Ina e hanaʻole na luna makaʻainana i ko kakou makemake alaila, e holehole aku i ko lakou mau iwi*" or "If the representatives do not do as we wish, then, we shall burn their bodies and strip their bones of their flesh."[113]

Some in the crowd tried to find seats in the assembly hall's viewing gallery, but most remained outside where they were harangued by speakers trying to be heard above the din punctuated by cheers for Queen Emma or Prince Kalākaua.

Inside at precisely 12:00 noon the meeting was called to order, the legislature was organized with Governor Nahaolelua as president, the oath was administered to the forty-five new legislators by Judge Alfred S. Hartwell, and then the balloting began. One by one, each legislator, beginning with the sorrowing Charles Kana'ina, Lunalilo's father, was called and walked alone to the secretary's table to deposit his ballot.[114] One of the *luna maka'ainana* (representatives) who voted was John Cummins, the "Lord of Waimanalo," a part-Hawaiian representative, who worked for Kalākaua's election because he felt Queen Emma was controlled by the English church; moreover, she was a woman. His own *ali'i* family was divided over their support for the queen, but Cummins was fond of saying, "I believe in beautiful women and fine horses, but no petticoat shall rule me."[115] His machismo was more characteristic of American prejudices than Hawaiian ones.

In contrast to the commotion prevailing outside, an eerie calm hung over the legislators and spectators, many dressed in mourning black (Lunalilo's body was still lying in state). The "exquisite dignity" of the procedure was marred only by the behavior of the last member from Kaua'i who was too drunk to know where the ballot box was located.[116] When the ballots were counted at about 3:45 p.m., Kalākaua was the overwhelming victor with thirty-nine votes to Queen Emma's six.

When the crowd heard the results, pandemonium erupted. The cheers of Kalākaua's backers were drowned out by the yells and cries of rage from the queen's supporters. An eyewitness reported they "were surging wildly hither and thither, a perfect tempest of shouts in which all words were commingled into one fierce roar."[117] Feeling rejected and betrayed, they turned their anger against the legislators for voting against their queen, shouting *"Inu na luna maka'ainana i ka wai awaawa,"* "They will drink of bitter waters!" The peaceful demonstration quickly erupted into a riot.

Because the front entrance was guarded by police, a group of protestors rushed to the back door of the courthouse where the five members of the committee selected to notify Kalākaua of the decision were about to enter their waiting carriage. The crowd seized the carriage and literally tore it to pieces. Using these pieces as clubs, they attacked the defenseless members of the committee before they could retreat into the building, severely injuring two. Representative Aholo, who slid under the carriage, escaped harm's way by shouting, "I'm not from your *kuleana* [jurisdiction]. I'm from Lahaina."[118] Although they tried not to harm any foreigners, a British subject who was aiding the committee members was knocked down and beaten.[119]

The mob next surged around to the front entrance and demanded that the legislators show their faces. When one was seen in the upper window, they shook their fists and sticks at him. Some government officials, foreign diplomats, and legislators tried to pacify the crowd but to no avail. One legislator, Nahaolelua, appeared on the courthouse balcony but could scarcely be heard over the cries of "*Pepehi, hailuku, puhi ka hale,*" "Kill, stone to death, burn the house."[120] When William L. Green, British vice consul, tried to quiet the crowd with his eloquence, he was "hissed off."[121]

The crowd next began to bombard the building with volleys of stones that shattered nearly every pane of glass and window sash. People yelled, "Break in the doors!" With no resistance from the police, they burst through the front and side doors and destroyed everything they could find: chairs, tables, papers, and books, except for those in the library and for the court, which a cool Marshal Parke had persuaded them to preserve. All the while, the rioters were breaking down trees to use as clubs and searching the blood-splattered building for any legislators trying to hide. When one was found, they yelled insults and beat him with clubs. They threw Representative Haupu of Hilo out of a second-story window, and when he landed eighteen feet below, he was beaten by the crowd. In the end, thirteen legislators, one foreigner, and one non-legislative native were injured, four seriously enough to require several weeks of recovery.[122]

At the height of the riot, several persons went to Queen Emma to request that she call off her supporters only to be treated, according to the *Pacific Commercial Advertiser,* with indifference and told it was "no concern of hers."[123] Samuel Wilder, businessman, reported that the queen told him that they should let events take their course and that the legislature should reconsider its vote. R. Stirling, a member of the House of Nobles, also tried to talk the queen into intervening. She said she was willing to intervene but did not.[124] When Sanford Dole went to Rooke House, he found her retainers in such "hysterical excitement" he could not get an audience.[125] Paul Nahaolelua may have been the first to speak to the queen, who reportedly sent him back to the rioters with a note stating that "if they could not obtain their desires now, perhaps they had better wait until the morrow, when a new election for Sovereign could be had."[126]

This note may have been a response to an alleged incident: a *haole* government official had appeared on a balcony during the riot and advised the crowd to disperse because the election was illegal, hence null and void, and that another election would take place when Queen Emma would have another opportunity for the throne, at which the crowd cheered and calmed down.[127]

The queen's reluctance to go to the scene may have also reflected her fear for her own safety, which was no doubt shared by her mother and friends who had gathered around her at Rooke House. Or it may have been a firm decision that the responsibility to restore law and order was not hers but rather that of the police and militia. In fairness to the queen, it should be noted that neither did Kalākaua go to the scene to suppress the disturbance. Both during and following the riot, according to Drs. Trousseau and C. T. Gulick, he hid in a wooden house opposite the palace.[128] Another account said that the "timid" Kalākaua hid in Dr. Trousseau's home.[129]

As soon as the riot started, a call went out for the volunteer Rifles and Artillery Companies to report for duty, but so few responded that they were of no use. To make matters worse, although Marshal Parke had repeatedly tried to disperse the mob peacefully, his sixty-man police force did almost nothing to quell the tumult. Many took off their badges and disappeared into the crowd, some even sympathizing with the Emmaites.[130]

With the government rendered helpless, with a few hundred natives still looking for legislators' blood, and with evening approaching—it was about 4:30 p. m.—Charles Bishop and Governor Dominis sought the new king's help to restore order. He agreed that they should ask the American Minister Henry Peirce and the British High Commissioner James H. Wodehouse to send armed marines ashore.[131] Anchored in the harbor were two American warships, the U.S.S. *Tuscarora* and U.S.S. *Portsmouth,* and one British gunboat, the *Tenedos.* Both Peirce and Wodehouse had anticipated trouble and had forewarned their respective commanders well in advance. As a result, by noon of the 12th—that is even before the riot began—the American marines had been fully equipped, with their arms stacked on the deck and their launches afloat in the water, waiting for their orders. Ten minutes after the orders came, about 150 sailors and marines were onshore marching at the double, with their Gatling machine gun in tow, toward the courthouse. Most of the people watched the spectacle with sadness and shared Castle's patriotic sentiments: "We could only look on in silence while we saw the Hawaiian flag disgraced for the first time by the landing on our soil of a lot of foreign bayonets, to maintain order among ourselves."[132]

A squad of American marines entered the courthouse to clear out the rioters on the second floor. One of the marines later wrote: "This did not take long, although a few violent ones talked a great deal and offered a slight resistance, but when the marines formed in the line and started for them with fixed bayonets most of them made for the side door and the windows in a hurry. One ringleader stood his ground until a bayonet touched him and then, with a yell, made for the door."[133]

Nearly thirty arrests were made, the crowd dispersed, many of them proceeded in a body back to the queen's residence and shouted that tomorrow they would return to see that she was chosen queen.[134] At Rooke House they continued "hurrahing and making speeches" until about seventy or eighty British marines arrived.[135] The Emmaites cheered the bluejackets and expected them to aid their cause because it was well known that the British supported Queen Emma. But they were keenly disappointed when the Britishers began to disperse them. The queen was doubly disappointed because she had always considered Commissioner Wodehouse as a supporter of her cause. To add insult to injury, the accompanying policemen proceeded to arrest several of her followers on her own premises.[136]

One of those in the retreating crowd was Thomas Kamukamu Bell, a ringleader in the riot who had fled to Rooke House with Marshal Parke on his heels. Before Parke could search the house, however, Lucy Peabody gave him one of her black *holokus* and Sarah Weed put her hat on his head. Feigning sleep, he lay on a sofa while the Marshal and his officers searched the house. He made his escape and swore allegiance to the queen "forever."[137]

That night American and British forces mounted guards at Rooke House, the palace, the apartments where Kalākaua and his family were ensconced, the residences of John Dominis and Prince Leleiōhoku, the barracks, armory, and government offices, including the courthouse. Except for scattered gunfire, with some shots fired at a guard posted at the courthouse and a few men presumed to be rioters prowling about in the darkness, Honolulu rested quietly under the protection of the United States and Great Britain.[138]

Not quite everyone, however, rested quietly. *Ka Nūpepa Kūʻokoʻa* reported that a strong tremor was felt in Hilo on the night of the 12th of February of 1874. The newspaper said it was "probably a sign from the mystical woman [*Pele*] acknowledging the actions committed by the people in Honolulu."[139]

19

The Queen's Party

Liliʻuokalani describes Queen Emma's election loss as the "great disappointment" from which she "never recovered."[1] That Emma was greatly disappointed there can be no question, but the implication that her disappointment somehow incapacitated her, mentally or spiritually, for the rest of her life is debatable. After all, she had endured setbacks even greater than that of losing to the Kalākauas, setbacks that demonstrated her great strengths of perseverance and resiliency. So when Emma had earlier admonished Peter to "Never despond," she acted accordingly in the wake of her defeat. The fact was that, at no time, either in the days immediately following the riot or in the months and years thereafter, did Emma exhibit any signs of abject despondency or moribund depression that might have turned her into a recluse and Rooke House into a hermitage. In contrast, the events of February 12, 1874, seemed to galvanize her resolve to be "ambitious and bold" in holding high the "ancestral renown" of the Kamehamehas. Instead of being a recluse, she became involved in grassroots politics, helping Emmaites get elected to office, taking a stand on key issues, and keeping in check the "D.K.s" (Kalākaua and his people). In the process Emma initiated the beginnings of a political party system in Hawaiʻi.

The Bitter Aftermath

On the morning after the riot, Queen Emma sent for Governor Paul Nahaolelua and, according to Liliʻuokalani, "demanded of him if it were

Lili'uokalani was David Kalākaua's sister. As king, he made her regent during his 1887 world tour, which exacerbated the tension between Lili'uokalani and Dowager Queen Emma. When Kalākaua died in 1891, Lili'uokalani ascended to the throne.

not possible to ask for another vote in the legislature."[2] As the titular leader of the Emmaites, she felt obligated to salvage whatever she could from their defeat. Because the special session of the legislature was still open and Nahaolelua was its elected president, she thought she still might have a chance, however slim. But the reality was that neither she nor her popular majority could overcome the power behind Kalākaua's throne: the American business community and the missionaries, now backed by U.S. and British bayonets.

At the same time, a nervous Kalākaua and his advisers acted swiftly and decisively to consolidate his position to forestall any further agitation. The king and Charles Bishop immediately asked the American, British, and French diplomats for assurance that they recognized David Kalākaua as sovereign of the Hawaiian kingdom. American Commissioner Henry Peirce, acting on behalf of his foreign colleagues, called on Dowager Queen Emma and "in a friendly manner" informed her that they had acknowledged Kalākaua as king and that they "recommended her to accept the fact of the legality of his election as King, and to urge her people to likewise do the same, and not to commit any more acts of violence or disorder."[3]

Their decision was to have Kalākaua take the oath of office as soon as possible "so as to remove all causes that prevented the restoration of quiet." At 11:30 a.m. on February 13, 1874, the inauguration ceremony was performed, not at Kawaiahaʻo Church as had been the custom, but rather at Kīnaʻu Hale, the former residence of Emma's uncle. From two to three hundred people, including foreign diplomats and officers of the three warships in the harbor, were quickly assembled for the king's inaugural speech. It was a short speech of 200 words and was peppered with references to the "disturbance," which, as far as King Kalākaua was concerned, was far from over.[4]

Meanwhile, the volunteers of the Artillery Company had gone to the top of Punchbowl to fire the royal salute to the new king. It was accompanied by a guard of thirty to forty armed marines to make sure the "rascals" did not turn the cannon on the town folk below.[5] When the Punchbowl battery boomed forth, it signaled the beginning of the reign of the Kalākauas.

That afternoon the dowager queen assembled her supporters at Rooke House to tell them that she had met with Henry Peirce earlier and had sent a message to Kalākaua acknowledging him as sovereign and informing him her people would do the same.[6] At best, the gesture was a begrudging acknowledgment and by no means constituted a guarantee that any of her adherents would do the same. They revered her, but some were beyond her reach, like those who talked about marching to the station house (jail) right then and there to release those who had been arrested.[7]

Later in the evening many of her followers took up lighted torches and paraded on the streets. They were described as "an ugly scowling crowd." Positioned among the spectators along the route were armed volunteers, like Alfred Castle and Sanford Dole, who had been warned that the "Emma men" intended to use their torches to burn down the town and even to launch an assault on King Kalākaua. Except for a few rockets and firecrackers, however, the parade ended quietly and peacefully.[8]

The next morning, February 14th, King Kalākaua called in person on the dowager queen in an attempt to reestablish friendly relations. It was more an act of politics than one of magnanimity. He had every reason to believe that she and her followers posed the greatest internal threat to his rule, and he wanted to minimize, if not eliminate, that danger. But he also empathized with Emma whom he had known since their days at the Chiefs' Children's School and whose husband he had loyally served as aide-de-camp. As for Emma, though she had once expressed a grudging respect for Kalākaua at the height of the campaign, she was not about to accept the unquestioned friendship of someone who, as Peter wrote, "everyone knows [won by] unfair means, with the basest of falsehoods" directed against her.[9] The attempt at rapprochement failed, and, in Ralph Kuykendall's words, "no cordiality existed between Queen Emma and the new royal family."[10]

At 10 a.m. the legislators, including the walking wounded, met in the damaged courthouse to close the special session. The *Hawaiian Gazette* reported that "It was a sad spectacle to witness the representatives seated around the half-furnished hall, with heads bandaged, and arms resting in slings—a sight that has never before been seen here since the establishment of a constitutional government."[11] Before it closed, the assembly passed a resolution thanking the officers and men of the warships for their generous assistance in preserving law and order. The attorney general, who was being blamed, along with his privy council members, for not providing an armed force at the courthouse to prevent violence, defended the cabinet's decision. He explained that while they had previously discussed the matter and expected "great excitement and loud words," they felt they were safe in trusting the people who had always behaved peacefully even in periods of crisis.[12]

When the king prorogued the session at noon, Queen Emma's last sliver of hope to undo the election in some constitutional way vanished. But in a system that provided no mechanisms for a loyal opposition, any alternative scheme to attempt such action, as Liliʻuokalani correctly observed, was "nothing less than treason."[13]

Later that day Queen Emma went to the palace to ask King Kalākaua to release the seventy some people who had been arrested. It seems odd that she would have come to see him on the same day that he had earlier visited her to make amends only to be turned away. Nevertheless, the king's response was predictable: his hands were tied as he had sworn to uphold the law of the land.

Queen Emma was accustomed to being sniped at from court circles but not from the newspapers. She was jolted the next day to read the first open and harsh criticism of her by a newspaper. The *Pacific Commercial Advertiser* said it deeply regretted that "the immediate occasion for the outbreak of lawlessness and violence should be furnished by the acts and exaggerated published manifestoes of a lady who, until now, has stood so high in the public estimation."[14] Two weeks later the *Hawaiian Gazette* followed suit with an article entitled "Our Misfortune," which began: "There is no use in dissembling the fact that the most intense indignation was felt and expressed during and since the riot, against the noble lady who was the rival candidate for the throne. That she did not act discreetly in not promptly seeking to stay the destruction of property and injury to the persons of the Representatives, by calling off her supporters is also evident, but what her reasons were, we do not know."[15]

Such criticism of the queen only confirmed the views held by many foreigners such as Harvey Hitchcock who wrote, "Her saintly reputation is gone, and she appears before the public, unmasked, as an intriguing politician and nothing more. Everybody is down on her."[16]

Queen Emma was now viewed as a "rebel," as revealed in a lei chant composed after the elections by one of her supporters from Kaua'i:

He Lei Kēia no Ema	
He lei kēia no Ema,	This is a lei chant for Emma,
Kō lei taulana i ke tipi,	A lei chant for you who are known as a rebel.
Ua kau kō lei i ka waha	Your name is mentioned everywhere
I ka lehelehe o ka loko 'ino.	By the lips of heartless people.
Tueka'a pau 'ia mai,	Everything rolls out,
Nā kui nā 'oi o loko.	Like nails and sharp things from within.
He kōlea kau 'āhua	They who speak are but mound-perching plovers,
Noinoi 'oihana aupuni.	They who seek to hold government offices,
I ka hana loko maita'i ia,	Though they have been kindly treated
Eka na'au lani ha'aha'a.	By the gracious-hearted chiefs.
Ua pono nō 'oe ke lino,	You have something to boast of,
Ua lohe nā kupa o Kahiti	For it is heard in foreign lands
'Elua 'oi o ke ao nei—	That there are but two great (women)—
Witolia kō Lākana	Victoria of London
'O Kuini Ema kō Hawai'i.	And Queen Emma of Hawai'i.
Kohukohu I ka moho kalaunu,	These two are fit to occupy thrones.
Ha'ina 'ia mai ka puana	This is the end of our chant
Kaleleonālani he inoa.	In praise of Kaleleonālani.[17]

The Arrests and Trial

Scores of people were arrested. *Ka Nūpepa Kū'oko'a* published their names and while it regarded them as criminals, the Emmaites saw them as heroes: Kealakua, Kanealii, Puweuweu, Kinilau, Kaiama, Kahelemauna, Kihei, Kuaana, Keailuwale, Koalii, Paaoao, Kapilau, Kamaheu, Opiopio, Kawika, Kilohi, Moluhi, Nanoo, Kalua, Kamakea, Kaihehau, Kapule, Pa, Moio, Alohikea, Kapou, Keku, Kanepaiki, Amohe, I Mahoe, Keoki, Kahele, Maalewa, Kaluaioahu, Keakui, Kailiuakea, Piko, Kekoa, Hapa, Maikai, William Brown, Kanui, Piipiilani, Kele, Wailele, Kahaunaele, Kaluumau, Pake, Lohiau, Kaanuana, Kaoliko, E Kupele, Koloa, Hoopii, S. Kailau, Piiopio, S.W. Mahelona, J. Kaulahea, Kamakamu (George Bell).[18] Except for a few men (there were no females) who came from Kāne'ohe and 'Ewa, they were all from Honolulu. And contrary to Lili'uokalani's claim that they were "all" Emma's retainers, almost none of her retainers were involved.

On the eve of the trial, Attorney General Alfred Hartwell called personally on Queen Emma to obtain her signature on a document announcing formally her allegiance to King Kalākaua and her disapproval of the riotous actions at the courthouse. It read:

> Many entirely false reports have been made concerning the Queen Dowager since the election of King Kalakaua. The Queen Dowager did not at first think it necessary to notice or deny them. But so great are the misrepresentations, that she now takes occasion to say through the newspapers that the reports are utterly false and without foundation which declare that she desires to see ill feeling stirred up against His Majesty the King. It has even been stated that she intends to send to the Queen of England for assistance in placing her on the Throne. It is all so absurd that she would not think it worth noticing if some people did not seek to think that some foundation exists for such reports.
>
> The Queen Dowager is too loyal a subject of King Kalakaua, and too true a friend to Hawai'i, to lend any sanction to anything that is opposed to the laws and peace of the Realm, or to allegiance to the King. She does not for one moment countenance the violent acts of the mob at the Court House, nor does she wish her name to be associated with any who wish to violate the law of the land.[19]

No evidence exists that Emma ever signed Hartwell's document, which would indicate that she did not agree with his characterization of her feelings toward Kalākaua or the riot or the law of the land. Hartwell, no doubt acting on behalf of the king, wanted to force her to abandon any hopes she had either to the throne or to her loyal supporters, neither of which she was willing to do.

At least seventy men were arraigned and brought to trial in early April 1874 in what was called "the most important trial ever held in Hawai'i." Hulu, the man named as the leader of the riot, testified that three days before the special session, a committee of thirteen had been appointed to take measures to secure the election for the queen. Part of the scheme called for an attack on the courthouse and those who had voted for Kalākaua.[20]

Hulu's testimony is corroborated in a letter by William F. Allen to his father Chief Justice Elisha Allen on February 23. In it he stated that the night before the session, a group of Emmaites had met privately and "agreed among themselves in case Emma was not elected to make an attack on the Court House, & kill the members of the Legislature who did not vote for Emma, burn the building and all other Government buildings, but not to touch foreigners or any of the Nobles."[21]

Hulu was not about to take the full blame; he insisted that he was only a tool in the hands of the real leaders, and he demanded that they too be punished. Associate Justice Charles Harris, who presided over the proceedings, agreed that many others could be held guilty because "[any] person who has counseled violence, during the last eighteen months, who, by speech or publication, has suggested it, or who has spoken of it in terms implying approbation, or when speaking of it has not met it with prompt disapproval, is answerable in no small degree to his own conscience and at the bar of public opinion for the disturbance now under our consideration, yet the law may not reach them." He was clearly alluding to the committee of thirteen. Harris knew who they were and so did the authorities, but they were not able to arrest them, let alone bring them to trial, because of insufficient evidence.[22]

Of those arrested, the court convicted forty-one. Four were sentenced to five years, five (including Hulu) to three years, one to two years, and three to eighteen months. Twenty-seven were condemned to pay fines ranging from one dollar up to 200 dollars. In discharging the all-Hawaiian jury, Judge Harris stated, "It does not appear to me that any of those who have been convicted can possibly think that all the evidence and every circumstance in their favor has not been duly weighed by you, while in looking upon the acquittals, I can truly say that there has been in all of them at least a reasonable doubt, and your verdicts have been equally creditable to you."[23]

Was She Guilty?

The queen was neither tried nor convicted for any of her actions connected directly or indirectly with the riot. But if Justice Harris' standard of guilt had been applied, it would have been difficult to hold Emma guiltless. The *Pacific Commercial Advertiser* editorialized that the lawlessness and violence were related to Emma.[24]

Not only the Honolulu newspapers but also the newspapers in California, where the riot had received widespread coverage, indicted the queen. After reviewing the events (somewhat inaccurately), the *Alta* of San Francisco concluded, "Such are the facts . . . [that] leave us with the impression that Emma is entirely unfit for the position to which she aspired and that her conduct was disgracefully indiscreet, to say the least of it."[25]

Most Americans residing in Honolulu would have agreed with Mrs. Alfred Castle that "the Queen of the mob ought to sit in sack cloth and ashes" for her involvement with the disturbance.[26] Even after the trial was over, the *Pacific Commercial Advertiser* continued to discredit the queen. It reported there were widespread rumors that she had encouraged the mob and was in one way or another involved in the rioting.[27] The suspicions of the public were heightened by the fact that at no time during this period did the dowager queen publicly object to the rioters or deny the rumors. (This same rationale was used in the document prepared by Attorney General Hartwell for the queen's signature.)

Feelings against Queen Emma were running high, and reports were circulated that attempts on her life were being made. On April 20, Attorney General Hartwell informed the queen that he had asked Marshal William Parke to place a guard at Rooke House to "prevent any anxiety on your part owing to what are undoubtedly idle rumors."[28] One of the threats was couched in a warning that came from the "Two Biting Lions," Lieutenant J. K. Naone and Corporal J. Aylett of the Prince's Company, who told the queen to be cautious when taking drinks of any kind in socializing with either dignitaries or commoners because "there may be evil people among them with treacherous intentions."[29]

A more serious threat came when Paul Nahaolelua, now serving as King Kalākaua's new minister of finance, received word that an attempt was to be made on the queen's life on a certain day at midnight. As with the other threats, she was not inclined to take this one seriously and had to be persuaded to leave Rooke House and spend the night at the priory. To avert any suspicions, the grounds of the cathedral were decorated with lanterns; Kalākaua had returned that day [Friday April 23] from his grand tour of O'ahu and a procession was held in his honor. One of the Sisters and a lady-in-waiting kept watch over the queen. While she slept in the parlor, some of the queen's men hid under the building to be ready in case of any trouble. When she awoke about 2:00 a.m. and asked for the time, she said quietly, "Thank God." The midnight hour had passed, and she was still alive.[30]

It was not clear, however, whether Hartwell's order to Marshal Parke was to keep intruders out or the queen in because he also warned her that she must not allow any assembling of her supporters on her premises that would lead to riots or sedition. He had reason for his suspicions because unrepentant Emmaites were still voicing their support for the queen's accession, and some even continued to conspire against the new regime. One Emmaite was the imprisoned Hulu who was plotting with Kahelemauna and other rioters about escaping from jail and conferring with the queen.[31] The intended subject of this discussion is not clear, but presumably it was directed against Kalākaua because of the king's "lies and boastings." Hulu had earlier written to the queen warning her "to watch out for yourself and keep away. We are giving our lives for your cause until victory is gained and our wish granted."[32] To complicate matters, another supporter warned the queen to be careful of Hulu who could not be trusted. She was advised not to meet with him for he was "trouble," and if she did meet with him, to make sure he was body-searched beforehand.[33]

Despite her equivocal allegiance to the new government and the subsequent attacks on King Kalākaua's efforts toward a reciprocity treaty, the dowager queen was invited to attend the opening of the legislature in its new assembly hall. The king's invitation may have been prompted by his feelings of confidence after his triumphal tour of the Islands where cheering throngs had welcomed their new sovereign with "hearts near bursting with joy."[34] He also honored her by seating her on the right of the dais with Queen Kapiʻolani, Prince Leleiōhoku, and Princesses Keʻelikōlani, Liliʻuokalani, and Likelike. Moreover, in his opening speech he remarked on the "disturbance occasioned by the actions of a few turbulent men" but refrained from any mention of her involvement. All these conciliatory actions indicate the king's willingness to defuse the combustible relationship with the dowager queen.[35] A month later both Emma and the king demonstrated their goodwill by attending the wedding of Carrie Brickwood at St. Andrew's Cathedral. According to the *Hawaiian Gazette*, the bride was "brought up and educated by the late King Kamehameha V as his own child."[36]

As far as the British commissioner Wodehouse was concerned, however, the situation in Honolulu was still volatile. He reported to his superiors in London that "The king is not popular in this Island [where the queen's support was the strongest], and were Honolulu left without the protection of a Ship-of-War, in my opinion, there would be a Revolution in which He would lose His Throne, and possibly His life. It is the fear of foreign intervention alone that keeps the Hawaiians quiet."[37]

The American commissioner Peirce agreed with his British colleague that disaffection persisted among the king's opponents but felt that the lack of capable leaders in this opposition would prevent it from being dangerous. "The Queen's party is weak in numbers, unorganized, unarmed and without an active head. Had an Hawaiian, endowed with prestige of popularity, ability & courage presented himself as their leader, some attempt would doubtless have been made ere this to dethrone King Kalakaua & place Emma upon the throne. As matters now are, they give promise of continued peace & quietness."[38]

Kepelino's Treason

The aftermath of the February riot has one last story: Kepelino's trial for treason. In the summer of 1874 the queen's private secretary was charged with circulating a petition addressed to the French commissioner, Theo Ballieu, requesting that French warships be allowed to dethrone the king and place Queen Emma on the throne. The lengthy document listed various reasons for this course of action: (1) King Lunalilo had named Emma to be his successor; (2) Kalākaua and his lieutenants in the legislature had through bribery and other devious means coerced the representatives to vote for him; (3) on February 11, Queen Emma received 3,091 votes from the people; (4) this fact had been presented to the legislative assembly with a request to postpone the special session, but it was totally ignored; had the petition been heeded, "there would have been no riot"; (5) the people rioted only after being ignored; (6) Kalākaua is hence a false king who intends to destroy Hawai'i's independence by mortgaging the kingdom to some foreign government; and (7) Queen Emma was the only legitimate sovereign by virtue of her Kamehameha lineage, being Lunalilo's heir, being chosen by the people, and being "amiable and good and suited to the people."[39]

Kepelino stated that the petition was signed by 346 people. But the twelve-person jury was told that few of the names were authentic and only about a dozen people had ever seen the petition. They were also told that the petition had never reached the French official to whom it was addressed.[40]

Witnesses at the trial—the first trial for treason since the establishment of a constitutional monarchy in 1840—testified that the petition was actually written by the French commissioner and given to Kepelino to circulate. When challenged by Peirce and Wodehouse, the French commissioner Ballieu denied the charge. But Peirce was convinced that "The affair is doubtlessly a French and Jesuit intrigue." Wodehouse opined that the French diplomat was probably "prompted mostly by a desire to increase his own importance here & that of the French Govt. in the political affairs of this people."[41]

A strong case can be made for Kepelino, however. The petition, after all, was not the first such document he had ever written. While David Kalākaua was acting postmaster, Kepelino had written letters to the king of Italy and to Queen Victoria asking for warships to support Queen Emma's accession to the throne.[42] In March of 1874 he had informed the queen that he was writing another petition. It read: "We, the Hawaiian people, will make petitions to the great countries Great Britain and France stating . . . 1. The majority of the Representatives were bribed with money and clothes so D. Kalākaua could become King. And Queen Emma, who has the loyalty of the native people, lost. 2. The King has appointed foreigners, against the wishes of the native people, to departments in the Government such as Mr. Green, A. F. Judd, Hitchcock and so forth. These men had signed their names to give away Pu'uloa to the United States. 3. These Americans here and their missionaries are looking for trouble so that Hawai'i will be seized by America. 4. If they get 2/3 of the fee simple land then they will control this Kingdom."[43] The similarity of the points in this letter and those stated in the petition indicate that Kepelino, who was both intelligent and talented, was quite capable of generating ideas and articulating them on paper.

In any case, Peirce found the French involvement with the "Queen's party" difficult to fathom because, repeating a position he had stated earlier, it was "weak in numbers, without leaders of ability & respectability, unorganized, unarmed and without pecuniary resources." He concluded that any attempt to dethrone King Kalākaua seemed to be of "a hopeless and desperate character."[44]

It is not known whether Queen Emma was involved in any part of the trial, either sub rosa or in the public court proceedings. The queen and Kepelino may have had a falling out months before the trial. He had written her in March, asking, "How could you act without compassion toward me?" He appealed to her to be patient with him and to ignore the malicious gossip and lies about him. He all but blamed his loyalty to her as the reason for his being considered persona non grata by the French, an enemy to the king, and "friendless."[45]

At the trial, Kepelino provided some perspective on events surrounding the riot but also raised serious questions about his own credibility. When Justice Harris asked him if he had anything to tell the court before sentence was pronounced, he replied that the king had no subject more loyal than himself and that he would willingly risk his life for him. This response, of course, contradicted the statements he had made in the petition favoring the queen. It is easy to recant when the death penalty is imminent. He also told the justice that on February 12 he had tried to persuade the queen to come to the courthouse to quell the riot. However, as noted earlier, none of the accounts of the riot mentions his name.

A letter from Albert Kūnuiākea to the dowager queen's supporters was introduced into the trial as extenuating evidence of Kepelino's complicity. It read: "To you, the friends who keep the peace. Salutations: 1. In order to facilitate and secure your guardianship, and keeping of order, I ask you to be pleased not to oppose the government, the peace and the laws of the land. 2. And as I cannot personally be present to guard my cousin the Queen, I do hereby appoint John P. Z. Kahoalii as my deputy. The verbal directions, or rules that he may make, shall be binding. 3. And I shall be gratified if my cousin the Queen confirms this. Done by my hand this 6th day of May, 1874."[46] There is no evidence that the queen confirmed the letter. She must have found the first item presumptuous because she herself had never issued such an order and the second point odd because Albert had never before offered to guard the queen. (If anyone needed guarding, it was Albert for whom the queen had sought for some time to be his guardian "as he is a spendthrift.")[47]

Defense counsel J. Porter Green read a statement on behalf of Kepelino, asking the court to recommend him to the king's mercy for the following reasons: (1) that he was led on by advice of others to draw up the offending petition, (2) that just as Kalākaua sought the aid of foreign troops to quell the riot, so could the friends of the queen seek the aid of a friendly foreign power to intervene on her behalf, and (3) that he labored under the mistaken notion that any petition produced for general circulation could not be considered as treasonable material.

Justice Harris, however, dismissed his contentions of innocence. "You declare that you endeavored to quell the riot. . . . Your memorial would indicate the contrary, for therein you say: 'We shed the blood of the Representatives, and destroyed the property of the Government.' You say you was [sic] led into your course by advice. This is a too frequent excuse by Hawaiians."

Harris concluded with a statement that seemed to all but exculpate the queen dowager from any of the defendant's actions: "The letter read to-day in your defense . . . indicates that you were appointed the leader of a party. But there is nothing in that letter to authorize you to counsel acts of violence; but only to keep watch and ward over the safety of a lady, who was and is just as safe as she was during the lifetime of her Royal husband. All men in this Kingdom of every class, would peril their lives in her defense."[48]

The jury's finding, which was reached in about twenty minutes, was a unanimous verdict of guilty. Kepelino was sent to prison and sentenced to hang, but the sentence was later commuted. Kalākaua granted him a full pardon in September 1876. Kepelino went on to earn a niche in Hawaiian history not for playing a role in the riot but rather for authoring *Traditions of Hawai'i*, which places him with Samuel M. Kamakau, David Malo, and John Papa 'Ī'ī in the front ranks of native-born preservers and interpreters of Hawai'i's ancient culture.

The Queen Emma Paper Lei

While the queen's name was being bandied about as an accomplice and rebel during Kepelino's trial, Peter was promoting the use of her name in an ingenious way. The *Hawaiian Gazette* reported that "a new lei composed of paper stars, and worn on the hat, is now [December 1874] the rage with Hawaiians, male and female, in Honolulu to the disadvantage, no doubt, of the flower-lei business."[49] Emma had sent him a couple of these paper leis that she had made, which he promptly placed on his hat and named after the queen. He wrote, "When I got to the Beach, my Wreath attracted the Natives' attention . . . and I gave its name as Queen Emma."[50] The name spread quickly because the Captain of the *Warwick* told Peter that "Because the whites like Queen Emma so much, and so do the Hawaiians, therefore, they wear them on their hats and call them "Queen Emma's lei."[51] The lei was a far more appropriate symbol for the queen than a rebellion.

Omens, Signs, and Prophecies

If there was one constant in Queen Emma's life, it was her Anglican faith, which left little room for the vestiges of the ancient Hawaiian priesthood and practices. She dismissed outright the claims of the new *kāhuna*, the sorcerers and mediums, and the shamanic healers. In 1873 she wrote to Peter about Paniku Hua, who was also a leper at Kalaupapa and whom he had credited with curing one of his ailments. Emma stated: "I have no faith in any one like her and believe not her prophesies."[52]

Also a Christian, Peter at first was as dismissive of the *kāhuna* as Emma, but in the wretched and lonely life of a leper, his interest grew in Hua's healing and prophetic prowess. His letters to Emma began to describe frequently and in detail many of Hua's predictions about Emma's own future. Peter wrote, for example, in November 1873 that Hua had prophesied that Emma would one day rule as queen, that Lunalilo would not live long, and that if the queen were to remarry she would have one more child, a girl who would be her last offspring.[53] In April 1874 he wrote that Hua had told him, "Be patient and do not worry about your cousin. God is watching over her and He will set her up on high."[54] Two months later Peter informed the queen that Hua had seen Kalākaua's calabash turned upside down with its content of bones scattered and then turned into ashes. When he had asked its meaning, Hua replied that it was the death of the Kalākauas and that the only way the "D.K.s" could prevent it was to "place Emma on the throne."[55] Again, Peter wrote that after Hua had read the signs in the heavens she said: "Here is Emma standing, visible everywhere. I know that Emma will reign, and it will not be long before we all shall see it happen. This woman's goodness of heart has been famous from the time she shared the Throne with her husband the King. She was never haughty nor proud. During their reign no man was debased. But with D.K. all men are thrust down."[56]

Unfortunately, much of the correspondence between Emma and Peter during this period (1873–1876) was either destroyed or lost; consequently, it is impossible to know exactly when she began to change. But by the end of 1875, her attitude had completely turned from one of total disdain toward *kāhuna* to complete absorption in their prophecies. This change is revealed in her letter to Peter dated December 17, 1875:

> She (Paalua) [Ruth Ke'elikōlani's servant] came to tell me the other day the Kahuna (the man's name is Kaiu) who predicted long ago from Waianae, "Rising—vanishing—rising—and entirely vanishing," has been to her and said I must remain steadfast in prayer in January, for in February next a sovereign will be crowned—either Albert or myself. All the D.K.s are going to die. Predictions are again rife as to my accession, four having been told me without each knowing of the other's previous informant. . . .
>
> Oh! I must go back to the old woman's predictions. She gave Pilipo and I the request of fasting Monday, Wednesday, and today (Friday) of this week, which we have done strictly, nothing but water passing my lips. . . . We were all to pray that God would please place me on the Hawaiian Throne, and on coming Monday at noon, December 20th, we should have a little feast. A young lamb should be eaten [with] it at noon, and three drops of its heart's blood with three drops of its gaul should be mixed in a glass of brandy, which I am to drink before eating at noon, representing the heart's blood of natives and the gall to represent the passage of time and the movement of events should be turned towards me. . . . On that day the heavens will be cloudless

> and some wonderful sign appear . . . and something will happen within ten days after our feast (which will happen on the 20th). She says that the tree with all its roots, branches, etc., will be cut off, meaning the D.K. [party] will all die off.

By this time Emma was also receiving both oral and written prophecies from many *kahuna* sources. One was from J. K. Lonokeawe who wrote to tell the queen that she saw in the omens and signs her sitting upon the throne.[57]

What caused Emma to change? By this time (1875) she may have lost some faith and patience with Providence. Then too she may have been worn down by events and thus become susceptible to the testimonies of Peter and to the prophecies of the *kāhuna*. Finally, her fiery, almost obsessive, desire to be queen may have predisposed her to believe in the hopeful assurances and the *mana* of the prophecies. Perhaps a combination of beliefs sustained her in carrying on a contest that most people felt neither she nor her supporters could win. In summary, Emma's change was a matter not so much of faith but of politics—the politics of winning.

Grand Tour of O'ahu

In October 1875 the queen decided to take a trek around the Islands. She asked part-Hawaiian John A. Cummins, a member of the House of Representatives and the owner-manager of Waimānalo ranch and sugar plantation, to organize the trek and to accompany her.[58] He was surprised at her request because he had opposed her election. In fact, he was the culprit who scribbled on her campaign poster: "We do not wish to see the petticoat putting on breeches." Moreover, he continued to be one of Kalākaua's strongest backers. Politics aside, Cummins had been an intimate friend of her husband Alexander Liholiho and had entertained them and performed many favors for the royal couple. In addition, only a man of his considerable resources, including hundreds of horses, could have carried out a grand tour of this kind.[59]

Thus on the morning of November 5, 1874, with Queen Emma and Cummins in the lead, followed by Fanny and other chiefs, the procession left Honolulu amidst a light rain. The cavalcade included 140 women, riding astride, all dressed in colorful, long-flowing *pā'ū*, reminiscent of the queen's first progress tour of Kaua'i following her marriage nearly twenty years before. As they rode through Honolulu, the streets were "thronged with people to witness the grand sight." From Honolulu, they passed through the parched lands of Wai'alae, Kuli'ou'ou, and Maunalua and on to Makapu'u. There the royal party was met by six mounted knights in red costume and red visors, carrying torches—both she and Kalākaua were entitled to the *kapu* of burning torches in the daytime. In fact, Cummins had organized almost the same royal welcome earlier in 1874 for King Kālakaua when he made his obligatory grand tour.[60]

As the procession wended its way to Waimānalo, four miles distant, a lighted arch appeared every 300 yards bearing a motto in Hawaiian. When they reached Mauna Rose, Cummins' three-story manor, they were welcomed by a corps of men blowing horns made from *lauhala* (pandanus leaves) and by residents prostrating themselves on the ground as the queen dowager passed. Although the custom had all but disappeared and Emma had not expected it, the gesture symbolized the esteem in which she was still held. From Mauna Rose, Cummins commanded the operation of an estate renowned for its great herds of cattle and sheep and its expansive sugar cane fields. It was also renowned for its tremendous parties numbering hundreds of guests (whom he conveyed over to Waimānalo on his schooners and lodged in cottages that surrounded the estate).

On this occasion the entertainment began with a *lū'au* for the 200 guests. It started at 5:30 p.m. and at 8:30 p.m. the hula dancers and singers performed throughout the night in the illumination of 300 kerosene-lit torches. The hula was still going on when the sun rose. After a night of continuous entertainment, these same 200 guests breakfasted at 8:00 a.m. at a table that displayed as much food as the night before. The next three days consisted of continuous feasts and hula and music and other spectacular diversions.

For the queen's pleasure, Cummins, the host extraordinaire, had his men stage a rare *he'e pu'ewai* or surfing up stream on the nearby Puha River. When the men created a twenty-foot opening in the sand that dammed the stream, the water rushed out at the rate of thirty knots, and only two men and two women dared to ride the bore of wild surf. To reward their feat, the queen presented each with $100 and four pairs of red blankets. The next day, after a few lessons from her host, the queen excelled at rifle shooting, smashing a bottle at 140 yards and cutting a twine from a long distance. To the queen's great delight, Cummins, one of the great horsemen of Hawai'i, also staged a horse race on his own racetrack that featured his prize horses in competition against the Islands' best.

As the cavalcade moved around Lanikai and Mōkapu to Kāne'ohe, then to Waikāne, Punalu'u, and beyond, the people continued to arrive with *ho'okupu* or gifts of foodstuffs for the queen. The amount was so immense that Cummins thrice had to summon a schooner to convey to Rooke House all the gifts, which included thirty live hogs, eleven smaller pigs, four sheep, 800 dried *'anae* (full-sized mullet), eight bundles of dried mullet, sixteen barrels of poi, ninety-six fowls, thirty-six turkeys, twelve white geese, ten bags of rice, and twenty sacks of sweet potatoes. If a people's love could be calculated in weights and measures, the queen had a supply sufficient to last the rest of her years. For her part, the queen gave away large quantities of blankets, calico or cotton cloth, and shirts called *ue wahine*, among other items.

Queen Emma tested her penchant for daring in Punalu'u when she and Cummins got in an outrigger canoe, which was attached by 100 fathoms of rope to a pair of horses that galloped for four miles on the beach parallel to the water. Cummins described the scene: "The beach was crowded with people to witness the great sight of a Queen taking a perilous ride in the surf. . . . Her Majesty enjoyed [it] . . . although she was wet through and through when we landed. . . ." The people then carried both the queen and Cummins a mile up the valley to Kaliuwa'a (now known as Sacred Falls). At the base of the eighty-five-foot high waterfall is a clear pool where they all bathed, swam, high jumped, and dove amidst great hilarity. At this time both the queen and Cummins were nearly forty years old.

At Lā'ie Malo'o the queen and her party were entertained by Kapuaokahala, "the great hula man," who, according to Cummins, "had the reputation [of] being the best hula player in Hawaii-nei." He and his three daughters performed an impressive variety of hula dances, including the *pūniu* (a small knee drum), *'āla'a papa* (dance done without a *pahu* or drum), *'ili'ulī* (probably the *'ulī'ulī* or gourd rattle), and *pa'i umauma* (chest-slapping).[61]

In Waialua, where they partied for four days, the number of women in the procession had increased to over 300 who "looked fat and smiling and every face was wreathed in smiles." Their last *lū'au*, which exceeded all previous experiences, was given by Princess Ruth Ke'elikōlani at her estate at Moanalua. There they were joined by another 200 people who had come from Honolulu to escort the queen's party home. By the time they reached Honolulu, the number in the cavalcade had climbed to nearly 800, all on horseback and all bedecked with leis of *lehua* and *pīkake*. When they reached Rooke House in Nu'uanu, everyone dismounted and bade farewell to Queen Emma, thereby ending fifteen days that were described by Cummins as the "merriest, wildest jaunt of my life . . . unlikely that such could ever be repeated."[62]

Why did Emma take the risk? Neither the queen nor Cummins gave any reasons. But the tour may have been politically motivated. She may have wanted to ascertain the extent of her popular support outside Honolulu and also perhaps to test the probabilities of the *kahuna* prophecies. The timing of the tour—just before the key election of 1876 that the Emmaites sought to win—suggests further that politics may have been the motive for the tour.

Why did Cummins, a strong supporter of King Kalākaua, agree to sponsor the trek? Possibly it was part of his conciliatory approach toward the queen. Of greater likelihood, however, is that Cummins merely wanted to mend an old friendship fractured by partisan politics. In an interesting aside, Cummins recalled that at one point in the tour the queen told him that if he had caused her to be elected she assuredly would have appointed him one of her ministers. He replied that "Although my father was an Englishman, he believed it was for the best interest of the country that there should be a king at the head of the nation rather than a queen, and that it was preferable that American influence should sway the throne rather than English, as we feared it would be if we elected Her Majesty." He also mentioned that he reminded the queen that she had assured him at one time that she did not contemplate being a candidate for election to the throne. (Cummins's remark is not supported by any of the evidence presented so far.)[63]

The Election of 1876

A major factor that unified Emma and her supporters was their common opposition to Kalākaua's campaign for a reciprocity treaty with the United States. Since the election of 1874 Emma and her British friends had been actively campaigning against reciprocity. In early January 1876, Wodehouse informed London: "I believe that a large proportion of the natives are very suspicious of the King and view with dislike his policy in the matter of the Treaty of Reciprocity with the U. States which altho they have not seen, they fear is fraught with danger to the independence of this Kingdom; and I confess . . . that King Kalakaua's conduct in, undoubtedly, 'coquetting' with the U. States fully justifies this feeling on their part which may some day lead to fresh disturbances."[64]

The queen's first and principal objection to the reciprocity treaty was her fear that Pearl Harbor might be ceded in the exchange leading to the loss of Hawaiian sovereignty. In fairness to King Kalākaua, he too opposed any diminution of Hawaiian sovereignty but believed that he could secure a treaty without giving up any territory. The queen's second fear was that a treaty would virtually guarantee an American monopoly on Hawaiian trade and thereby further reduce the kingdom's already weak ties to Great Britain.

As far as the queen's supporters were concerned, the reciprocity treaty was their number-one issue in the 1876 campaign for the election of representatives in the legislative assembly. Consequently, they supported several candidates in Honolulu and elsewhere. William F. Allen wrote to his father, Chief Justice Elisha Allen: "The Emmaites have fully organized for the coming election, they have candidates in every district, and will elect the most of them, the British residents all over the Islands favor the Emma candidates. They are pledged to pass no laws to raise any revenue in place of what may be lost by the treaty."[65]

A few days before the election, Walter Murray Gibson, the *Nuhou*'s editor, tried to rally support for the treaty and for King Kalākaua and wrote: "I regret to say that I hear mention made among you of an 'Emma party'; . . . the persons who pretend to form such a so-called party, and who advise any disloyalty to the reigning Sovereign, are fomenting a most foolish and dangerous discussion."[66]

After the election was over, the queen cheered the results: of the four seats allotted to Honolulu two of her candidates, Samuel M. Kamakau and Kalaukoa, had won. The other two winners were Henry Waterhouse who, though not an Emmaite, opposed the reciprocity treaty and Edward K. Lilikalani, a Kalākaua protégé.[67] Outside Honolulu the queen's men had also won in North Kona with Reverend Pilipo, in Puna, Hawai'i with D. Joseph Nawahi, in Kaua'i with J. Kauai, and in Waianae with S. W. Mahelona. Other Emmaites, such as David P. Eldredge who ran in the Wailuku, Maui district, lost narrowly.[68]

In analyzing the election for Peter, Emma described Kalaukoa as a common laborer who made his living on the streets as a boatboy, drayman, and cartboy; yet he was one of the speakers at the courthouse who encouraged the people to support her. Although the venerable Kamakau garnered fewer votes (686 to Kalaukoa's 702), she felt that he was the one to whom people looked for stability and solid arguments on issues.[69]

She was not so charitable, however, in describing Lilikalani as King Kalākaua's "mouthpiece" in the legislature and a "fufu" or softy who "got in by tremendously heavy bribes of cash." She said he choked with fright every time he spoke to a crowd, yet she was convinced that Kalākaua would "succeed in making a man out of him." She reminded Peter that "practice is the only way to make perfect anything," something Kalākaua himself had proved. "To be sure, he is not all we want, still he has made his name by his own determined effort. So therefore we must do likewise."[70]

While Emma was willing to recognize Kalākaua's perseverance and ambition, she was always quick to condemn some of his actions. She told Peter that before the election the king was so frightened that he had summoned all the military to the palace to guard him. Everyone was armed with firearms of all sorts, which were always loaded. Even the whites feared an uprising against the king. She accused King Kalākaua of trying to make people believe that she was "conspiring to overturn" him.[71]

Peirce confirmed the queen's portrayal of events when he wrote on the morning of the 1876 election, "It is apparent that there exists among a large part of the native population of this island [Oahu], a disrespect for their King and his brother, the heir apparent; which, if it continues to increase; may ultimately endanger, if it does not destroy the present dynasty."[72]

As it turned out, the election, according to the *Pacific Commercial Advertiser*, "passed off without noise or excitement" but not without some humor. One episode involved a well-known gentleman who deposited what he thought was his ballot, carefully enclosed in an envelope, but which when the ballots were being counted, turned out to be a bill for the tuition of one of his children.[73]

Queen Emma praised the bloodless election of 1876 by declaring, "The beauty of the whole thing is that the people never planned to attack or shed blood that day."[74] She was sufficiently knowledgeable about democratic political mechanisms to understand that the idea of an election is to allow for the smooth and peaceable transfer of power. Otherwise she would have had little motivation to work as hard as she did to campaign for her candidates and for the issues and principles she and her followers espoused. Even if she did not trust King Kalākaua, she had some faith in the principles and institutions of the kingdom's constitutional monarchy. In the process, she and her adherents created the political entity that Peirce and Gibson called the "Queen's party." Beginning in 1876 even Queen Emma herself used the term "party" when referring to the Emmaites in the Legislature.

For example, once the representatives were in session, she wrote to

Peter: "Our *party* (emphasis added) in Parliament is the wisest and has the law at their fingers' ends, disconcerting the Nobles. But in spite of it they gain because they have 2/3 of the whole House. Simon and Kamakini are the only workers and speakers on the Nobles' part to oppose our *party* (emphasis added). The hall is full, crowded with natives all day, listening to the debates and cheering our side but calling against those who speak against our speakers."[75] Presumably, the queen was also present at the proceedings. But she seemed resigned to the fact that her party could never win because "the opposition is always 2/3 of the house and we are only 1/3."[76]

By conventional standards, the Emmaites were not a political party with an articulated platform, an organized leadership and membership, a formal slate of candidates, and so on. But modern historians do agree that one unintended consequence of the election of 1876 was the emergence of the embryonic "Queen's party" that evolved into Hawai'i's first political party system.[77]

20

Rifts and Conspiracies

Queen Emma was now the acknowledged leader of a nascent political party. However, this party was not viewed as the "loyal opposition" by those in power; indeed, they viewed both the queen and her partisans as disloyal. In 1874 the one word that described the relationship between the royal "ins" and the royal "outs" was distrust. It exacerbated the conflicts between Emma and Lili'uokalani, which in turn tainted the relationships of many around them by forcing them to take sides. In this pervasive atmosphere of distrust, Emma resorted to her "conspiratorial impulses" not only to rescue Peter Ka'eo from Kalaupapa but also to obstruct the path of the Kalākauas.

The Rift with Kapi'olani

The close friendship between Kapi'olani and Emma, according to Lili'uokalani, disintegrated after the riot, and she blamed Emma. She devoted three pages of her autobiography (*Hawaii's Story*) to a harsh criticism of Emma for her treatment of Kapi'olani and accused her of being disrespectful and at times even insulting. Lili'uokalani found Emma's behavior difficult to understand and attributed it to her bitter disappointment over losing the election of 1874 to her brother David Kalākaua.

Lili'uokalani wrote of a specific incident at the palace when Dowager Queen Emma sought the king's release of those Emmaites who were arrested after the riot. Just before the king was to receive Emma, he had asked both Lili'uokalani and Kapi'olani to accompany him in receiving her, but before they could comply, Emma had held her audience with the king, had made her request, and then, had hastily withdrawn without waiting for the entrance of Queen Kapiʻolani or herself. Liliʻuokalani thought Emma's failure to wait and greet them demonstrated exceedingly poor manners.[1]

Liliʻuokalani wrote, "Why she should cherish such bitterness of spirit against the queen is past my comprehension. Queen Kapiolani had been aunt to Queen Emma, having been the wife of her uncle Namakeha, and had nursed the young prince, the son of Alexander Liholiho, although her rank not only equaled, but was superior to, that of Queen Emma, the child's mother."[2]

She then wrote of Kapiʻolani: "The sweet disposition and amiable temper of Queen Kapiolani never allowed her to resent in the least the queen dowager's bitterness, nor would she permit herself to utter one word of reproach against the mother of the child she had herself so deeply loved. In this respect my brother's wife showed her truly Christian character, and there were occasions when the lack of courtesy on the part of Queen Emma became something very like insult."

Apparently, Emma displayed her lack of manners on more than one occasion. As Liliʻuokalani wrote: "Even in the residence of my brother visiting the palace at the invitation of the king, if the queen were present she avoided recognizing her, and would at times rise and leave when Queen Kapiolani entered, saluting no one but the king as she retired; although this was an outrageous impertinence to the queen under her own roof, it was through Christian charity ignored by its recipient."[3]

But in the first specific instance, was Emma as spiteful and malicious toward Kapiʻolani as alleged? Is it not possible that Emma was so distraught over the events of the previous days and so unhappy about the king's refusal to grant the release of her followers that she decided to exit the palace as quickly as possible? Perhaps it was not a case of bitterness but rather of disappointment and hurt, which Kapiʻolani understood and Liliʻuokalani did not. And how could Emma have so easily forgotten or ignored the fact that Kapiʻolani had been married to her uncle Namakeha and had cared for and nursed Prince Albert? These associations were too precious and enduring for her to forget, even for a moment. In addition, Emma still enjoyed a good relationship with Kapiʻolani's younger sister, Kapoʻoloku Poʻomaikelani, who had served as one of her trusted ladies-in-waiting for many years and had just left Emma's employ to join her sister at court, as was the custom.[4] Furthermore, Emma's fight was not with Kapiʻolani but rather with her husband Kalākaua.

Unfortunately, Lili'uokalani's intemperate, unforgiving, and one-sided account is the only one available. Kapi'olani, who spoke only Hawaiian although she was educated in English and Hawaiian, did not leave any memoirs. While Emma left numerous letters and bits and pieces of journals and other written material, nothing of importance refers to Kapi'olani after 1874. In fact, among all the letters exchanged between Emma and Peter not one mention is made of Kapi'olani. If their relationship was as bitter as Lili'uokalani described, Emma or her correspondents, Fanny, Peter, or Lucy Peabody, probably would have mentioned it.

Over the years of Kalākaua's reign it is entirely plausible that Emma would have had an occasional dispute with Kapi'olani. Any situation with two living queens, who are almost neighbors, would have a natural potential for conflict. After all, Kapi'olani was a member of a new dynasty that was determined to establish its own identity and reputation; in this process, protocol and precedence inevitably became fundamental issues.

One such conflict occurred immediately after Kalākaua's accession to the throne. An objection was made to Emma's name being placed before that of Kapi'olani in the prayer for the royal family in the Anglican church because in the *aloali'i* (court) Kapi'olani, the queen consort, was second in rank to the king. It was also a delicate matter for Bishop Alfred Willis because both queens were members of the church. He settled it publicly in a letter to the editor of the *Hawaiian Gazette* and stated that, based on Anglican practice in Great Britain, a queen dowager took precedence over the consort of the reigning sovereign.[5]

Another example pertained to the place of Emma's carriage in Lunalilo's funeral procession, but this time the issue may have been raised by Peter. He wrote to Emma, "I see in the Funeral Programme that you come in the third, but let them have their way, for I hope that they will find out before long that the majority will yet rule."[6] Her carriage came after the one carrying Princesses Ruth Ke'elikōlani, Lili'uokalani, Likelike, and Bernice Pauahi Bishop. In the first carriage rode King Kalākaua, Queen Kapi'olani, Prince Leleiōhoku, and Kana'ina, Lunalilo's father.[7]

There would be many such conflicts, for, as Curtis Iaukea, Kalākaua's aide-de-camp, put it, "The question of precedence frequently arose to plague us at Court."[8]

Another conflict involved actions that honored one queen over the other as in the relocation of the site of the Royal Hawaiian Band concerts. Since 1872 the popular concerts had been held at Emma Square, but in March 1877 it was decided to move the concerts to a new site to be called Kapiʻolani Square. The decision required the construction of a new park at Pohukaina, a large lot adjoining the palace.[9] Later, however, after Captain Berger had returned from Europe in mid-1877, he reinstated the concerts at Emma Square but judiciously continued the concerts at Kapiʻolani Square.[10]

Suffice it to say, such decisions were most likely made by officials or advisers, including Liliʻuokalani, rather than by Queen Kapiʻolani herself so that any conflicts with Emma were more with them than with the queen consort herself. Over the years the cumulative effect of such conflicts, however minor, might have annoyed Dowager Queen Emma to the point where she may have occasionally turned in frustration and anger against Queen Kapiʻolani. Liliʻuokalani may have used the specific instances that she witnessed to exaggerate a pattern of disrespectful behavior.

The irony is that the bulk of the evidence reveals a rift between Emma and Liliʻuokalani rather than between Emma and Kapiʻolani. Liliʻuokalani admitted: "I confess that my own patience with such displays was not equal to a like forbearance; and, as I would not stoop to court her favor, nor could accept, without proper and dignified notice, her overbearing demeanor towards myself, Queen Emma never forgave me my own rank and position in the family which was chosen to reign over the Hawaiian people. It did not trouble me at all, but I simply allowed her to remain in the position in which she chose to place herself."[11]

Emma may not have posed a threat to Kapiʻolani, but she was an obstacle to Liliʻuokalani's own ambitions of accession to the throne. When Leleiōhoku, the talented and popular heir to the throne, died on April 10, 1877, Keʻelikōlani quickly claimed her right to be named heir to the throne on the grounds that she was his *hānai* mother. (Leleiōhoku was actually Kalākaua's youngest brother whom Princess Ruth Keʻelikōlani had adopted as a baby.) Her claim was rejected by the cabinet on the grounds that if she was appointed heir, then Mrs. Pauahi Bishop would be the next heir because they were first cousins.[12] That Keʻelikōlani's candidacy was supported by the Emmaites was of course dismissed. Although Liliʻuokalani was immediately named as heir apparent, at least one observer saw Emma as her major challenger. The British commissioner Wodehouse reported:

> It is useless to disguise the fact that the death of the Prince is a most serious blow to the new Dynasty, and although it was immediately followed by the Proclamation as Successor to the King, should he die

> without issue, of his Sister the Princess Lydia who is married to an American but is childless, few believe, that in such an event, she would be allowed to ascend the vacant Throne without a struggle, the result of which might, and in the absence of Foreign intervention, probably would end in the elevation of Her Majesty the Queen Dowager Emma, if she wished it, to the Throne of Hawaii . . . Queen Emma is much, and deservedly so, beloved by the mass of the Hawaiian people, and they consider that she has an undoubted right to succeed the present Sovereign.[13]

That Lili'uokalani was keenly aware of Emma's popularity is revealed in her account of her own grand tour of O'ahu, which she made following the death of Leleiōhoku. She stated that as heir to the throne it was only "proper and necessary" to tour the Islands to meet her future subjects. Part way through the tour Likelike, who was accompanying her sister, received a letter from her husband, Governor Archibald Cleghorn, to return to Honolulu because his opinion was that if the purpose of the tour was "to meet the people and cultivate their love, the time spent on the route would be wasted, because they were all zealous partisans of Queen Emma."[14] Likelike decided to stay, a decision that Lili'uokalani claimed not to have influenced. It would have been a great mistake had she returned, Lili'uokalani wrote, because the people had proved, even "the most zealous of Queen Emma's people," that "no heir to the throne could have been more royally received by all than I had been."

At the end of the tour, she wrote that as they entered Honolulu, "there was scarcely space for our cavalcade to pass between the throngs of people which lined our way. From Leleo to Alakea Street it was a mass of moving heads, through which only slowly could our carriages, horses, and outriders pass." In what might have been a thinly veiled jab at Emma, Lili'uokalani concluded, "It was understood and accepted as a victorious procession; and out of sympathy for the disappointed dowager queen, our people refrained from noisy demonstrations and loud cheering, and instead the men removed their hats, and the women saluted as we passed [Rooke House on the way to Lili'uokalani's residence, Washington Place]."[15]

The Plot to Rescue Peter

Lili'uokalani may have exaggerated Emma's capacity for causing mischief, but she was not entirely off the mark. As the author Alfons Korn put it, at times Emma found it difficult to satisfy her "suppressed but restless conspiratorial impulses."[16] This particular time, while she waged political battle with the "D.K.s" in the election of 1876, she also plotted the rescue of her cousin Peter from Kalaupapa. She had the help of a close personal friend and adviser, Edward Preston, an Englishman who arrived in Hawai'i six years before to practice law. The audacious plan was to have Peter smuggled back to O'ahu by canoe under the cover of darkness. The canoe was to be manned by two accomplices, Robert Charlton, a loyal Emmaite, and Jack Smith, one of Peter's cronies. They were to pick up Peter on the beach opposite his cottage, transport him across the channel, and then land him at a secluded spot on O'ahu.

The plot was not only audacious but also, had it been carried out, patently illegal. Under the Penal Code it was a misdemeanor to visit a leper without written permission of the Board of Health or to knowingly harbor, secrete, or conceal a leper. If found guilty, the perpetrators risked a fine of $100 and imprisonment at hard labor.[17] But the plan was aborted because Robert Charlton talked too much. In Emma's words, "he had been so indiscrete as to tell many people . . . your brother [Albert Kūnuiākea] being one of them, who instantly circulated the tale, and everyone had it on the tip of their tongues."[18] Her greatest fear was that once the government found out, it "would overstep the mark and take the law into their own hands."[19] Although it was only a misdemeanor, the queen was worried that King Kalākaua might throw Peter and his co-conspirators into jail and even try them for treason, as had been the case with Kepelino.[20]

Despite her fears, she did not cease to plan Peter's escape. She told him that Kalawaianui, a loyal Emmaite and a distant relative through their grandmother Ka'ōana'eha, had come up with a plan of his own. Emma wrote: "[He} now knows the coast of that part of Molokai and can very well land at night, walk up to your house and come down together with you and pull off to ship. His destination is Punaluu, Koolau [windward side of O'ahu], and [he] says he can well stand off and on at Kalaupapa for you."[21] For whatever reason, Kalawaianui's plan was not carried out.

Betraying her role as an arch conspirator, Emma wrote: "In order to carry on the pretense that I knew nothing of the plans for your rescue (should you have come), I sent as usual every article of food save the sheep or pig. I did not care who gets them in case you did come down, and wrote a non-committal letter which I was not afraid to have read by . . . others, in case you had left."[22]

Why was the queen willing not only to break the law but also to be duplicitous? She had always prayed that her cousin, whom she considered more like a brother, would recover and leave Kalaupapa. He, of course, yearned to return to Honolulu and to repossess his *ali'i*-hood. But sentiment alone would not have motivated Emma's conspiracy; otherwise, she might have planned his rescue long before. The true reason was politics: she must have thought the risk worthwhile so that Peter could regain his seat in the House of Nobles and thereby strengthen her party's position in the legislature.

The exact time when the queen began to plan Peter's rescue is not known, but Peter had written to her in March 1876 stating that he had heard a rumor from Honolulu about his being called to take his seat in the legislature.[23] She promptly replied: "So you have heard of the rheumor of your coming to your seat at this Legislature. There is a report of such [a] thing, but because I have not yet found it tenable I have not told you of it, but should I know it as a fact then will write."[24] Evidently, at this time she had not yet formulated plans for his rescue. After making inquiries, she must have learned from some of her supporters such as Representative Pilipo that the legislature was seriously talking about bringing him back.[25] It was probably in April 1876 when she formulated the plot with Edward Preston and others. As she explained to Peter, "[Preston] said throughout, that once you landed here everyone would be in defence of your rights and probably that would bring things to a climax. He said a stir is wanted now to check the present unscrupulous management of Government."[26] Preston's argument implied that so many people would be sympathetic to Peter's return that whatever actions they took would be justified by the end result. When viewed in this context, the plot was neither reckless nor ignoble, insofar as Emma was concerned.

Although the queen had failed, Peter was unexpectedly released in June. A new "Committee of Thirteen," composed of leading legislators including Pilipo, visited the colony to investigate conditions. As they were leaving the settlement, they paused to take refreshments at Peter's cottage. Without any medical advice, they simply announced to Peter that he was "not a leper" and that he could accompany them back to Honolulu. After he had packed his things and was waiting on the beach, he was told he could not leave without the permission of the Board of Health. A few days later, he was granted his release, based on the recommendation of Dr. Robert McKibbin, a close friend of Queen Emma.[27]

Although nothing is known about his reception in Honolulu, certainly Peter was happily and gratefully welcomed at Rooke House by his cousin Emma, aunt Fanny, Lucy, and others. Emma was eager for him to resume his seat in the House of Nobles and to reassert their "ancestral renown even in high places." After retaking his seat in 1878, he faithfully attended his meetings and voted a straight "party ticket" for the issues that Queen Emma either supported or opposed, but he seldom spoke on the floor and introduced no legislation of any significance. However, Peter was among exceedingly illustrious peers who included Charles Bishop, Archibald Cleghorn, Samuel Castle, Alfred Hartwell, John Kapena, James Dowsett, J. Mott Smith, Samuel Wilder, John Parker, and Edward Preston.

ʻIolani Palace

On December 31, 1879, the cornerstone for the new ʻIolani Palace was laid with full Masonic rites, not unlike those that Kamehameha IV had used in 1860 for the Queen's Hospital. Those attending the ceremony were members of the royal court, ministers and legislators, foreign dignitaries, as well as throngs of native and foreign residents. Emma was undoubtedly invited, but whether she attended is not known. She was not averse to building a new palace; it had been talked about and planned for, and funds had been appropriated by the legislature under Kamehameha V.[28] Given her penchant for thriftiness, she opposed extravagant expenditures, as some of the king's critics had predicted. Indeed, the costs soared from $50,000 to $343,000.[29]

Had Emma been present at the ceremony, she would have heard John Kapena, Minister of Foreign Affairs, speak of Alexander Liholiho. He spoke of the three Masonic principles of "Faith, Hope, and Charity" and he compared Kamehameha IV to Faith, Kamehameha V to Hope, and Kalākaua to Charity. Of Kamehameha IV, he said: "For Liholiho, Kamehameha IV, believed the people might be saved by curing the diseases—as witness his exertions in procuring the erection of the Queen's Hospital as proof of his Faith." He compared Kamehameha V to Hope because he "hoped for the perpetuity of Hawaiian independence." However, Emma would not have agreed with Kapena's comparison of Kalākaua with Charity, "the noblest virtue" nor his being praised for braving "the wintry cold of the Rocky Mountains and . . . the icy precincts" of Niagara Falls in his efforts to secure the "boom of Reciprocity."[30]

Because this event occurred on New Year's Eve, Emma's attention may have been focused on the imminent elections of 1880 in which her cousin, Albert Kūnuiākea, was a promising candidate.

Return of the Prodigal Cousin

Queen Emma was probably shocked at the 1880 election results: Albert Kūnuiākea, in his first campaign, was elected to the legislative assembly with the greatest number of votes. Despite the D.K.s' strong opposition to his candidacy, Albert garnered 643 votes, 23 more than the second vote getter, E. K. Lilikalani, the king's protege.[31] Running on the Queen Emma party ticket, in which Albert was known as *ke keiki ali'i* or the young chief, his victory was interpreted by some observers as "proof of the strength of Queen Emma's influence among the people."[32]

The details of Albert's victory and his reconciliation with Emma are not clear, but both events must have been a great relief to her. Four years earlier, in January 1876, when Governor Nahaolelua lost his patience and gave up his guardianship, Emma had petitioned the court that some suitable person be appointed guardian to control Albert's wasteful spending and other bad habits. Once Emma herself was appointed guardian, Albert repeatedly tried to have the court dismiss her. He did not help his cause, however, by fighting and getting drunk. Emma wrote to Peter: "Your brother was taken to Station house on Ash Wednesday the 1st of this month for fighting (whilst under the influence of liquer) in the streets at Paalua's house. They let him off however with a warning not to make a row. Next day I went to see him and he was all smiles. He had however said that he had vowed never to see or know me again, but I took him by surprise and he could not help himself."[33]

During Emma's guardianship, Albert complained bitterly about how she treated him, especially about how she doled out his allowance.[34] Emma wrote Peter: "I had for two months made him live on the $30—food, clothing, and squander money [included] in it all—[but] he could not endure it, so complained of me finally. I gave up trying to save his money for house, because he got so dreadfully abusive of me—it was worry for no use, because he was determined to go against me in everything. The last thing he did was to go to Cartwright and ask him to take his property in hand, as he cannot stand my treatment of him and property."[35]

Despite his behavior, Emma predictably persevered. When she reminded Peter of his illustrious ancestry and encouraged him to keep his station "high as well as renowned," she included Albert.[36] And when she urged Peter to "make a name" for himself and to "add another laurel to the ancestral tree," she specifically asked Peter to help his brother.[37]

Once Peter had asked, "What ever will become of poor Albert?" But now back in Honolulu, Peter had the opportunity to help Albert revitalize his self-esteem and his public image. At the same time, Albert's once stormy relations with Emma subsided as she began to mentor him in his new role of carrying the family as well as the party banner. Basically, he rose to the new level of his responsibilities.

His change was confirmed not only by his election but also by his release from the guardianship with Emma.

Immediately after the February 1880 elections, Queen Emma accompanied Princess Ruth Ke'elikōlani as her guest on a two-week tour to the Island of Hawai'i. The *Pacific Commercial Advertiser* wondered whether the trip had "any political significance" given the recent election.[38] It could have well been an innocent trip because the two were close friends and because Emma had properties in Wai'aha (Kona) to look after. However, the trip could have been politically motivated because it would have given Emma the opportunity to speak with and encourage her supporters, especially in Kona and Kohala, which were Emmaite strongholds. Although Ke'elikōlani was no longer the governess of Hawai'i, having been replaced by Princess Likelike, the king's sister, she was still a force to be reckoned with because of her status in the royal court and her enormous wealth.

Coincidentally, Emma shared many of the same friends with Princess Ruth Ke'elikōlani, including Claus Spreckels, the San Francisco sugar refiner, who at the time was trying to purchase the fee for 24,000 acres of leased sugar land on Maui. In an ingenious strategy, he approached Ke'elikōlani to buy out her claim to a part interest in the crown lands of the kingdom, which would have then given him the fee title. She had asserted that she was entitled to half the crown lands based on the assumption that the crown lands were the private property of the Kamehamehas. After the death of Alexander Liholiho, Emma had made the same claim and the court had agreed, only to have the government pass legislation nullifying the right of the heirs and successors to the throne to make such a claim.[39] Ke'elikōlani probably knew about Emma's case. Whether or not she knew about the legislation, Ke'elikōlani asserted that she was entitled to half the crown lands and sold Spreckles her claim for $10,000. The transaction caused a huge uproar because the land was estimated at $750,000. Many people felt that Ke'elikōlani had outwitted the Sugar King because she knew her claim to the crown lands was worthless.[40]

Sad Endings

If 1880 had begun happily with the triumph of Albert, it ended sadly with the demise of Fanny and Peter. Emma's natural mother, Fanny Young Kekuiapoiwa Kekelaokalani Kailikulani Leleoili Kuiua, died on the morning of September 4. At the age of seventy-six she had outlived her sister Grace Kamaʻikuʻi Rooke by fourteen years. In the *hānai* tradition, Emma always regarded them both equally as her mothers. If Grace dominated the first half of Emma's life, Fanny naturally dominated the second because Grace had been largely absent. No one will truly know the full extent of Fanny's influence on Emma as well as on some major actors and events of the times. In its obituary, the *Hawaiian Gazette* stated: "The deceased lady was universally respected for her virtues which was reflected in the distinguished daughter who is thus bereft of her nearest earthly support."[41]

Fanny was accorded the burial honors befitting her rank as a high chiefess—an impressively long funeral procession and burial among the *aliʻi* at Maunaʻala.[42] However, notably absent from the procession were King Kalākaua, Queen Kapiʻolani, and Princesses Liliʻuokalani and Likelike, a fact that "excited some comment."[43]

After a five-day illness, Peter died at night in his Honolulu residence on November 26, at the age of forty-four, less than five years after his release from Kalaupapa.[44] In contrast to Fanny, his death went almost unnoticed except for a brief one-paragraph announcement in the newspaper. He was quickly buried two days later on a Sunday afternoon at Maunaʻala, but with none of the elaborate ritual accorded to royals.[45]

Emma's seemingly endless sorrow from the deaths of her father, husband, son, her two mothers, uncles and aunts, and now her beloved cousin is revealed in a letter she wrote in early 1881 to Sarah Von Pfister, her former governess:

"Thanks so much for your kind letter of October received when I was again entered into mourning for my dear Cousin Peter Kekuaokalani. I ought to have answered it before this but really have not had the courage to speak or write of the sorrowful events which have come to me. Not quite three months had passed after my dear Mother was so suddenly taken from me, when the Cousin who had always been as a brother to me also passed, after only five days illness, to the unseen world which now holds all that is dearest. The loneliness of those left behind came over me once more as I seemed to feel well nigh overcome. [The] near presence of child and husband float near to comfort me."[46]

In December 1880 Queen Emma visited Kaua'i for two weeks with Princess Ruth Ke'elikōlani.[47] Although the details are not available, she probably tarried in Lāwa'i, where she had once celebrated Peter's thirty-fifth birthday, to revisit her property and home, Maunakilohana. In 1872 when Emma had promised her faithful housekeeper, Keli'imoewai, that she would come back to repair the blocked ditch and care for the dying plants, she had not intended it to take eight years.

Reaction to Kalākaua's Round-the-World Trip

During the last months of 1880 King Kalākaua had traveled throughout the Islands discussing, among other topics, his intention to journey around the world. His stated purposes were to "recuperate" his own health and to find the means for "recuperating" his people by the introduction of foreign immigrants.[48] He sought young men for two reasons: to meet the sugar plantations' demand for a steady supply of labor due to the dwindling number of native Hawaiians and to help increase the Hawaiian population. The king assured his people that the immigrants would be of a "cognate race" with similar values and hence would be compatible with the Hawaiian character. An additional, albeit unstated, purpose for the trip was his own intellectual curiosity about the world. After announcing publicly his decision to take the tour, he added that Lili'uokalani would act as regent during his absence.

What was Queen Emma's reaction? On January 20, 1881, the day that King Kalākaua departed Honolulu, she wrote in her diary that the trip was "his tour of pleasure & self praise." She implied that it was an ego trip for him as the first king of Hawai'i to tour the world. Furthermore, she felt that there was "a latent feeling of suspicion in the minds of foreigners" as well as native Hawaiians that the purpose of his trip was to "further some secret agreement arranged between Mr. Moreno & himself, may be to sell these Islands."[49] Although King Kalākaua had never intended to sell any Island, the rumor gained wide currency during the ensuing months.

One of those who believed the story was the American Secretary of State James G. Blaine. He said that the king was "a false and intriguing man, and that the principal object of this journey was to endeavor to sell his kingdom to some European Power."[50] To make matters worse, American President James Garfield shared Blaine's opinion. Even the *New York Times* flatly stated that Kalākaua's mission was for "the purpose of selling his kingdom."[51] Sir Edward Thornton, the British minister in Washington, D.C., with whom Blaine had earlier shared his concern, wrote to London stating that the United States, fearing complications arising from King Kalākaua's "expedition," was ready to take "some early measures for securing to itself the entire control of the Islands."[52]

In the meantime, British Commissioner Wodehouse had obtained a copy of Thornton's dispatch and showed it to Queen Emma. He reported, "She was deeply distressed at its contents." She then wrote the following letter to Wodehouse:

> The sudden and bold uncovering of America's long cherished wish (which they have always denied) to possess these Islands . . . has caused me great, great grief and anxiety. . . . I consider that America is now our open enemy, and that to England would be our natural course to look for strengthening, and that as we have bounden friends in England and France, America cannot carry out her high-handed policy with regard to these Hawaiian Islands. . . .
>
> The Native Hawaiians . . . are one with me in the love of our country, and determined not to let Hawaii become a part of the United States of America. We have yet the right to dispose of our country as we wish, and be assured that it will never be to a Republic![53]

Emma's defiant rejection of republicanism revealed the extent of her dedication to monarchy. She once wrote Peter that if Hawaiʻi became a republic, "It will make us like shiftless France in time."[54] To Emma, a sovereign and independent kingdom always meant a monarchy, preferably a monarchy ruled by a Kamehameha.

She concluded her letter to Wodehouse, "I do not wish to inveigle you into committing yourself or your Government, but for our safety, I repeat a question once put to you confidentially by a relative of mine from the Throne, Kamehameha V, whether, in case of emergency, England would take these Islands should we give ourselves up to her?"[55]

In replying, Wodehouse pointed out that the course she had suggested would certainly involve England in a war with the United States, which would be in violation of an agreement between England and France that they were bound to recognize the independence of the Hawaiian Islands and not to take possession of them under any form. He then sent a copy of Queen Emma's letter and his reply to his home office in England.[56]

Emma had anticipated Wodehouse's answer, but she always had hope because she saw no other alternative. Kuykendall observed that she misjudged the temper of the American people and the policy of their government toward the Hawaiian Islands. He cited the *New York*

Tribune's statement that "We do not covet them, but we could not consent to their transfer to any European naval power. . . . Such a thing as forcible annexation is not thought of in this country."[57] Emma had heard such pronouncements before, and they seemed only to have the opposite effect on her. Until her death she nurtured an abiding and enduring distrust of American intentions toward Hawai'i.

21

No Seclusion

Contrary to suggestions that Emma's final years were "spent in relative seclusion," the fact is she led an astoundingly active life.[1] She endured the smallpox epidemic of 1881 while quarantined for several trying months in her home with forty-one members of her household. She continued to strengthen the Anglican cause and to help fund the construction of the cathedral. She regularly visited and followed closely the progress of her two major charities, St. Andrew's Priory and the Queen's Hospital. She tended her gardens, planting, and weeding alongside her gardeners, cleaned house with her servants, played tennis with her ladies-in-waiting, and rode horseback over miles of barren lava and forested trails in Puna. She continued to challenge the Kalākauas on a wide range of issues, especially the validity of her lineage and her precedence in the royal court.

Lili'uokalani as the New Regent

In 1881, King Kalākaua decided to appoint Lili'uokalani as regent during his world-tour absence. Initially, however, his cabinet did not approve. Instead, it proposed the establishment of a Council of Regency, which she would head and with which she would exercise joint authority. But she believed that this arrangement was another ploy by the "missionary party" to undermine the Hawaiian monarchy at every opportunity. Concurrently, when the king asked for her opinion, Lili'uokalani told him "in terms too plain to admit of the least misunderstanding between us" that such a Council of Regency was unnecessary and that she should be the sole regent with full executive authority.[2]

The *Pacific Commercial Advertiser* heartily approved of her appointment and also rejected the idea of a Council of Regency. It said that the new regent possessed so fully "the *aloha ali'i* [love of the chiefs] of the people" and that her "sound sense and judgment" were so widely recognized that she would secure the "approbation of all sections" of the public. It added that its confidence in her appointment as regent was also enhanced by the fact that her consort of "much judgment and of such long experience" would be at her side.[3]

Understandably, the newspaper did not mention the fact that her consort, Mr. John Dominis was not always "at her side." Dr. George Trousseau, the Dominis's family physician, described him as being an "irregular husband" who had "affairs" but "never a regular mistress" and who caused her "great unhappiness by his inconsistencies."[4] In any event, she may have preferred being alone; she termed her husband "boring" and was happy to send him away because she couldn't stand "any more of his dreary stories."[5]

Queen Emma, who was keeping a diary at the time, certainly knew about this unhappy marriage because it was widely talked about, but she never mentioned the subject in her diary. Instead, she talked about "Mrs. Dominis" (she never used "Lili'uokalani") who was desperately seeking the help of an "all powerful" *kahuna* (priest) on Maui. Emma had heard that Lili'uokalani was trying to contact this particular female *kahuna* who had a spirit named Mohailani. This spirit told Lili'uokalani how to behave because many dreadful predictions had been made of her family dying and her brother "D.K." never returning. Emma wrote, "So her anxiety is very great to consult & secure the good offices of that wonderful female who is supposed to be all powerful."[6]

Meanwhile, Emma herself was a subject of dire warnings of *kāhuna*, as she reveals in the following entry in her diary:

> At four o'clock [this] afternoon two men came to tell me of a dream which one of them drempt concerning me. He has been accustomed to dream of similar dreams & certain results have usually followed, generally pertaining to the former kings. They began narrating part of dream then left part of it to finish tomorrow. The commencement was a fishing seine made up of three size mesh nets Makahi, Malua & Makolu. These form the bag of net or Mole. The other or second net was made up of Malua, Makolu, Maha which likewise formed Eke or

> Mole of it. These nets were let into the sea & a dreamer saw & heard Ruth Keelikolani say Oh, the fish is caught and that little woman is caught in it. She called Kapo (Pooloku), Oh, you pull the net quick so as to secure that little woman (kapi wahine) which was myself. Dreamer saw me & lo! I was covered all over with hair save the middle of my body [which was] quite round. He says had I been covered all over with hair it is certain speedy death, but not entirely covered gives me a chance of seeing life from amongst skilled Kahuna but it must be done soon or I die. Dreamer has drempt similar ones before—Uncle John's [Keoni Ana Young], all Kings, my Mother's recent death. He says he has always spoken of it beforehand—what silly falsehood to play on people. They think to frighten me, their ignorance is pitiable. Tomorrow they will want money.[7]

A few days later Emma wrote of another incident. "It seems that Olohana went to consult a kahuna who is continually possessed with the spirit of Kamiki reputed to be a very powerful spirit who gives straight forward interpretations & foretells events accurately. How laughable all this is about Akuas [gods] & Spirits, yet poor superstitious Hawaiians are as great believers in incantations etc. as ever they were in olden days—so this Spirit told him the dream has an evil significance, but she alone will ward [it off]."[8]

Finally, the following encounter illustrates how Emma lost all patience with *kāhuna* like Pahua. "Oh! She is the most tiresome teadious person one could wish to be bored with. She instantly knelt before me, kissed my hand & commenced praying to the effect that she was about to lay her hands on my head in the act of blessing as preparatory to another person's anointing, meaning the Crown is to be laid on my head signifying my accession to the Throne. But during her prayer, a person came up the steps & it was Kahelemauna. I motioned to her and she ended her devotions, but when he was gone, she coolly said to me that we are fallen to the ground & all by my own act again."[9]

Despite her earlier interest in *kāhuna*, as expressed in her letters to Peter, Emma was clearly no longer interested in their powers as of 1881. Moreover, Lili'uokalani was as fervent and devout a Christian as Emma, and she did not place much credence in the *kāhuna* either. Lili'uokalani was just as apt to dismiss them as false beliefs or superstitious fears as, for example, she did when she journeyed to Hilo in August 1881 and led local churches in prayers to the "Almighty Ruler" to turn the course of the fiery lava flowing from the erupting Mauna Loa away from Hilo. She even hinted that God might stop the flow if the people also obeyed the First Commandment and observed the Sabbath as a holy day.[10] The scene reminded Lili'uokalani of the "brave acts" of her aunt Kapi'olani who, more than fifty-five years before, had defied the fire-goddess at the edge of Kilauea by breaking the *kapu* and proclaiming the might of Jehovah.[11]

But among those "superstitious" Hawaiians who tried to appease *Pele* with bottles of whiskey or brandy was Princess Ruth Ke'elikōlani who spent a night on her bed next to the lava flow's edge only to wake up the next morning to see the lava had stopped, some said, within a yard of her bed. Some believed it was her intercession and *mana,* not Jehovah's, that tamed *Pele.*[12]

In matters of Christian faith, both Emma and Lili'uokalani were in fundamental agreement. Yet even the gospel of love could not bridge the vast gulf of distrust and resentment that still divided them.

Perhaps the best evidence of this enmity is that during the ten months of Lili'uokalani's regency, Emma did not attend any official or unofficial reception, ball, banquet, tour, or charity event at which either Lili'uokalani or Kapi'olani was present. Because Dowager Queen Emma was an official member of the court, her absence was quite conspicuous at court functions, which were attended by all the other court members. (These members, as listed in rank order in the City Directory of 1880, were King Kalākaua, Queen Kapi'olani, Lili'uokalani, Princess Miriam Likelike, and Queen Emma followed by Princess Ruth Ke'elikōlani and Lord Chamberlain, Col. Charles H. Judd.)[13] Specific, conspicuous events that the dowager queen did not attend were Lili'uokalani's birthday celebration at Ali'iolani Hale,[14] the receptions for high foreign officials and guests such as American Admiral Stevens of the *U.S.S. Pensacola*[15] and the new Minister of Foreign Affairs, W. L. Green,[16] and the laying of the foundation stone of the Lunalilo Home.[17] The one event, a marriage ceremony, that Emma did attend with other members of the court, i.e., Princesses Likelike and Ke'elikōlani, was the one that neither Lili'uokalani nor Kapi'olani attended.[18]

It should be noted that Emma's relationship with Princess Likelike, or Mrs. Cleghorn, was generally quite friendly. Emma wrote in her diary that one afternoon the Cleghorns, with their little daughter Ka'iulani, called on her at Rooke House and that "They were very cordial." They spoke of the new theater and its "nice arrangements," and Mr. Cleghorn mentioned that the plants at Emma's "marine" residence in Waikīkī needed some care because they were dying. Emma closed her entry with "Mrs. C[leghorn] hoped I would go out & see them again."[19]

Because the Cleghorns were neighbors who lived right across the ʻĀpuakēhau Stream at ʻĀinahau, the name of their famed residence, they had frequent opportunities to meet and socialize with one another.[20]

One of the few activities in which Liliʻuokalani, Queen Kapiʻolani, and the queen dowager were collectively involved was that of preparing clothing, conveniences, and other comforts for those suffering from the smallpox epidemic.[21]

Quarantine

A smallpox epidemic ravaged Honolulu in 1881. The disease was brought to Honolulu by infected passengers arriving onboard ships. Isolated cases had occurred in October and December 1880, but the disease began to spread in January when a deserter from the German steamer *Quinta* hid in the neighborhood of Rooke House and passed the disease to several people with whom he came in contact. By February forty-two cases were reported along with four deaths.[22] The Board of Health attempted to control the spread of the disease by vaccinating residents or placing them in quarantine. If arriving ships had any suspected cases, all passengers were quarantined at the station in Kakaʻako. The afflicted were removed to the hospital on the reef of Kaholaloa, which was often referred to as the "pest house on the reef" (now Sand Island).[23] Curiously, Queen's Hospital was off-limits to smallpox patients; not even those who were well but attending the sick were allowed to visit the hospital during the epidemic.[24] Unlike the disastrous epidemic of 1853, however, this time the health officials were better prepared, and also native Hawaiians were more "obedient to foreign medical direction." Nevertheless, many suffered, including Emma and her household.[25]

Rooke House was one of the first locales to succumb. Emma reported on February 2 that there was already "a great deal of feaver amongst our servants . . . Lameka, Mrs. William Healstead, her daughter Johanna, Hawane, Pua (boy) Pahia, Kanehoa and Kaeo."[26] When Kaeo, who lived over the coach house, broke out in spots, Emma sent for Dr. McKibbin who, after seeing the boy, threw up his hands and pronounced it a "veritable case of smallpox. . . . The Dr. was very wrathy for not being told of it before." The Board of Health immediately placed a quarantine on those staying in the coach house, which included Kaeo's wife, his sister, her year-and-a-half-old baby, and two young boys aged ten years. Emma wrote, "The little ones are the most to be pitied, poor little dears. They have all been vaccinated, thank God. So we hope if they do take ill, it will fall lightly."[27]

The next day the police arrived and ordered the removal of Kaeo to Kaholaloa hospital and the fumigation of the coach house. When Kaeo was taken away, his wife and sister wailed loudly. The rooms were then disinfected and shut for five hours during which time, "They all sat out on the verandah till night, food water and everything had to be left at the foot of the stairs."[28]

The following day the police planned to take Pua away on the "pest cart," but he "walked off quite in a jolly mood, laughing & biding the folks goodbye."[29] He was fortunate because, more often than not, the afflicted were forced to dress hurriedly and placed in an open cart. In feverish condition, they were driven over "windswept roads and across the reef while exposed to the blasts of seawater."[30]

On February 7, 1881, Emma wrote: "Everyday many fresh cases of smallpox amongst the natives come out, [but] only one death so far & I hope it may be the only one."[31] It was a forlorn hope because every day thereafter the number of new cases mounted together with the number of deaths. The newspapers not only reported the number of new cases, deaths, and the cured or discharged but also printed each of their names and even locales, including "Queen Emma's."

By now the entire Rooke House was off-limits. Emma listed the quarantined household members, all forty-one of them: Men: (1) George Davis, (2) John Davis, (3) Kalua, (4) I, (5) Kanehoa, (6) Ikaaka, (7) Milikaa, (8) Laanui, (9) Kupina, (10) Kini, (11) Pahia, (12) Ahi, (13) Pilipo, (14) Kaai; Women: (1) Kahakui, (2) Pioe, (3) Auloa, (4) Kalua, (5) Mary, (6) Clio, (7) Kaaka, (8) Kahikona, (9) Kamana, (10) Kaelehiwa, (11) Nakai, (12) Kahaanapilo, (13) Lucy Peabody, (14) Mrs. Healstead (Lameka), (15) Johanna Healstead, (16) Hawane, (17) Kealoha Hanaiole, (18) Kaleleonālani; Children: (1) Keahilalapoli (g), (2) Kaaluwea (g), (3) Kapulahaole (g), (4) Kalanikiekie (g), (5) Kaleonahenahe (g), (6) Manelelehua (g), (7) Naliimahiai (b), (8) Mililani (b), (9) Nailima (b).[32] On February 10 Dr. McKibbin came to Rooke House to vaccinate seven members including Emma, and the rest went to the hospital the next day to be vaccinated.

A few days later the Board of Health insisted on a stricter confinement of Emma's household because of complaints that its members were out too often. Some of her staff were seen shopping and going back and forth to Pā Aloha (one of Emma's nearby dwellings). She replied that the restrictions were too vague but agreed that "no one is to go out after this and none to come in." She had to refuse the request of William Pflueger, whom she had met in England, for an audience with her.[33]

Still, the board continued to receive complaints and thus sent one of its agents to issue another warning. When the agent commented that they probably did not feel confined because the premises were so large and open, Emma quickly corrected him. She also complained that she was paying her day laborers $2 and $3 a day, as well as feeding and clothing them, but that because of the quarantine they had not been able to work. When the agent left, he ordered her to keep the gates chained.[34] The next day the authorities attached yellow flags to both the front and back gates.[35]

In a reflection of the ongoing friction between the palace and Rooke House, people at the palace grumbled because the yellow flags had not been put up earlier. Simon Kaʻai, however, defended Queen Emma, insisting that the fault was not hers.[36] A few weeks later, Queen Emma in turn complained about the palace. One of the policemen posted at her gate said that some people residing at the palace had smallpox; yet no restrictions had been placed on them. Emma wrote, "Mrs. Dominis drives out daily & all their folks, sentr[ies] as well, go out."[37]

The quarantine tried both nerves and friendships. Emma remarked that two friends were afraid to even come near her gate. "I am really surprised that these two could not come outside at least & leave inquiries or send in little trifles by way of sympathy. How true it is circumstances try the friendship of our acquaintances."[38] She was particularly happy when "good Kini Mahoe" was the first of all of her "friends, acquaintances, retainers & makainana" to send a kind message and a gift showing that she remembered them. The gift contained two squids, a bowl of *lipoa,* another bowl of *ʻaʻalaʻula,* and other varieties of seaweed. Emma said, "Of course, they were very acceptable, but it is not so much the articles as the kind thought bestowed which shewed a true & not pretended friendship, for adversities try such. Every one of us felt the spirit & feeling that dictated the act & I shall remember it & repay when I can."[39] Unfortunately, Mahoe contracted smallpox, according to an announcement in the *Pacific Commercial Advertiser,* which published the names of everyone who had the disease.[40]

Every day either Dr. McKibbin of Queen's or Dr. Ferdinand W. Hutchison of the Board of Health called to check on Emma's household. One by one each broke out "in spots on face and body" and had to be carted away, crying and worrying about whether they would ever return. The best medicine the *haole* physicians could provide did not impress the natives, including her own household. Emma observed, "They always consult native kahuna, so I never ask after them for advice."[41] Yet, on one occasion when Kealoha Hanaiole, her late husband's aging retainer, seemed to grow faint and cold, she sent someone to obtain relief from a native healer. He prescribed four little dried leaves from a certain plant with instructions that the patient chew the leaves and apply the residue over her face. Emma sympathized for the "poor old soul" who had to take the medicine.[42] On another occasion she noted that one of the herbal remedies that the people were freely using was eucalyptus leaf baths.[43]

On a fine but overcast morning, Emma wrote that she and Lucy and others worked at mending, patching, and renovating her old clothes for the patients at Kaholaloa, which included "20 holokus, 5 night dresses, 6 chimeses, 3 petticoats, 6 stockings, 1 pea jacket, 2 water proof wrappers. . . ." At the same time they made "one very large bundle of linnens, rags, towels, handkerchiefs for Queens Hosp[ital]."[44] When contagious garments had to be thrown out and burned, she and her group also made new garments for the household members who were sick.

Lucy Peabody told Dr. Hutchison that if Dr. McKibbin asked Emma to go to the quarantine hospital to help, she would go quite willingly. Although Dr. Hutchison knew that such a request would never be made, he replied that apart from the queen, few people would volunteer to perform such acts of mercy and love.[45] In fact, the hospital was in desperate need of help. By the end of February it had over 120 patients with no nurses and only one physician who could make only one visit a day because he also attended to the 1,000 people quarantined in Kakaʻako. The *Pacific Commercial Advertiser* made public appeals for "a self-sacrificing" resident physician as well as "a noble Florence Nightingale and a saintly Sister Dora" to care for the patients on the reef.[46]

Emma mourned the loss of several of her servants, but she particularly mourned the fate of the boy Laweoki. "Poor boy, if only Lucy & I could get to him I feel sure we might save his life. I have preyed so earnestly with very heavy heart that our good good God may spare his young life and alter his future living & character for all that is good to God & man. . . . May God in his infinite mercy, spare him dear little fellow, he has no Mother nor a kindly hand and voice to sooth his pains & dangerous illness. . . . Poor child of the Almighty's hard work. Father in thy loving mercy consider his low estate & mold him for future glory to thee."[47]

She also prayed fervently for Kealoha Hanaiole as she lay dying. Emma wrote, "I came upstares & poured out my heavy hearted petitions to Almighty God, that he may shew the Glory of his loving kindness unto the multitude in restoring his faithful handmaiden to health, that the enemy may not say, 'There she is deserted by her God in the day of her dire distress.' Lord make her to bless thee for thy tender mercys & which she undoubtingly trusts. Lord, hear our prayers & let our crys come unto thee."[48] She and Lucy took turns feeding Kealoha a diet of Brandy Punch, arrowroot beef tea, poi, and "a little cooked mullet mashed to a fine pulp & thinned with water."[49] Emma was impressed with Lucy's "minutely attentions & care," staying up night and day, spending every moment in her room "watching her every wish & symptom," and snatching "10 minutes of sleep here & there through the day & night."[50]

Emma had asked Mr. Blackburn, one of Bishop Willis's assistants, to come to Rooke House to read the liturgy and to intercede on behalf of its sick members. He came willingly, but he paid a price: he was barred from visiting the patients at the Queen's Hospital and the Sisters and students of St. Andrew's Priory until the end of the quarantine.[51]

By May 1881 the epidemic steadily declined, and when it was over, 780 cases of smallpox had been reported and 282 had died.[52] With the removal of the yellow flags, Rooke House returned to a semblance of normalcy.

Cameos from Emma's Diary

Emma tried to keep a daily diary during the first half of 1881. However, she kept it only intermittently (from January 1 to June 18) because it has only fifty-one entries. Nonetheless, next to her letters to Peter, the diary provides the most revealing cameos of some of her habits and thoughts.

Like Alexander Liholiho, she was by middle age an early riser. Arising at 5:00 a.m. seemed to be a habit, no matter how late she went to bed. One morning she woke at four and then wakened the whole household by chanting these sentences in her morning prayer, "I will arise & go to my Father, Love not, I would the Pope's gay life were mine."

Clearly Emma preferred the mornings because she described them more often than any other part of the day and in some of her best prose. For example, "Another lovely morning fresh from the cool dewy night, and the bright warm sun out, glorifying all the glad earth. Not a breath of air. How I should enjoy a brisk canter on a good horse with pleasant company."[53] Of another morning she wrote, "It has been raining since 4 o'clock till dark. Then all wind, rain & cold lulled & the most delicious quiet & calm succeeded. The quiet is the most pleasant."[54] And of the next day's beginnings she wrote, "The sun came out bright this morning, making a fine warm sunny day but the whole premises is standing in one sheet of water from the heavy rains of last night, but even as I write, it is fast sinking into the ground, and the folks can walk on ouzy ground from house to house."[55] Of course, there were some enchanting evenings as when she wrote, "The moonlight is most lovely tonight & the music of the Band from Emma Square comes floating delightfully on the still cool air."[56]

The Bible was a constant source of inspiration for Emma. Early on January 31 she "spent much time hunting out the historys of penitents mentioned in 'Litany of Penitents' in my '*Vade Mecum*,' reading King David's humble confession, also of Solomon's grand history. The reading of these historical events was exceedingly interesting & really they seemed like new reading to me." She remembered that it was the anniversary of "poor Lunalilo's birthday."[57]

On a typical Sabbath she attended the morning and afternoon Anglican services. On one particular Sunday she rode her buggy to and from church in a downpour. She did not hesitate to mix business with worship because after the service she gave the bishop $58 to cover the school tuition for two of her wards, Loe and Maude. En route home, she stopped to visit Aunt Hikoni and found her still complaining about nothing in particular. Following the afternoon church service she visited the priory to take her customary tea with the Sisters.[58]

The last day of the month was payday (for Emma the income probably was from her estate rather than from her government stipend). Instead of collecting the money herself, she sent Lucy Peabody and Mary Liwai to Alexander J. Cartwright's to retrieve it. She then paid her "servants, pensioners etc. etc. two great bills, to Holt the butcher $124, & Mrs. Griffin $49.90."[59]

The reminders of her son Albert were constant, such as the Fire Department's Annual Parade on February 3. She, Lucy, Johanna, and other members of her retinue had decorated No. 2 Fire Engine rather than No. 1, which was the one the little prince rode on in his last parade. As this parade passed in front of Rooke House, one spectator took his hat off to the queen—he was Sam Parker, owner of the Parker Ranch and a close friend.[60] Parker had visited the queen two days before and laughingly threatened to call the police to arrest the persons who had removed his framed photographs of the queen.[61]

On another occasion, as Emma was rearranging the items in her jewelry box, she found "my own dear little Prince of Hawaii's 'Navel' in amongst them together with Grandfather's [John Young's] two last teeth, which dear Mother [Mrs. Rooke] always had kept with such affection."[62] (Emma was following a standard Hawaiian custom of preserving a child's *piko* or umbilical cord, which was venerated because it was the link between the infant and the mother.)[63]

Emma cherished her extensive jewelry collection and could identify each piece and the person who gave it: the gold chain with pearl pendants was from Robert C. Wyllie, the California gold necklace was made by her father as one of his wedding presents to her, the little pearl drop earrings were given to her in Kōloa on her wedding tour in 1856, the turquoise and pearl ring was from Ruth Ke'elikōlani, the plain gold ring came from the captain of the U.S. warship *Vanderbilt,* which transported her home from San Francisco, and a diamond ring that was her "very dear own Alex's Christmas present."[64]

Emma still delighted in giving gifts but seemed to enjoy the shopping as much as the giving. Interestingly, she took pains in recording their every feature and cost. Of one purchase, for example, she wrote, "I bought 18 rolls of buff or light straw Pongee silk, 19 yds in the piece at $8 a roll. So it cost $144. 27 women will be supplied with a dress of 12 yds each from Rooke House to Pa Aloha." She bought for herself a roll of white figured silk for night dresses and underclothes. She thought it was "very pretty stuff."[65] Emma described the wedding presents she bought for two future brides: "A pair of gold bracelets, $23, for Nawahi's intended, Aima, two bangles, silver, with her name on one & Aloha Oe on the other. . . . Likeness of myself was boxed up to send Nawahi as his present." The other bride was Lydia Keōmailani Crowningburg whom the queen had sent to school in England and who was about to marry Wray Taylor, the new organist and choirmaster at St. Andrew's. Her wedding present was "a broach & ear drops of Tigar claw set in gold" that cost $50. Emma also bought, apparently for herself, another "Tigar claw set, the exact copy or match to my present necklace" for $125.[66]

Emma had always enjoyed the theater, not only as a spectator but also as an active participant. To amuse her quarantined household, she directed and produced several tableaus (as she had done ten years before in Waimea, Kaua'i, after her Alaka'i Swamp adventure).[67] On March 1, 1881, she wrote that she, Johanna, and Lameka "have been hard at work preparing the outfits of our Tableaus tonight."[68] Unfortunately, she did not report on the audience as a critic.

Tennis was another activity she resumed as a consequence of the long confinement and the need for amusement. First, Emma unpacked the tennis box and installed the net between the main house and coach house. To make more room for the balls, she also had her boys cut some of the tree branches along the verandah of the coach house. She commented that the servant boys "commenced the game & enjoyed it immensely, but could not at first handle the ball" because they were more accustomed to baseball.[69] Two days later, on February 18, she wrote, "Johanna, Hawane, Lameka & I had a practice at throwing & hitting properly—well, we did it rather poorly but improved towards the end after two hours of exercise."[70]

The physical activity that Emma missed the most was horseback riding and driving her buggy. She had to put five of her horses, including her two black ponies, out to pasture in Wailupe at a cost of $2 per head per month.[71] Once the quarantine was lifted, she resumed her morning routine of driving her buggy for two hours, frequently on her favorite route around Diamond Head and along the then lonely and uninhabited coast.[72]

Her passion for gardening continued unabated. "I have been gardening with Kewiki & Ahi taking up young petunias, curiopeis, & carditufis, to save [them] in the nursery for replanting the beds after weeding them."[73] On another occasion, she and Philip Laʻanui "cleaned out the Fernery & slipped three boxes full of euphobia for church and Kaluaokau " (her residence in Waikīkī).[74] Though she could have easily had her boys and Asun, her "Celestial" (or Chinese) gardener, do the work, she preferred to work alongside them. But a few weeks later she fired Asun because he was too lazy and hired Leleva, a Gilbertese, to do some of the gardening.[75] "This has been a wet day throughout, but I have been out with the boys all day gardening, weeding the flower beds & setting out young plants which I sowed last fortnight . . . petunias, floxes, many varieties of morning glory, evening primroses, larkspurs, nesturtians, etc."[76]

Her passion for gardening was intertwined with her love of nature, which is revealed in this passage from her diary: "How very lovely the early mornings & moonlight nights have been of late & this morning is no exception. It is so calm & delightful, the golden sunlight of the early day bathing the different foliage of Tamarind, the great feathery arms of Cocoa nut leaf, the gorgeous bloom of the purple Bougainvillea which makes my Mother's cottage Polihale one gay mass, the fine delicate foliage of the Poinciana, & the still more delicate Algaroba, all in its golden sheen. How very lovely all nature is to be sure."[77]

During the quarantine, Nailipelapela, her housekeeper in Waikīkī, reported that he had harvested the first "tarrows" planted a year ago and had made some poi from them.[78] He sent a barrel of poi to Emma along with six *awa* (milkfish) from her fish pond and a bucket of *līpoa* seaweed.[79]

Dowager queen or not, Emma had no compunctions about cleaning house. With the help of the servant boys, for example, she cleaned out the messy stone house and carted off eight "oat bags full" of rubbish. They then thoroughly washed out the interior and left it open to dry.[80] In June 1881, when the epidemic had subsided, Emma left Rooke House for Waikīkī with an express wagon, two buggies, and several saddle horses to finish cleaning the rooms in Lunalilo's small cottage.[81] For Emma cleaning was a very normal part of her life.

An avid reader, she kept up with current events around the world by subscribing to foreign newspapers and periodicals, which arrived regularly by steamer. She read them thoroughly as indicated by the statement: "All the day I have given to my newspapers."[82] They ranged from the *Illustrated London News* and the *Telegram* to the *Sacramento Union*. Not only did she read but also she discussed the news with a detailed understanding of what she read as she demonstrated to Dr. McKibbin one day. "We talked on the European news. He is not an admirer of Gladstone & had bragged before Lord Beaconsfield's fall from office at the late elections that Mr. Gladstone will never get into office as Prime Minister & that if he should, he himself will almost be ashamed to call himself an Englishman."[83] She also clipped interesting items that she shared with Lucy and others. One such clipping preserved in her diary was entitled "Secrets of the Latest Fashions," a subject in which she had an abiding interest.

The Saga of the Bees

An instructive anecdote from her diary reveals Emma's occasional impulsiveness as well as her eclectic interests. After she purchased a swarm of bees, she told the following story:

> After breakfast a great crowd gathered on Nuuanu St. in front of my flower garden all eyes gazing up to the Tamarind tree nearest Chaplain Lane corner. There was a swarm of Bees on a branch up on a tree. Presently a young Chinese boy came to say they belonged to his father who had 10 hives & this swarm was tampered with by some boys yesterday. I allowed him to take them away. So together with his father & younger brother who held a sugar keg & burnt sandalwood joy sticks,

> he ascended the tree & cut off the branch on which the Bees were hanging from. It fell & the swarm scattered like dried leaves, finally settling on the euphobia bush. They covered [the bush with] the keg & so got them all in, smoakin the sticks the meanwhile. I was so taken up with them that I bought the swarm for $5 & [paid] 25 cts. for the keg. They are now upstairs on my back verandah. I shall have a proper glass hive for them made in 4[?] months time when they swarm again.[84]

Two days later when the swarm escaped, she wrote: "My swarm of Bees came out thick outside of the keg. So I sent for the little Chinaman & he assured me, it was only the heat that had driven them out, but that by 4 o'clock they would all go in again. However, at that time the whole swarm left the barrel & settled in a crevis of the boards outside the mauka room on the verandah. Ahi the Chinese cabinet maker came up to make a glass hive for them."[85] A few days later, she reported that she was still having "a time with the Bees" but that Ahi had completed his work and that the swarm was finally moved from inside to outside the house.[86]

Queen Victoria

Emma's last contact with Queen Victoria was her letter in October 1879 thanking the queen for the steel engravings of the British royal family.[87] Now on March 20, 1881, Emma wrote in her diary that she had "very strangely drempt of Queen Victoria. I saw her in Polihale."[88] Polihale was her mother's home at Kulaokahua, located between Alapai and Punahou Streets. She did not attempt to explain what her dream might have meant, and its significance may be only that she thought it important enough to record it in her diary.

On July 11 King Kalākaua had an audience with Queen Victoria at Windsor Castle. Queen Victoria recorded in her journal that "King Kalakaua is tall, darker than Queen Emma, but with the same cast of features.[89] William N. Armstrong, writing of his trip around the world with King Kalākaua, remembered that Queen Victoria had asked the king for news of Queen Emma and had told him: "She is a charming young woman; I was very fond of her."[90] It is not known whether Queen Victoria was aware of the conflicts between the king and the dowager queen or whether her sentiments about Queen Emma had any impact on him.

Restarting the Cathedral

Despite the costs of maintaining a half dozen homes, plus her ladies-in-waiting, housekeepers, gardeners, wards, and others, numbering as many as fifty people, Queen Emma continued to make charitable contributions to important causes. One of these was the building fund of St. Andrew's Cathedral. She had given Bishop Willis $99 in February and $101 in March and had agreed to solicit contributions from others, including Ruth Ke'elikōlani, a confirmed non-believer. The bishop had specifically asked Queen Emma to persuade Ke'elikōlani to give at least $10,000, but the queen thought that that sum was too much even for the wealthiest woman in the Islands. She told him that it would be "impossible," that Ke'elikōlani might give $2,000 but not much more, and that the amount would depend on Simon Ka'ai, the steward of Princess Ruth's estates.[91] In fact, $2,000 was the top amount that the king and

The Cathedral Church of St. Andrew (Episcopal) was founded in 1862 by Queen Emma and King Kamehameha IV who were Anglicans. After the king's death in 1863, the dowager queen traveled to England to raise the funds for the construction of the cathedral. Drawing on her love of French Gothic churches, Emma also influenced its architecture.

St. Andrew's Great West Window with detail of King Kamehameha IV and Queen Emma (located on the right side of the entrance).

queen, Mr. and Mrs. Charles Bishop, and Emma herself would give over the next two years.[92]

At the beginning of 1881 the cut stone for the arches and windows that the queen had shipped from England in 1866 still lay unused in crates. Several members in the congregation favored selling the English stone and erecting a modest brick building that would have cost less—and would have served well for their worship. But the one consideration that stopped this plan was the impact that such a decision would have had on Queen Emma. Theo. H. Davies, the same who walked Emma across the operatic stage in 1861, now spearheaded the building fund drive. He wrote: "I confess that I was influenced by the thought of the blow it would give her stricken heart to see that memorial of one whom she has loved and mourned like a true woman, abandoned for some building that might be as good a church, but would be no memorial, and which would leave the very cornerstone that was laid when her grief was fresh as a monument only of her disappointment.

"Trusting to the eventual completion of this memorial church, Queen Emma has gone on paying in money as she could spare it . . . and I for one had not the heart to say a word that would tend to her disappointment."[93]

By the end of 1881 construction on the cathedral had resumed. In the year 1882 a start was made on the walls, which used beach stone brought by schooners from beyond Barber's Point.[94] Needless to say, Emma was happy and relieved that the project was finally taking tangible shape.

"John Sugarcane"

Queen Emma was visiting Maui in the fall of 1882 when she received a call one night from John D. Spreckels (the son of Claus Spreckels) whom she nicknamed "John Sugarcane." He invited her to his father's Mill Number One to inspect the "concentrated daylight." The lights had been installed on September 22, making the mill the first edifice in the Islands (five years before ʻIolani Palace) to be lighted by electricity.[95] Emma wrote to her friend Ihilani (Flora) Jones:

> I must write & tell you of the very pleasant visit we are making here, everybody has been so extremely good & kind to us. Last night Mr. J. D. Spreckles called & invited me to go & see the electric light, which they use at the mill, so this evening we started by train [from Kahului] with a party of nearly 600 people for Puunene where his mill stands.

> Everything is carried on the most extensive scale, and the newest inventions are used of machinery, etc. Mr. Spreckels showed us the electric machines where electricity is made & conducted through wires to every part of the mill. You have seen the light no doubt, so can fancy how like unto day was the entire interior & exterior of [the] building. It really was wonderfully grand, he explained the various process[es] of sugar making, giving scientific names & meanings of things, he was awfully patient with us. There was music, vocal & instrumental, wine & cake at his house & music in [the] train."[96]

Several months later (March 1882) in Honolulu, Spreckles invited Emma to look at his new home in Kapunahou (the former name for the area of Punahou). Accompanying him in another carriage was William G. Irwin, his father's partner and owner of a leading sugar factoring company. The queen rode with Spreckels and Hannah Kaninau, and Jennie Stillman rode with William Irwin. They drove along King Street past Government House where the sugar planters had been invited to dine with the king. The planters had convened in Honolulu to support the renewal of the reciprocity treaty and the importation of laborers for their plantations, among other things. Emma tells what happened next: "When I covered my face with a veil, he firmly demanded I open it. He wanted all those people to see us. I did not open my veil. At that time he said he did not want to socialize with liars or those who break their promises to friends as D.K. did to his father. I replied, don't talk that way about your friends. He was irritated and said they were not his friends."[97]

She told Lucy that she thought young Spreckels was a pretentious show-off. He insisted on showing Emma his home, after which she concluded that Princess Ruth Keʻelikōlani's home was "much nicer from top to bottom."[98] A few evenings later he and Irwin visited Rooke House unannounced, bringing oysters from Puʻuloa (Pearl Harbor) and champagne and staying till one o'clock in the morning.[99]

Keʻelikōlani's "home" was her sparkling new Victorian mansion, Keōua Hale, on her Emma Street property. Some people felt it exceeded in grandeur any home ever built in Honolulu and was the equal of the still unfinished ʻIolani Palace. Keʻelikōlani was said to have spared no expense in its construction because she wanted to outdo the Kalākauas partly out of spite over their attacks on her ancestry.[100]

Both as a housewarming party and as a celebration of her birthday, Princess Keʻelikōlani had invited about 1,000 people to her home for a grand *lū'au* and ball. A few days before the event, Emma had written Julia Akana, one of her wards in Maui, that she expected the ball to be "most brilliant" with "ladies' dresses fashionably made."[101] Indeed, the ball as well as the entire evening was deemed to be "a perfect success."[102]

The Election of 1882

As the symbolic head of the native Hawaiian opposition to King Kalākaua, Dowager Queen Emma regarded every election with extreme interest. She had cause for concern in this election because neither she nor her leaders had been able to form a truly cohesive party to oppose the king.[103] In fact, buoyed by his recent world travels and by Hawai'i's prosperity, the king was a far more confident and formidable force than he had been two years earlier. Conversely, the Queen's party seemed to be less of a force. In the press reports covering the election of 1882, for example, almost no mention was made of the Queen's party, the Emmaites or the Queenites. The party's top vote-getter in the 1880 campaign, Albert Kūnuiākea, lost the election, coming in ninth place with 277 votes.[104] Lilikalani and Lahilahi, the king's men, whom Albert had bested the last time, each had twice as many votes as he. And only three of her strong supporters, Joseph Nawahi in Hilo, George W. Pilipo in Kona, Hawai'i, and J. Kauai on Kaua'i, were reelected.

The "man of the hour" was Walter M. Gibson, the adventurer turned politician, who received 1,153 votes out of the 1,451 ballots cast in Honolulu. As publisher of the Hawaiian-English newspaper, *Ka Nūpepa Nuhou*, he had opposed Queen Emma in 1874 and urged the support of David Kalākaua. Gibson continued to back the king thereafter on every major issue from the reciprocity treaty to Hawaiian independence. Now, with his commanding popular support due in no small measure to his "Hawai'i for Hawaiians" platform, King Kalākaua would name Gibson his new prime minister, making him in effect, the second most powerful person in the kingdom.

Last Correspondence

As the election faded into the background, Emma turned to her domestic interests, especially gardening. On March 21, 1882, she wrote to Lucy Peabody that she had just purchased 775 coconuts from Tahiti for her home in Pu'uloa. Because she had learned that coconuts in Hōnaunau could be bought for $2.00 per hundred she intended to purchase these. In addition, she had already planted a hundred coconut trees and some algaroba or *kiawe* trees at Hānaiakamalama.[105]

The next morning Emma awoke to learn of the attempted assassination of Queen Victoria. A deranged man had shot the queen as she was leaving the station at Windsor, but she was not hurt.[106] Distressed by yet another attempt on the queen's life, Emma wrote her a sympathetic note:

> Hānaiakamalama
> April 9, 1882
>
> Your Majesty & Dear Friend
> How shall I express my horror and grief over the narrow escape Your Majesty's valuable life had met at the hands of an insane person. The news gave me such a shock—but that great love upon which you have so often taught me to rely was even then as ever protecting Your Majesty and I thank God fervently in common with the rest of mankind for this signal kindness placing undoubting trust in that care which may never fail over your safety & happiness to add many more years of usefulness good reign over your people. I need hardly say that this news was felt almost as a personal calamity by every native Hawaiian so much have they learnt to respect yourself.
>
> I must at this opportunity thank Your Majesty so very very much for the kind message and enquiries made after me which His Majesty The King Kalakaua delivered immediately on his return from England giving the constant proofs of condescending remembrances for myself which I value more than I can say. The King enjoyed his visit to your country greatly and was so pleased with Your Majesty's kind reception of himself.
>
> With repeated earnest prayers that no harm in the future may befall yourself,
> I remain your sincere and grateful friend
> Emma

Sometime later Queen Victoria wrote back to thank Emma for her letter and asked to be remembered to King Kalākaua.[107] This letter was the last in the correspondence between the two queens.

To Ka'ū on Impulse

In early April 1882 Emma decided, without informing anyone, to travel to Ka'ū, Hawai'i. She chose Ka'ū because the younger Spreckels had mentioned that whenever she visited Ka'ū, Mr. Buck, the manager of the Hutchison Plantation in Na'alehu, would make her welcome and place his home at her disposal. Jennie Stillman tells of the morning when Queen Emma came to her bedroom, which she shared with Lucy Peabody, woke them up, and told them to pack because they were going to Ka'ū that day. Emma took them by complete surprise. "She spoke softly as if she was sorry for disturbing us," Jennie recalled. By 5:00 that evening they were off on the steamer *Iwalani* and arrived at Honuapo Bay in Kaʻū at 6:00 the next morning. No one was there to greet them because the queen had not told anyone, including Mr. Buck, of their trip. He graciously surrendered his home to the royal party, and that evening the queen reciprocated by holding a reception, including hula and music, for the plantation employees.[108]

Jennie and Lucy probably were not aware of the adventurous queen's next plan: a trip on horseback of over eighty-five miles, from Naʻalehu at sea level, up the volcano trail to the crater summit and down to Kaimū (the black sand beach in Kalapana) over a difficult terrain of barren lava fields, and through a desert, and then tropical rain forests. The queen's wish was their command, however, and the next morning they rode to Hīlea to dine with Mr. and Mrs. Charles Spencer who persuaded the queen and party to stay overnight rather than endure the rough ride back to Naʻalehu that same day. The following day they proceeded to the oasis of Waiʻōhinu, which Lady Franklin and Sophia Cracroft had visited in 1861 with their guide, David Kalākaua, then aide-de-camp to Emma's Alexander Liholiho. They stayed with the William Smithers who entertained them with a *lūʻau* and hula dances. Mr. Buck, back at Naʻalehu, was not to be outdone by the Smithers; he hosted a sumptuous *lūʻau*. Jennie noted: "It was a surprise to us to see a Hawaiian feast at a haole table." The next day they went to see Lizzy Pratt and her husband Frank at Kapāpala Ranch, where they spent two nights. The ranch comprised 200,000 acres located on the slopes of Mauna Loa and had been leased to William Reed by Kamehameha IV in 1860.

Their odyssey next took them to upper Puna and then down the Kalapana trail and turned into a virtual "nightmare." They rode for miles over barren lava beds in intense heat. At times, they had to rest the unshod horses and walk; and when they did, the horses carrying their lunches disappeared, forcing them to eat the wild berries and guavas in the forest. Eventually, the party came to a stone wall, which their guide assured them was the correct path. Jennie wrote: "We followed the wall for miles and miles . . . [until] there was nothing left to our shoes. When night came, we had not yet come to the end of the wall, and the Queen who was very tired, said, 'When will we ever come to the end of this stone wall?' I remember hearing her say many times after we had come back to Honolulu, 'I can still see that endless wall.' "[109]

When at last they saw a lighted house and were welcomed inside to eat and rest, the queen thought the journey was over. She learned to her disappointment, however, that they had five more miles to travel to reach their destination, the village of Kaimū. By the time they had arrived there, it was past 10:00 p.m. Although exhausted, Emma invited the ladies to use her room until their clothes arrived. Jennie expressed the following: "The Queen always carried a Ni'ihau mat wrapped in a shawl in front of her saddle to use as a pommel. This she had us spread on the floor, and we all three lay down on it, and exhausted, fell asleep. The Queen, always thoughtful of others, refused to lie on the bed prepared for her."[110]

When high *ali'i* visited Kalapana they were asked, according to custom, to pull down a small coconut tree without uprooting it. This feat was accomplished by tying a rope to the tree and then pulling until the tree was flat on the ground, thereby allowing it to continue to grow. When the queen performed this ceremony, she was aided by others who did the pulling while she placed her hands on the tree and then wrote her name on it. A coconut tree pulled down in this manner was called *niu moe o Kalapana* (the supine coconut palm of Kalapana). In 1950 two such trees were still growing in Kalapana.[111]

Once in Puna, they stayed with Mr. William "Willie" Shipman, the founder of W. H. Shipman Limited, and his part-Hawaiian wife, Mary Kahiwaaiali'i Johnson. Caroline Robinson, Mary Shipman's sister, took the queen and her party to visit the warm-spring pool of Waiwelawela in Kapoho (which was covered by the 1960 lava flow) and nearby Waiapele (the ancient name for Green Lake).[112]

After the queen and entourage had finally ended their journey in Hilo, she conferred for several hours with one of her party's leaders, Joseph Nawahi, who had recently been reelected to the legislative assembly. When she departed Hilo she was gifted with a chant commemorating her journey:

Ka wai lani kapu ae keia	This [person] is the sacred heavenly water
A ka iwalani e hii mai nei	of a handsome person that is cherished;
Ka Kekelaokalani Kuiapoina	She is Kekelaokalani Kuiapoina's [sic] daughter;
Mo'opuna a Kaniniu o Kalani.	and the granddaughter of Kaniniuokalani.[113]

Walter Murray Gibson

Queen Emma returned to Honolulu before the opening of the legislative assembly in July 1882. Apparently she attended some of its sessions.[114] She may have been drawn to the assembly sessions by its star attraction, Walter Murray Gibson, prime minister under Kalākaua. He was not only a mesmerizing speaker but also its dominant figure.

What did the dowager queen think of Gibson? Although no written opinions exist, she could not have faulted his two basic goals: preservation of the Hawaiian race by improving its health and the preservation of Hawaiian sovereignty by holding off the Americans who sought annexation to the United States.[115] She especially applauded his efforts to increase appropriations for improving the work of the Board of Health and for expanding the branch hospitals. However, she vigorously opposed Gibson's obsequious behavior toward King Kalākaua, which caused him to approve of the king's extravagances such as the cost overruns for ʻIolani Palace, the creation of a Board of Genealogy of Hawaiian Chiefs, and the purchase of a $1,200 feather cloak. As a connoisseur of Hawaiian collectibles, Emma may have been especially piqued about being outbid by Gibson for the feather cloak. The cloak had some sentimental value to Emma because it had belonged to Kalaimamahu, King Lunalilo's grandfather, and was part of an auction of the effects of Charles Kanaʻina (Lunalilo's father) of whom she had been fond.[116]

Assemblyman George Washington Pilipo, the "Lion of North Kohala," who remained one of the queen's staunchest supporters, attacked a measure introduced by Gibson on the assembly floor.[117] The measure was a bill to authorize the conveyance to Claus Spreckels of 24,000 acres in Wailuku. Spreckels had leased the land from the government in exchange for a quit claim to the interest in a half million acres of crown lands, worth $750,000. He had purchased this land from Princess Ruth Keʻelikōlani for $10,000, even though some doubt existed about her legal right to dispose of the land in the first place. Pilipo declared his feeling about this issue:

> This is not a matter that will please the Hawaiian people . . . [Gibson] . . . a man whose mouth is full of aloha for Hawaiians, but whose actions are not? . . . think that taking crown lands away from the crown and giving them to another person is a step toward destroying the independence of the country.
>
> The Minister [Gibson] knocks at the door of the Members of this House and asks them to join him at lunch at his home. I am informed that he said to those present that a conciliatory policy was best, that it is better to give this small tract of crown land to prevent trouble. Where will this trouble come from? . . .
>
> Where is the danger? Is it from Great Britain, from Germany or the United States? No! It is from one man—a merchant [Spreckels]. . . .
>
> Perhaps one or two, or three or more of the Ministry are in the clutches of this man. Perhaps he holds their papers. If this bill passes,

> it will relieve them. . . . It may be that the Ministry are doing what they are told to do by a higher power. Is it the King? What is the matter with the King? Is he in the power of the same man?[118]

The extent to which Pilipo's views reflected those of Queen Emma is not clear. Suffice it to say, the queen probably concluded that she did not trust either one of them.

Precedence at the Coronation

Certain signs indicated that the hostility between Queen Emma and King Kalākaua was mellowing.

In July 1882 the Royal Hawaiian Band had honored Mr. and Mrs. William Atwater with a program of musical entertainment followed by an impromptu dance. The king was present along with many others, including the queen dowager. The next day she invited the Atwaters to attend a legislative assembly and sit with her. That evening she prepared a hula program for their entertainment and hosted a ball in their honor.[119] Two weeks later she attended Prize Day at ʻIolani College to hear the students sing and recite. The king presided over the award ceremonies and was accompanied by Princess Liliʻuokalani, Wodehouse, the British commissioner, and other dignitaries.[120] Later in the fall, the king himself, without any invitation, appeared unexpectedly at one of Queen Emma's lively evening parties in Waikīkī. She wrote to Ihilani Jones that "to our surprise, the King was announced, but I was very glad as I had a message to deliver to him from Queen Victoria [who wished] to be remembered by him; he was rather a little merry with wine . . . [however] kept quiet on the verandah."[121]

The fact that King Kalākaua had a conciliatory approach toward Emma is supported by Curtis Iaukea, his aide-de-camp, who wrote that the king "continued to show his friendly feelings . . . and show every courtesy and regard for her position as the Dowager Queen."[122]

In February 1883 the king made a special effort to prove his sincerity during the events surrounding his coronation. Although he had acceded to the throne in 1874, Kalākaua had postponed his coronation because of the volatile situation following the riot at the courthouse. Once his round-the-world trip was completed, he decided he should be properly crowned like the other monarchs of the world and assigned the ceremony to Gibson. *The Fantastic Life of Walter Murray Gibson* gives this description: "To provide a stage for the investiture, he ordered the construction of a pavilion before newly completed Iolani Palace, to be linked by a long wooden passageway to its spacious lanai. Surrounding the pavilion was a covered grandstand to provide seating for several thousand guests, invited to represent other kingdoms and republics throughout the world, as well as each major island in the Hawaiian Kingdom. The statue of Kamehameha the Great, handsome in bronze and gold, was placed on its pedestal near King Street across from the palace and readied for the unveiling. Orders were given to the King's Guard and to the Royal Hawaiian Band. Luaus, balls, receptions, dinners, fireworks, and horse races were arranged. Thousands of invitations were sent out."[123] Queen Emma received one of the invitations.

On February 10, two days before the coronation, King Kalākaua took the unprecedented step of issuing four separate "Letters Patent under the Great Seal of the Kingdom." The first granted Queen Kapi'olani "precedence above all other subjects," except, of course, his sovereign self. The second granted Emma Kaleleonālani "precedence under the title of Queen Dowager next to Her Majesty Queen Kapiolani and above other subjects." The third granted precedence to Lili'uokalani "next to the Queen Dowager," while the fourth granted the same to John Dominis "during their joint lives."[124]

Clearly, King Kalākaua intended this action to resolve the nettlesome protocol issue that had exacerbated the antagonistic relationships between his family and Emma. He even looked forward to Emma's attendance at the coronation and the state dinner that was to follow.

When Lili'uokalani learned that the king had placed her below Queen Emma in precedence, she was furious. To add insult to injury, the king had not told her of his decision before he announced it to the press. She immediately wrote the king expressing her indignation:

> My dear Brother:
> Without meaning any disrespect, after reading the notice given in this morning's paper, it had made us (sister and myself) feel that we would not be doing justice to ourselves should we permit the Queen Dowager Emma to take precedence to ourselves in any State occasions in the future. This being the first consideration, we and our husbands beg respectfully to decline being present at the dinner this eve.
>
> Liliuokalani[125]

According to Iaukea, Lili'uokalani's "ungracious action" received little sympathy at court and apparently none at home because both their husbands, John Dominis and Archibald Cleghorn, did attend the dinner.[126]

As for Emma, she attended the dinner but not the coronation.[127]

Why? In issuing the "letters of patent," King Kalākaua had failed to recognize the *ali'i* status of Princess Ruth Ke'elikōlani and Mrs. Bernice Pauahi Bishop. In fact, *Ko Hawai'i Pae 'Āina* called the king's action an act of "contempt against these ali'i" (both of whom had stronger bloodlines to Kamehameha than Emma).[128] It is difficult to explain the king's rationale because both Ke'elikōlani and Pauahi had supported him in his 1874 election, had been on friendly terms with both him and his queen, and had willingly participated in many other court activities.

Pauahi and Ke'elikōlani took umbrage against the king and decided not to attend the coronation. But they did decide to attend the state dinner. Out of sympathy and loyalty to the Kamehamehas, Emma had chosen to do the same.

The dinner was held in the palace. As the guests gathered in the spacious entrance hall, they were marshaled in order of precedence led by the king and queen with Queen Emma immediately behind them. King Kalākaua sat at the center of the table with Queen Kapi'olani directly opposite and with Queen Emma on his right.[129] Unfortunately, no account exists of what transpired between Emma and Kapi'olani at dinner, but, with Lili'uokalani sulking at home, the dinner may actually have been quite pleasant.

King Kalākaua's efforts at reconciliation with Queen Emma continued even after the coronation. Isobel Field, the daughter of Robert Louis Stevenson, told of the king's meeting with the dowager queen on board the U.S.S. *Adams*. She wrote:

> Breathlessly the crowd below watched His Majesty mount the companionway; when he reached the quarter-deck he was greeted by the Captain who motioned toward the throne where Queen Emma stood. Kalakaua stepped forward, a gallant figure in white and gold, bowed low to the lady in black, and offered her his hand, which she took and was about to kiss. With a quick, dexterous movement he gave her a little whirl and a push that seated her on the throne. Queen Emma's surprised face was almost comic when the King bowed again before her. Then she smiled sweetly, he leaned over and they talked together with such evident friendliness that we all felt like applauding. After that the two were friends and I often saw Queen Emma at the King's formal parties.[130]

Alas, their friendship was short-lived. The Dowager Queen Emma and the Kalākauas soon became embroiled in a testy genealogical debate.

22

The Last Flight

During the two years before Queen Emma's death in 1885, three recurring themes predominated. The first was the unending challenge to her royal bloodline. The second theme was the maintenance of her political influence—not to regain the throne but rather to preserve the honor of the Kamehamehas. And the third great leitmotiv of her life and times was illness and death. When the people buried Queen Emma in one of Hawai'i's largest royal funerals, they honored all of the Kamehamehas—and Emma as the last.

Ruth Ke'elikōlani's Passing

In the midst of King Kalākaua's coronation celebrations in 1883, Princess Ruth Ke'elikōlani celebrated her fifty-sixth birthday at her new mansion, Keōua Hale, located on Emma Street. Not to be outdone by the Kalākauas, she invited a thousand guests to a party that lasted three days. Emma was there to enjoy the festivities. But the party may have provided too much excitement for Ke'elikōlani because the next day she fell ill and was ordered by her doctor to go to Kona to rest. She retired to her thatched hut near the place where her great-grandfather, Kamehameha I, had died.

Emma had two reasons to be concerned about Ruth Ke'elikōlani's condition. The first of course was her health. The second involved a decision on the suit they had filed jointly for the recovery of a plot of land in Honolulu, which was one of several pieces of crown lands that

Emma claimed.[1] The reason for Keʻelikōlani's involvement is not clear. Certainly she did not need any more land because she already owned 353,000 acres, more land than any one in Hawaiʻi. (These were the Kamehameha lands that Princess Keʻelikōlani had inherited and then willed to Bernice Pauahi Bishop to form the corpus of the Bishop Estate.) Also not known is the extent to which Keʻelikōlani helped Emma eventually win the suit and the plot of land.[2]

Meanwhile, Ruth Keʻelikōlani seemed to be improving. Lying "propped up by her familiar stacks of yellow cushions," she received a stream of well-wishers.[3] She even finished composing her own *kanikau*, the chant to mourn her passing. In it, she bid a poetic farewell to her favorite Island of Hawaiʻi, the great mountains, the waves, the ocean, the beach, the familiar places, her homes, and her friends.[4]

In late May 1883, unbeknownst to Keʻelikōlani, her servants had sent a note to Bernice Pauahi Bishop informing her of how ill she was and urging her to send a doctor. Upon receiving the note, Bernice Pauahi and Emma immediately left Honolulu for Kona. In a letter to Ihilani Jones, who had become a close friend of the queen, Emma wrote that Keʻelikōlani was "very annoyed" when she learned what her servants had done because she did not think she was so ill. In fact, when Emma saw her on the evening of their arrival, "she was so cheerful and full of jokes, sitting up and asking all about the latest news of Honolulu . . . giving directions to her people what to do about our accommodations."[5] The king, who was en route to Hilo, also arrived, but when he was told that she was in no danger, he proceeded on to Hilo. Emma and Pauahi chose to remain at her bedside. During the night Keʻelikōlani had a high fever and the next morning she died. According to Emma, she "breathed her last at 9 o'clock precisely on the morning of the 24th, Queen Victoria's birthday."[6]

Ruth Keʻelikōlani's body was taken back to Honolulu and for the next three weeks lay in state in her mansion, guarded day and night by six men who constantly waved *kāhili*. Emma and Pauahi were the chief mourners, and seated next to them were Liliʻuokalani and Likelike. Because it was the custom for the mourners of rank to stay in the same house where the body lay in state, for three weeks Liliʻuokalani and Emma sat together keeping vigil by the coffin.[7]

The "watch" was an unusual opportunity for them to patch up some of their differences, and on the surface it appears they did. Liliʻuokalani did not raise the precedence issue when Emma sat at the head of the coffin, in front of the king and queen and other members of the court.[8]

And Emma, as a possible gesture of goodwill, had just written to a friend to squelch the false reports that were being repeatedly circulated about "Mrs. Dominis" giving birth to an heir.[9] But, sadly, as subsequent events would show, the reconciliation was only superficial.

Genealogical Fighting

Even before Princess Ruth's demise, the genealogists in the Emma and the Kalākaua camps were engaged in a nasty fight, which had been precipitated when Emma's supporters defended her decision not to attend the coronation. They boldly asserted that Kalākaua was not of "sufficient ali'i lineage" to be on the throne and that the only eligible candidate was Queen Emma.[10] It was a charge that the Kalākauas could not ignore. In fact, the quarrel concerned not only Emma but also the Kamehamehas because Bernice Pauahi Bishop and Ruth Ke'elikōlani, the other principal representatives of the dynasty, had chosen not to attend the coronation either.

In earlier times such a dispute would have been settled on the battlefield, but in 1883 it was confined to the pages of the Hawaiian language newspapers, two in particular: *Ko Hawai'i Pae'āina,* which took Emma's side, and *Ka 'Elele Poakolu,* which took Kalākaua's. After the latter newspaper attacked Emma's royal lineage, the former accused it of "grabbing at nothing," "grumbling," and "crying." "We can see the meetings they hold, and the lists on their side, so that they are well prepared to fight; however we haven't gotten anything, just things from unskilled people." When *Ka 'Elele Poakolu* denied that Queen Emma was descended from Keli'imaika'i, the half-brother of Kamehameha I, *Ko Hawai'i Pae'āina* shot back, "Your mouth is spreading foolishness. Keliimaikai was the husband of Kalikookalani, and Kaoanaeha was their child. . . . We are standing firm behind our beliefs, because we have ample for our resources, our accuracy and the truth."[11] The newspaper backed its claim with detailed narratives and charts going back to 'Umi a Liloa, the fifteenth-century progenitor of the Kamehamehas. When *Ka 'Elele Poakolu* denied this claim as well, *Ko Hawai'i Pae'āina* replied, "open your dumb eyes, and look carefully, and don't try to teach the people false facts, before stretching the truth gets you into trouble, and you grovel blindly."[12] Four months later the same newspaper was still firing verbal salvos at its journalistic rival: "Your side is always denying, just like when you denied Ke'elikōlani and her relationship to Kamehameha, but you were the one who lost with disappointment. You stuck out your fingers only to be burned. . . . You can just squirm, you can't succeed, because you have been charred, discolored, cancered which will not disappear even if you tried to scrub it out with soap."[13] The skirmishing between the genealogists continued well into 1884.[14]

The fight was of course not new. In 1856 High Chief Kapa'akea, the father of Lili'uokalani and David Kalākaua, had opposed the marriage of Emma and Alexander Liholiho on the grounds that Emma's lineage was not high enough. (See Chapter 5.) During the events leading up to the riot on the 12th of February 1874, *Ka Nūhou Hawai'i* published an article by a Kalākaua genealogist repudiating Samuel M. Kamakau's genealogy linking Queen Emma to Keli'imaika'i. The king's genealogist argued that Keli'imaika'i "himself denied publicly that he had a child named Kaoanaeha" and "that it was accepted by the chiefs of that time. . . . [So] how can SMK [Samuel M. Kamakau] turn the truth into a lie, when he knows the true genealogy of the Queen?"[15]

This ongoing genealogical battle underscores the fact that although nearly ten years had passed since Queen Emma's loss in the 1874 election, a hard core of Queenites still believed that she should be enthroned. *Ko Hawai'i Pae'āina* declared: "Here is the Hawaiian people with their thoughts, to treasure her to this day. Their hands are forever greeting her and awaiting for the day she comes before us, on each one of the islands."[16]

Queen Emma was not involved in this journalistic battle, at least not publicly; she was never quoted, either directly or indirectly, by the newspapers. Neither was Lili'uokalani, but her position was clear as she later revealed in her autobiography. In it she repudiated Emma's descent from Kamehameha. She wrote that Queen Emma could not have descended from Keli'imaika'i because he "had no issue." He was supposed to have been married to a chiefess named Kiilaweau, but, according to Lili'uokalani, Kiilaweau was not a woman but rather a man.[17]

First Seizure

If Queen Emma remained above the genealogical fray, it was not for lack of energy. She wrote to her friend Ihilani Jones in July 1883 that she had been cleaning her residence at Pu'uloa and that she had already done a special cleaning at Hānaiakamalama for the Sisters at the Priory who intended to stay there for a few days. She added that she was proceeding to her "marine" residence in Waikīkī to do still more cleaning. In addition, she related plans for hiking up Mānoa Valley to the "pretty spring" of Waiakeakua and then camping, still two of her favorite pastimes.[18] According to Jennie Stillman, they camped there for a week "in a fern shelter, roughly thrown together."[19]

Emma still indulged in her habit of driving her carriage every morning for two hours, sometimes around Diamond Head or, in the guava season, up Nuʻuanu Valley to gather fruit. Jane Smythe recalled, "She particularly delighted in the Diamond Head drive, along a lonely and uninhabited coast, and I shared her delight, for she allowed me to handle the reins."[20]

Such activity shows that Emma was still healthy and strong in the fall of 1883. In fact, she had never been seriously ill in her life. So, it was a cause for concern when in October Dr. George Trousseau was called to her bedside in Waikīkī. According to Jennie Stillman, the queen had fallen off her chair and became "quite insensible," unable to recognize anyone. When Dr. Trousseau examined her, he said it was just "a bit of indigestion."[21] Unless Stillman erred in her recording of what he said, it was a strange diagnosis because it did not fit the symptoms described by Stillman. *Ko Hawaiʻi Paeʻāina* reported Emma was stricken by *lolo kaʻa* (literally rolling brains) or a "small stroke."[22] This would explain the sudden weakness, the fall from the chair, the blackout, the resulting weak vision in her right eye, and the subsequent recurring headaches.[23]

In November Emma was still complaining about being "weary." "The work at Waikīkī has kept me going back and forth. I get so weary and faint sometime after the day's work [that] I lay up quite after it."[24] But the anniversary of Alexander Liholiho's passing had never been a happy month for Emma. When she received an invitation to a party on the 30th, for example, she declined because, as she wrote to Ihilani, "it is a day full of sadness. You never know what it is to be in sorrow and grief for your loneliness, but God knows alone what is best for those gone before and those left behind. His must be praised for all things."[25]

The Demise of the Queen's Party

While weariness, illness, and grief may have sapped some of her strength, she was not entirely distracted from the forthcoming 1884 election. She had reason to be concerned because of the dwindling influence of her party and the challenges faced by her supporters, especially the few running for office. She was reminded of this by a letter from the Rev. George W. Pilipo in December in which he reported on his meetings with constituents in Kohala, Mahukona, Puna, and Hilo and on the electoral chances of Joseph Nawahi and other party candidates.[26]

The plight of her party is revealed in the public discussions generated by the campaign regarding the existence, or non-existence, of political parties in the kingdom. Part of the discussion involved an exchange between *The Hawaiian Monthly* and the *Pacific Commercial Ad-*

vertiser. The former argued that while there was much talk about a "palace party," "independent party," "administration party," "people's party," "&c., &c.," political parties as such did not exist in Hawai'i. Because of the changes in the character and composition of the population, the growing complexity of public affairs, and the magnitude of the public revenue and expenditures, the *Hawaiian Monthly* said the time had come for the creation of a well-organized and well-managed political party system.[27]

In contrast, the *Pacific Commercial Advertiser* stated: "it is an unmistakable fact that there are two parties in this land and that their proper designations are the 'Hawaiian' and the 'Foreign' parties." Although neither of them had "that peculiar machine organization" that characterized parties in America, the paper maintained that they were quite as fully organized as any political parties found in England or France.[28] It described the "foreign party" as made up of "heterogeneous elements" of white foreigners ranging from "the absolute annexationist" to "the moderate man disposed to treat" the existing government with fairness. The Hawaiian party comprised "the whole native race" whose binding principle was "Hawaii for the Hawaiians," although the newspaper acknowledged that a certain number of Hawaiians did "stand aloof" from the king and his policies. The *Advertiser* concluded: "We affirm, without any hesitation, that the tendency of things since 1880, has been to the formation of two distinct parties here and that the real characteristics of these parties are that one is a foreign party and the other a native party."[29]

Kuykendall points out that the *Pacific Commercial Advertiser* was in error in implying that the political division had an exclusively racial basis. "In the election campaign then in progress, there were two groups resembling political parties, one supporting and the other opposing the Gibson administration; each group included both native Hawaiians and haoles."[30] One was called the National party, whose candidates were exclusively Hawaiian or part-Hawaiian, and the other the Independent party, one-fourth of whose candidates were non-Hawaiian.[31]

Conspicuously absent from the public debate on political parties was any mention of the "Queen's party," although the *Pacific Commercial Advertiser*'s reference to "the tendency of things since 1880" may have been a veiled acknowledgement of the role of the dowager queen and her party in that election. Not even the Hawaiian language newspapers mentioned the Queen's party. For example, *Ko Hawai'i Pae'āina*, which was friendly to the queen, declared that there were only two parties: the bread-and-butter party and the independent party.[32]

Why was there no mention of the "Queen's party"? For one reason, the party was no longer a power. In the election of 1884, for example, Kūnuiākea ran as a candidate not for the Queen's party but rather for the Independent party. Had there been a viable Queen's party, he would have surely been its candidate. On the eve of the election, the *Hawaiian Gazette* said of him, "Kunuiakea, a Alii stands for the Independent ticket. He is a well known protégé of Queen Emma, and on these grounds he is a most acceptable candidate to all."[33] And the *Pacific Commercial Advertiser* stated that Kūnuiākea is a candidate who "places his trust in his relatives" and for whom "a great deal of money is being expended."[34] As it turned out, Kūnuiākea lost the election and came in a poor sixth place.[35]

Although Queen Emma made no public statement about the decline of her party, her support of her cousin's candidacy as an Independent may be taken as evidence of that fact. Several reasons can be advanced for the gradual disappearance of her party: competition from other parties, lack of leadership, loss of members, shifts in public opinion, and demographic changes. However, the main reason was the consolidation of King Kalākaua's power and the corresponding diminution of the queen's. Her party suffered the fate of all single-issue parties: when the issue disappears, the party disappears.

The queen may have been consoled by the reelection of the "last of the Emmaites," Joseph Nawahi in Hilo, Rev. George Washington Pilipo in Kohala, and J. Kauai in Kaua'i.[36]

Second Seizure

By the spring of 1884 Emma had apparently regained much of her strength. In May she wrote to Ihilani that she was "extremely busy" planting and transplanting trees "together with house attending" at Pu'uloa. She had 2,000 coconut trees planted, in addition to tamarind trees, royal palms, and dozens of bougainvillea vines.[37] She had previously spent a week cutting firewood.[38]

Queen Emma also continued her charitable activities such as fundraising. She reported that the Library Fair had raised more than $3,000 over a three-day period and that she expected the Police Ball to raise another $400. Working with Mrs. Alfred Willis and other members of the Anglican church, she made various products to be sold at fairs on behalf of the cathedral building fund. For example, she had asked Ihilani to collect and send sugar cane leaves out of which they intended to make hats for the fair.[39]

In June 1884 when Prince El Darago of Italy and Prince Oscar of

Sweden visited Honolulu, the queen threw a lavish *lūʻau* for them at her "marine" residence in Waikīkī. It was said of Prince Oscar that "because of the niceties of royal etiquette, he was unable to refuse the proffered delicacy of roasted dog" and that the experience "intrigued" him.[40] Jennie Stillman revealed the "kindly humour" of the queen on the morning after the party. "Greeting me at breakfast, she remarked with mock seriousness: You seem to take it as a matter of course. Puzzled, I asked: What, your Majesty? She smiled winningly, What a child; I give you three princes to dance with, and you think it an ordinary event." The third prince at the ball was her cousin, Kūnuiākea.[41]

Queen Emma spent the month of July in Kohala as the houseguest of Clements Kynnersely, a lay reader, who founded Kohala's St. Augustine Church, and his wife. After many receptions, teas, and outings, her hosts honored the queen on her last night with a dinner and ball at the local English Club. She and her party then spent a week as the houseguests of a not-too-distant neighbor Mrs. Woods. En route she and her party stopped for lunch. Jennie Stillman and Sister Eldress Phoebe tell what happened next: "She ate heartily . . . mounted her horse" and was riding "very fast in the burning sun" when she "felt something coming on." She stopped and asked "to be let down from her horse" and fainted. That "was the last she saw of everything."[42] This time there was no question about the diagnosis: it was another stroke.

Lucy Peabody left immediately for Honolulu and returned with Dr. McKibbin and the queen's business agent, Alexander Cartwright (for she had not yet made a will). Stillman wrote: "The so-called doctor there [in Kohala] had not done the first thing for her" and only the prompt action of Dr. McKibbin saved the queen. In fact, Dr. McKibbin told members of the party that had he arrived two hours later, "it would have been all over with her." When he insisted on moving the queen to Honolulu, some were opposed, saying it would kill her.[43]

They left Kawaihae August 17 onboard the *Likelike.* The queen became conscious during the night and asked where she was. Dr. McKibbin told her "You are going home. You have been very ill," to which she replied, "Oh, no. I don't think so. It has been very dark the last five days."[44]

After their arrival in Honolulu two days later, Stillman reported that "the queen "is certainly steadily improving" and that they had "good grounds to hope" for a speedy recovery.[45] But on August 25, 1884, Stillman wrote that while the queen was improving every day, she was in and out of consciousness. "She talks and laughs with you one moment and forgets within the next."[46]

On August 31, Sister Phoebe, who was tending Emma "day and night," along with Jennie Stillman and Mrs. Wodehouse, wrote that the queen was "quite sensible about everything except her own illness and place of abode. [She] says she is not ill [and] can't understand why she is to take medicine, and [why] she is in bed. [She] also fancies she is still in Kohala and can't understand why she is in Honolulu and in her own house. Her bed was placed in the large drawing room of Rooke House because it was more airy. [She] looks at the ceiling and pictures, but still is continually wandering back to Kohala, travelling . . . her memory quite fails her on this subject. She remembers all that she did up to when she was seized with the fainting on her horse."[47]

Sister Phoebe was not as sanguine as Jennie Stillman about the chances for the queen's recovery. She was partially paralyzed and could not see out of her right eye. The doctors had told her that the queen would "have to be very careful, for a third attack would be instantaneous death."[48] At this point in her letter, Sister Phoebe worried about the queen "being taken" before she made her will. She had heard that all of her property was going to be bequeathed to Prince Albert Kūnuiākea. "What would become of the rest of her dependents?" she asked. The answer would come in two months.

Pauahi's Passing

In May 1884 Emma had written Ihilani about Mrs. Bernice Pauahi Bishop's departure for San Francisco for treatment of breast cancer. She mentioned how she prayed that "God in his infinite love to humankind may spare her life . . . [as] every year lessens our numbers."[49] In recent years Emma and Pauahi had grown closer. The esteem that Pauahi felt for Emma was revealed in her will in which she bequeathed to Emma the fishpond called "Kawa" located in Kawaa (near today's O'ahu Prison) and a property in Lāi'mi, near Hānaiakamalama in Nu'uanu.[50]

After Pauahi's return, however, her condition worsened and she died on October 16. Emma attended both the wake and the funeral and found herself seated next to Lili'uokalani, as had been the case with Ruth Ke'elikōlani's services. Interestingly, in the funeral procession, any protocol issue of precedence was prevented by pairing Emma and Charles Bishop on one side of the hearse and placing Lili'uokalani, who was Mrs. Bishop's *hānai* sister, on the other side.[51]

The effects of Emma's stroke must have been quite visible because Lili'uokalani observed in her autobiography that at the funeral "Queen Emma showed plainly by her peculiar actions that she was suffering from some malady."[52] Such a characterization of Emma's actions at the time may have contributed to the rumor then that she "had gone queer."[53]

Emma's Will

Five days after Pauahi's death, Emma answered Sister Phoebe's question when she signed her last will and testament in the presence of Cartwright and J. M. Monsarrat (the attorney and son of Victoria's lover; see Chapter 6). She bequeathed St. Andrew's Priory $600 per annum for the maintenance of four annual scholarships of $150 each to be called the "Queen Emma Scholarships" and instructed that the money be entrusted to the Head Sister (Sister Phoebe).[54]

She gave $100 to her servants Kekii, Mamaina, and Kuhina, $300 to Jennie Stillman, Katie Montgomery, and Sarah Weed, and annuities of $900 to Lucy Peabody, $600 to Hikoni, and $300 each to Grace Kahoalii and Mary Liwai. She also gave Grace a house lot in Honolulu and the

Albert Kūnuiākea was the natural son of King Kamehameha III and Jane Young. Jane was the younger sister of Fanny and Grace Young, Emma's natural and hānai mothers, respectively. As such, Albert was Emma's cousin. Albert was a perennial worry not only to Emma but also to his family, teachers, and guardians. Queen Emma willed her property to Albert, but when he died without issue, all property reverted to her estate, which has as its main beneficiary The Queen's Medical Center.

ahupuaʻa of Papaʻakoko and Kahanaiki in Oʻahu's districts of Koʻolauloa and Koʻolaupoko, respectively; Mary received the *ʻili ʻāina* (a land area in an *ahupuaʻa*) of Kalaepōhaku in Mōʻiliʻili.

She bequeathed to Elizabeth Kekaʻanīʻau Pratt, her classmate and life-long friend, one-half of an *ʻili ʻāina* in Makiki and to Stella Keomailani one parcel known as "Kaʻalaʻa-luna" in Nuʻuanu, a house lot on Queen Street, and a taro patch known as "Waianae" in Lahaina, Maui.

The remainder of her landholdings were bequeathed to her cousin Albert Kūnuiākea, and business agent, Alexander Cartwright. The devises to Cartwright were in trust; he received nothing personally. The properties he received, such as Lāwaʻi, Hālawa, and Kaluaokau, were to be used to pay the annuities and scholarships. When the annuitants died, the value was to be divided, one-half to the hospital and half to remain in trust for the life of Albert Kūnuiākea, with the balance to be paid to Albert's issue at his death. The other properties that Cartwright received in trust, such as Kawaihae and Waikahekahe in Puna, were to provide income to Albert for life. At his death, his issue were to receive the lands from Cartwright. But in the event of Albert's death without issue, the hospital was to receive all of the lands.

Thus, if Albert Kūnuiākea had been survived by children or grandchildren, the bulk of Queen Emma's estate would have passed to them, free of trust. (In legal terms, the hospital was a contingent charitable remainder beneficiary.) But because he actually died childless, Queen's Hospital became the main beneficiary. The queen's will did not direct how her lands or income therefrom were to be used by the hospital.

She left her entire collection of books and pamphlets to the Honolulu Library and Reading Room Association.[55] Notably absent from her will as beneficiaries were St. Andrew's Cathedral and what is now the Episcopal church.

Apparently, she had forgotten to mention in her will the disposition of her collection of Hawaiian valuables. A month after signing her will, Emma declared: "As I am about to embark on the steamer Kinau for a visit to Hilo, Hawaii, I make this codicil to my last will and testament." In it she bequeathed to Charles Bishop her collection of "native curiosities, such as kahilis, calabashes, feather capes and leis" and the silver baptismal vase given her by Queen Victoria on condition that the objects would go to what is now known as the Bishop Museum. (Some of these treasures are also on exhibit at the Queen Emma Summer Palace in Nuʻuanu.)

Queen Emma's last trip was to Hilo. Partly because of her support

THE LATE QUEEN EMMA.

The death, on April 25, at Honolulu, of Emma Kaleleonalani Queen Dowager of Hawaii or the Sandwich Islands, has occasioned much regret. This lady, who had received an English education, visited Europe nearly twenty years ago, leaving her home in May, 1865, and returning in October, 1866; she made many friends in England, one among them being Queen Victoria, with whom she has often since corresponded. She was born in January, 1836, the daughter of Naea, a chief of high rank, her mother being Fanny Young Kekelaokalani, niece to King Kamehameha I. She was brought up in the house of Dr. T. C. B. Rooke, an English physician, who had married her aunt, Grace Kamaikui Young, sister to Fanny Young Kekelaokalani. Dr. Rooke was a native of Hertfordshire, well connected, having two brothers in the Indian Army; he had studied for the medical profession in London, and went out to the Sandwich Islands in 1830; there he married, and resided till his death, in 1858. The future Queen received instruction in her girlhood from Mr. and Mrs. Cooke, directors of the Royal School for children of native chiefs, and from a private governess, Mrs. Von Pfister, a German lady. In 1856, she was married to the late King Kamehameha IV. (Alexander Liholiho), and as Queen Consort, till the lamented death of her husband, in 1863, shared all his plans and efforts to promote the welfare of the people. They had one child, a little boy, who was taken from them by a short illness at four years of age, and whose death was soon followed by that of his father.

The funeral, of which we give some Illustrations, was attended by many of the chief personages at Honolulu, and by a large assemblage of the people. The coffin lay in state, covered with a purple pall richly embroidered, in a room of the late Queen's house, which is in Nuuanu-street, and the garden-front of which is shown in one of our Views. Young women or girls, prostrate or kneeling on the ground outside the house, uttered wailing cries of lamentation, as prescribed by native custom. Within the house, or in the verandah, were the friends of the deceased, including Princess Liliuokalani, Princess Likelike, Governor Dominis, and several officers of the King's Staff and Household. At eight o'clock in the evening, the coffin was placed on the hearse, and was conducted by a torchlight procession, with a military escort, to Kawaiahao church, where the clergy performed the funeral service. The figures of attendants, shown in our correspondent's sketches, are represented as holding the ceremonial "kahilis," which are maces surmounted with a splendid arrangement of plumes, black, white, crimson, or yellow, made of the precious dyed feathers of a famous Hawaiian bird which has become extinct. The hearse or bier was drawn all the way by members of the Poola Society; and the effect of this gorgeous plumage under the flashing torchlight was very beautiful. A Portrait of the late Queen Emma is included among our Illustrations.

Queen Emma's funeral was described in the *Illustrated London News,* June 12, 1885.

for the popular Joseph Nawahi, the queen had won many friends in Hilo. When she attended a diorama of Hawaiian and Australasian views and images, which displayed "a splendidly colored picture" of herself, the audience gave a "great applause."[56]

"Queen Emma is Dead!"

On January 2, 1885, the queen celebrated her forty-ninth birthday with a large reception at Rooke House. Throughout the day a crowd of well-wishers, both natives and foreigners, called on her.[57] Numerous other Hawaiians celebrated the occasion, including the inmates of the branch (leper) hospital who, along with so many others, endearingly called her "Mother."[58]

She appeared to be in good health, except for the recurring headaches. Dr. McKibbin was worried that she had not been maintaining her physical exercise. She spent less and less time tending to her residences and gardens, and, against her physician's advice, she continued to "gratify her large appetite" and consequently had gained considerable weight.[59]

In mid-April a curious incident occurred in Kona, Hawai'i; swarms of *akule* (goggle or big-eyed scad) came ashore.[60] Hawaiians believed that such events portended the death of an *ali'i.* Five days later Queen Emma was dying. Dr. McKibbin describes her last hours:

> Yesterday evening [Friday, April 24] she complained of a headache and Miss Peabody asked me to call and see her. I called last night, and found that she had a slight headache and had taken a little medicine. There were no alarming symptoms, and I apprehended nothing except the natural anxiety with which, as her physician, I watched her recurring headaches.
>
> I called on her again this morning, and found her lying on a sofa. She complained of her head, but said it was not a very bad headache. She was very hungry and wanted her breakfast. I would not permit her to eat anything, however, except a little tea and toast. On leaving the Queen's residence, I met Mr. Cartwright . . . and I told him that I was anxious about the headaches to which she was subject.
>
> I then went to the hospital and returned to my own house about ten minutes after 1 o'clock. As I entered I was called by telephone. I recognized Miss Peabody's voice, asking me to come very quick as the Queen had another attack.
>
> I went immediately to the house, and as soon as I saw her, I directed Dr. Trousseau and Mr. Cartwright to be telephoned for, as from her

appearance I knew that she was very ill. Her breathing was stertorous, and she had hardly any pulse.

Dr. Trousseau soon came in, and we administered medicine. She recovered somewhat and her pulse became stronger; so much so that the doctors were about to leave. She arose, and when passing from one room to another, she was seized with another attack of convulsions, and died at ten minutes before two o'clock, the attack from the beginning lasting barely an hour. Her death was caused by effusion of blood into the base of the brain.[61]

Uwē Helu (Wailing)

Two hours later King Kalākaua, accompanied by his aide Colonel Curtis Iaukea, visited the "house of mourning" and returned later that same night.[62] It is impossible to fathom all his thoughts at the time, but the king must have felt genuine sadness—and perhaps some relief as well. Relief because, as Paul Isenberg, a member of the House of Nobles put it, with Queen Emma's death, "The last fear that Kalakaua had is now passed away."[63] And with Ruth Keʻelikōlani and Pauahi gone, he was also free of the Kamehamehas (except for Kūnuiākea who posed no threat).

The news of the queen's death had quickly spread and people began to gather at Rooke House. A group of the queen's old retainers chanted "sweetly and mournfully" the *kanikau* (lament) that they had composed. Relieving each other at intervals, they chanted and wailed throughout the night so that "the sounds of grief never ceased."[64] As they wept, the rain fell. *"Kulu ka waimaka, uwē ka ʻōpua."* "The tears fall; the clouds weep."[65] By evening when it was announced that the body of the queen would be on view from 9:00 a.m. to 1:00 p.m. the next day (Sunday), a large crowd had already assembled at the residence.

The queen's body, clothed in white silk trimmed with gold, was placed on a bier located in the drawing room (which was located on the second floor). On her head was a circlet of jewels and on her arms were gold and jeweled bracelets. At her feet was a crucifix surrounded by fragrant white flowers. On a table in the room was the silver vase presented by Queen Victoria at the birth of Ka Haku O Hawaiʻi. Stationed next to the bier were female retainers waving small *kāhili* over the queen, while male retainers dressed in black held the large *kāhili.* Positioned around the bier was a distinguished Guard of Honor including Colonel Curtis Iaukea, Colonel James H. Boyd, Colonel Charles H. Judd, Colonel E. W. Purvis, and G. W. Macfarlane.[66]

The first mourners allowed to enter were the boarding students at

St. Andrew's Priory, all dressed in white with mourning ribbons around their waists.[67] Among the accompanying sisters was Sister Albertina who only the day before had tended the dying queen.[68]

They were followed by members of the royal court, government ministers, the diplomatic corps, other leading citizens, and ordinary folk, both natives and foreigners. By 1:00 p. m. nearly 2,000 mourners had filed past the bier.[69]

In the nearby Anglican pro-cathedral, within earshot of the wailing, the Reverend George Wallace eulogized "the noble lady . . . who has been always a queen, a mother, and a friend to her people." He spoke: "Her life speaks eloquently to the women of her race and to the women of every race dwelling among us, telling how she passed through the temptations of high estate without a stain, how she maintained the sacred domestic relations of wife and mother with beautiful fidelity, and how she used her income in a graceful hospitality, a noble munificence, and Christian charity."[70]

He reminded his parishioners that they had inherited the work of establishing the Anglican mission that Queen Emma and Kamehameha IV had initiated. Acknowledging that the work had not yet been a "visible success," he said that they shared in the responsibility of building the mission and the cathedral whose stones still lay uncrated.[71]

The body was to lie for the next three weeks—the time it took the carpenters to make the coffin and sarcophagus. After two weeks it was decided to move the coffin and the viewing from Rooke House to the more spacious Congregational Kawaiahaʻo Church. It was also decided that the funeral services would be held there rather than in the small pro-cathedral in order to accommodate the expected crowds.

This decision was not well received, however. In fact, it drew heavy criticism, especially from Liliʻuokalani who was a member of Kawaiahaʻo. She wrote: "Queen Emma was not an attendant there. On the contrary, she had been chiefly instrumental in the founding of the Anglican Mission, and was an Episcopalian. Why, then, supposing it had been at all necessary to select a church for her funeral, did they not select the Episcopal church? That was her own church, and she should have been buried therefrom; for while living she had shown strong attachment to it, and an equally strong feeling of opposition to other denominations."[72]

Liliʻuokalani, who had forsaken her Anglican faith, was overruled by King Kalākaua who was still an active Anglican as evidenced by his support of Bishop Willis and the cathedral building fund.

During the week that the queen lay in state at the "Stone Church," thousands of mourners—the vast majority of whom were not Anglicans—from all parts of the Islands came to pay their respects.

The Final Procession

The funeral service was held on Sunday, May 17, 1885. By noon the church overflowed with people inside and outside. Foreigners seemed to outnumber the natives. All the members of the court were present: King Kalākaua and Queen Kapiʻolani, Princesses Liliʻuokalani and Likelike along with Kaʻiulani. The *Hawaiian Gazette* reported that Queen Kapiʻolani was "in heavy mourning" but said nothing about Liliʻuokalani.[73]

Before the Anglican service began, King Kalākaua had arranged for the Reverend H. H. Parker to conduct a Congregational ceremony and give a eulogy in Hawaiian. Surprisingly, he began by clearly reaffirming Queen Emma's Kamehameha lineage, thus ignoring the claims of King Kalākaua's "skillful genealogist." After recounting the events of her life, her joys, and her sorrows, Rev. Parker asked: "How did it come about that the late Queen Dowager held so supreme a place in the hearts of this people?" He answered:

> She loved the people. Love begets love. The common people believed that Queen Emma did really care for them. The Hospital that bears her name will ever remain a memorial of her regard for the Hawaiian race. So long as a Hawaiian lives, when sick, he may go to the Queen's Hospital and have all that love and skill can do for him, free of charge.[74] The Queen also disbursed much of her means in a quiet way, among the poor and the sick. She gave to foreigners as well as to natives, whom she believed to be in need. The poor will miss her.
>
> Motherhood and womanhood were blended in Queen Emma's nature in such a way as to make up a lovely character. That motherly nature was another element that drew the hearts of the people towards herself. . . . This was more especially marked in the influence she won over the young of her own sex, many of whom looked to her as they would look to a mother. They will miss her.

Another source of her influence, according to Reverend Henry H. Parker, was that "she had religious faith. She held to her convictions of the truth. These traits won for her the respect of very many good men and women." He concluded, "Emma, Queen of the hearts of the people, we bring today our tribute of aloha to your memory. Happy are the

Mauna'ala or Royal Mausoleum. *Top:* The marble shaft to the right of the chapel commemorates the family of the Kalākauas. *Bottom:* Queen Emma and King Kamehameha IV and their son, Prince Albert, are buried in the Kamehameha Vault.

thoughts you have left behind you, thrice happy your example of faith, of patience, and courage."[75] The service concluded with Reverend Willis reading from the liturgy of the Anglican church. Afterward the massive coffin, made of *koa* and *kou*, was placed in the large catafalque at the church entrance. Two hundred native men, members of the Kawaiahaʻo and Kaumakapili churches, then began pulling the wheeled platform toward Maunaʻala, as the battery on Punchbowl announced that the procession had started. The procession was nearly a mile and a half long with over 2,000 people, including the Honolulu Rifles, King's Guard, Fire Department, Improved Order of Red Men, Knights of Pythias, Ancient Order of Foresters, American Legion of Honor, Catholic, Protestant and Anglican clergy, attending physicians, the *konohiki* (managers) of the queen's lands, her retainers, and the officer bearing her decorations and jewels. Notably absent from the official list of organizations in the procession was Queen Emma's principal beneficiary: the Queen's Hospital.[76]

Thousands of spectators lined King and Nuʻuanu streets. Out of respect to Queen Emma's Christian faith, except for an occasional cry of a *kupuna* (an elderly person), almost no wailing was heard along the way. It took more than two hours and several halts before the procession reached Maunaʻala. This was the largest Hawaiian funeral-of-state honoring any dowager queen (past or future).

Waiting in the Royal Mausoleum were the king and queen and other members of the royal family including Liliʻuokalani, the king's ministers, members of the diplomatic corps, and other dignitaries who had preceded the procession by carriage. The coffin was removed from the catafalque and placed in the anteroom where Bishop Willis concluded the service as the choir, dressed in white surplices, sang the hymn "Now the Laborer's Task Is O'er." Outside the Household Troops fired three volleys of musketry in a tribute rarely given in honor of a woman. Four hundred female mourners gathered around the entrance and chanted their last *uwē*. The Royal Hawaiian Band played a solemn dirge. Then one by one the mourners departed, leaving Queen Emma sleeping by the side of her husband and her son.[77]

The *Pacific Commercial Advertiser* penned its own poignant farewell lament that expressed to one degree or another the sentiments of everyone:

Auwe! Auwe! The bitter wail resounds,
　　From far Kauai to bold Hawaii's shore;
The people's grief and sorrow know no bounds,
　　For their loved Ema-lani is no more.

A Chieftain's daughter lies in regal state;
Kahilis, royal emblems, wave on high,
And soldiers, guards of honor, round her wait;
While every isle takes up the mournful cry.

The royal diadem beside her head,
The purple pall emblazoned with her crest,
These mutely tell us that a Queen is dead,
The crucifix—A Christian laid to rest. . . .

Auwe! Auwe! The mourning nation cries;
Auwe! Auwe! She does not heed its grief;
Auwe! No more she wipes the weeping eyes,
No more she gives the sick and poor relief.

The King and lowliest native equal share
The common grief, for each has lost a friend,
And closer draws the bond of sympathy—
The throne and hut unite their tears to blend.

And not alone Hawaiians grieving cry,
The Haoles join the universal moan;
America extends her sympathy,
And England's Queen will mourn a sister gone. . . .

Low droops the Royal standard on its mast;
Loud sounds the brazen cannon's hoarse farewell;
Sway the kahilis; while our tears drop fast,
O'er her whom rich and poor have loved so well.

Toll, toll ye bells; beat, beat, ye muffled drums;
Ye trumpets wait the funeral dirge aloud;
Weep, weep, ye people in your island homes,
Let every head in bitter grief be bowed.

Sing on ye choirs, of death and grave destroyed;
Sing of our Ema-lani's happy state;
Sing on, of bliss and pleasure unalloyed;
Our hearts are heavy, but our hopes are great.

Kaleleonalani is not dead!
She sleeps on earth, but wakes in Paradise;
Rejoice we then and lift the drooping head,
She is but veiled from our mortal eyes.

And so we leave her sleeping sweet in God.[78]

23

The Legacy

Queen Emma did not fear death itself. What she feared instead was death with insignificance. However, the tens of thousands of her "heirs"—the school girls and teachers of the priory, the worshippers at St. Andrew's, the patients, physicians, nurses, and staff at The Queen's Medical Center, the Hawaiians and Hawaiians-at-heart—all attest to the fact that Emma did not die with insignificance. The tangible monuments of her legacy, which are situated near the heart of downtown Honolulu, bear witness to her remarkable life: St. Andrew's Priory, St. Andrew's Cathedral, and The Queen's Medical Center.

St. Andrew's Priory stands on the same ground on which it was originally built in 1867. As Hawai'i's first all-girls school, the priory remains a girls' school, with a current enrollment of 500 students in grades kindergarten through twelve. Although Queen Emma had envisioned a school for girls of Hawaiian descent, today only a small minority of the students are of Hawaiian ancestry. Instead, the students represent most ethic and religious groups in Hawai'i and come mainly from business and professional families; more than 98 percent of its graduates go on to higher education. As a liberal arts and college preparatory school, St. Andrew's Priory has over 3,500 alumnae who include accomplished artists, businesspersons, composers, doctors, engineers, lawyers, managers, performing artists, and teachers.[1] From its original wood-frame classrooms, the present campus boasts up-to-date classroom buildings, two libraries, three computer labs, a modern multipurpose athletic complex, and art and music rooms. More than 130 years later, the priory still proudly proclaims that it "exists to continue Queen Emma's efforts in directing young women toward ever widening horizons" in a Christian environment of "acceptance, encouragement, and love."[2]

A few steps from the priory stands St. Andrew's Cathedral, for which the queen had labored so tirelessly. That she did not live long enough to see its completion was probably one of her greatest disappointments. Construction on the first phase (the chancel and first two bays of the nave), which began in 1867, resumed in 1882, and was completed in 1888. The final phases, consisting of two additional bays, the narthex, the vestibules, and the great stained glass window, were not completed until 1958, ninety-one years after the queen had returned from England with the original plans and the initial funding.[3]

Today the cathedral complex contains the imposing Mackintosh Tower, Davies Hall or the Parish House, and Parke Chapel. The architecture of these complementing structures is in harmony with the French Gothic style that the queen favored. In recognition and honor of its architectural, religious, and historical importance, St. Andrew's Cathedral was placed on the National Historical Register in 1973.

St. Andrew's Cathedral is, of course, the mother church of the Episcopal church in Hawai'i, which had no stronger defender than Queen Emma. Indeed, at the initiative of Hawai'i's Episcopalians, both Queen Emma and Alexander Liholiho Kamehameha IV have been placed on the church's "Calendar of Saints."[4] These "Royal Monarchs" are now honored in special services on the last Sunday of each November. Today the church she helped to found in the Islands boasts over 10,000 members, constituting nearly 3 percent of the total religious adherents in Hawai'i. With its forty parishes located on all the major Islands and its affiliated schools including the renowned 'Iolani, the Episcopalian church today enjoys a position of influence in Hawai'i far out of proportion to its relatively small membership.[5]

At the foot of Punchbowl is The Queen's Medical Center, the oldest and largest private hospital in Hawai'i and the Pacific Basin. Starting with 124 beds, it is now licensed to operate with 530 acute care beds. In addition, it has more than 3,500 employees, including 850 nurses and 1,000 physicians on staff. In 1997 the hospital admitted over 18,000 patients and provided outpatient services to over 200,000 people of all races. As the leading medical referral center in Hawai'i, it is best known for its programs in cancer, cardiology, neuroscience, orthopedics, surgery, and trauma. The hospital offers several residency programs in conjunction with the John A. Burns School of Medicine at the University of Hawai'i. It is also affiliated with the Voluntary Hospitals of America (VHA), an association of more than 1,000 hospitals nationwide.[6]

Although The Queen's Medical Center scarcely resembles its humble beginnings, it is still committed to a mission of "preserving, protecting and perpetuating the health of all the people of Hawaii, recognizing the special health needs of Native Hawaiians." It seeks to accomplish this goal "in the spirit of Aloha, as guided by the vision and ideals of our founders, Queen Emma and King Kamehameha IV."[7]

Queen's also operates and subsidizes the Moloka'i General Hospital, a small thirty-bed rural facility that serves the Island's 7,000 residents, most of whom are Hawaiians. And through its Queen Emma Clinics, Queen's offers low-cost medical services to all people; in fact, it is the leading provider of charity care in the state of Hawai'i.

The Queen Emma Summer Palace was built in 1848 and sold to Emma's uncle, John Young II (Keoni Ana) in 1850. Young named the home Hānaiakamalama and later willed it to his niece, Emma. She and her husband, King Kamehameha IV, used it as a retreat from downtown Honolulu. Today the Daughters of Hawai'i maintain Hānaiakamalama as a museum to honor the memory of the royal couple.

The Queen's Medical Center is now part of a network of healthcare companies called The Queen's Health Systems that reflects the complexity of modern healthcare. Its subsidiaries include the largest not-for-profit home care operation in the state and one of Hawai'i's largest accredited medical laboratories serving people throughout the Pacific. In 1997 these two companies served more than one million ambulatory patients.[8]

When Queen Emma died in 1885, she left a substantial estate of lands and other properties that were valued at over a million dollars.[9] Although large parcels were sold to pay the queen's debts, the estate retained approximately 10,000 acres of the *ahupua'a* of Kawaihae on Hawai'i Island, 2,600 acres in Hālawa on O'ahu, and 18.5 acres of prime real estate in Waikīkī.[10] These lands today are worth many millions; in fact, the Waikīkī property generates 75 percent of the total income of the financial legacy. These lands are managed by The Queen Emma Foundation, a not-for-profit, charitable foundation that deploys its revenues to support and advance healthcare in Hawai'i. The foundation's current emphasis is on community health programs involving areas largely populated with native Hawaiians.

The $13,500 that Queen Emma and King Kamehameha IV raised in 1859 for construction of the Queen's Hospital has now grown to $800 million, the current value of the total assets of The Queen's Health Systems, with revenues of $500 million.

By any standard, this heritage is impressive. But just as balance sheets cannot account for the intangible assets of an organization, so these lasting monuments of school buildings, gothic structures, and modern medical facilities do not reveal the full measure of Queen Emma's legacy.

Ultimately, that legacy can be found only in the deepest wellsprings of the choices she made in her life, that is, her values, those enduring beliefs about what she held to be right or wrong, important or unimportant, good or bad. These values and beliefs include her ceaseless quest for knowledge, her unbridled curiosity, her passion for reading and conversation, and her dedication to improving the opportunities for young women; her uncompromising belief in God, her piety, and faith in the power of prayer; her aloha, compassion, and caring for the sick, the poor, and the unfortunate; her unswerving commitment to the sovereignty of the Kingdom of Hawai'i and loyalty to her "ancestral renown"; her love of plants and nature—"the dashing waves, rosy pink clouds, black majestic mountains and rocks"—indeed "everything God has made"; her integrity, openness, and humility; her moral, intellectual, spiritual, and physical courage; her daring and love of adventure; her practice-makes-perfect persistence and self-discipline; her openness and cosmopolitan embrace of all people; her strong sense of personal accountability and, ultimately, her constancy of purpose.

Hers is a glorious living legacy.

Notes

Abbreviations

AH	Archives of Hawai'i
BM	Bishop Museum
DOH	Daughters of Hawai'i
HMCS	Hawaiian Mission Children's Society
KHS	Kaua'i Historical Society
QMC	Queen's Medical Center
UH	University of Hawai'i

1 The Beginnings

1. Kathleen Mellen, *The Lonely Warrior: The Life and Times of Kamehameha the Great of Hawaii.* New York: Hastings House, Publishers, Inc., 1949, 17.
2. Helena G. Allen, *Kalākaua—Renaissance King.* Honolulu: Mutual Publishing, 1994, 1.
3. *Polynesian,* December 11, 1858.
4. *Hawaiian Gazette,* April 29, 1885.
5. *Polynesian,* December 11, 1885.
6. Alfons L. Korn, ed., *News from Molokai, Letters between Peter Kaeo and Queen Emma, 1873–1876.* Honolulu: University of Hawai'i Press, 1976, xv.
7. E. S. Craighill Handy and Mary Kawena Puku'i, *The Polynesian Family System in Ka'u, Hawai'i.* Rutland, Vermont: Charles E. Tuttle Company, 1981, 72.
8. Lorna J. Desha, "The Story of Queen Emma." Unpublished paper, Daughters of Hawai'i, 1964, 21.
9. Mary Kawena Puku'i, E. W. Haertig, and Catherine A. Lee, *Nānā I Ke Kumu (Look to the Source).* Honolulu: Hui Hānai, 1979, vol. 2, 36.
10. *Hawai'i Ponoʻī,* February 18, 1874; and *Ka Nūhou Hawai'i,* February 17, 1874.
11. *Ko Hawai'i Pae'āina,* June 16, 1883.
12. Paper read before the Daughters of Hawai'i by Mrs. Edgar Henriques, April 1917.
13. Clarice Taylor, *Honolulu Star-Bulletin,* July 9, 1853.
14. Samuel M. Kamakau, *Ruling Chiefs of Hawaii.* Honolulu: Kamehameha Schools Press, 1992, 143. His given name was Kalanimalokulokuikepo'ookalani.
15. Ibid., 155.
16. John Papa 'Ī'ī, *Fragments of Hawaiian History.* Honolulu: Bishop Museum Press, 1973, 59.
17. Clarice Taylor, *Honolulu Star-Bulletin,* July 17, 1953.

18. Ralph S. Kuykendall, *The Hawaiian Kingdom.* Honolulu: University of Hawaiʻi Press, 1957, vol. 1, 25, 27, 50–51.
19. Ibid., 35, 40, 42–44, 54, and 58.
20. Levi Chamberlain, *Journal, 1822–1849.* HMCS, vol. 20, 7.
21. Young was also called Olohana, a name he was given because of his frequent use of the boatswain's call, "all hands," during battle.
22. William Barrera and Marion Kelly, *Archaelogical and Historical Surveys of the Waimea to Kawaihae Road Corridor, Island of Hawaii,* Report 74-1, 16.
23. Russell A. Apple, *Pahukanilua: Homestead of John Young, Kawaihae, Kohala, Island of Hawaiʻi.* National Park Service, Hawaiʻi State Office, 1978.
24. Henry E. P. Kekahuna, "Waiʻaha—kahi i hanau ai o Queen Emma," Hawaii (No. 2 South Kona, "Historical Satellites of Kailua," Drafts), #47, M-445 H. E. P. Kekahuna and T. Kelsey Collection, AH; *Hilo Tribune Herald,* March 15, 1854.
25. Research Report to Daughters of Hawaii Collections Committee, Subject: Oil Painting Offered by Mrs. Marks, compiled by Mariajane C. Mee, July 7, 1976, DOH.
26. George S. Kanahele, *Pauahi, The Kamehameha Legacy.* Honolulu: Kamehameha Schools Press, 1986, 12.
27. Chamberlain, *Journal,* vol. 20, 7, HMCS.
28. Isabella L. Bird, *Six Months in the Sandwich Islands.* Rutland, Vermont: Charles E. Tuttle Company, 1988, 157. Edna Williamson Stall mistakenly claims that Rooke House was built in 1833 or three years before Emma's birth. *Historic Homes of Hawaii, From Clipper Ship to Clipper Ship.* Privately printed, 1937, 74.
29. *Hawaiian Annual,* 1904, 74.
30. Joseph Feher, *Hawaii: A Pictorial History.* Bernice P. Bishop Museum, Special Publication No. 58. Honolulu: Bishop Museum Press, 1969, 276.

2 *Ulu Ke Keiki,* The Child Grows

1. David Malo, *Hawaiian Antiquities (Moʻolelo Hawaiʻi).* B. P. Bishop Museum, Special Publication 2. Honolulu: Bishop Museum Press, 1951, 90.
2. Patricia Grimshaw, *Paths of Duty: American Missionary Wives in Nineteenth-Century Hawaii.* Honolulu: University of Hawaiʻi Press, 1989, 138.
3. Pukuʻi, et al., *Nānā I Ke Kumu,* vol. 2, 30.
4. Ibid., 35.
5. O. A. Bushnell, *The Gifts of Civilization: Germs and Genocide in Hawaiʻi.* Honolulu: University of Hawaiʻi Press, 1993, 291.
6. Marjorie Sinclair, *Nahiʻenaʻena, Sacred Daughter of Hawaiʻi.* Honolulu: University of Hawaiʻi Press, 1976, 16.
7. Kanahele, *Pauahi,* 22.
8. Ibid., 33.
9. For a modern day affirmation of infant massage, see Vimala Schneider, *Infant Massage.* New York: Bantam, 1982.
10. Pukuʻi, et al., *Nānā I Ke Kumu,* vol. 2, 32.
11. Handy and Pukuʻi, *The Polynesian Family System,* 91.
12. As cited in Eleanor C. Nordyke, *The Peopling of Hawaii.* Honolulu: University Press of Hawaiʻi, 1977, 18.

13. O. A. Bushnell, *The Gifts of Civilization,* 269.
14. Alfons L. Korn, *Victorian Visitors.* Honolulu: University of Hawai'i Press, 1958, 118.
15. Eleanor H. Davis, *Abraham Fornander.* Honolulu: University of Hawai'i Press, 1979, 50.
16. Puku'i, et al., *Nānā I Ke Kumu,* vol. 2, 37.
17. Barbara B. Peterson, ed., *Notable Women of Hawaii.* Honolulu: University of Hawai'i Press, 1984, 342.
18. Laura Fish Judd, *Honolulu: Sketches of the Life, Social, Political, and Religious in the Hawaiian Islands from 1828 to 1861.* Honolulu: privately printed, 1928, 62.
19. James J. Jarves, *History of the Hawaiian or Sandwich Islands.* Boston: Tappan and Dennet, 1843, 181.
20. Sinclair, *Nahi'ena'ena,* 157–159.
21. Davis, *Abraham Fornander,* 50.
22. Correspondence, Oct. 4, 1838, Henriques Collection, BM.
23. Korn, *News from Molokai,* 19.
24. Queen Emma Collection, AH. Dr. Rooke had all but closed his private medical practice from 1839 to 1841 due to illness, which may have forced him to slow down. *The Friend,* July, 1844.
25. *The Transactions of the Royal Hawaiian Agricultural Society, Fourth Annual Meeting,* June 1854, vol. 2, no. 1, 29–30.
26. Kuykendall, *The Hawaiian Kingdom,* vol. 1, 189.
27. Christiaan P. Klieger, *Nā Maka o Hālawa, A History of Hālawa Ahupua'a, O'ahu.* B. P. Bishop Museum Technical Report 7. Honolulu: Bishop Museum Press, December 1995, 42.
28. Thomas C. B. Rooke, "General Table of Meteorological Observations at Honolulu, from July 1, 1837, to January 1, 1838," *The Hawaiian Spectator,* vol. I, no. 3, July, 1838, 104.
29. Davis, *Abraham Fornander,* 50.
30. Gorham D. Gilman, "Streets of Honolulu in the Early Forties," *Hawaiian Annual,* 1904, 79.
31. A. Grove Day, *History Makers of Hawaii.* Honolulu: Mutual Publishing of Honolulu, 1984, 37.
32. Puku'i, et al., *Nānā I Ke Kumu,* vol. 2, 49.

3 *Ka 'Ike O Ke Keiki,* The Child Learns

1. In 1838 Richards was appointed by King Kamehameha III to be his "Chaplain, Teacher and Translator." Kuykendall, vol. 1, 154.
2. 'Ī'ī, *Fragments of Hawaiian History,* 164.
3. Kuykendall, *The Hawaiian Kingdom,* vol. 1, 110.
4. Kanahele, *Pauahi,* 24.
5. Mary Atherton Richards, *The Chiefs' Children's School.* Honolulu: *Honolulu Star-Bulletin,* 1937, 70.
6. Ibid., 49.
7. Juliette Montague Cooke to Sally Smith, March 30, 1846, Missionary Letters, HMCS.
8. Richards, *The Chiefs' Children's School,* 107.
9. Elizabeth Keka'anī'au Pratt, "A Brief Sketch of the Life of Queen Emma Kaleleokalani," unpublished paper, January 2, 1928, DOH.
10. Lili'uokalani, *Hawai'i's Story by Hawai'i's Queen.* Rutland, Vermont: Ellis Company, 1906, 5–6.
11. Amos S. Cooke, *Journal,* unpub-

lished, vol. 7, Jan. 7, 1842, 184, HMCS.

12. Richards, *The Chiefs' Children's School,* 201.
13. Ibid., 212.
14. Ibid., 208.
15. Mary Atherton Richards, *Amos Starr Cooke and Juliette Montague Cooke: Their Autobiographies Gleaned from Their Journals and Letters.* Honolulu: Daughters of Hawai'i, 1987, 225.
16. Ibid., 203.
17. Cooke, *Journal,* unpublished, vol. 5, July 25, 1840, 273, HMCS.
18. Ibid., August 13, 1839, 116.
19. Ibid., vol. 7, December 20, 1843, 117.
20. Linda K. Menton, "Everything Lovely and of Good Report, The Chiefs' Children's School 1839–1850." Ph.D. dissertation, University of Hawai'i, 1983, 131.
21. Amos Starr Cooke, Reports of the Chiefs' Children's School to the American Board of Commissioners for Foreign Missions, 1841, HMCS.
22. Cooke, *Journal,* unpublished, vol. 7, July 20, 1843, 117, HMCS.
23. Lili'uokalani, *Hawai'i's Story,* 5.
24. Cooke, Reports of the Chief's Children's School, 1842, HMCS.
25. Ibid., 1843.
26. *Polynesian,* July 4, 1840.
27. Richards, *The Chiefs' Children's School,* 108.
28. Richards, *Amos Starr Cooke and Juliette Montague Cooke,* 225.
29. Amos Cooke to David Greene, March 22, 1845, ABCFM-Hawaii Papers, Houghton, HMCS.
30. Kanahele, *Pauahi,* 33–34.
31. Cooke, Reports of the Chief's Children's School, 1842, HMCS.
32. Cooke, *Journal,* unpublished, vol. 7, October 26, 1842, 13, HMCS.
33. Ibid., October 30, 1843, 165.
34. Richards, *Amos Starr Cooke and Juliette Montague Cooke,* 265.
35. Cooke, *Journal,* unpublished, vol. 8, October 24, 1846, 6, HMCS.
36. Ibid., vol. 7, December 16, 1845, 357.
37. Pratt, "A Brief Sketch of the Life of Queen Emma Kaleleonalani."
38. Cooke, *Journal,* unpublished, vol. 8, February 28, 1847, 33, HMCS.
39. Ibid., January 6, 1847, 22.
40. Juliette M. Cooke to Fanny Montague, August 28, 1847, Missionary Letters, HMCS.
41. Letters of Amos S. and Juliette M. Cooke, 1836–1850, August 25, 1844, HMCS.
42. Ibid., March 12, 1845.
43. Ibid., December 11, 1845.
44. Richards, *Amos S. Cooke and Juliette M. Cooke,* 267.
45. Cooke, Reports of the Chiefs' Children's School Report, 1841, HMCS.
46. Juliette M. Cooke to Fanny Montague, December 3, 1840, HMCS.
47. *The Diary of Bernice Pauahi Bishop,* February 2, 1843, BM.
48. Cooke, *Journal,* unpublished, vol. 7, May 28, 1842, 252, HMCS.
49. Ibid., June 18, 1842, 260.
50. Elspeth P. Sterling and Catherine C. Summers, *Sites of Oahu.* Honolulu: Bernice P. Bishop Museum, 1978, 307.
51. Richards, *The Chiefs' Children's School,* 252.
52. Juliette M. Cooke to Martha Montague, November 5, 1844, Missionary Letters, HMCS.
53. Cooke, *Journal,* unpublished, vol. 7, January 29, 1842, 192, HMCS.

54. Cooke, Reports of the Chiefs' Children's School, 1841, HMCS.
55. Kanahele, *Pauahi,* 49.
56. Cooke, *Journal,* unpublished, vol. 7, October 26, 1843, 162, HMCS.
57. Richards, *The Chiefs' Children's School,* 203.
58. Ibid., 142.
59. Ibid., 143.
60. Ibid., 254.
61. Ibid.
62. Ibid., 263; and Alexander Liholiho to Juliette M. Cooke, July 14, 1846, HMCS.
63. Richards, *The Chiefs' Children's School,* 258.
64. Ibid., 187–188.
65. Ibid., 314.
66. Ibid., 319.
67. Ibid., 313
68. Amos S. Cooke to Martha Montague, January 6, 1849, Missionary Letters, HMCS.
69. Menton, "Everything Lovely and of Good Report," 239.
70. Ibid.
71. Sterling and Summers, *Sites of Oahu,* 307.

4 Growing Up

1. Korn, *News From Molokai,* xviii.
2. *Polynesian,* October 28, 1848.
3. Malcolm Brown, *Reminiscences of a Pioneer Kauai Family with References and Anecdotes of Early Honolulu, 1804–1917.* T. McVeagh, 1918, 15.
4. Ibid.
5. Maude Jones, "Emma-Lani." Unpublished paper, no date, DOH.
6. Charles Victor Crosnier de Varigny, *Fourteen Years In the Sandwich Islands 1855–1868.* Honolulu: University of Hawai'i Press, 1981, 266.
7. David Lawrence Gregg, *The Diaries of David Lawrence Gregg: An American Diplomat in Hawaii 1853–1858,* edited by Pauline King. Honolulu: Hawaiian Historical Society, 1982, 85.
8. Minutes of the Honolulu Amateur Musical Society, 1853–1894, 6, HMCS. Also Lynne Johnson, "The Role of Women in the Honolulu Amateur Musical Society 1853–1894: A Reflection of Changing Social Values." Unpublished paper, 1996. Interestingly, the society's musical programs were solemn occasions because only silent applause was permitted after a performance.
9. Varigny, *Fourteen Years in the Sandwich Islands,* 166.
10. Brown, *Reminiscences,* 16.
11. *Polynesian,* December 11, 1858.
12. Ibid., January 26, 1850.
13. Apple, *Pahukanilua: Homestead of John Young,* 75–77.
14. Ka'ōana'eha is buried with John Young at Mauna'ala, the Royal Mausoleum.
15. Kanehoa is buried at Mauna'ala together with his adopted nephew Keli'imaika'i Ka'eo, who died just two weeks after his foster father.
16. William C. Parke, *Personal Reminiscences of William Cooper Parke, Marshal of the Hawaiian Islands, from 1850–1884.* Cambridge University Press, 1891, 56. Kamakau states that 10,000 people died throughout the kingdom. *Ruling Chiefs,* 418. Actually, no one knows how many died.
17. Kamakau, *Ruling Chiefs,* 417.
18. Parke, *Personal Reminiscences,* 55.
19. Edgar Henriques, "Nae'a." Unpublished paper. April 1977, DOH.

20. Wyllie to Admiral Thomas, July 27, 1855, AH.
21. Fredrick Anderson, Michael B. Frank, and Kenneth M. Sanderson, eds., *Mark Twain's Notebooks and Journals,* vol. 1, 1855–1873. Berkeley: University of California Press, 1975, 220.
22. *Honolulu Star-Bulletin,* April 1, 1960.
23. Authur A. St. Mouritz, *The Path of the Destroyer, The History of Leprosy in the Hawaiian Islands and Thirty Years Research into the Means by Which It Has Been Spread.* Honolulu: *Honolulu Star-Bulletin,* 1916, 29–30. The origin of the name had to do not with Nae'a but rather with a chief from the suite of Kekauluohi, the premier under Kamehameha III, who was first treated for leprosy by the missionary doctor, Dwight Baldwin. Francis John Halford, *Nine Doctors and God.* Honolulu: University of Hawai'i Press, 1954, 223–224.

5 Courtship and Marriage

1. Russell E. Benton, *Emma Naea Rooke (1836–1885), Beloved Queen of Hawaii.* Lewiston, New York: Edwin Mellen Press, 1988, 13.
2. Lili'uokalani, *Hawaii's Story,* 7.
3. Richards, *The Chiefs' Children's School,* 304.
4. Ibid., 246.
5. Ibid., 235–238.
6. Alexander Liholiho, *The Journal of Prince Alexander Liholiho,* edited by Jacob Adler. Honolulu: University of Hawai'i Press, 1967, 111.
7. Ibid., 121.
8. Ibid., 124.
9. Ibid., 127.
10. Ibid., 50.
11. Varigny, *Fourteen Years in the Sandwich Islands,* 64.
12. Gregg, *The Diaries,* 85.
13. Neilson to mother, March 4 and June 4, 1856, AH.
14. Gregg, *The Diaries,* 85.
15. *Polynesian,* April 13, 1852.
16. Gregg, *The Diaries,* 193.
17. Sylvester K. Stevens, *American Expansion in Hawaii.* Harrisburg, Pennsylvania: Archives Publishing Company, 1945, 63.
18. Ibid., 62.
19. Ibid., 64.
20. *The Friend,* February 1855, 10.
21. David Lawrence Gregg, *Diary,* unpublished, January 24, 1855, AH; and Stevens, *American Expansion in Hawaii,* 72.
22. *The Transactions of the Royal Hawaiian Agricultural Society,* vol. 2, no. 1, 1854, 10.
23. *Roster Legislatures of Hawaii 1841–1918.* Honolulu: The Hawaiian Gazette Co., Ltd., 1918, 59.
24. Liholiho to Emma, September 21, and October 27, 1855, AH.
25. Jones, "Emma-Lani," DOH.
26. Privy Council Record, IX, July 12, 1855, 171, AH.
27. Maude Jones to Miss Adams, December 20, 1937, DOH.
28. Gregg, *The Diaries,* 241.
29. Richards, *Amos S. Cooke and Juliette M. Cooke,* 434.
30. Ibid., 437.
31. Ibid.
32. Desha, "Story of Queen Emma," 6, DOH.
33. Richards, *Amos S. Cooke and Juliette M. Cooke,* 434; and Varigny, *Fourteen Years in the Sandwich Islands,* 64.
34. Emma, *Diary,* May 25, 1854, BM.
35. Ibid., May 28, 1854.

36. As cited in *Honolulu Star-Bulletin,* October 31, 1957.
37. Korn, *Victorian Visitors,* 128.
38. Benton, *Emma Naea Rooke,* 13; and Feher, *Hawaii: A Pictorial History,* 246.
39. Puku'i, et al., *Nānā I Ke Kumu,* vol. 2, 89; and Handy and Puku'i, *Polynesian Family System,* 105.
40. *Ko Hawai'i Pae'āina,* June 23, 1883.
41. Ibid., June 30, 1883.
42. Varigny, *Fourteen Years in the Sandwich Islands,* 64.
43. Wyllie to Admiral Thomas, July 27, 1855, AH.
44. Lili'uokalani, *Hawaii's Story,* 12.
45. Gregg, *The Diaries,* 317.
46. Ibid.
47. *Pacific Commercial Advertiser,* July 2, 1856.
48. *Polynesian,* June 21, 1856.
49. Parke, *Personal Reminiscences,* 85.
50. *Polynesian,* June 21, 1856.
51. Ibid.
52. *Pacific Commercial Advertiser,* November 20, 1856.
53. Gregg, *The Diaries,* 330.
54. Ibid., 362.
55. Dr. Rooke had a second reason to celebrate: the establishment of the Hawaiian Medical Society of which he was a founding member together with Drs. William Hillebrand and Robert McKibbin, physicians who would play important roles in the development of Hawai'i's first public hospital. The other founding physicians were A. Lathrop, R. W. Wood, E. Hoffman, Charles F. Guillou, S. P. Ford, and Thomas Welsd. The society was established on May 18, 1856. *Polynesian,* August 30, 1856.
56. Lucy Peabody, handwritten notes, n.d., DOH.

6 The New Life At Court

1. See "Lei no Emalani" in *The Echo of Our Song, Chants and Poems of the Hawaiians,* translated and edited by Mary Kawena Puku'i and Alfons L. Korn. Honolulu: University of Hawai'i Press, 1973, 75–79.
2. Korn, *Victorian Visitors,* 161.
3. Charles E. Peterson, "The Iolani Palaces and the Barracks," *Journal of the Society of Architectural Historians,* May 1963, Vol. XXII, Number 3, 91–92.
4. Gavan Daws, *Shoal of Time.* Honolulu: University of Hawai'i Press, 1982, 160.
5. *Hawaiian Annual,* 1906, 75.
6. Gregg, *The Diaries,* 333.
7. Korn, *News from Molokai,* 90.
8. Korn, *The Victorian Visitors,* 332
9. Gregg, *The Diaries,* 61.
10. Ibid., 379.
11. Ibid., 333
12. Korn, *Victorian Visitors,* 118.
13. Anya P. Royce, *The Anthropology of Dance.* Bloomington: Indiana University Press, 1977, 123.
14. Gregg, *The Diaries,* 332, 377.
15. *Pacific Commercial Advertiser,* June 7, 1856.
16. Bob Dye, "The Great Chinese Merchants' Ball of 1856," *The Hawaiian Journal of History,* vol. 28 (1994), 69–76.
17. *Pacific Commercial Advertiser,* November 20, 1856.
18. *Ka Hae Hawai'i,* November 19, 1856.
19. Gregg, *The Diaries,* 368.
20. Ibid., 368–369.
21. Ibid., 333.
22. *Pacific Commercial Advertiser,* September 11, 1856.
23. Cited in Richard A. Greer, "Honolulu in 1847," *Hawaiian*

Journal of History, vol. 4, 1970, 71.
24. *Polynesian*, July 21, 1856; and *Pacific Commercial Advertiser*, July 24, 1856.
25. *Pacific Commercial Advertiser*, August 7, 1856.
26. *Polynesian*, August 2, 1856.
27. Kathleen Mellen, *The Gods Depart: A Saga of the Hawaiian Kingdom, 1832–1873*. New York: Hastings House, 1956, 124.
28. *Pacific Commercial Advertiser*, August 7, 1856; and *Ka Hae Hawai'i*, November 12, 1856.
29. Neilson to mother, January 4, 1857; and Emma to Dr. Rooke, August 31, 1856, AH.
30. Ruth M. Tabrah, *Ni'ihau, The Last Hawaiian Island*. Honolulu: Press Pacifica, 1987, 86–87.
31. Neilson to mother, January 4, 1857, AH.
32. Ibid.
33. Emma to Dr. Rooke, August 31, 1856, AH.
34. Emma to Kate Staley, May 1868, as cited in Katherine Shirley Thompson, *Queen Emma and the Bishop*. Honolulu: Daughters of Hawai'i, 1987, 47.
35. Edward Joesting, *Kauai: The Separate Kingdom*. Honolulu: University of Hawai'i Press, 1984, 154–155.
36. Ibid.
37. Neilson to mother, January 4, 1857, AH.
38. *Ka Lae Hawai'i*, November 12, 1856.
39. Neilson to mother, January 4, 1857, AH.
40. Mellen, *The Gods Depart*, 119–121.
41. Gregg, *The Diaries*, 359.
42. Minutes of the Privy Council, November 10, 1856, AH.
43. Gregg, *The Diaries*, 385.
44. Korn, *Victorian Visitors*, 129.
45. Gregg, *The Diaries*, 388.
46. Ibid., 388.
47. Ibid.
48. *Polynesian*, July 25, 1857.

7 The Birth of an Heir

1. *Polynesian*, October 3, 1857.
2. Ibid., October 10, 1857.
3. Gregg, *The Diaries*, 459.
4. Ibid., 458–459.
5. Ibid., 461.
6. Gregg, *Diary*, unpublished, March 7, 1858, AH.
7. Gregg, *The Diaries*, 465.
8. Ibid., 467.
9. Ibid.
10. Ibid.
11. Ibid., 471.
12. Ibid., 470.
13. Ibid., 471–472.
14. Ibid., 472.
15. Ibid., 476.
16. Ibid., 472.
17. Ibid., 472–473.
18. Ibid., 476.
19. Ibid., 477.
20. *Polynesian*, January 23, 1858.
21. Ibid., March 20, 1858.
22. Ibid.
23. Gregg, *The Diaries*, 490.
24. *Polynesian*, May 29, 1858.
25. Varigny, *Fourteen Years in the Sandwich Islands*, 97.
26. Malo, *Hawaiian Antiquities*, 136.
27. Desha, "The Story of Queen Emma," 12, DOH.
28. *Polynesian*, June 17, 1858.
29. Puku'i, et al., *Nānā I ke Kumu*, II, 4.
30. Ibid., 29.
31. *Pacific Commercial Advertiser*, May 26, 1858.
32. Ibid., May 20, 1858.
33. Ibid., May 26, 1858.
34. Minutes of the Privy Council, May 24, 1858, AH.
35. *Polynesian*, June 17, 1858.

36. Ibid., June 12, 1858.
37. *Polynesian,* October 9, 1858. *He Wahine Holo Lio* ("A Woman Horse Rider") is a well-known modern *mele* that tells of Queen Emma's riding style and habits.
38. Ibid., September 11, 1858.
39. Ibid.
40. *Polynesian,* October 23, 1858.
41. Neilson to mother, February 16, 1859, AH.
42. Ibid.
43. *Polynesian,* December 11, 1858.
44. Ibid.
45. *Ka Nūpepa Kū'oko'a,* January 25, 1862.

8 The Queen's Hospital

1. *Pacific Commercial Advertiser,* December 31, 1858.
2. *The Friend,* May 14, 1859.
3. *Polynesian,* May 1, 1858.
4. *Pacific Commercial Advertiser,* April 29, 1858.
5. Kuykendall, 2, 71.
6. *Polynesian,* April 30, 1859.
7. *Pacific Commercial Advertiser,* May 5, 1859.
8. *Ka Hae Hawai'i,* May 11, 1859.
9. *Hawaiian Annual,* 1905–06, 91.
10. *Ka Hae Hawai'i,* May 11, 1859.
11. *Pacific Commercial Advertiser,* May 5, 1859.
12. Ibid., May 5, 1859.
13. The list of subscribers was printed in *The Friend,* May, 1859, 37.
14. Varigny, *Fourteen Years in the Sandwich Islands,* 266.
15. *Polynesian,* May 28, 1859.
16. Ibid.
17. Cabinet Council Minute Book, III, November 1856–May 28, 1859, 137, AH.
18. *Pacific Commercial Advertiser,* December 6, 1860.
19. *Ka Nūpepa Kū'oko'a,* January 25, 1862.
20. *Polynesian,* May 28, 1859.
21. Gregg, *Diary,* unpublished, May 29, 1859, AH.
22. *Polynesian,* May 28, 1859.
23. Some notable *ali'i*—and family-connected—names, such as Ruth Ke'elikōlani, Jane Lahilahi, and Peter Ka'eo, were absent.
24. *Polynesian,* May 28, 1859.
25. Gregg, *Diary,* unpublished, June 6, 1859, AH.
26. Ibid., June 9, 1859.
27. Ibid., June 29, 1859.
28. Record of the Trustees Meetings, 1859–1907, Queen's Hospital, 185.
29. Ibid., 29.
30. Ibid., 26.
31. Ibid., 26–27.
32. Ibid., 28.
33. *Polynesian,* June 23, 1860.
34. The Trustees Minutes, Queen's Hospital, 34.
35. Ibid., 36.
36. Ibid., 11–13, 30–31.
37. Ibid., 15.
38. Ibid., 13–14.
39. Ibid., 14.
40. *Pacific Commercial Advertiser,* August 4, 1859.
41. *Polynesian,* October 22, 1859.
42. The Trustees Minutes, Queen's Hospital, 45.
43. The first trained nurse at Queen's was Mrs. Mary Adams who was hired in 1886.
44. *Polynesian,* January 14, 1860.
45. *Pacific Commercial Advertiser,* January 26, 1860.
46. Queen's Hospital Annual Report 1873.
47. *Pacific Commercial Advertiser,* August 4, 1859.
48. Ibid.
49. *Polynesian,* June 23, 1860 and June 29, 1861.

50. Kamakau, *Ruling Chiefs,* 292; and Sterling and Summers, *Sites of Oahu,* 309. Also, Mary Kawena Puku'i, Samuel H. Elbert, and Esther T. Mookini, *Place Names of Hawai'i.* Honolulu: University Press of Hawai'i, 1974, 145.
51. The Trustees Minutes, Queen's Hospital, 46.
52. *Polynesian,* June 23, 1860.
53. The Trustees Minutes, Queen's Hospital, 44–45.
54. *Pacific Commercial Advertiser,* January 17, 1861.
55. The Trustees Minutes, Queen's Hospital, 42–43.
56. Ibid., 48.
57. *Polynesian,* May 28, 1859.
58. Ibid., November 12, 1859; and Gregg, *Diary,* unpublished, November 9, 1859, AH.
59. *Polynesian,* November 24, 1860.
60. For example, an *"aha'aina loko-maika'i"* or fund-raising banquet was held on April 19, 1862. It generated $3,000 of which $2,000 went to the hospital. *Ka Nūpepa Kū'oko'a,* April 26, 1862.
61. The Trustees Minutes, Queen's Hospital, 39.
62. *Pacific Commercial Advertiser,* August 4, 1859.
63. *Polynesian,* May 26, 1860.
64. The Trustees Minutes, Queen's Hospital, 56.
65. *Pacific Commercial Advertiser,* December 6, 1860.
66. *Polynesian,* July 14, 1860.
67. *Pacific Commercial Advertiser,* July 19, 1860.
68. *The Friend,* August 1, 1860, 58.
69. *Pacific Commercial Advertiser,* December 6, 1860.
70. Theodore C. Heuck, "Translations of Letters, 1850–1866," AH.

9 The Neilson Ordeal

1. Pratt, "A Brief Sketch of the Life of Queen Emma Kaleleokalani," DOH.
2. Ibid.
3. Kuykendall, *The Hawaiian Kingdom,* vol. 2, 86.
4. Neilson to Bleecker Neilson, October 25, 1859, AH. Lady Franklin's account of this part of the incident says that the king first went to the queen's apartment and "overwhelmed her with the most disgraceful epithets." Her account should be read with caution because it contains several errors of both fact and interpretation. See Korn, *Victorian Visitors,* 30.
5. Neilson to Bleecker Neilson, October 25, 1859, AH.
6. Ibid.
7. Varigny, *Fourteen Years in the Sandwich Islands,* 101.
8. Kuykendall, *The Hawaiian Kingdom,* vol. 2, 152; and *Polynesian,* September 10, 1859. Also, Charles S. Meyer, *Meyer and Molokai,* ed., Yolla Forbes. Alden, Iowa: Graphi-Agri Business Ltd., 1982, 26.
9. Kamehameha V to Privy Council, September 16, 1859, AH.
10. Wyllie to Kamehameha IV, September 17, 1859, AH.
11. Kamehameha IV to Wyllie, September 19, 1859, AH.
12. *Pacific Commercial Advertiser,* September 24, 1859.
13. Wyllie to Kamehameha VI, September 24, 1859, AH.
14. Foreign Office, Ministerial Conference, 1856–1863, vol. 2, AH.
15. Kamehameha IV to Wyllie, September 26, 1859.
16. Wyllie to Kamehameha IV, September 27, 1859.

17. Liliʻuokalani made essentially the same argument but from a Hawaiian point of view. She stated: "There were causes which were apparent to any of our people for something very like righteous anger on the part of the king. His Majesty was trying to make us each and all happy; yet even during moments of realization, undue familiarity, absence of etiquette, rudeness, or any other form which implied or suggested disrespect to royalty in any manner whatsoever, would never be tolerated by any one of the native chiefs of the Hawaiian people. To allow any such breach of good manners to pass unnoticed would be looked upon by his own retainers as belittling to him, and they would be the first to demand the punishment of the offender." *Hawaii's Story,* 19.
18. *Pacific Commercial Advertiser,* September 18, 1859.
19. As cited in Mellen, *The Gods Depart,* 170–171.
20. *Polynesian,* October 1, 1859.
21. Kuykendall, *The Hawaiian Kingdom,* vol. 2, 86; and Liliʻuokalani, *Hawaii's Story,* 19.
22. Cabinet Council 1856–1863, Cabinet Council Meeting, 11 a.m., Oct. 1, 1859.
23. *Polynesian,* October 8, 1859.
24. Kamehameha IV to Neilson, October 12, 1859, AH. The king always misspelled the name by putting the "i" before the "e".
25. Varigny, *Fourteen Years in the Sandwich Islands,* 101.
26. Liliʻuokalani, *Hawaii's Story,* 19.
27. Varigny, *Fourteen Years in the Sandwich Islands,* 101.
28. Emma to Kamehameha IV, November 15, 1859, AH.
29. Kamehameha IV to Webster, October 11, 1859, AH.
30. Emma to Kamehameha IV, November 16, 1859, AH.
31. *The Friend,* 1859.
32. Kamehameha IV to Webster, November 1859, AH.
33. Kamehameha IV to Emma, November 11, 1859, AH.

10 The Flight of the Heavenly Chief

1. *Pacific Commercial Advertiser,* May 26, 1859.
2. *Honolulu,* July 1, 1858.
3. Jane "Jennie" Stillman Smythe.
4. Liliʻuokalani, *Hawaii's Story,* 18.
5. Mellen, *The Gods Depart,* 158.
6. Liliʻuokalani, *Hawaii's Story,* 18.
7. Emma to Liholiho, November 15, 1859, AH.
8. Emma to Liholiho, August, no date, 1859, AH.
9. Meiric Dutton, *Ka Haku o Hawaii, His Royal Highness the Prince of Hawaii,* unpaginated. Honolulu: Paradise of the Pacific Press, 1915.
10. Korn, *Victorian Visitors,* 137–138.
11. "A Royal Holiday in Kauai," *Hawaiian Chronicle,* March 1969, 5. See also "Queen Emma on Kauai," handwritten paper, DOH.
12. Korn, *Victorian Visitors,* 139–140.
13. *Hawaiian Chronicle,* March 1969, 5.
14. Ibid.
15. Dutton, *Ka Haku o Hawaii.*
16. Allen, *Kalakaua,* 28.
17. Peterson, *Notable Women of Hawaii,* 204.
18. *Hawaiian Chronicle,* March 1969, 4.
19. *Pacific Commercial Advertiser,* July 25, 1861.

20. Edwin P. Hoyt. *Davies: The Inside Story of a British-American Family in the Pacific and Its Business Enterprises.* Honolulu: Topgallant Publishing Company, 1983, 60.
21. Korn, *Victorian Visitors,* 31–32.
22. Ibid., 33.
23. Ibid., 89.
24. Ibid., 110.
25. Ibid., 90.
26. Ibid., 34.
27. Ibid., 92.
28. Ibid.
29. Ibid., 128.
30. Ibid.
31. Ibid., 86.
32. Ibid., 87.
33. *Pacific Commercial Advertiser,* June 27, 1861.
34. Interior Department Lands, March 24, 1865, and April 25, 1866, AH.
35. *Polynesian,* September 12, 1861.
36. Rhoda Hackler, "Albert Edward Kauikeaouli Leiopapa a Kamehameha, Prince of Hawai'i," *Hawaiian Journal of History,* vol. 26, 1992, 26.
37. Ibid., 25.
38. Ibid., 27
39. Jane K. Smythe, "Queen Emma, The Person," *Paradise of the Pacific,* February 1931, 5–6.
40. Ibid.
41. Emma to Mary Allen, October 24, 1861, AH.
42. Ibid.
43. Ibid.
44. Emma to Mary Allen, December 20, 1861, AH.
45. *Pacific Commercial Advertiser,* January 23, 1862.
46. Elizabeth Waldron, *Liholiho and Emma, King Kamehameha IV and his Queen.* Honolulu: Daughters of Hawai'i, 1986, 15.
47. Curtis Piehu Iaukea, "Reminiscences of the Court of Kamehameha IV and Queen Emma," Papers of the Hawaiian Historical Society, No. 17, 18.
48. Hackler, "Albert Edward . . . ," 29.
49. Ibid., 29–30.
50. Ibid., 30.
51. Ibid., 33.
52. Ibid.
53. *Pacific Commercial Advertiser,* August 28, 1862, and September 1, 1862.
54. Hackler, "Albert Edward . . . ," 34.
55. Kuykendall, *The Hawaiian Kingdom,* vol. 2, 95.
56. Hackler, "Albert Edward . . . ," 34–35.
57. Ibid., 36.
58. Lili'uokalani, *Hawaii's Story,* 19–20.
59. C. R. Bennett, "The Reign of Kamehameha IV—Alexander Liholiho." *Queen's Hospital Bulletin,* vol. XII, nos. 1–6 (January 1936), 16.
60. Alfred D. Morris, "The Death of the Prince of Hawai'i: A Retrospective Diagnosis," *Hawaiian Journal of History,* vol. 28, 1994, 80–81.
61. Bennett, "The Reign of Kamehameha IV," 16.
62. *Pacific Commercial Advertiser,* August 28, 1862.
63. Hackler, "Albert Edward . . . ," 39.
64. *Pacific Commercial Advertiser,* September 9, 1862.
65. Hackler, "Albert Edward . . . ," 40–41.
66. Kaleleokalani may also be translated as "The Flight of the Heavenly Chief." For further commentary on Hawaiian names, see John S. Charlot, *The Chanting Universe: Hawaiian Religious Cul-*

ture. Hong Kong: Emphasis International, 1979, 96.
67. *Ka Hōkū o ka Pākipika,* August–September, 1862.

11 Establishment of the Anglican Church in Hawai'i

1. Kuykendall, *The Hawaiian Kingdom,* vol. 2, 86.
2. Rianna M. Williams, *From Royal Garden to Gothic Splendor, The History of St. Andrew's Cathedral.* Honolulu: St. Andrew's Cathedral, 1996, 8.
3. Liholiho, *The Journal,* 88.
4. Ibid., 92.
5. Ibid., 97.
6. Ibid., 109.
7. Korn, *Victorian Visitors,* 87.
8. Kuykendall, *The Hawaiian Kingdom,* vol. 1, 346–347; and Henry B. Restarick, *Hawaii, 1778–1920 from the Viewpoint of a Bishop.* Honolulu: Paradise of the Pacific, 1942, 55–60.
9. Kuykendall, *The Hawaiian Kingdom,* vol. 2, 92.
10. *Polynesian,* June 5, 1858.
11. *Pacific Commercial Advertiser,* December 15, 1859.
12. Kuykendall, *The Hawaiian Kingdom,* vol. 2, 85.
13. Ibid., 87.
14. Ibid.
15. Ibid., 88.
16. *Pacific Commercial Advertiser,* December 15, 1859.
17. Manley Hopkins, *Hawaii: The Past, Present, and Future of Its Island Kingdom.* London: Longman, 1862, 342.
18. Kuykendall, *The Hawaiian Kingdom,* vol. 2, 89.
19. Ibid.
20. Ibid.
21. *Pacific Commercial Advertiser,* September 5, 1861.
22. Judd, *Honolulu: Sketches of Life in the Hawaiian Islands from 1828 to 1861,* 199.
23. Kuykendall, *The Hawaiian Kingdom,* vol. 2, 93.
24. Kamehameha IV to William Webster, September, 1861, AH.
25. Wyllie to William Miller, December 1, 1857, cited in Kuykendall, *The Hawaiian Kingdom,* vol. 2, 94.
26. Korn, *Victorian Visitors,* 159.
27. Ibid., 186.
28. Williams, *From Royal Garden to Gothic Splendor,* 30.
29. *Pacific Commercial Advertiser,* November 5, 1862.
30. Thomas N. Staley, *Five Years' Church Work in the Kingdom of Hawaii.* London: Rivingtons, 1868, 26–28.
31. Ibid., 23.
32. Restarick, *Hawaii, 1778–1920,* 63.
33. Ibid., 64.
34. Hopkins, *Hawaii: Past, Present, and Future of Its Island Kingdom.* 428–431.
35. Ibid., 431–432.
36. Williams, *From Royal Garden to Gothic Splendor,* 12.
37. As cited in Mildred E. Staley, "The Story of Iolani School," *Hawaiian Church Chronicle,* vol. 22, no. 4, June 1933, 4.
38. *Pacific Commercial Advertiser,* April 2, 1863.
39. Mildred E. Staley, ed., "Bishop Staley's Journal," April 15, 1863, cited in "Bishop Staley's Journal," *Hawaiian Church Chronicle,* vol. XXIV, March 1934, 6.
40. *Polynesian,* November 8, 1862.
41. Ernest G. Villers, "A History of Iolani School," ME thesis, University of Hawai'i, 1940, 30–32.
42. Staley, "Bishop Staley's Journal," April 15, 1863.

43. Monica Mary Heyes, "The History of St. Andrew's Priory, 1867–1918," MA thesis, University of Hawai'i, 1951, 39.

12 Celebrations Amidst the Sick

1. Jarves, *History of the Hawaiian Islands,* 463.
2. *Pacific Commercial Advertiser,* January 1, 1863.
3. Roger Bye, *How Christmas Came to Hawai'i.* Honolulu: Hawaiian Dredging Company, 1951, 19.
4. *Pacific Commercial Advertiser,* January 1, 1863.
5. Jarves, *History of the Hawaiian Islands,* 463–464.
6. Ibid., 454.
7. Ibid.
8. *Pacific Commercial Advertiser,* January 1, 1863.
9. *Polynesian,* January 3, 1863.
10. *Pacific Commercial Advertiser,* January 8, 1863.
11. Ibid., January 7, 1863.
12. *Ka Hōkū o ka Pākipika,* February 12, 1863.
13. Ibid., February, 5, 1863.
14. *Ka Nūpepa Kū'oko'a,* February 14, 1863.
15. *Ka Hōkū o ka Pākipika,* February 12, 1863.
16. Jarves, *History of the Hawaiian Islands,* 466.
17. Mildred Staley, "A Great Woman, Queen Emma Kaleleonālani of Hawaii," paper presented to the Daughters of Hawai'i, May 15, 1940, 6, DOH.
18. *Ka Hōkū o ka Pākipika,* February 12, 1863.
19. Staley, "A Great Woman, Queen Emma Kaleleonālani of Hawaii," 5, DOH.
20. *Pacific Commercial Advertiser,* February 5, 1863.
21. Jarves, *History of the Hawaiian Islands,* 466.
22. *Pacific Commercial Advertiser,* April 18, 1863.
23. Ibid., April 23, 1863.
24. *Polynesian,* April 18, 1863.
25. *Ka Nūpepa Kū'oko'a,* April 25, 1863.
26. Ibid., August 22, 1863.

13 Oh, My Husband

1. *Polynesian,* February 14, 1863.
2. *Pacific Commercial Advertiser,* February 12, 1863.
3. Jarves, *History of the Hawaiian Islands,* 438–439.
4. Ibid., 439–440.
5. *Polynesian,* March 14, 1863.
6. Emma to Kapi'olani, March 19, 1863, AH.
7. Allen, *Kalakaua,* 32–33.
8. *Polynesian,* April 18, 1863.
9. Lot to Nahaolelua, April 16, 1863, AH.
10. *Pacific Commercial Advertiser,* April 30, 1863.
11. Staley, *Five Years' Church Work in the Kingdom of Hawai'i,* 29–33.
12. *Ka Nūpepa Kū'okoa,* November 28, 1863.
13. Grace to Emma, March 31, 1863, AH.
14. *Pacific Commercial Advertiser,* October 17, 1861.
15. George S. Kanahele, *Waikīkī: 100 B.C. to 1900 A.D.: An Untold Story.* Honolulu: University of Hawai'i Press, 1995, 121–122.
16. Korn, *Victorian Visitors,* 194.
17. Jarves, *History of the Hawaiian Islands,* 436.
18. Ibid., 437.
19. Staley, *Five Years' Church Work in the Kingdom of Hawai'i,* 33.
20. Jarves, *History of the Hawaiian Islands,* 437.

21. Varigny, *Fourteen Years in the Sandwich Islands,* 123.
22. Staley, *Five Years' Church Work in the Kingdom of Hawai'i,* 32.
23. *Pacific Commercial Advertiser,* December 13, 1863.
24. Staley, *Five Years' Church Work in the Kingdom of Hawai'i,* 30; and Jarves, *History of the Hawaiian Islands,* 442–443. The time of death was 9:15 a.m., according to the *Pacific Commercial Advertiser,* December 3, 1863 and *Ka Nūpepa Kū'oko'a,* December 5, 1863.
25. Staley, *Five Years' Church Work in the Kingdom of Hawai'i,* 31.
26. Privy Council Book, November 30, 1863, and December 2, 1863, AH.
27. Varigny, *Fourteen Years in the Sandwich Islands,* 128.
28. Privy Council Book, December 3, 1863, AH.
29. Staley, *Five Years' Church Work in the Kingdom of Hawai'i,* 32. Several of the queen's Anglican lady friends scarcely left her side during this long vigil.
30. *Polynesian,* February 6, 1864.
31. *Pacific Commercial Advertiser,* November 4, 1865.
32. Korn, *Victorian Visitors,* 192.
33. *Hawaiian Gazette,* October 7, 1874.
34. *Polynesian,* December 5, 1863.
35. *Pacific Commercial Advertiser,* December 3, 1863.
36. *Ka Nūpepa Kū'oko'a,* January 2, 1864. Translated by Rubellite Johnson.

14 New Love, Old Grief

1. *Pacific Commercial Advertiser,* February 27, 1864.
2. Kuykendall, *The Hawaiian Kingdom,* vol. 2, 153.
3. *Polynesian,* May 24, 1856.
4. *Pacific Commercial Advertiser,* May 14, 1864.
5. Varigny, *Fourteen Years in the Sandwich Islands,* 127.
6. *Pacific Commercial Advertiser,* January 21, 1865.
7. Korn, *Victorian Visitors,* 192.
8. *Pacific Commercial Advertiser,* April 11, 1865.
9. Kanahele, *Pauahi,* 104–105.
10. Varigny, *Fourteen Years in the Sandwich Islands,* 199.
11. William Bliss, *Paradise in the Pacific: A Book of Travel, Adventure, and Facts.* New York: Sheldon, 1873, 70.
12. Rhoda E. A. Hackler, "My Dear Friend: Letters of Queen Victoria and Queen Emma." *Hawaiian Journal of History,* vol. 22, 1988, 109.
13. Varigny, *Fourteen Years in the Sandwich Islands,* 194.
14. Kuykendall, *The Hawaiian Kindgom,* vol. 2, 201.
15. Ibid.
16. Korn, *Victorian Visitors,* 193.
17. As cited in Korn, *Victorian Visitors,* 193.
18. Ibid., 196.
19. Emma to Lady Franklin, April 30, 1864, AH.
20. As cited in Korn, *Victorian Visitors,* 197.
21. *Pacific Commercial Advertiser,* November 5, 1864.
22. Merze Tate, *The United States and the Hawaiian Kingdom: A Political History.* Westport, Conn.: Greenwood Press, 1980, 28–29.
23. *Pacific Commercial Advertiser,* December 17, 1864.

15 Travels Abroad

1. *Pacific Commercial Advertiser,* May 13, 1865.
2. *Ke Au 'Oko'a,* September 1, 1865.

3. Williams, *From Royal Garden to Gothic Splendor,* 32.
4. Emma to Kamehameha V, June 7, 1865, AH.
5. As cited in the *London Times,* June 15, 1865.
6. Emma to Kamehameha V, June 29, 1865, AH.
7. Emma, *Diary,* June 22, 1865, BM.
8. *London Times,* July 15, 1865.
9. Korn, *Victorian Visitors,* 204–205.
10. Emma, *Diary,* July 17, 1865, BM.
11. Ibid.
12. Emma, *Diary,* July 18, 1865, BM.
13. Ibid., July 24, 1865, BM.
14. Ibid., August 7, 1865, BM.
15. Ibid., July 18, 1865, BM.
16. Ibid., July 24, 1865, BM.
17. Korn, *Victorian Visitors,* 229.
18. Ibid.
19. Emma, *Diary,* July 23, 1865, BM.
20. Korn, *Victorian Visitors,* 254. Queen Emma may have also visited an asylum for the blind.
21. *Illustrated London News,* August 12, 1865.
22. As reprinted in *The Friend,* June 1, 1866, 41–44.
23. As cited in Thompson, *Queen Emma and the Bishop,* 17. The queen's itinerary was of great interest to her subjects, and the Hawaiian-language newspapers followed her movements with regular monthly reports. See *Ke Au 'Oko'a* July 17, 31, August 21, September 18, 25, October 23, November 20, 1865, and January 8, 1866.
24. Restarick, *Hawaii, 1778–1920,* 257.
25. *Wells Journal,* November 4, 1865.
26. Ibid.
27. *Wells Journal,* November 4, 1865; and Restarick, *Hawaii, 1778–1920,* 259.
28. Hackler, *The Cathedral Church of Saint Andrew,* 6; and Restarick, *Hawaii, 1778–1920,* 260.
29. Williams, *From Royal Garden to Gothic Splendor,* 32.
30. Korn, *Victorian Visitors,* 234.
31. Ibid.
32. Emma, *Diary,* July 30, 1865, BM.
33. Korn, *Victorian Visitors,* 224–228.
34. Emma, *Diary,* July 26, 1865, BM.
35. Ibid., August 9, 1865.
36. Korn, *Victorian Visitors,* 235.
37. Restarick, *Hawaii, 1778–1920,* 259.
38. Emma, *Diary,* July 27, 1865, BM.
39. Ibid., July 22, 1865.
40. Korn, *Victorian Visitors,* 238.
41. Lou Taylor, *Mourning Dress: A Costume and Social History.* Boston: G. Allen and Unwin, 1983, 136, 141–146.
42. Korn, *Victorian Visitors,* 241.
43. Emma to Kamehameha V, September 9, 1865, AH.
44. As cited in Korn, *Victorian Visitors,* 243.
45. Korn, *Victorian Visitors,* 248.
46. Ibid. An unflattering account of the queen's visit is given by Robert B. Martin in his biography of Tennyson. He described Emma as the "young black queen of the Sandwich Islands," who "was pretty and good-natured, but she was an awkward guest." She was "so indolent that she would sometimes get up in the middle of dinner to go and rest on a sofa." Martin described the Reverend Hoapili as one "whose womanizing was a constant embarrassment, as was his wish to fling off his clothes and bathe in the Serpentine." Martin also described Hoapili's wife as being "six feet tall with a black moustache, stupid, and even more tor-

pid

pid than her mistress." *Tennyson, the Unquiet Heart.* Oxford: Oxford University Press, 1980, 463.

47. Emma to Lady Franklin, December 5, 1865, AH.
48. Dispatch No. 1,044 to Secretary of State, William H. Seward, from Charles F. Adams, Sep 14, 1865, as cited in *Hawaiian Gazette,* March 25, 1868.
49. Hopkins to Wyllie, September 23, 1865, AH.
50. Kuykendall, *The Hawaiian Kingdom,* vol. 2, 205–206.
51. Korn, *Victorian Visitors,* 254.
52. Emma to Kamehameha V, December 4, 1865, AH.
53. Emma to Kapo, January 13, 1866, AH.
54. Emma to Kamehameha V, December 9, 1865, AH.
55. Emma to Carry Poor, December 11, 1865, AH.
56. Emma to Kamehameha V, December 9, 1865, AH.
57. Emma to Kahanawai, February 21, 1866, AH.
58. Emma to Kamehameha V, December 9, 1865, AH.
59. Emma to Kapo, January 13, 1866, AH.
60. Ibid.
61. Emma to Peter Ka'eo, February 18, 1866, AH.
62. Emma to Lady Devon, January 1, 1866, AH.
63. *Pacific Commercial Advertiser,* February 3, 1866.
64. Emma to Kamehameha V, January 26, 1866, AH.
65. Kamehameha V to Emma, February 28, 1866, AH.
66. Ibid., May 24, 1866.
67. Legislative Journal, 1866 Session, 92–93.
68. Emma, *Diary,* January 1, 1866, BM.
69. Ibid., January 2, 1866.
70. Ibid., January 3, 1866.
71. Ibid., January 6, 1866.
72. Ibid., January 20, 1866.
73. Emma to Kamehameha V, February 14, 1866, AH.
74. Ibid.
75. Emma to Peter, February 18, 1866, AH.
76. Emma to Kahanawai, February 21, 1866, AH.
77. Emma to David Kalākaua, January 20, 1866, AH.
78. Korn, *Victorian Visitors,* 274.
79. As cited in Korn, *Victorian Visitors,* 272.
80. Korn, *Victorian Visitors,* 273.
81. Ibid.
82. Emma, *Diary,* April 3, 1866, BM.
83. Emma to Bishop Staley, April 6, 1866, AH.
84. Cited in Andrew F. Muir, "William Hoapili Kaauwai: A Hawaiian in Holy Orders," *Sixty-first Annual Report of the Hawaiian Historical Society for the Year 1952* (1953), 7.
85. Ibid., 10.
86. Emma, *Diary,* April 6, 1866, BM.
87. Niklaus R. Schweizer, *Hawai'i and the German Speaking Peoples.* Honolulu: Topgallant, 1982, 141.
88. Emma, *Diary,* May 23, 1866, BM.
89. *Journal de Genève,* May 27, 1866.
90. Emma, *Diary,* May 21, 1866, BM.
91. Korn, *Victorian Visitors,* 273.
92. Emma, *Diary,* June 2, 1866, BM.
93. *Pacific Commercial Advertiser,* June 2, 1866.
94. Nahaolelua to Emma, June 2, 1866, AH.
95. Kamehameha V to Emma, October 23, 1865, AH.
96. Ibid.
97. Kamehameha V to Emma, June 15, 1866, AH.
98. Emma to Kamehameha V, June 9, 1866, AH.

99. *Hawaiian Historical Society, Annual Report*, 1927, 25.
100. *Hawaiian Gazette*, August 11, 1866.
101. Emma, *Diary*, July 2, 1866, BM.
102. Ibid., July 4, 1866.
103. Ibid., July 23, 1866.
104. Ibid., July 4, 1866.
105. Ibid., July 16, 1866.
106. Ibid., July 17, 1866.
107. Ibid., July 23, 1866.
108. Williams, *From Royal Garden to Gothic Splendor*, 13.
109. Emma, *Diary*, July 24, 1866, BM.
110. Ibid., July 25, 1866.
111. Ibid., July 26, 1866.
112. Ibid., July 28, 1866.
113. Ibid., July 30, 1866.
114. Kamehameha V to Emma, May 24, 1866, AH.
115. *New York Times*, August 9, 1866.
116. *The Friend*, November, 1866, 101.
117. *New York Times*, August 9, 1866.
118. Ibid.
119. Ibid.
120. *New York World*, August 13, 1866, as cited in the *Pacific Commercial Advertiser*, October 6, 1866.
121. Odell to Charles de Varigny, August 11, 1866, AH.
122. *New York Times*, August 16, 1866.
123. Thomas Lately, *The First President Johnson*. New York: William Morrow and Company, 1968, 478–479.
124. *Pacific Commercial Advertiser*, October 13, 1866.
125. Benjamin Pitman to Emma, January 18, 1867, AH.
126. *Hawaiian Gazette*, October 20, 1866.
127. Kuykendall, *The Hawaiian Kingdom*, vol. 2, 205.
128. *Hawaiian Gazette*, October 27, 1866.

16 The Anglican Visionary

1. Kamehameha V to Emma, October 18, 1866, AH.
2. Emma to Kamehameha V, October 29, 1866, AH.
3. Kamehameha V to Emma, December 18, 1866, AH.
4. Charles Victor Crosnier de Varigny, "Emma Reine des Iles Havai," *Revue des Deux Mondes* (Paris), LXXII (1885), 101. Note: The words "he loved the queen" or "*il aimait la reine*" appear only in this article and not in Varigny's book, in either the original French version or its English translation.
5. *Hawaiian Gazette*, January 23, 1867.
6. Ibid., 102.
7. *Hawaiian Gazette*, March 6, 1867.
8. Ibid.
9. Ibid.
10. Restarick, *Hawaii, 1778–1920*, 260.
11. Ibid., 280.
12. Emma to Kamehameha V, May 15, 1867, AH.
13. Heyes, "The History of St. Andrew's Priory," 44.
14. Ibid., 47.
15. Ibid., 49.
16. Ibid., 54.
17. Ibid., 49.
18. Emma to Kamehameha V, June 5, 1867, AH.
19. Heyes, "The History of St. Andrew's Priory," 65.
20. Restarick, *Hawaii, 1778–1920*, 129.
21. Heyes, "The History of St. Andrew's Priory," 71.
22. Ibid. Many of the Sisters had worked with Florence Nightingale in the Crimean war of 1856–57. Sister Beatrice and Mother Sellon were both close friends of

the "founder of modern nursing." Mildred E. Staley, *A Tapestry of Memories, An Autobiography.* Hilo, Hawai'i: The *Hilo Tribune Herald,* 1944, 138.

23. Heyes, "The History of St. Andrew's Priory," 144.
24. Ibid., 72.
25. Ibid., 73.
26. Staley, *Five Years' Church Work in the Kingdom of Hawai'i,* 56.
27. Heyes, "The History of St. Andrew's Priory," 40.
28. Staley, *Five Years' Church Work in the Kingdom of Hawai'i,* 58.
29. Bird, *Six Months in the Sandwich Islands,* 148–149.
30. Heyes, "The History of St. Andrew's Priory," 40.
31. January 9, 1866, AH.
32. Bird, *Six Months in the Sandwich Islands,* 149–150.
33. As cited in Staley, "A Great Woman, Queen Emma Kaleleonalani," DOH.
34. Staley, *Five Years' Church Work in the Kingdom of Hawai'i,* 62–63.
35. Ibid., 60–61.
36. Ibid., 79.
37. *Ke Au 'Oko'a,* April 15, 1867.
38. Staley, *Five Years' Church Work in the Kingdom of Hawai'i,* 76.
39. Kalākaua may have had in mind the complaint by the newspaper *Ka Nūpepa Kū'oko'a* (September 15, 1866) that Hawaiians were inattentive and disrespectful in church.
40. Personal communication from Jean Greenwell, Christ Church (Kealakekua, Hawai'i), based on Archives of St. Augustine's Missionary College, Canterbury, Kent, England. Letter dated February 28, 1998.
41. Restarick, *Hawaii, 1778–1920,* 366–367.
42. Williamson to the Secretary of the Society for the Propagation of the Gospel, May 21, 1867, Kona Historical Society.
43. Ibid.
44. Parke, *Personal Reminiscences,* 99–102.
45. Emma to Kamehameha V, January 29, 1868, AH.
46. Restarick, *Hawaii, 1778–1920,* 366–367.
47. Amoe Ha'alelea to Emma, April 6, 1868, AH.
48. *Hawaiian Gazette,* May 6, 1868.
49. Heyes, "The History of St. Andrew's Priory," 54.
50. Emma to Kamehameha V, June 4, 1867, AH.
51. Kuykendall, *The Hawaiian Kingdom,* vol. 2, 221. British Commissioner Wodehouse must have placed some stock in what the queen said because he immediately reported this conversation to the Foreign Office in London. Coincidentally, the queen had only recently rented her mother's home to Wodehouse and his family at a time when a severe housing shortage existed in Honolulu.
52. As cited in Kuykendall, *The Hawaiian Kingdom,* vol. 2, 227.
53. Emma to Kamehameha V, January 9, 1868, AH.
54. Ibid.
55. Restarick, *Hawaii, 1778–1920,* 120–121; and Heyes, "The History of St. Andrew's Priory," 14–16.
56. Staley, *Five Years' Church Work in the Kingdom of Hawai'i,* 85.
57. Kuykendall, *The Hawaiian Kingdom,* vol. 2, 98.
58. Staley, *Five Years' Church Work in the Kingdom of Hawai'i,* 91.
59. Ibid., 93.

60. Emma to Bishop Staley, July 1868, as cited in Thompson, *Queen Emma and the Bishop*, 48.
61. Emma to Mrs. Staley, May 1868, as cited in Thompson, *Queen Emma and the Bishop*, 47.
62. Emma to Bishop Staley, October 1868, as cited in Thompson, *Queen Emma and the Bishop*, 49.
63. As cited in Restarick, *Hawaii, 1778–1920*, 120.
64. *Pacific Commercial Advertiser*, January 1, 1870.
65. Kuykendall, *The Hawaiian Kingdom*, vol. 2, 98.
66. Emma to Kamehameha V, April 7, 1871, AH.
67. Ibid., June 4, 1867.
68. *Hawaiian Gazette*, July 22, 1868, AH.
69. Ibid., March 25, 1868.
70. *Pacific Commercial Advertiser*, July 24, 1869.
71. Emma to Lucy Peabody, August 21, 1869, Henriques Collection, BM.
72. *Pacific Commercial Advertiser*, August 4, 1869.
73. Emma to Lucy Peabody, August 9, 1869, Henriques Collection, BM.
74. Liliʻuokalani, *Hawaii's Story*, 33.
75. *Hawaiian Gazette*, July 24, 1869.
76. *Pacific Commercial Advertiser*, August 7, 1869.
77. Liliʻuokalani, *Hawaii's Story*, 34.

17 Lāwaʻi Adventures

1. Probate #1222, Will of Dr. Thomas C. B. Rooke, May 1858, AH.
2. *Honolulu Star-Bulletin*, January 17, 1935. Estimates of Lāwaʻi's acreage vary from 2,100 to 4,200 acres. The "Certificate of the Boundaries of the Land of Lawai," which was filed by John Dominis for Queen Emma on July 8, 1873, failed to include any acreage information. Certificate #10, Bureau of Conveyances, State of Hawaiʻi, LCA 43, 3414, 3416, 3417, 3612, 9188.
3. Dated September 13, 1851.
4. Bureau of Conveyances Liber 32, 5.
5. Emma to Kamehameha V, December 31, 1870, AH.
6. Ibid.
7. Daniel Dole to Dr. Baldwin, January 2, 1871, HMCS.
8. David Forbes, *Queen Emma and Lawai*. Kauaʻi Historical Society, April 1970, 5.
9. The Alakaʻi Swamp was not Queen Emma's first strenuous hike according to a chant that tells of her climb up Mauna Kea on the Island of Hawaiʻi in the early 1860s. In fact, because of the queen's fondness for mountain climbing, she was affectionately called *Ke Aliʻi Piʻi Kuahiwi* or the Mountain Climbing Chiefess.
10. Eric Knudsen, "Queen Emma Goes to Alakai Swamp," paper read at the Twenty-sixth Annual Meeting of the Kauaʻi Historical Society, May 27, 1940, 1, KHS.
11. *Ke Au ʻOkoʻa*, February 16, 1871.
12. Knudsen, "Queen Emma Goes to Alakai Swamp," 2–3.
13. Emma to Kamehameha V, March 11, 1871, AH.
14. Kathryn C. Hulme, "The Timeless Kauai Swamp," *Atlantic Monthly*, January, 1965, 69.
15. Knudsen, "Queen Emma Goes to Alakai Swamp," 3.
16. *Ke Au ʻOkoʻa*, February 16, 1871.
17. Ibid.
18. Emma to Fanny, January 28, 1871, AH. Today the Alakaʻi Swamp trail is not as physically challenging as

it was in Queen Emma's day. Although the six-and-one-half-mile hike is still rated as "strenuous," a boardwalk has been constructed through the swamp, making it a safe and easy jaunt.

19. Emma to Kamehameha V, March 11, 1871, AH.
20. Kamehameha V to Emma, February 11, 1871, AH.
21. Nahaolelua to Emma, March 16, 1871, AH.
22. Chant Collection, BM.
23. Emma to Fanny, February 1, 1871, AH.
24. Ibid.
25. *Ke Au 'Oko'a,* January 26, 1871.
26. Emma to Fanny, February 1, 1871, AH.
27. Emma to Elizabeth Pratt, February 15, 1871, AH.
28. Fanny to Emma, April 2, 1871, AH.
29. Emma to Kamehameha V, February 14, 1871, AH.
30. Emma to Fanny, February 13, 1871, AH.
31. Emma to Kamehameha V, March 11, 1871, AH.
32. Emma to Fanny, March 11, 1871, AH.
33. Forbes, *Queen Emma and Lawai,* 9.
34. Emma to Fanny, March 6,1871, AH.
35. Horace F. Clay, and James C. Hubbard, *The Hawai'i Garden, Tropical Exotics.* Honolulu: University of Hawai'i Press, 1977, 126.
36. Emma to Sarah Weed, March 29, 1871, AH.
37. Forbes, *Queen Emma and Lawai,* 9.
38. *Honolulu Star-Bulletin,* January 17, 1935.
39. Emma to Williamson, March 25, 1869, AH.
40. Linda Paik Moriarty, *Ni'ihau Shell Leis.* Honolulu: University of Hawai'i Press, 1986, 18.
41. Emma to Fanny, February 15, 1871, AH.
42. Ibid., March 6, 1871.
43. Ibid., February 15, 1871.
44. Ibid., March 6, 1871.
45. Irving Jenkins, *The Hawaiian Calabash.* Honolulu: Editions Limited, 1989, 77.
46. Emma to Fanny, March 13, 1871, AH.
47. Ibid., March 14, 1871.
48. Jenkins, *The Hawaiian Calabash,* 208.
49. Emma to Fanny, February 15, 1871, AH.
50. Ibid.
51. Jenkins, *The Hawaiian Calabash,* 183.
52. Emma to Fanny, February 15, 1871, AH.
53. Emma to Elizabeth Pratt, February 15, 1871, AH.
54. Emma to Sarah Weed, March 20, 1871, AH.
55. Fanny to Emma, April 18, 1871, AH.
56. Ibid.
57. Emma to Fanny, February 13, 1871, AH.
58. Ibid., February 15, 1871.
59. Ibid.
60. Emma to Fanny, February 13, 1871, AH.
61. Ibid., February 14, 1871.
62. Emma to Sarah Weed, March 20, 1871, AH.
63. Ibid., March 29, 1871.
64. Ibid.
65. Kalani E. Flores, "Lawa'i, No. 37, Verdant Valley," and Reginald P. Gage, II, "A Short History of the Land Tenure of Lawai," unpaginated, both papers presented to the Kaua'i Historical Society, 1995.

66. Emma to Sarah Weed, March 29, 1871, AH.
67. Emma to Fanny, March 6, 1871, AH.
68. Emma to Elizabeth Pratt, February 15, 1871, AH.
69. Emma to Fanny, February 15, 1871, AH.
70. Fanny to Emma, January 14, 1871, AH.
71. Nahaolelua to Emma, March 16, 1871, AH.
72. Fanny to Emma, March 5, 1871, AH.
73. Ibid., March 13, 1871.
74. Ibid., March 31, 1871.
75. Ibid., April 18, 1871.
76. Emma to Kamehameha V, April 7, 1871, AH.
77. Cited in Forbes, *Queen Emma and Lawai,* 13.
78. Emma to Keliʻimoewai, October 24, 1872, AH.
79. *Pacific Commercial Advertiser,* May 13, 1871.
80. Ibid., February 12, 1876.
81. Isobel Strong, *The Girl From Home: A Story of Honolulu.* Honolulu: Crossroads Bookshop, 1912, 99.
82. David Wayne Bandy, "The History of the Royal Hawaiian Band 1836–1980 with a Concentration on the Era of Bandmaster Henry Berger." MA thesis, University of Hawaiʻi, 1980, 16–19.

18 The Battles of Succession

1. Kamehameha V to Bishop Staley, January 20, 1868, AH.
2. Muir, "William Hoapili Kaauwai: A Hawaiian in Holy Orders," 10.
3. Fanny to Emma, November 15, 1872, AH.
4. Ethel M. Damon, *Sanford Ballard Dole and His Hawaii.* Palo Alto, Calif.: Pacific Books, 1957, 107–108.
5. Nahaolelua to Emma, November 15, 1872, AH.
6. Rufus A. Lyman, "Recollections of Kamehameha V," *Third Annual Report of the Hawaiian Historical Society for the Year 1895* (Honolulu, 1896), 19.
7. Ibid.
8. Liliʻuokalani, *Hawaii's Story,* 35; Iaukea and Watson, *By Royal Command,* 21; and Letter from John Dominis to Charles R. Bishop, January 7, 1873, as cited in the *Sixth Annual Report of the Hawaiian Historical Society for the Year 1898,* 11–16.
9. Dominis to Bishop, January 7, 1873, as cited in the *Sixth Annual Report of the Hawaiian Historical Society for the Year 1898,* 11–16.
10. Iaukea and Watson, *By Royal Command,* 22.
11. Ibid.
12. Kuykendall, *The Hawaiian Kingdom,* vol. 2, 241.
13. Emma to Mrs. Wodehouse, January 17 and 19, 1873, AH.
14. Dominis to Bishop, January 7, 1873, as cited in the *Sixth Annual Report of the Hawaiian Historical Society for the Year 1898,* 11–16.
15. Nahaolelua to Emma, February, no date, 1873, AH.
16. Emma to the Molokai Committee, December, no date, 1872, AH. This brief letter is notable because it is one of the rare times when Queen Emma referred to her deceased husband as *ʻIolani,* the heavenly hawk.
17. Korn, *News from Molokai,* xi-xv.
18. Kuykendall, *The Hawaiian Kingdom,* vol. 2, 242–243.

19. Sanford Dole, "Thirty Days of Hawaiian History," *Twenty-third Annual Report of the Hawaiian Historical Society for the Year 1914,* 37.
20. Ibid., 36.
21. *Pacific Commercial Advertiser,* January 4, 1873.
22. Emma to Peter, January 19, 1873, AH.
23. Dole, "Thirty Days of Hawaiian History," 45–46.
24. Alfred Stedman Hartwell, "Judge Alfred Stedman Hartwell," *Fifty-fourth Annual Report of the Hawaiian Historical Society for the Year 1945,* 16.
25. Nahaolelua to Emma, December 28, 1872, AH.
26. Ibid.
27. Ibid., February 14, 1873.
28. Nahaolelua to Emma, February, no date, 1873, AH.
29. Ibid., February 14, 1873.
30. Emma to Peter, August 20, 1873, AH.
31. Ibid., September 2, 1873.
32. Ibid.
33. Ibid.
34. *Ka Nūhou Hawai'i,* August 8, 1873.
35. August 8, 1873, AH.
36. Emma to Peter, August 18, 1873, AH.
37. Emma to Keli'imoewai, August 20, 1873, AH.
38. Emma to Peter, August 7, 1873, AH.
39. Ibid., July 29, 1873.
40. Ibid., August 20, 1873.
41. Ibid., September 2, 1873.
42. Ibid.
43. Ibid., September 3, 1873.
44. Ibid., September 4, 1873.
45. Ibid., September 3, 1873.
46. Ibid.
47. Ibid., September 17, 1873.
48. Ibid.
49. Ibid., September 3, 1873.
50. Kuykendall, *The Hawaiian Kindgom,* vol. 2, 261.
51. Emma to Peter, September 10, 1873, AH.
52. Ibid., September 24, 1873.
53. Ibid., September 2, 1873.
54. Korn, *News from Molokai,* 95.
55. Emma to Peter, September 3, 1873, AH.
56. Ibid., September 26, 1873. Lunalilo was not the only sick person the queen cared for. One of two sick people she specifically mentioned in her letters was Kiliwehi, who was her lady-in-waiting during her travels abroad. She was brought to Honolulu from Wailuku for treatment for a bleeding condition in her lungs. After consultations with Dr. McKibbin, the medical director at Queen's Hospital, Kiliwehi was housed "in the most comfortable room at the Waikiki end of the women's wards upstairs looking out on the plains, cocoanut grove, Diamond Hill, and the blue sea." Emma to Peter, October 13, 1873, AH. The second person was Lanakila who was also at the hospital where the queen was to have gone with Bishop Alfred Willis (who had succeeded Bishop Staley) to translate for him as he confirmed Lanakila a member of the church. Emma to Peter, September 20, 1873, AH.
57. Emma to Lucy Peabody, November 22, 1873, AH.
58. Cabinet Council Minute Book, September 16 and 17, 1873, AH.
59. Emma to Peter, August 25, 1873, AH.
60. Ibid., July 29, 1873.
61. Ibid., September 3, 1873.
62. Ibid.

63. Ibid., September 2, 1873.
64. Ibid., October 20, 1873.
65. Ibid., September 26, 1873.
66. Ibid., September 3, 1873.
67. Ibid.
68. Ibid., October 27, 1873.
69. Ibid.
70. Charles R. Bishop, "An Inside View of the Reign of Lunalilo," *Forty-ninth Annual Report of the Hawaiian Historical Society for the Year 1940* (1941), 26. See also Kanahele, *Pauahi,* 122–126.
71. Emma to Peter, September 2, 1873, AH.
72. Ibid., January 6, 1874.
73. Ibid., July 29, 1873.
74. Ibid., July 18, 1873.
75. Ibid., July 29, 1873.
76. Ibid., September 20, 1873.
77. Liliʻuokalani, *Hawaii's Story,* 39–40.
78. Emma to Lucy Peabody, January 19, 1874, AH.
79. Charles Castle to Claire Castle, January 20, 1874, HMCS.
80. Ibid.
81. *Ka Nūhou Hawaiʻi,* January 20, 1874.
82. Charles Castle to Claire Castle, February 8, 1874, HMCS.
83. Ibid., January 31, 1874.
84. *Pacific Commercial Advertiser,* February 7, 1874.
85. Korn, *News from Molokai,* 164.
86. *Ka Nūpepa Kūʻokoʻa,* February 7, 1874; *Pacific Commercial Advertiser,* February 7, 1874; and Curtis Lyons to Folks, February 14, 1874, AH.
87. *Ka Nūpepa Kūʻokoʻa,* February 7, 1874; and *Honolulu,* February 15, 1874.
88. *Hawaiian Gazette,* February 4, 1874.
89. *Ka Nūpepa Kūʻokoʻa,* February 7, 1874.
90. Privy Council Record XII, 27–33, February 6, 1874, AH.
91. Curtis Lyons to Folks, February 14, 1874, AH.
92. Charles Castle to Claire Castle, February 8, 1874, HMCS; and Lyons to Folks, February 14, 1874, AH.
93. Helena B. Allen, *Sanford Ballard Dole, Hawaiʻi's Only President, 1844–1926.* Glendale, California: Arthur H. Clark Company, 1988, 95.
94. Charles Castle to Claire Castle, February 11, 1874, HMCS.
95. *Hawaiian Gazette,* February 11, 1874.
96. Parke to Everett, February 9, 1874, AH.
97. Allen, *Sanford Ballard Dole,* 95.
98. Harvey R. Hitchcock to Brothers, February 11, 1874, AH; and Jean Dabagh, "A King Is Elected: 100 Years Ago," *Hawaiian Journal of History* 8 (1974), 83.
99. Kepelino, "Kepelino's Hawaiian Collection: His Hooiliili Havaii, Pepa I, 1858," translated and annotated by Bacil F. Kirtley and Esther T. Mookini, *Hawaiian Journal of History* 11 (1977), 39–40. Kepelino is a Hawaiian transliteration of "Zephyrin," the name given him at baptism.
100. Korn, *News from Molokai,* 165.
101. Liliʻuokalani, *Hawaii's Story,* 44.
102. J. Nathan Kaiʻiaikawaha to Emma, February 9, 1874, AH.
103. Committees to Emma, February, no date, 1874, AH.
104. Harvey R. Hitchcock to Brothers, February 11, 1874, AH; and Dabagh, "A King Is Elected," 83.
105. *Hawaiian Gazette,* February 11, 1874.
106. *Hawaiʻi Ponoʻī Extra,* February 7, 1874.

107. Allen, *Sanford Ballard Dole,* 51.
108. *Ka Nūhou Hawai'i,* February 10, 1874. Gibson described it as a "slovenly literary production," which reflected little credit on Her Majesty's Secretary, Kepelino, who wrote it.
109. Charles Castle to Claire Castle, February 8, 1874, HMCS.
110. Lili'uokalani, *Hawaii's Story,* 44.
111. Charles Castle to Claire Castle, February 11, 1874 , HMCS.
112. Iaukea and Watson, *By Royal Command,* 23.
113. *Ka Nūpepa Kū'oko'a,* February 14, 1874.
114. *Pacific Commercial Advertiser,* February 14, 1874.
115. Emma Ahuena Taylor, *Honolulu Star-Bulletin,* February 2, 1935.
116. Lyons to Folks, February 14, 1874, AH.
117. Ibid.
118. *Ka Nūpepa Kū'oko'a,* February 14, 1874.
119. *Pacific Commercial Advertiser,* February 14, 1874; and *Hawaiian Gazette,* March 4, 1874.
120. *Ka Nūhou Hawai'i,* March 10, 1874.
121. Hitchcock to Brothers, February 11, 1874, AH; and Dabagh, "A King Is Elected," 83.
122. *Pacific Commercial Advertiser,* February 14, 1874; *Hawaiian Gazette,* February 18, 1874; *Hawai'i Pono'ī,* February 18 and 25, 1874; and Lyons to Folks, February 14, 1874, AH.
123. *Pacific Commercial Advertiser,* February 14, 1874.
124. Charles Castle to Claire Castle, February 18, 1874, HMCS.
125. Damon, *Sanford Ballard Dole and His Hawai'i,* 127.
126. *Pacific Commercial Advertiser,* February 4, 1874.
127. *Ka Nūhou Hawai'i,* April 7, 1874.
128. Alfred S. Hartwell, "Forty Years of Hawaii Nei," *Fifty-fourth Annual Report of the Hawaiian Historical Society for the Year 1945,* 17.
129. Damon, *Sanford Ballard Dole,* 127.
130. *Ka Nūpepa Kū'oko'a,* February 21, 1874; Lili'uokalani, *Hawaii's Story,* 47; and *Pacific Commercial Advertiser,* February 14, 1874.
131. *Hawaiian Gazette,* March 4, 1874.
132. Charles Castle to Claire Castle, February 15, 1874, HMCS.
133. Admiral W. H. H. Southerland, "Incidents Connected with the Election of King Kalakaua in February, 1874," 21 *Hawaiian Historical Society Report,* 1913, 12–14.
134. *Ka Nūpepa Kū'oko'a,* February 14, 1874.
135. *Hawaiian Gazette,* February 18, 1874; and *Pacific Commercial Advertiser,* February 14, 1874.
136. *Hawaiian Gazette,* March 4, 1874.
137. Ahuena Taylor, *Honolulu Star-Bulletin,* February 2, 1935.
138. *Pacific Commercial Advertiser,* February 14, 1874.
139. *Ka Nūpepa Kū'oko'a,* February 21, 1874.

19 The Queen's Party

1. Lili'uokalani, *Hawaii's Story,* 49.
2. Ibid.
3. Kuykendall, *The Hawaiian Kingdom,* vol. 3, 11.
4. *Hawaiian Gazette,* February 18, 1874.
5. Alfred Castle to Claire Castle, February 15, 1874, HMCS.
6. Kuykendall, *The Hawaiian Kingdom,* vol. 3, 11.
7. Alfred Castle to Claire Castle, February 15, 1874, HMCS.
8. Ibid.

9. Peter to Emma, February 23, 1874, AH.
10. Kuykendall, *The Hawaiian Kingdom,* vol. 3, 11.
11. *Hawaiian Gazette,* February 18, 1874.
12. Ibid.
13. Liliʻuokalani, *Hawaii's Story,* 49.
14. *Pacific Commercial Advertiser,* February 14, 1874.
15. *Hawaiian Gazette,* February 18, 1874.
16. Hitchcock to Brothers, February 11, 1874, AH.
17. Mary Kawena Pukuʻi, *Nā Mele Welo, Songs of Our Heritage,* arranged and edited by Pat Namaka Bacon and Nathan Napoka. Honolulu: Bishop Museum, 1995, 54–55.
18. *Ka Nūpepa Kūʻokoʻa,* February 28, 1874.
19. Korn, *News from Molokai,* 181.
20. *Hawaiian Gazette,* April 15, 1874.
21. Allen to Allen, February 23, 1874, AH.
22. *Hawaiian Gazette,* April 15, 1874.
23. *Pacific Commercial Advertiser,* April 18, 1874.
24. *Pacific Commercial Advertiser,* February 14, 1874.
25. *Alta,* March 21, 1874, as cited in *Pacific Commercial Advertiser,* April 11, 1874.
26. Claire Castle to M. J. Bella, February 17, 1874, HMCS.
27. *Pacific Commercial Advertiser,* April 14, 1874.
28. Alfred Hartwell to Emma, April 20, 1874, AH.
29. J. K. Naone and J. Aylett to Emma, April 16, 1874, AH.
30. Restarick, *Hawaii, 1778–1920 from the Viewpoint of a Bishop,* 280–281.
31. Eldredge to Emma, April 19, 1874, AH.
32. Hulu to Emma, February, n.d., 1874, AH.
33. Eldredge to Emma, April 19, 1874, AH.
34. *Hawaiian Gazette,* April 29, 1874.
35. Ibid., May 6, 1874.
36. Ibid., June 17, 1874.
37. Kuykendall, *The Hawaiian Kingdom,* vol. 3, 14.
38. Ibid.
39. As cited in Kuykendall, *The Hawaiian Kingdom,* vol. 3, footnote 32, 653.
40. *Hawaiian Gazette,* October 14, 1874.
41. Ibid.
42. "Kepelino's Hawaiian Collection: His Hooiliili Havaii, Pepa 1, 1858," 39–40.
43. Kepelino to Emma, March 27, 1874, AH.
44. As cited in Kuykendall, *The Hawaiian Kingdom,* vol. 3, footnote 32, 653.
45. Kepelino to Emma, March 23, 1874, AH.
46. *Pacific Commercial Advertiser,* October 17, 1874.
47. The queen was appointed his guardian by the court two years later, in January 1876.
48. *Pacific Commercial Advertiser,* October 17, 1874.
49. *Hawaiian Gazette,* December 16, 1874.
50. Peter to Emma, December 16, 1874, AH.
51. Ibid. "A natural flower lei also associated with Queen Emma was the *pīkake* lei. Star-shaped flowers of paper may have been intended to imitate the smallish blossoms of *pīkake-hōkū,* or star jasmine *(Jasminum pubescens),* a shrubby vine from India, still very popular in Hawaiʻi." Korn, *News from Molokai,* 273.

52. Emma to Peter, September 3, 1873, AH.
53. Peter to Emma, November 8, 1873, AH.
54. Ibid., April 10, 1874.
55. Ibid., June 16, 1874.
56. Ibid., June 23, 1874.
57. J. K. Lonokeawe to Emma, no date, AH.
58. "A Prominent Hawaiian," *Paradise of the Pacific,* December 1904, 38.
59. John A. Cummins, "Around Oahu in Days of Old," *The Mid-Pacific Magazine,* vol. VI, no. 3, September 1913, 233–243.
60. *Pacific Commercial Advertiser,* April 25, 1874.
61. Cummins, "Around Oahu in Days of Old," 241.
62. Ibid., 243.
63. Ibid., 237.
64. Kuykendall, *The Hawaiian Kingdom,* vol. 3, 15.
65. Ibid.
66. *Ka Nūhou Hawai'i,* January 31, 1876.
67. Emma to Peter, February 4, 1876, AH.
68. *Pacific Commercial Advertiser,* February 5, 1876.
69. Emma to Peter, February 4, 1876, AH.
70. Ibid.
71. Ibid.
72. Kuykendall, *The Hawaiian Kingdom,* vol. 3, 16.
73. *Pacific Commercial Advertiser,* February 5, 1876.
74. Emma to Peter, February 4, 1876, AH.
75. Ibid., May 10, 1876.
76. Ibid.
77. Daws, *Shoal of Time,* 205; and Kuykendall, *The Hawaiian Kingdom,* vol. 3, 14.

20 Rifts and Conspiracies

1. Lili'uokalani, *Hawaii's Story,* 49.
2. Ibid.
3. Ibid., 50–51.
4. Peter to Emma, February 23, 1874, AH.
5. *Hawaiian Gazette,* February 16, 1874.
6. Peter to Emma, March 1, 1874, AH.
7. *Pacific Commercial Advertiser,* March 7, 1874.
8. Iaukea and Watson, *By Royal Command,* 50.
9. *Pacific Commercial Advertiser,* March 7, 1874.
10. Ibid., July 28, 1877.
11. Lili'uokalani, *Hawaii's Story,* 51.
12. Ibid., 55.
13. Kuykendall, *The Hawaiian Kingdom,* vol. 3, 197.
14. Lili'uokalani, *Hawaii's Story,* 58.
15. Ibid., 59.
16. Korn, *News from Molokai,* 279.
17. Section 992 and Section 996, The Penal Laws of the Hawaiian Islands, 1897.
18. Emma to Peter, May 10, 1876, AH.
19. Ibid.
20. Korn, *News from Molokai,* 280.
21. Emma to Peter, May 10, 1876, AH.
22. Ibid.
23. Peter to Emma, March 21, 1876, AH.
24. Emma to Peter, March, n.d., 1878, AH.
25. *Hawaiian Gazette,* May 31, 1876.
26. Emma to Peter, May 10, 1876, AH.
27. *Pacific Commercial Advertiser,* June 28, 1876.
28. Allen, *Kalakaua,* 103.
29. Rhoda E. A. Hackler, *'Iolani Palace: Hawai'i's Royal Palace, Official Residence of King Kalakaua and Queen Lili'uokalani,*

the Last Monarchs of Hawai'i, 1882–1893. Honolulu: Friends of 'Iolani Palace, 1987, 5.

30. Allen, *Kalakaua,* 99–100.
31. *Pacific Commercial Advertiser,* February 7, 1880.
32. Kuykendall, *The Hawaiian Kingdom,* vol. 3, 206.
33. Emma to Peter, March 6, 1876, AH.
34. Albert Kūnuiākea to Emma, April 2, 1876, AH.
35. Emma to Peter, May 10, 1876, AH.
36. Ibid., January 6, 1874.
37. Ibid.
38. *Pacific Commercial Advertiser,* February 14, 1880.
39. Ibid., September 25, 1880.
40. Kristin Zambucka, *The High Chiefess Ruth Ke'elikōlani.* Honolulu: Mana Publishing Company, 1977, 54.
41. *Hawaiian Gazette,* September 8, 1880.
42. *Pacific Commercial Advertiser,* October 2, 1880.
43. *Hawaiian Gazette,* October 6, 1880.
44. *Pacific Commercial Advertiser,* November 27, 1880.
45. Ibid., December 4, 1880.
46. Emma to Sarah Rhodes Von Pfister, January 17, 1881, AH.
47. *Hawaiian Gazette,* December 22, 1880.
48. Ibid., January 19, 1881.
49. Emma, *Diary,* January 20, 1881, BM. Celso Moreno was an American businessman with a tainted past; when King Kalākaua appointed him prime minister, so much anger was aroused that the king was forced to dismiss Moreno only five days after his appointment. Kuykendall, *The Hawaiian Kingdom,* vol. 3, 207–226.
50. Kuykendall, *The Hawaiian Kingdom,* vol. 3, 238.
51. Ibid., 241.
52. Ibid., 239.
53. Ibid., 242.
54. Emma to Peter, January 25, 1876, AH.
55. Kuykendall, *The Hawaiian Kingdom,* vol. 3, 242.
56. Ibid., 243.
57. Ibid.

21 No Seclusion

1. Korn, *News from Molokai,* 321.
2. Lili'uokalani, *Hawaii's Story,* 75–76.
3. *Pacific Commercial Advertiser,* January 15, 1881.
4. Blount's Report, as cited in Allen, *The Betrayal of Lili'uokalani,* 159.
5. Helena G. Allen, *The Betrayal of Lili'uokalani—Last Queen of Hawaii 1838–1917.* Honolulu: Mutual Publishing, 1982, 149.
6. Emma, *Diary,* January 30, 1881, BM.
7. Ibid., February 7, 1881.
8. Ibid., February 10, 1881.
9. Ibid., April 1, 1881.
10. *Pacific Commercial Advertiser,* August 20, 1881.
11. Lili'uokalani, *Hawaii's Story,* 82, 72.
12. Zambucka, *The High Chiefess Ruth Ke'elikōlani,* 67.
13. *Pacific Commercial Advertiser,* December 4, 1880.
14. Ibid., October 3, 1881.
15. Ibid., May 7, 1881.
16. Ibid., September 3, 1881.
17. Ibid., April 9 and 16, 1881.
18. Ibid., June 25, 1881.
19. Emma, *Diary,* February 2, 1881, BM.
20. Ibid., June 18, 1881.
21. *Pacific Commercial Advertiser,* March 19, 1881.

22. Ibid.
23. Report of the President of the Board of Health to the Legislative Assembly of 1882, *Board of Health Reports,* 1866–88, AH.
24. *Pacific Commercial Advertiser,* March 7, 1881.
25. Ibid., March 5, 1881.
26. Emma, *Diary,* February 3, 1881, BM.
27. Ibid., February 4, 1881.
28. Ibid., February 5, 1881.
29. Ibid., February 6, 1881.
30. *Pacific Commercial Advertiser,* March 5, 1881.
31. Emma, *Diary,* February 7, 1881, BM.
32. Ibid., February 11, 1881.
33. Ibid., February 15, 1881.
34. Ibid., February 16, 1881.
35. Ibid., February 17, 1881.
36. Ibid., February 19, 1881.
37. Ibid., March 7, 1881.
38. Ibid., February 7, 1881.
39. Ibid., February 26, 1881.
40. *Pacific Commercial Advertiser,* February 12 and 19, March 5 and 12, and April 19, 1881.
41. Emma, *Diary,* February 3, 1881, BM.
42. Ibid., March 7, 1881.
43. Ibid., February 16, 1881.
44. Ibid., February 14, 1881.
45. Ibid., March 5, 1881.
46. *Pacific Commercial Advertiser,* February 26, 1881.
47. Emma, *Diary,* March 6, 1881, BM.
48. Ibid., March, 8, 1881.
49. Ibid., March 9, 1881.
50. Ibid., March 9, 1881.
51. Ibid., March 7, 1881.
52. *Board of Health Reports,* 38, AH.
53. Emma, *Diary,* February 11, 1881, BM.
54. Ibid., February 7, 1881.
55. Ibid., February 8, 1881.
56. Ibid., February 14, 1898.
57. Ibid., January 31, 1881.
58. Ibid., January 30, 1881.
59. Ibid.
60. Ibid., February 3, 1881.
61. Ibid., February 1, 1881.
62. Ibid., February 13, 1881.
63. Puku'i, et al., *Nānā I Ke Kumu,* vol. 1, 183.
64. Emma, *Diary,* February 13, 1881, BM.
65. Ibid., February 8, 1881.
66. Ibid., February 7, 1881.
67. Ibid., February 23, 1881.
68. Ibid., March 1, 1881.
69. Ibid., February 16, 1881.
70. Ibid., February 18, 1881.
71. Ibid., February 14, 1881.
72. Smythe, "Queen Emma, The Person," 5.
73. Emma, *Diary,* February 21, 1881, BM.
74. Ibid., February 9, 1881.
75. Ibid., April 8, 1881.
76. Ibid., March 4, 1881.
77. Ibid., February 15, 1881.
78. Ibid., March 6, 1881.
79. Ibid., March 8, 1881.
80. Ibid., February 12, 1881.
81. Ibid., June 18, 1881.
82. Ibid., February 23, 1881.
83. Ibid.
84. Ibid., April 7, 1881.
85. Ibid., April 10, 1881.
86. Ibid., April 13, 1881, BM.
87. *Pacific Commercial Advertiser,* October 19, 1879.
88. Emma, *Diary,* March 20, 1881, BM.
89. As cited in Hackler, "My Dear Friend," 127.
90. William N. Armstrong, *Around the World with a King.* Rutland, Vermont: Charles E. Tuttle Company, 1981, 225.
91. Emma, *Diary,* April 4, 1881, BM.

92. Letter from Theo. H. Davies to John Waterhouse, November 7, 1883, as cited in Williams, *From Royal Garden to Gothic Splendor,* 26–27.
93. Ibid.
94. Episcopal Church, *The Episcopal Church in Hawaii, Ninety Years of Service, 1862–1952,* written by Meiric Dutton with the assistance of Rev. C. Fletcher Howe. Honolulu: The Missionary District of Honolulu, 1952, 18.
95. Jacob Adler, *Claus Spreckels: The Sugar King in Hawaii.* Honolulu: University Press of Hawai'i, 1966, 74–75.
96. Emma to Ihilani Jones, November 17, 1881, AH.
97. Emma to Lucy Peabody, March 25, 1882, AH.
98. Ibid.
99. Ibid.
100. Kanahele, *Pauahi,* 161.
101. Emma to Julia Akana, February 7, 1882, AH.
102. *Pacific Commercial Advertiser,* February 15, 1882.
103. Ibid., February 11, 1882.
104. *Hawaiian Gazette,* February 8, 1882.
105. Emma to Lucy Peabody, March 21 and March 25, 1882, AH.
106. *Hawaiian Gazette,* March 22, 1882.
107. Hackler, "My Dear Friend," 127–128.
108. Jane "Jennie" Stillman Smythe, "Reminiscences of My Trip to Ka'u, Hawai'i, with Queen Emma," unpublished paper, no date, DOH.
109. Ibid.
110. Ibid.
111. After several months the ropes that held the tree down would be untied and the trunk would grow in this supine position. In 1950 two such trees were still growing in Kalapana. Mary Kawena Puku'i and Samuel H. Elbert, *Hawaiian Dictionary,* rev. and enlarged ed. Honolulu: University of Hawai'i Press, 1986, 267.
112. Smythe, "Reminiscences of My Trip to Ka'u," DOH. A quite different account of the queen's visit to Puna was given by Russ and Peg Apple in their newspaper column "Tales of Hawaii." They stated that the queen visited Puna in 1883 rather than 1882, that she rode directly from Hilo by horseback to Puna rather than starting from Honuapo Bay in Ka'u, and that she returned after only a week because she observed a comet in the sky that she took as a sign of the imminent death of someone important. "Tales of Hawaii," *Honolulu Star-Bulletin,* April 5, 1975. Interestingly, the queen may have actually seen a comet because one did appear in late 1882 and early 1883. David A. Seargent, *Comets, Vagabonds of Space.* Garden City, New York: Doubleday, 1982, 118–120.
113. Smythe, "Reminiscences of My Trip to Ka'u."
114. *Pacific Commercial Advertiser,* July 14, 1882.
115. Adler, *Claus Spreckles,* 112–113.
116. *Pacific Commercial Advertiser,* July 27, 1882.
117. Jacob Adler and Robert M. Kamins, *The Fantastic Life of Walter Murray Gibson: Hawaii's Minister of Everything.* Honolulu: University of Hawai'i Press, 1986, 133–134.
118. *Hawaiian Gazette,* July 26, 1882.
119. *Pacific Commercial Advertiser,* July 14, 1882.

120. Ibid., July 28, 1882.
121. Emma to Ihilani Jones, October 31, 1882, AH.
122. Iaukea and Watson, *By Royal Command,* 50.
123. Adler and Kamins, *The Fantastic Life of Walter Murray Gibson,* 137.
124. *Pacific Commercial Advertiser,* February 15, 1883.
125. Iaukea and Watson, *By Royal Command,* 50.
126. Ibid.
127. *Pacific Commercial Advertiser,* February 17, 1883.
128. *Ko Hawaiʻi Paeʻāina,* February 24, 1883, AH.
129. Iaukea and Watson, *By Royal Command,* 51.
130. Isobel O. Field, *This Life I've Loved.* New York: Longmans, Green, 1937, 185.

22 The Last Flight

1. *Pacific Commercial Advertiser,* March 8, 1883.
2. Kanahele, *Pauahi,* 165.
3. Ibid., 164-165.
4. *Hawaiian Gazette,* May 30, 1883.
5. Emma to Ihilani Jones, May 29, 1883, AH.
6. Ibid.
7. Liliʻuokalani, *Hawaii's Story,* 107.
8. *The Friend,* July 1883, 60.
9. Emma to Ihilani Jones, May 8, 1883, AH.
10. Allen, *Kalakaua,* 151.
11. *Ko Hawaiʻi Paeʻāina,* June 23, 1883.
12. Ibid.
13. *Ko Hawaiʻi Paeʻāina,* September 22, 1888.
14. *Ka ʻElele Poakolu,* March 19, 1884, and April 2, 1884.
15. *Ka Nūhou Hawaiʻi,* February 3, 1874. For Kamakau's genealogy of Queen Emma, see *Ka Nūpepa Kūʻokoʻa,* October 5, 1867.
16. *Ko Hawaiʻi Paeʻāina,* June 16, 1883.
17. Liliʻuokalani, *Hawaii's Story,* 404.
18. Emma to Ihilani Jones, July 10, 1883, AH.
19. Smythe, "Queen Emma, The Person," 5.
20. Ibid.
21. Stillman to Ihilani Jones, October 16, 1883, AH.
22. *Ko Hawaiʻi Paeʻāina,* May 2, 1885.
23. Sister Phoebe to Flora (Ihilani) Jones, August 31, 1884, AH.
24. Emma to Ihilani Jones, November 13, 1883, AH.
25. Ibid., November 27, 1883.
26. Pilipo to Emma, December 28, 1883, AH. She may have also been amused by his recounting of the rumor on Hawaiʻi that he was dead. It had spread to Hilo, and when he arrived there, he found the people "were in mourning for me and I was found howling."
27. *The Hawaiian Monthly,* vol. 1, no. 2, February 1884, 39–40.
28. *Pacific Commercial Advertiser,* February 5, 1884.
29. Ibid., February 9, 1884.
30. Kuykendall, *The Hawaiian Kingdom,* vol. 3, 270.
31. Ibid.
32. Quoted in *Saturday Press,* February 24, 1883.
33. *Hawaiian Gazette,* February 6, 1884.
34. *Pacific Commercial Advertiser,* January 18, 1884.
35. Ibid., February 9, 1884.
36. Nawahi to Emma, February 7, 1884, AH.
37. Emma to Ihilani Jones, April 19, 1884 and May 20, 1884, AH.
38. Ibid., February 29, 1884.
39. Albertine Loomis, *The Best of Friends: The Story of Hawaiʻi's Libraries and Their Friends 1879–*

1979. Kailua: Friends of the Library of Hawaii, Press Pacifica, 1979, 12–13.
40. Emma to Ihilani Jones, May 20, 1884, AH.
41. Davis, *Abraham Fornander,* 235.
42. Smythe, "Queen Emma, The Person," 6.
43. Stillman to Flora (Ihilani) Jones, August 25, 1884, AH.
44. Ibid., August 19, 1884.
45. Ibid.
46. Stillman to Flora (Ihilani) Jones, August 25, 1884, AH.
47. Sister Phoebe to Flora (Ihilani) Jones, August 31, 1884, AH.
48. Ibid.
49. Emma to Ihilani Jones, May 13, 1884, AH.
50. *Pacific Commercial Advertiser,* November 3, 1884.
51. Ibid.
52. Lili'uokalani, *Hawaii's Story,* 108.
53. Allen, *The Betrayal of Lili'uokalani,* 181.
54. Heyes, "The History of St. Andrew's Priory," 58. The first two scholarships went to Fannie Mahulani, who had been supported by the queen prior to her death, and to Maude Niaupio, her cousin.
55. Emma's bequest of 600 books was the first and the largest the library had received. Loomis, *The Best of Friends,* 18–19. Some of the books in her library included Walter Scott, *Life of Napoleon Bonaparte,* vol. 1, John Keble, *Christian Year,* P. Blot, *Handbook of Practical Cookery,* Daniel Defoe, *Robinson Crusoe,* Webster's *Dictionary* (1850), Robert Brett, *Doctrine of the Cross,* John B. Newman, *Parlor Book of Flowers,* and Charles Mills, *The History of Machiavellianism.* The above-mentioned books are on exhibit at the Queen Emma Summer Palace.
56. *Pacific Commercial Advertiser,* December 1, 1884.
57. Ibid., January 3, 1885.
58. Ibid.
59. Ibid., April 27, 1885.
60. Ibid., May 19, 1885.
61. Ibid., April 27, 1885; *Hawaiian Gazette,* April 29, 1885; and *Ko Hawai'i Pae'āina,* April 17, 1885.
62. *Pacific Commercial Advertiser,* April 27, 1885.
63. Damon, *Koamalu,* vol. 2, 782.
64. *Pacific Commercial Advertiser,* April 28, 1885.
65. Mary Kawena Puku'i, *'Ōlelo No'eau: Hawaiian Proverbs and Poetical Sayings.* Bishop Museum Special Publication 71. Honolulu: Bishop Museum Press, 1983, 206.
66. *Pacific Commercial Advertiser,* April 27, 1885.
67. *Ko Hawai'i Pae'āina,* May 2, 1885; and Heyes, "The History of St. Andrew's Priory," 57–58.
68. *Honolulu Advertiser,* February 24, 1926.
69. *Pacific Commercial Advertiser,* April 27, 1885.
70. *Hawaiian Gazette,* April 29, 1885.
71. Ibid.
72. Lili'uokalani, *Hawaii's Story,* 109.
73. *Hawaiian Gazette,* May 20, 1885.
74. Reverend Parker was not entirely accurate. Only needy Hawaiians could expect treatment "free of charge" and only as long as sufficient government funding was available to the hospital.
75. *Hawaiian Gazette,* May 20, 1885.
76. The hospital may have been represented by Dr. McKibbin who was one of the attending physicians in the procession. The grateful hospital had Reverend MacIntosh conduct a special memorial ser-

vice for the queen on its premises on Sunday morning, May 9, 1885. *Ko Hawai'i Pae'āina*, May 9, 1885. The hospital board passed the following resolution honoring the queen:

> Whereas it has pleased God to take from us by death the Queen Dowager Emma, one of the founders and the financial patrons of the Queen's Hospital, an institution which has been of great value to this community and which will be a lasting blessing to the natives and foreigners in this country in time to come and in which the beloved Queen took the deepest interest from its conception to the end of her life, and for the support of which she gave a large part of her estate.
>
> Therefore be it resolved: That in the death of Queen Dowager Emma the nation has lost a great and good friend, distinguished for her kindness to the poor and the sick and whose memory should be honored and cherished by all who value nobility and purity of character and of life as a rich legacy of her countrymen and friends. . . .
>
> That all who may hereafter avail themselves of the advantages of the Hospital will, like those who have received them in the past, have reason to remember with gratitude the kind hearted and benevolent Queen Emma. . . .

Record of the Trustees Meetings, 1859–1907, Queen's Hospital, 185.

77. *Pacific Commercial Advertiser,* May 18, 1885; and *Hawaiian Gazette,* May 20, 1885.
78. *Pacific Commercial Advertiser,* May 18, 1885.

23 The Legacy

1. St. Andrew's Priory, *The Student and Parent Handbook,* 1998.
2. Ibid.
3. Hackler, *The Cathedral Church of Saint Andrew,* 11, 15.
4. Interview with Father Norio Sasaki, Episcopal church historiographer, Honolulu, August 4, 1998. See sermon by Rev. John Paul Engeloke, May 16, 1976, Episcopal Collections, St. Andrew's Cathedral.
5. Hawaii Department of Business, Economic Development and Tourism, *The State of Hawaii Data Book: A Statistical Abstract.* Honolulu: Department of Business, Economic Development and Tourism, 1990, 57.
6. The Queen's Health Systems, *Overview,* 1998.
7. "Mission of The Queen's Medical Center," Approved, Board of Trustees, The Queen's Medical Center, November 1990.
8. The Queen's Health Systems, *Overview,* 1998.
9. The queen's debts totaled at least $60,000. Some of her lands were sold to raise $74,000 to pay these debts and other expenses. Letter from Robert Bruce Graham, Jr., attorney at law, August 20, 1998.
10. Emma to Peter, September 26, AH.

Glossary of Hawaiian Words

All definitions are from the *Hawaiian Dictionary* by Mary Kawena Puku'i and Samuel H. Elbert. Honolulu: University of Hawai'i Press, 1986.

'A'ala'ula. (wāwae'iole) A variety of seaweed.
'Aha'aina. Feast, party, banquet.
'Ahahui. Association, society, club, organization.
Ahupua'a. Usually a wedge-shaped portion of land running from the mountains to the sea.
'Aikupika. Home of Pākī and Konia (the parents of Bernice Pauahi Bishop).
'Āina. Land or lands.
Akua. God, goddess, spirit, devil, ghost, image, idol.
Akule. Goggle or big-eyed scad.
Alaka'i. To lead, guide; leader.
Ali'i. Chief, chiefess, monarch, king, queen, noble, royal.
Ali'i ma'i. Sickness of the chief.
Ali'i nui. Great or high chief.
Aloali'i. In the presence of chiefs, royal court.
Aloha. Love, affection, compassion, mercy, sympathy.
Aloha ali'i. Love of the chiefs.
'Anae. Full-sized mullet.
Auwai. Ditch.
Auwē. Alas.
Awa. Milkfish.
'Ehu. Ruddy.
Haku. Lord, master; to compose.
Haku mele. Composer, poet; to compose a song or chant.
Hale. House, hut, building, institution.
Hānai. Foster child, adopted child; to raise, feed.
Haole. White person, Caucasian, American; formerly, any foreigner.
Haole ho'ohaunaele. Brawling foreigners.
Hapa haole. Part-white person.
Hau. A lowland tree, some spreading horizontally over the ground forming impenetrable thickets, and some trained on trellises.

He'e. To surf, slide.
He'e pu'ewai. Surfing up stream.
Heiau. Pre-Christian place of worship, shrine, temple.
Hilahila. Shyness or embarrassment.
Hīmeni. Hymns.
Hina. A goddess.
Hoa. Companion, friend, associate.
Hoa 'ai wai. Companion at the breast.
Hō'ailona. Portents, omens.
Holokū. A loose, seamed dress with a yoke and usually with a train, patterned after the Mother Hubbards of the missionaries.
Ho'okipa. To entertain, treat hospitably; hospitality.
Ho'okupu. Tribute, a ceremonial gift-giving to a chief as a sign of honor and respect.
Ho'omanamana. To impart *mana.*
Ho'opalau. To pair or join, as in a betrothal.
Ho'opū'ā. The practice of feeding babies, whereby a mother would chew a bit of solid food and then place it in the mouth of the infant being fed.
Hui. Club, association, organization, group, band.
Huli(s). Taro plantings.
Humuhumu. Trigger fish.
'Ili 'āina. Land section, next in importance to *ahupua'a* and usually a subsection of an *ahupua'a.*
'Io. Hawk.
Ipu. The bottle gourd, a wide-spreading vine; a drum made of a single or two large gourds joined together; any container.
Ka Haku O Hawai'i. The Prince of Hawaii.
Ka'a. To roll, turn, twist.
Kahili. Feathered royal standard. (Plural: *kāhili*)
Kahu. Honored attendant, guardian, servant, nurse, pastor, minister.
Kahuna. Priest, expert in any profession. (Plural: *kāhuna*).
Kāhuna ho'opunipuni. Fake and lying *kāhuna.*
Kahuna la'au lapa'au. Herbal physician.
Kahuna lapa'au. Physician.
Kaikamahine. Girl, daughter.
Kaikamahine kolohe. Naughty girl.
Kalo. Taro.
Kamani. A large tree with shiny oblong leaves, found along the shore.
Kāne. Male, husband, man; the leading god of the four great Hawaiian gods; god of fresh water and agriculture.
Kanikau. Lamentation, chant of mourning.
Kapa. Tapa, barkcloth as made from *wauke* or *māmaki* bark.
Kapu. Taboo, prohibition; sacredness, forbidden; no trespassing, keep out.

Kaua. War, battle.
Kauhale. Group of houses comprising a Hawaiian home, formerly consisting of men's eating house, women's eating house, sleeping house, cook house, etc.; hamlet or settlement.
Kawowo. Seedling; progeny.
Keiki. Child, offspring.
Kī. A woody plant, with long, slender, and unbranched leaves.
Kileka. Cypress.
Kino. Body.
Koa. The largest of native forest trees.
Koali. Some kinds of morning glory.
Kōkua. To care for; help, helper.
Kolohe. Mischievous, naughty.
Konohiki. Headman of an *ahupua'a* under the chief.
Kou. A tree with large ovate leaves and orange tubular flowers.
Kū. Ancient Hawaiian god of war.
Kua'āina. Person from the country, countrified, country.
Kuhina nui. In the days of the monarchy, a prime minister or premier who shared executive power with the monarch.
Kuleana. jurisdiction; responsibility.
Kupuna. Grandparent, ancestor, elder.
Lā. Sun; day, date.
Laua'e. A fragrant fern.
Lauhala. Pandanus leaf.
Lehua. Flower of the *'ōhi'a* tree.
Līpoa. Bladelike, branched brown seaweeds.
Lo'i. Irrigated terrace, especially for taro; patch, paddy.
Lolo. Brain.
Lolo ka'a. Literally rolling brains; stroke.
Lomi. Massage.
Lū'au. Feast or party; taro leaves.
Luna. Foreman, boss, overseer.
Luna maka'āinana. Representative.
Mahele. Portion, division, section; land division of 1848.
Ma kai. Toward the sea.
Ma uka. Toward the mountains.
Ma'i. Sickness, illness.
Ma'i lēpela. Leprosy.
Ma'i pu'upu'u li'ili'i. Smallpox.
Ma'i pu'upu'u 'ula. Measles.
Maka'āinana. Commoner, populace.
Makahiki. Year, age.
Makamaka. Close friend.

Mana. Supernatural or divine power; universal energy.
Mauna'ala. Site of Royal Mausoleum.
Mele. Song, anthem, or chant of any kind.
Mele inoa. A name chant.
Mo'o. Lizard, reptile of any kind, dragon; gecko.
Nīele. Inquisitiveness.
Niu. Coconut.
Niu moe o Kalapana. Supine coconut palm of Kalapana.
Noe. Mist, fog.
Nu'akea. Goddess of lactation.
'Ōahi. Fireworks.
'Ohana. Family, relative, kin group.
'Ohe. Bamboo.
'Ohe hano ihu. Nose flute.
'Ōhi'a 'ai. Mountain apple.
Oli. Chant that is not accompanied by dance.
One. Sand.
Pa'i umauma. Chest slapping hula.
Pā'ū. Woman's skirt; skirt worn by female horseback riders.
Pahu. Drum.
Pākōlea. To train to grow straight, as an infant's crooked limb.
Pele. Goddess of fire and volcano.
Pepehi, hailuku, puhi ka hale. Kill, stone to death, burn houses.
Pia. Arrowroot.
Pīkake. White jasmine.
Piko. Navel, umbilical cord.
Pili. Type of grass formerly used for thatching houses in old Hawai'i.
Pule. Prayer.
Pūlo'ulo'u. A tapa-covered ball on a stick carried before a chief as insignia of taboo.
Punahele. Favorite or pet; to treat as a favorite (as a child).
Pūniu. Small knee drum made out of a coconut shell with a fishskin cover.
Ua. Rain.
Ua noe. Misty rain.
Uē, uwē, helu. Wailing call of grief and love, recounting deeds of a loved one and shared experiences; to weep and speak thus.
Ue wahine. Type of shirt.
Ukuhi. To wean, as a child.
Ulī'ulī. Gourd rattle.
'Ūpepe. Flat-nosed.
Wahine. Female, woman.
Wai. Fresh water.

Bibliography

Adler, Jacob. *Claus Spreckles: The Sugar King in Hawaii.* Honolulu: University of Hawai'i Press, 1966.

Adler, Jacob, and Gwynn Barrett, eds. *The Diaries of Walter Murray Gibson, 1886–1887.* Honolulu: University Press of Hawai'i, 1973.

Adler, Jacob, and Robert Kamins. *The Fantastic Life of Walter Murray Gibson: Hawai'i's Minister of Everything.* Honolulu: University of Hawai'i Press, 1986.

Allen, Helena G. *The Betrayal of Liliuokalani—Last Queen of Hawaii 1838–1917.* Honolulu: Mutual Publishing, 1982.

———. *Kalakaua—Renaissance King.* Honolulu: Mutual Publishing, 1994.

———. *Sanford Ballard Dole, Hawaii's Only President, 1844–1926.* Glendale, California: Arthur H. Clark Company, 1988.

Anderson, Fredrick, Michael B. Frank, and Kenneth M. Sanderson, eds. *Mark Twain's Notebooks and Journals,* vol. 1 (1855–1873). Berkeley: University of California Press, 1975.

Apple, Russell A. *Pahukanilua, Homestead of John Young, Kawaihae, Kohala, Island of Hawai'i.* National Park Service, Hawaii State Office, 1978.

Armstrong, William N. *Around the World with a King.* Rutland, Vermont: Charles E. Tuttle Company, 1981.

Bandy, David Wayne. "The History of the Royal Hawaiian Band 1836–1980 with a Concentration on the Era of Bandmaster Henry Berger." MA thesis, University of Hawai'i, 1980.

Barrera, William, and Marion Kelly. *Archaeological and Historical Surveys of the Waimea to Kawaihae Road Corridor, Island of Hawaii.* Report 74-1. Honolulu: Bishop Museum Department of Anthropology, 1974.

Bennett, C. R. "The Reign of Kamehameha IV—Alexander Liholiho." *Queen's Hospital Bulletin,* vol. XII, nos. 1–6 (January 1936).

Benton, Russel E. *Emma Naea Rooke (1836–1885), Beloved Queen of Hawaii.* Lewiston, New York: Edwin Mellen Press, 1988.

Bird, Isabella L. *Six Months in the Sandwich Islands.* Rutland, Vermont: Charles E. Tuttle Company, 1988.

Bishop, Bernice Pauahi. *Diary.* No date. Bishop Museum.

Bishop, Charles R. "An Inside View of the Reign of Lunalilo." *Forty-ninth Annual Report of the Hawaiian Historical Society for the Year 1940* (1941), 12–28.

Bliss, William. *Paradise in the Pacific: A Book of Travel, Adventure, and Facts.* New York: Sheldon, 1873.

Board of Commissioners of Public Archives. *Roster Legislatures of Hawaii 1841–1918,* compiled by Robert C. Lydecker. Honolulu: Hawaiian Gazette Company, 1918.

Brown, Malcolm. *Reminiscences of a Pioneer Kauai Family with References and Anecdotes of Early Honolulu, 1804–1917.* T. McVeagh, 1918.

Bureau of Conveyances, Records. State of Hawai‘i, Honolulu.

Bushnell, O. A. *The Gifts of Civilization: Germs and Genocide in Hawai‘i.* Honolulu: University of Hawai‘i Press, 1993.

Bye, Roger. *How Christmas Came to Hawai‘i.* Honolulu: Hawaiian Dredging Company, 1951.

Cabinet Council (Kingdom of Hawai‘i). Minutes Book. Hawai‘i State Archives.

Cahill, Emmett. *The Shipmans of East Hawai‘i.* Honolulu: University of Hawai‘i Press, 1996.

Castle, William Richards, Jr. *Life of Samuel Northrup Castle.* Honolulu: Samuel N. and Mary Castle Foundation, 1960.

Chamberlain, Levi. *Journal, 1822–1849.* Hawai‘i Mission Children's Society.

Charlot, John. *Chanting the Universe: Hawaiian Religious Culture.* Hong Kong: Emphasis International, 1983.

Clay, Horace F., and James C. Hubbard. *The Hawai‘i Garden, Tropical Exotics.* Honolulu: University of Hawai‘i Press, 1977.

Cooke, Amos S. *Journal.* Unpublished. Hawaii Mission Children's Society.

———. Reports of the Chiefs' Children's School to the American Board of Commissioners for Foreign Missions, 1841–1844, Hawai‘i Mission Children's Society.

Cummins, John A. "Around Oahu in Days of Old." *The Mid-Pacific Magazine,* vol. VI (3) (September 1913), 233–243.

Dabagh, Jean. "A King Is Elected: 100 Years Ago." *Hawaiian Journal of History* 8 (1874).

Damon, Ethel M. *Koamalu,* 2 vols. Honolulu: Star-Bulletin, 1931.

———. *Sanford Ballard Dole and His Hawai‘i.* Palo Alto, Calif.: Pacific Books, 1957.

Davis, Eleanor H. *Abraham Fornander.* Honolulu: University of Hawai‘i Press, 1979.

Davis, Robert G. "Reports of a Portion of the Decisions Rendered by the Supreme Court of the Hawaiian Islands in Law, Equity, Admiralty and Probate, 1857–1865." *Hawaiian Reports,* vol. II (1866).

Daws, Gavan. *Holy Man: Father Damien of Molokai.* New York: Harper and Row, 1973.

———. *Shoal of Time.* Honolulu: University of Hawai‘i Press, 1982.

Day, A. Grove. *History Makers of Hawaii.* Honolulu: Mutual Publishing of Honolulu, 1984.

Desha, Lorna J. "Story of Queen Emma." Unpublished paper, Daughters of Hawai'i, 1964.

Dole, Sanford. "Thirty Days of Hawaiian History." *Twenty-third Annual Report of the Hawaiian Historical Society for the Year 1914* (1915), 28–40.

Dutton, Meiric. *Ka Haku o Hawaii, His Royal Highness the Prince of Hawaii.* Honolulu: Paradise of the Pacific Press, 1915.

Dye, Bob. "The Great Chinese Merchants' Ball of 1856." *The Hawaiian Journal of History* 28 (1994): 69–76.

———. *Merchant Prince of the Sandalwood Mountains, Afong and the Chinese in Hawai'i.* Honolulu: University of Hawai'i Press, 1997.

Ellis, Nalani. "Queen Emma." Address presented to Daughters of Hawai'i, January 1973.

Emerson, Oliver Pomeroy. *Pioneer Days In Hawaii.* Garden City, New York: Doubleday, Doran and Company, 1928.

Emma. *Diary, 1855–1881.* Hawai'i State Archives and Bishop Museum.

Episcopal Church. *The Episcopal Church in Hawaii, Ninety Years of Service, 1862–1952,* written by Meiric Dutton with the assistance of Rev. C. Fletcher Howe. Honolulu: The Missionary District of Honolulu, 1952.

Feher, Joseph. *Hawaii: A Pictorial History.* Bernice P. Bishop Museum Special Publication No. 58. Honolulu: Bishop Museum Press, 1969.

Field, Isobel O. *The Girl From Home, A Story of Honolulu.* Honolulu: Crossroads Bookshops, 1912.

———. *This Life I've Loved.* New York: Longmans, Green, 1937.

Flores, Kalani E. "Lawa'i, No. 37, Verdant Valley." Paper presented to the Kaua'i Historical Society (1995).

Forbes, David. *Queen Emma and Lawai.* Kaua'i Historical Society, April 1970.

Gage, Reginald P., II. "A Short History of the Land Tenure of Lawai." Paper presented to the Kaua'i Historical Society, 1995.

Gilman, Gorham D. "1848—Honolulu As It Is—Notes for Amplification," edited by Jean S. Sharpless and Richard A. Greer. *Hawaiian Journal of History* 4, 1970, 105–156.

———. "Streets of Honolulu in the Early Forties." *Hawaiian Annual,* 1904, 74–101.

Gospel Missionary. "Daily Life of Queen Emma of Honolulu." *The Gospel Missionary,* vol. 18. London: Bull and Daldy, 1868.

Greer, Richard A. "Honolulu in 1847." *Hawaiian Journal of History* 4, 1970, 59–95.

———. "The Founding of the Queen's Hospital." *Hawaiian Journal of History* 3 (1969), 110–145.

Gregg, David Lawrence. *The Diaries of David Lawrence Gregg: An American Diplomat in Hawaii 1853–1858,* edited by Pauline King. Honolulu: Hawaiian Historical Society, 1982.

———. *Diary.* Unpublished. Archives of Hawai'i.

Grimshaw, Patricia. *Paths of Duty: American Missionary Wives in Nineteenth-Century Hawaii.* Honolulu: University of Hawai'i Press, 1989.

Hackler, Rhoda E. A. "Albert Edward Kauikeaouli Leiopapa a Kamehameha, Prince of Hawai'i." *Hawaiian Journal of History* 26 (1992), 21–44.

———. *The Cathedral Church of Saint Andrew.* Honolulu: St. Andrew's Cathedral, 1991.

———. *'Iolani Palace: Hawai'i's Royal Palace, Official Residence of King Kalakaua and Queen Lili'uokalani, the Last Monarchs of Hawai'i, 1882–1893.* Honolulu: Friends of 'Iolani Palace, 1987.

———. "My Dear Friend: Letters of Queen Victoria and Queen Emma." *Hawaiian Journal of History* 22 (1988), 101–130.

Halford, Francis John. *Nine Doctors and God.* Honolulu: University of Hawai'i Press, 1954.

Handy, E. S. Craighill, and Mary Kawena Puku'i. *The Polynesian Family System in Ka'u, Hawai'i.* Rutland, Vermont: Charles E. Tuttle Company, 1981.

Hartwell, Alfred Stedman. "Judge Alfred Stedman Hartwell." *Fifty-fourth Annual Report of the Hawaiian Historical Society for the Year 1945* (1947), 7–8.

———. "Forty Years of Hawaii Nei." *Fifty-fourth Annual Report of the Hawaiian Historical Society for the Year 1945,* (1947) 9–24.

Hawaii Department of Business, Economic Development and Tourism. *The State of Hawaii Data Book: A Statistical Abstract.* Honolulu: Department of Business, Economic Development and Tourism, 1990, 57.

Hays, Hoffman Reynolds. *The Kingdom of Hawaii.* Greenwich, Connecticut: New York Geographic Society, 1964.

Henriques, Edgar. "Nae'a." Unpublished paper, Daughters of Hawaii, April 1977.

Heyes, Monica Mary. "The History of St. Andrew's Priory, 1867–1918." MA thesis, University of Hawai'i, 1970.

Hopkins, Manley. *Hawaii: The Past, Present, and Future of Its Island Kingdom.* London: Longman, 1862.

Hoyt, Edwin P. *Davies: The Inside Story of a British-American Family in the Pacific and Its Business Enterprises.* Honolulu: Topgallant Publishing Company, 1983.

Hulme, Kathryn C. "The Timeless Kauai Swamp." *Atlantic Monthly* (January 1965), 68–71.

Iaukea, Curtis Piehu. "Reminiscences of the Court of Kamehameha IV and Queen Emma." Papers of the Hawaiian Historical Society, (17) (1978), 17–24.

Iaukea, Curtis Piehu, and Lorna K. Iaukea Watson. *By Royal Command,* edited by Niklaus R. Schweizer. Honolulu: Hui Hānai, 1988.

'Ī'ī, John Papa. *Fragments of Hawaiian History.* Honolulu: Bishop Museum Press, 1973.

Jarves, James J. *History of the Hawaiian or Sandwich Islands.* Boston: Tappan and Dennet, 1843.

Jenkins, Irving. *The Hawaiian Calabash.* Honolulu: Editions Limited, 1989.

Joesting, Edward. *Kauai: The Separate Kingdom.* Honolulu: University of Hawai'i Press, 1984.

———. *Tides of Commerce.* Honolulu: First Hawaiian Bank, 1983.

Johnson, Lynne. "The Role of Women in the Honolulu Amateur Musical Society 1853–1894: A Reflection of Changing Social Values." Unpublished paper, December 11, 1996.

Jones, Maude. "Emma-lani." Unpublished paper, no date, Daughters of Hawai'i.

Judd, Laura Fish. *Honolulu: Sketches of the Life, Social, Political, and Religious, in the Hawaiian Islands from 1828 to 1861.* Honolulu: privately printed, 1928.

Kamakau, Samuel M. *Ruling Chiefs of Hawai'i.* Honolulu: Kamehameha Schools Press, 1992.

Kanahele, George S. *Kū Kanaka—Stand Tall, A Search for Hawaiian Values.* Honolulu: University of Hawai'i Press and Waiaha Foundation, 1986.

———. *Pauahi, The Kamehameha Legacy.* Honolulu: Kamehameha Schools Press, 1986.

———. "The Story of the Queen's Heritage." Unpublished paper, presented to The Queen's Medical Center, August 1987.

———. *Waikīkī: 100 B.C. to 1900 A.D.: An Untold Story.* Honolulu: University of Hawai'i Press, 1995.

Kekahuna, Henry E. P. "Wai'aha—kahi i hanau ai o Queen Emma," Hawai'i (No. 2 South Kona, "Historical Satellites of Kailua," Drafts), No. 47.

Kepelino. "Kepelino's Hawaiian Collection: His Hooiliili Havaii, Pepa I, 1858," translated and annotated by Bacil F. Kirtley and Esther T. Mookini, *Hawaiian Journal of History* 11 (1977), 39–40.

King, Josephine Wundenberg. "Queen Emma on Kauai." Paper presented to Daughters of Hawaii (1930?).

———. "A Royal Holiday on Kauai." Hawaiian Church Chronicle (March 1969), 4–5.

Klieger, Christiaan P. *Nā Maka o Hālawa, A History of Hālawa Ahupua'a, O'ahu.* Bishop Museum Technical Report 7. Honolulu: Bishop Museum Press, December 1995.

Korn, Alfons L., ed. *News from Molokai, Letters between Peter Kaeo and Queen Emma, 1873–1876.* Honolulu: University of Hawai'i Press, 1976.

———. *The Victorian Visitors.* Honolulu: University of Hawai'i Press, 1958.

Knudsen, Eric. "Queen Emma Goes to Alakai Swamp." Paper read at Twenty-sixth Annual Meeting, Kaua'i Historical Society, May 27, 1940.

Kuykendall, Ralph S. *The Hawaiian Kingdom.* 3 vols. Honolulu: University of Hawai'i Press, 1938, 1953, 1967.

"The Late Prince Albert" (Kūnuiākea)." *Paradise of the Pacific,* March 1903, 38.

Lately, Thomas. *The First President Johnson.* New York: William Morrow and Company, 1968.

Legislative Journal (Kingdom of Hawaii), 1866 Session.

Liholiho, Alexander. *The Journal of Prince Alexander Liholiho,* edited by Jacob Adler. Honolulu: University of Hawai'i Press, 1967.

Lili'uokalani. *Hawaii's Story by Hawaii's Queen.* Rutland, Vermont: Ellis Company, 1906.

Loomis, Albertine. *The Best of Friends: The Story of Hawaii's Libraries and Their Friends 1879–1979.* Kailua: Friends of the Library of Hawaii, Press Pacifica, 1979.

Lyman, Rufus A. "Recollections of Kamehameha V." *Third Annual Report of the Hawaiian Historical Society for the Year 1895* (1896).

Malo, David. *Hawaiian Antiquities (Mo'olelo Hawai'i).* B. P. Bishop Museum Bulletin, Special Publication 2. Honolulu: Bishop Museum Press, 1951.

Martin, Robert Bernard. *Tennyson, the Unquiet Heart.* Oxford University Press, 1980.

Mellen, Kathleen. *The Gods Depart: A Saga of the Hawaiian Kingdom, 1832–1873.* New York: Hastings House, 1956.

———. *An Island Kingdom Passes: Hawaii Becomes American.* New York: Hastings House, 1958.

———. *The Lonely Warrior: The Life and Times of Kamehameha the Great of Hawaii.* New York: Hastings House, 1949.

Menton, Linda K. "Everything Lovely and of Good Report, The Chiefs' Children's School 1839–1850." Ph.D. dissertation, University of Hawai'i, 1983.

Meyer, Charles S. *Meyer and Molokai,* edited by Yolla Meyer Forbes. Alden, Iowa: Graphic-Agri Business Ltd., 1982.

"Mission of The Queen's Medical Center," Approved, Board of Trustees, The Queen's Medical Center, November 1990.

Moriarty, Linda Paik. *Ni'ihau Shell Leis.* Honolulu: University of Hawai'i Press, 1986.

Morris, Alfred D. "The Death of the Prince of Hawai'i: A Retrospective Diagnosis." *Hawaiian Journal of History* 28 (1994), 79–85.

Mouritz, Authur A. St. *The Path of the Destroyer, The History of Leprosy in the Hawaiian Islands and Thirty Years Research into the Means by Which It Has Been Spread.* Honolulu: *Honolulu Star-Bulletin,* 1916.

Muir, Andrew F. "William Hoapili Kaauwai: A Hawaiian in Holy Orders." *Sixty-first Annual Report of the Hawaiian Historical Society for the Year 1952* (1953), 5–13.

Nordyke, Eleanor C. *The Peopling of Hawaii.* Honolulu: University Press of Hawai'i, 1977.

Parke, William C. *Personal Reminiscences of William Cooper Parke, Marshal of the Hawaiian Islands, from 1850–1884.* Cambridge University Press, 1891.

Peabody, Lucy. Handwritten paper, no date, DOH.

Penal Laws of the Hawaiian Islands 1897. Honolulu: Hawaiian Gazette, 1897.

Peterson, Barbara B., ed. *Notable Women of Hawaii.* Honolulu: University of Hawai'i Press, 1984.

Peterson, Charles E. "The Iolani Palace and the Barracks." *Journal of the Society of Architectural Historians* 22 (3) (May 1963): 91–103.

Pratt, Elizabeth Keka'anī'au. "A Brief Sketch of the Life of Queen Emma Kaleleokalani," unpublished paper, Daughters of Hawaii, January 2, 1928.

Privy Council (Kingdom of Hawai'i). Minute book. Hawai'i State Archives, Honolulu.

"A Prominent Hawaiian" (John A. Cummins). *Paradise of the Pacific,* December 1904, 38.

Puku'i, Mary Kawena. *'Ōlelo No'eau: Hawaiian Proverbs and Poetical Sayings.* Bishop Museum Special Publication 71. Honolulu: Bishop Museum Press, 1983.

———, trans. *Nā Mele Welo, Songs of Our Heritage,* arranged and edited by Pat Namaka Bacon and Nathan Napoka. Honolulu: Bishop Museum, 1995.

Puku'i, Mary Kawena, and Samuel H. Elbert. *Hawaiian Dictionary,* rev. and enlarged ed. Honolulu: University of Hawai'i Press, 1986.

Puku'i, Mary Kawena, Samuel H. Elbert, and Esther T. Mo'okini. *Place Names of Hawai'i.* Honolulu: University Press of Hawai'i, 1974.

Puku'i, Mary Kawena, E. W. Haertig, and Catherine A. Lee. *Nānā I Ke Kumu (Look to the Source),* 2 vols. Honolulu: Hui Hānai, 1979.

Puku'i, Mary Kawena, and Alfons L. Korn, eds. *The Echo of Our Song, Chants and Poems of the Hawaiians.* Honolulu: University of Hawai'i Press, 1973.

The Queen's Health Systems, *Overview,* 1998.

Queen's Hospital Annual Report 1873.

Record of the Trustees Minutes, 1859–1907, Queen's Hospital.

Research Report to Daughters of Hawai'i Collections Committee, Subject: Oil Painting Offered by Mrs. Marks, compiled by Mariajane C. Mee, July 7, 1976.

Restarick, Henry B. *Hawaii, 1778–1920 from the Viewpoint of a Bishop.* Honolulu: Paradise of the Pacific, 1942.

Richards, Mary Atherton. *Amos Starr Cooke and Juliette Montague Cooke, Their Autobiographies Gleaned from Their Journals and Letters.* Honolulu: Daughters of Hawaii, 1941.

———. *The Chiefs' Children's School.* Honolulu: *Honolulu Star-Bulletin,* 1937.

Rooke, Thomas C. B. "General Table of Meteorological Observations at Honolulu, from July 1, 1837 to January 1, 1838," *The Hawaiian Spectator,* vol. I, no. 3, July 1838.

Roster Legislatures of Hawaii 1841–1918. Honolulu: Hawaiian Gazette Co. Ltd., 1918.

Royce, Anya P. *The Anthropology of Dance.* Bloomington: Indiana University Press, 1977.

St. Andrew's Priory. *The Student and Parent Handbook, 1998.*

Schneider, Vimala. *Infant Massage.* New York: Bantam, 1982.

Schweizer, Niklaus R. *Hawai'i and the German Speaking Peoples.* Honolulu: Topgallant, 1982.

Scott, Edward B. *The Saga of the Sandwich Islands.* Lake Tahoe: Sierra-Tahoe Publishing Company, 1968.

Seargent, David A. *Comets, Vagabonds of Space.* Garden City, New York: Doubleday, 1982.

Sinclair, Marjorie. *Nahi'ena'ena, Sacred Daughter of Hawai'i.* Honolulu: University of Hawai'i Press, 1976.

Smythe, Jane "Jennie" Stillman. "Reminiscences of My Trip to Ka'u, Hawai'i, with Queen Emma." Unpublished paper, no date, Daughters of Hawai'i.

———. "Queen Emma, the Person." *Paradise of the Pacific* (February 1931), 5–6.

Southerland, W. H. H. "Incidents Connected with the Election of King Kalakaua in February, 1874." *Hawaiian Historical Society Report* 21 (1913), 12–15.

Staley, Mildred. "A Great Woman, Queen Emma Kaleleonalani of Hawaii," paper presented to the Daughters of Hawai'i, May 15, 1940.

———. "Queen Emma Kaleleonalani of Hawaii." Pan Pacific 3 (April–June 1939): 5–6.

———. "The Story of Iolani School." *Hawaiian Church Chronicle* XXII (4) (June 1933), 1–11

———. *A Tapestry of Memories, An Autobiography.* Hilo, Hawai'i: The *Hilo Tribune Herald,* 1944.

———, ed. "Bishop Staley's Journal." *Hawaiian Church Chronicle* XXIV (1) (March 1934), 6.

Staley, Thomas N. *Five Years' Church Work in the Kingdom of Hawaii.* London: Rivingtons, 1868.

Stall, Edna Williamson. *Historic Homes of Hawaii, From Clipper Ship to Clipper Ship.* Privately printed, 1937.

Sterling, Elspeth P., and Catherine C. Summers, comp. *Sites of Oahu.* Honolulu: Bernice P. Bishop Museum, 1978.

Stevens, Peter F. "Queen Emma's Historic Voyage." *Honolulu,* October 1991, 54–57.

Stevens, Sylvester K. *American Expansion in Hawaii.* Harrisburg, Pennsylvania: Archives Publishing Company, 1945.

Strong, Isobel. *The Girl from Home: A Story of Honolulu.* Honolulu: Crossroads Bookshop, 1912.

Tabrah, Ruth M. *Ni'ihau, The Last Hawaiian Island.* Honolulu: Press Pacifica, 1987.

Tate, Merze. *The United States and the Hawaiian Kingdom: A Political History.* Westport, Conn.: Greenwood Press, 1980.

Taylor, Lou. *Mourning Dress: A Costume and Social History.* Boston: G. Allen and Unwin, 1983.

Thomas, Mifflin. *Schooner from Windward: Two Centuries of Hawaiian Inter-island Shipping.* Honolulu: University of Hawai'i Press, 1983.

Thompson, Katharine Shirley. *Queen Emma and the Bishop.* Honolulu: Daughters of Hawai'i, 1987.

Transactions of the Royal Hawaiian Agricultural Society, Fourth Annual Meeting, June 1854, vol. 2, no. 1, 29–30.

Varigny, Charles Victor Crosnier de. "Emma Reine des Iles Havai." *Revue des Deux Mondes* (Paris) LXXII (1885), 101–102.

———. *Fourteen Years in the Sandwich Islands, 1855–1868.* Translated by Alfons L. Korn. Honolulu: University of Hawai'i Press, 1981.

Villers, Ernest G. "A History of Iolani School." ME thesis, University of Hawai'i, 1940.

Waldron, Elizabeth. *Liholiho and Emma, King Kamehameha IV and his Queen.* Honolulu: Daughters of Hawai'i, 1986.

Williams, Rianna M. *From Royal Garden to Gothic Splendor, The History of St. Andrew's Cathedral.* Honolulu: St. Andrew's Cathedral, 1996.

Zambucka, Kristin. *The High Chiefess Ruth Ke'elikōlani.* Honolulu: Mana Publishing Company, 1977.

———. *Princess Kaiulani, The Last Hope of Hawaii's Monarchy.* Honolulu: Mana Publishing, 1984.

PERIODICALS

Atlantic Monthly
Friend, The (Honolulu)
Hawaiian Almanac and Annual (Honolulu)
Hawaiian Annual
Hawaiian Chronicle
Hawaiian Gazette, The (Honolulu)
Hawaiian Monthly, The (Honolulu)
Hawaiian Spectator, The (Honolulu)
Hilo Tribune Herald
Honolulu
Honolulu Magazine
Honolulu Advertiser
Honolulu Star-Bulletin
Journal de Genève (Geneva, Switzerland)
Ka 'Elele Hawai'i (Honolulu)
Ka 'Elele Poakolu (Honolulu)
Ka Hae Hawai'i (Honolulu)
Ka Hōkū Loa o Hawai'i (Honolulu)
Ka Hōkū o ka Pākipika (Honolulu)
Ka Nūhou Hawai'i (Honolulu)

Ka Nūpepa Kūʻokoʻa
Ke Au ʻOkoʻa (Honolulu)
Ko Hawaiʻi Paeʻāina (Honolulu)
Ko Hawaiʻi Ponoʻī (Honolulu)
London Illustrated News
London Times
Mid-Pacific Magazine (Honolulu)
Neue Zuercher Zeitung (Zurich)
Pacific Commercial Advertiser (Honolulu)
Paradise of the Pacific (Honolulu)
Polynesian, The (Honolulu)
Queen's Hospital Bulletin, The
Revue des Deux Mondes (Paris)
Saturday Press (Honolulu)
Wells Journal, The

Index

Bold numbers indicate illustrations